W9-AQJ-820

Bloomfield
English
Fundamentals

Form A   *Twelfth Edition*

Donald W. Emery
Late of The University of Washington

John M. Kierzek
Late of Oregon State University

Peter Lindblom
Miami-Dade Community College

Allyn and Bacon
Boston • London • Toronto • Sydney • Tokyo • Singapore

Editor-in-Chief, Humanities: Joseph Opiela
Editorial Assistant: Kristen Desmond
Marketing Manager: Lisa Kimball
Cover Coordinator: Jenny Hart
Composition Buyer: Linda Cox
Manufacturing Buyer: Suzanne Lareau
Production Coordinator: Deborah Brown
Editorial-Production Service: Susan McNally
Electronic Composition: Omegatype Typography, Inc.

Library of Congress Cataloging-in-Publication Data

Emery, Donald W. (Donald William), 1906–
    English fundamentals, form A / Donald W. Emery, John M. Kierzek, Peter Lindblom.—
12th ed.
     p. cm.
    Includes index.
    ISBN 0-205-32239-5
     1. English language—Grammar—Problems, exercises, etc.   I. Kierzek, John M. 1891–   .
II. Lindblom, Peter D., 1938–   III. Title.

PE1112.E47   2000
428.2—dc21

                                               00-030606

Contents

Part 7

··

Writing Paragraphs and Essays 305

Part 8

··

Progress Tests 355

Appendixes

··

Preface

The twelfth edition of *English Fundamentals* builds upon the foundation of eleven successful editions to provide quality instruction in English. As the book has flourished through the years, it has retained in each subsequent edition the tried and true presentations that have made the book a success for so many years. In each new version there have been changes and refinements to keep the book on pace with contemporary students. This new book closely resembles the previous versions, but it also changes in ways that will make students' experiences with it richer and more rewarding. With these changes, however, the purpose and the audience have not changed since the first edition. All students who want to improve their ability to use English in writing and speaking can profit from this twelfth edition.

Organization of the Text

Certain important qualities have always been characteristic of *English Fundamentals:* clear, effective instruction in the fundamental principles of English; carefully crafted exercises designed to illustrate those principles; and a comprehensive testing system to diagnose problems and measure progress. The first lessons introduce students to the basic system of the language and provide carefully chosen examples of verb connections, basic sentence patterns, and the internal workings of the sentence. Simplified presentations make the book accessible both for developmental students and for those who have advanced in their study of the language. Because the first sections are cumulative, building step by step a foundation in the operating principles of the language, these early lessons should be studied first. Once the foundation is laid, the order for studying the remaining units is flexible. Work on spelling and capitalization, for example, can be undertaken at almost any point, even during study of another unit.

Building on the foundation of the early lessons, subsequent lessons explore the more complex structures and relationships of the language. Students examine the function of various clauses and phrases, first learning to recognize their structures, and then learning to use them through drills on sentence combining, embedding, and transformation. The drills are proven methods for helping students to develop flexibility and sophistication in their writing and to recognize effective, correct constructions when they revise.

The last instructional section surveys college writing. Students study the writing process, with special emphasis on techniques of invention, and then learn to apply that process to a wide range of writing assignments typical of college courses. These assignments range from personal essays to academic papers, with an additional focus on paragraph development. The section includes an examination of essay tests and test-taking. To accommodate the interests of a wide range of students, the examples and exercises throughout the book come from a number of disciplines, including science and business.

The text concludes with a set of twenty progress tests and three appendixes. The first appendix contains eleven sentence-combining exercises, each containing five or six units.

These exercises are in addition to the embedding, combining, and transformation drills found in the exercises attached to each lesson. These additional drills encourage the students to try out a variety of sentence-building strategies by combining the short sentences in each unit in as many ways as possible. The sentence-combining drills also require the students to review punctuation rules as they combine the sentences and properly punctuate the new, longer sentences. The second appendix offers diagnostic tests to analyze students' abilities in spelling, punctuation, sentence structure, and usage. The third appendix contains the answer key to the practice sheets. The book concludes with an index to help students use the text for references to specific concepts.

New to This Edition

The instructional material in all lessons has been significantly rewritten to make the concepts more accessible to the students. Explanations have been simplified, and examples have been updated to accommodate a wider range of students.

Over the past three editions, the number of practice sheets and exercises requiring active writing has increased so that there are now forty-five pages that ask students to write or rewrite sentences to reinforce the concepts taught in the lessons. The result is that every major concept is covered by drills that require both recognition and production. These new drills use sentence-combining, embedding, transformation, and rewriting to encourage the students to use the concepts taught in each lesson.

Practice Sheets

The twelfth edition continues the use of practice sheets. After every lesson there is at least one easily understood worksheet that provides examples of and practice with the concept introduced in that lesson. The sentences in the practice sheets are usually shorter and somewhat simpler than those in the exercise worksheets that follow. Thus, the practice sheets provide a starter exercise, a warm-up for students to begin work on each new concept. The practice sheets also allow teachers to use the book with students whose reading levels might require simplified material.

An answer key for every practice sheet may be found in Appendix C. Its presence allows students to use *English Fundamentals* independently as a drill and practice book. Students in composition classes who, for example, need extra work on punctuation for compound sentences can find that section in the index, read the instruction and commentary, work through the practice sheets, and correct their work by referring to the answer key in Appendix C.

Variety in Exercises

In the minds of some, English texts that focus on the fundamentals of the language often limit student work to recognition, identification, and correction—a sort of fill-in-the-blanks scheme that doesn't require much actual writing. *English Fundamentals* requires such work as is necessary to build certain skills but also incorporates a large number of exercises that require active production of sentences. Students will practice sentence combining and reducing independent clauses to various dependent clauses and phrases. They will learn to embed independent clauses in sentences and will rewrite sentences. They will transform active expressions to passive ones and vice versa, and change from direct to indirect quotation and from indirect to direct. They will write sentences to practice using various constructions. Research has shown, and we are convinced, that such active manipulation of the structures of language will greatly improve students' ability to write effectively and correctly.

Optional Testing Program

The twelfth edition, like the eleventh, offers additional tests. The Optional Testing Program consists of thirty tests sent to instructors on request. These tests are printed in a separate volume with perforated pages. The tests differ from the progress tests in the text in that they generalize, focusing on major concepts (for example, introductory subordinate elements) rather than specific constructions. The tests first ask for recognition of correct forms, then ask for generation of the new structure out of the basic parts. There is an answer key provided with the tests so that, in addition for use in evaluation, they can be used as higher-level practice exercises.

Acknowledgments

Our thanks go to all those who offered advice and suggestions for improving this and previous editions: Edwin J. Blesch, Jr., Nassau Community College; Ladson W. Bright, Cape Fear Community College; James Vanden Bosch, Calvin College; Bernadine Brown, Nassau Community College; Kitty Chen Dean, Nassau Community College; Patricia Derby, Chabot College; Neil G. Dodd, East Los Angeles College; Loris D. Galford, McNeese State University; Harold J. Herman, University of Maryland; William T. Hope, Jefferson Technical College; Sue D. Hopke, Broward Community College; Clifford J. Houston, East Los Angeles College; George L. Ives, North Idaho College; Edward F. James, University of Maryland; Thomas Mast, Montgomery College; Walter Mullen, Mississippi Gulf Coast Community College; Mary E. Owens, Montgomery College; Crystal Reynolds, Indiana State University; Bill Sartoris, Camden College; Albert Schoenberg, East Los Angeles Community College; Ines Shaw, North Dakota State University; Barbara Stout, Montgomery College; and Robert S. Sweazy, Vincennes University Junior College.

P. L.

Basic Sentence Patterns
Lessons, Practice Sheets, and Exercises

Lesson 1 — *The Simple Sentence; Subjects and Verbs*

While you might find it difficult to produce a satisfying definition, you probably know that the sentence is a basic unit of written or oral expression. Thus, if you were asked, you might define a sentence as "an orderly arrangement of words that makes sense." If you wished to be more specific and more formal, you might say a sentence is "a self-contained grammatical unit, usually containing a subject and a verb, that conveys a meaningful statement, question, command, or exclamation."

You need to understand the basic construction of the sentence in order to write and speak effectively and correctly. In the first few lessons of this book, you'll examine the parts that make up a sentence and the distinctive characteristics of a few types of sentences that serve as the basic structures of more complicated units.

To begin, be sure you can recognize the two indispensable parts of a sentence:

1. The **subject:** the unit about which something is said.
2. The **predicate:** the unit that says something about the subject.

Although the predicate usually includes other modifying words and phrases, the indispensable part of a predicate is the verb, the word (or words) that indicates what the subject does or is. Here are a few things to remember about the subject-verb relationship:

1. In a sentence that reports a specific action, the verb is easily recognized. For instance, to find the subject and verb in *The rusty bumper on the front of my truck rattles noisily,* ask the question, "What happens?" The answer, *rattles,* gives the verb. Then, by asking the question "Who or what rattles?" you will find with the subject, *bumper.* Notice that neither "front rattles" nor "truck rattles" makes the basic statement of the sentence.

2. Some sentences do not report an action. Instead, the sentence says something about the *condition* of the subject. It points out a descriptive quality of the subject or says that something else resembles or is the same thing as the subject. In this kind of sentence, you must look for verbs like *is, are, was, were, seem,* and *become.* Such types of verbs are often called *describing (linking) verbs.* They are words that are almost impossible to define because they lack the concrete exactness and action of verbs like *rattle, throw, smash,* and *explode.*

1

In a sentence using a describing verb, the subject usually reveals itself easily. For example, in the sentence "The long first chapter seemed particularly difficult," the verb is *seemed*. The question "Who or what seemed?" provides the subject, *chapter*. The other possible choices—*long, first, particularly,* and *difficult*—do not make sense as answers to the question "Who or what seemed?".

3. Very often the subject of a sentence has material between it and its verb:

   The *price* of potatoes *is* high. [The subject is *price*, not *potatoes*.]
   Each of my sisters *is* tall. [The subject is *each*, not *sisters*.]
   Only *one* of these watches *works*. [The subject is *one*, not *watches*.]

4. Most modern English sentences place the subject before the verb, but in some sentences, the verb precedes the subject:

   Behind the house *stood* [verb] an old *mill* [subject].
   Under the table *sat* [verb] a large *cat* [subject].

   A very common type of sentence with the verb–subject arrangement uses *here* or *there* preceding the verb:

   There *are* [verb] three willow *trees* [subject] in our yard.
   Here *is* [verb] the *list* [subject] of candidates.

5. Casual, informal language often combines short verbs and subjects with apostrophes representing the omitted letters:

   I'm (I am)   It's (It is)   You've (You have)   They're (They are)

For your first practice work you'll be using only a single subject for each sentence. Within this limitation the subject is always a noun or a pronoun. Before the first practice, it would be wise to review a few facts about nouns, pronouns, and verbs so that you can recognize them easily.

Nouns

A **noun** is a word that names something, such as a person, place, thing, quality, or idea. If the noun names just any member of a group or class, it is called a *common noun* and is not capitalized:

man, city, school, relative

A noun is a *proper noun* and is capitalized if it refers to a named individual in a group or class:

Albert Lawson, Toledo, Horace Mann Junior High School, Aunt Louise

Most nouns have two forms; they show whether the noun is naming one thing (singular number) or more than one thing (plural number, which adds *s* or *es* to the singular): one *coat*, two *coats*; a *lunch*, several *lunches*. Proper nouns are rarely pluralized, and some common nouns have no plural form, for example, *honesty, courage, ease,* and *hardness*. (Lesson 28 examines in detail the special spelling problems of plural nouns.)

Nouns often follow *the*, *a*, or *an*, words that are called **articles**. A descriptive word (an adjective) may come between the article and the noun, but the word that answers the question "What?" after an article is a noun:

Article	$\left(\begin{array}{c}optional\\adjective\end{array}\right)$	noun
A (or The)	happy	girl.

Another way to identify nouns is to recognize certain suffixes. A **suffix** is a unit added to the end of a word or to the base of a word. (See Supplement 1.)* Here are some of the common suffixes found on hundreds of nouns:

age [break*age*]; ance, ence [resist*ance*, insist*ence*]; dom [king*dom*]; hood [child*hood*]; ion [prevention]; ism [national*ism*]; ment [move*ment*]; ness [firm*ness*]; or, er [invest*or*, los*er*]; ure [expos*ure*]

Pronouns

A **pronoun** is a word that substitutes for a noun. There are several classes of pronouns. (See Supplement 2.) The following classes can function as subjects in the basic sentences that you will examine in these early lessons:

Personal pronouns substitute for definite persons or things: *I, you, he, she, it, we, they.*

Demonstrative pronouns substitute for things being pointed out: *this, that, these, those.*

Indefinite pronouns substitute for unknown or unspecified things: *each, either, neither, one, anyone, somebody, everything, all, few, many,* and so on.

Possessive pronouns substitute for things that are possessed: *mine, yours, his, hers, its, ours, theirs.*

Verbs

A **verb** is a word that expresses action, existence, or occurrence by combining with a subject to make a statement, to ask a question, or to give a command. One easy way to identify a word as a verb is to use the following test:

Let's _____
   (*action word*)

*In some lessons of this book you will find notations referring you to a supplement that appears at the end of the lesson. Read the supplement *after* you have thoroughly studied the lesson. The lesson contains the essential information that is vital to your understanding of subsequent lessons and exercises. The supplement presents material that has relevance to some points of the lesson. The supplements at the end of this lesson are found on page 4.

Any word that will complete the command is a verb: "Let's *leave*." "Let's *buy* some popcorn." "Let's *be* quiet." This test works only with the basic present form of the verb, not with forms that have endings added to them or that show action taking place in the past: "Let's *paint* the car" (not "Let's *painted* the car").

Supplement 1

Hundreds of nouns have distinctive suffix endings. The definitions of some of these suffixes are rather difficult to formulate, but you can quite readily figure out the meanings of most of them: *ness*, for instance, means "quality or state of" (thus *firmness* means "the state or quality of being firm"); *or* and *er* show the agent or doer of something (an *investor* is "one who invests").

A unit added to the beginning of a word is called a **prefix.** Thus, to the adjective *kind*, we add a prefix to derive another adjective, *unkind*, and a suffix to derive the nouns *kindness* and *unkindness*. An awareness of how prefixes and suffixes are used will do far more than aid you in your ability to recognize parts of speech: Your spelling will improve and your vocabulary will expand.

Supplement 2

Two classes of pronouns, the **interrogative** and the **relative,** are not listed here. Because they are used in questions and subordinate clauses but not in simple basic sentences, they will not be discussed until later lessons.

Another type of pronoun that you use regularly (but not as a true subject) is the **intensive** or **reflexive** pronoun, the "self" words used to add emphasis:

You *yourself* made the decision.

or to name the receiver of an action when the doer is the same as the receiver:

The boy fell and hurt *himself.*

The first example is the intensive use; the second is the reflexive. Pronouns used this way are *myself, yourself, himself* (not *hisself*), *herself, itself, ourselves, yourselves,* and *themselves* (not *themself, theirself,* or *theirselves*).

The "self" pronouns are properly used for only these two purposes. They should not be substituted for regular personal pronouns:

Mary and I [not *myself*] were invited to the dance.
Tom visited Eric and me [not *myself*] at our ranch.

A fourth type of pronoun is the **reciprocal** pronoun that denotes a mutual relationship, for example *one another, each other:*

We try to help *each other* with our homework.

NAME _____ SCORE _____

Directions: In the space at the left, copy the word that is the verb of the italicized subject.

_____ 1. *Some* of the students' problems seemed humorous to the faculty members.

_____ 2. A *woman* from the computer center knocked on the office door.

_____ 3. At the top of that tall tree sits a huge *nest.*

_____ 4. A light *rain* still fell softly on the open field.

_____ 5. Only a few *people* from the night shift came to the meeting.

_____ 6. *Neither* of the debaters offered much new information.

_____ 7. The new *rolls* for the history classes are now ready.

_____ 8. At the back of the shelf there's a new *box* of cookies.

_____ 9. *All* but one of those students own computers.

_____ 10. From the inner office echoed the deep *snores* of the president of the company.

_____ 11. Fewer than ten *people* attended class this morning.

_____ 12. On my desk stands a new *scanner.*

_____ 13. Only *one* of the lifeguards appeared at the pool today.

_____ 14. His *contributions* to the project became ever more valuable.

_____ 15. Here comes our team's new *captain.*

_____ 16. *Those* were my two favorite movies.

_____ 17. *Two* of the new members bought their pins.

_____ 18. The new *coach* soon hired three new assistants.

_____ 19. *Some* of the staff members left early today.

_____ 20. The *reason* for her hasty resignation made itself clear very soon.

6 · *Subjects and Verbs*

Directions: In the space at the left, copy the word that is the subject of the italicized verb.

_____ 1. The high-pitched whine of the chain saw *ruined* our sleep.

_____ 2. In that beautiful cabinet in the lobby *are* trophies from earlier sports triumphs.

_____ 3. Answers to our letter about the problem *came* from all fifty states.

_____ 4. There *were* several puddles of muddy water in the front hall.

_____ 5. Out in the middle of that prairie *stand* several tall, beautiful trees.

_____ 6. All those articles, plus several others, *are* available in the college library.

_____ 7. The first of the weary travelers *arrived* at about 3:00 A.M.

_____ 8. None of the sophomores in my class *passed* that test.

_____ 9. There *are* several pages of that magazine on the floor.

_____ 10. A shortage of crude oil *drove* the price up very quickly.

_____ 11. Around the track *raced* the most beautiful bay filly imaginable.

_____ 12. Jim's lack of patience *was* familiar to every employee.

_____ 13. The grades of the students in my history class *are* really quite high.

_____ 14. Only the oldest of the five cars *failed* inspection.

_____ 15. In the corner of the couch *slumped* a very tired little boy.

_____ 16. Even the slowest runner in the group *finished* ahead of me.

_____ 17. One of my mother's friends *holds* title to that property on the highway.

_____ 18. In that stack of library books *was* my lost textbook.

_____ 19. An urgent call *came* from the governor's office.

_____ 20. Even the shorter of the two obstacle courses *was* too difficult for Mary and Joanne.

NAME _____   SCORE _____

Directions: In the first space at the left, copy the subject of the sentence. In the second space, copy the verb.

_____   1. Some of the team's former captains attended the game.

_____   2. The investigation of the incident provided no useful information.

_____   3. Behind the counter at the fast food restaurant stood a kindly old man.

_____   4. Some of the brightest students in my high school never went to college.

_____   5. There's no more money in my checking account.

_____   6. The reasons for her departure were unknown.

_____   7. A group of reporters stood on the sidewalk in front of the house.

_____   8. In the basement of our house there is an old, leaky furnace.

_____   9. Only a few of my friends have jobs this summer.

_____   10. Martha's quite concerned about her grade in calculus.

_____   11. Yesterday was the last day of exam week.

_____   12. An orchid with five blooms on it hangs in the dining room.

_____   13. Under the porch crouched three frightened kittens.

_____   14. Hardly any of those students studied for the test.

_____   15. There were new orders on the bulletin board this morning.

_____   16. The athletic ability of the new quarterback amazed all the coaches.

_____   17. Several of the secretaries left for lunch a few minutes ago.

_____   18. I'm not surprised by your success in that class.

_____ 19. Yesterday after my first class, I went home for lunch.

_____ 20. Here are two more applications for that position.

_____ 21. That old hotel became a condominium.

_____ 22. After a poor start, Jane's grades improved at the end of the term.

_____ 23. There are always problems in a course such as this one.

_____ 24. Two former members of the Marathoners' Club joined us for yesterday's workout.

_____ 25. His last good season as a pitcher was in 1989.

_____ 26. She's the first arrival for today's interviews.

_____ 27. In yesterday's paper there is a very controversial editorial.

_____ 28. Each of those four scales gave a different weight.

_____ 29. From somewhere on the other side of the park came the sound of barking dogs.

_____ 30. The deep, throbbing sounds of the car's exhaust rattled the grandstands at the racetrack.

_____ 31. After the first drops of rain, all of the carpenters left the job.

_____ 32. Next to my raincoat hung a beautiful sweater.

_____ 33. During lunch hour my father always takes a brief nap.

_____ 34. None of the five lab assistants found that error in the new program.

_____ 35. During my first day as an assistant trainer, I taped ten players' ankles.

_____ 36. Here comes my little sister with her two obnoxious friends.

_____ 37. They're obviously the best-qualified candidates from that group.

_____ 38. The sale price of that fishing rod pleased my brother.

_____ 39. The last emergency call for that night came at 11:45 P.M.

_____ 40. A few of the better students in the class finished the test very early.

Lesson 2   *Verbs, Adjectives, Adverbs, and Prepositions*

In Lesson 1 you learned how to recognize a verb. Every verb has a **base** or **infinitive.** This form of the verb "names" the verb. But verbs change their form according to various conditions, three of which are person, number, and tense. You should learn these forms because they occur in nearly every sentence that you speak or write.

> **Person** specifies the person(s) speaking ("first" person: *I, we*); the person(s) spoken *to* ("second" person: *you*); and the person(s) or thing(s) spoken *about* ("third" person: *he, she, it, they*).
>
> **Number** shows whether the reference is to *one* thing (*singular* number) or to more than one thing (*plural* number).
>
> **Tense** refers to the time represented in the sentence, whether it applies to the present moment (I *believe* him) or to some other time (I *believed* him, I *will believe* him).

To demonstrate these changes in form, you can use a chart or arrangement called a *conjugation.* In the partial conjugation that follows, three verbs are used: *earn, grow,* and *be.* The personal pronoun subjects are included to show how the person and number of the subject affect the form of the verb.

Indicative Mood
Active Voice*

	Singular	*Plural*
	Present Tense	
1st Person	I earn, grow, am	We earn, grow, are
2nd Person	You earn, grow, are	You earn, grow, are
3rd Person	He earns, grows, is**	They earn, grow, are
	Past Tense	
1st Person	I earned, grew, was	We earned, grew, were
2nd Person	You earned, grew, were	You earned, grew, were
3rd Person	He earned, grew, was	They earned, grew, were
	Future Tense	
1st Person	I shall earn, grow, be	We shall earn, grow, be
2nd Person	You will earn, grow, be	You will earn, grow, be
3rd Person	He will earn, grow, be	They will earn, grow, be

*Indicative mood indicates that the verb expresses a fact as opposed to a wish, command, or possibility. *Active voice* indicates that the subject of the verb is the *doer,* rather than the receiver, of the action of the verb.

**The pronoun *he* is arbitrarily used here to represent the third-person singular subject, which may be any singular pronoun *(she, it, who, nobody)*; singular noun *(girl, neighbor, elephant, misunderstanding, Alice, Christopher Robert Klein III)*; or word groups constituting certain types of phrases or clauses that will be studied in later lessons.

Present Perfect Tense

1st Person	I have earned, grown, been	We have earned, grown, been
2nd Person	You have earned, grown, been	You have earned, grown, been
3rd Person	He has earned, grown, been	They have earned, grown, been

Past Perfect Tense

1st Person	I had earned, grown, been	We had earned, grown, been
2nd Person	You had earned, grown, been	You had earned, grown, been
3rd Person	He had earned, grown, been	They had earned, grown, been

Future Perfect Tense

1st Person	I shall have earned, grown, been	We shall have earned, grown, been
2nd Person	You will have earned, grown, been	You will have earned, grown, been
3rd Person	She will have earned, grown, been	They will have earned, grown, been

Notice that in the past tense, *earn* adds an *ed* ending, but *grow* changes to *grew*. This difference illustrates **regular** and **irregular** verbs, the two groups into which all English verbs are classified. *Earn* is a regular verb, *grow* is an irregular verb. (Lesson 21 discusses irregular verbs in more detail.)

Notice also that some verb forms consist of more than one word *(will earn, have grown, had earned, will have been)*. In such uses, *will, had,* and *have* are called **auxiliary verbs**. More auxiliary verbs are examined in Lesson 5.

With the "naming" words (nouns and pronouns) and the "action" words (verbs), you can construct true sentences:

Janice arrived.
He laughed.
Power corrupts.

But to make sentences more varied and complete, you need modifiers or "describing" words (adjectives and adverbs) and prepositional phrases.

Adjectives

An **adjective** is a word that describes or limits—that is, gives qualities to—a noun. Adjectives are found in three different positions in a sentence:

1. Preceding a noun that is in any of the noun positions within the sentence

   The *small* child left. He is a *small* child. I saw the *small* child. I gave it to the *small* child.

2. Following a describing (linking) verb and modifying the subject

   The child is *small*. Mary looked *unhappy*. We became *upset*.

3. Directly following the noun (less common than the two positions described above)

   He provided the money *necessary* for the trip. The hostess, *calm and serene*, entered the hall.

Certain characteristics of form and function help you to recognize adjectives. There are several suffixes that, when added to other words or roots of other words, form adjectives. Here again, an understanding of the meaning of a suffix can save trips to the dictionary. For instance, in the hundreds of adjectives ending in *able (ible)*, the suffix means "capable of" or "tending to"; thus *usable* means "capable of being used" and *changeable* means "tending to change."

> able, ible [read*able*, irresist*ible*]; al [internation*al*]; ant, ent [resist*ant*, diverg*ent*]; ar [lun*ar*]; ary [budget*ary*]; ful [meaning*ful*]; ic, ical [cosm*ic*, hyster*ical*]; ish [fool*ish*]; ive [invent*ive*]; less [blame*less*]; ous [glamor*ous*]; y [greas*y*]

One note of warning: Many other words in English end with these letters, but you can easily see that they are not employing a suffix. Ta*ble*, fer*ment*, ar*rive*, d*ish*, and pon*y*, for instance, are not adjectives. (See Supplement 1 for more information on adjectives.)

Adjectives Used in Comparisons

Nearly all adjectives, when they are used in comparisons, can be strengthened or can show degree by changing form or by using *more* and *most:*

> *great* trust, *greater* trust, *greatest* trust
> *sensible* answer, *more sensible* answer, *most sensible* answer

The base form (*great* trust, *sensible* answer) is the **positive degree.** The second form (*greater* trust, *more sensible* answer) is the **comparative degree:** it compares two things. The third form (*greatest* trust, *most sensible* answer) is the **superlative degree** and distinguishes among three or more things. (See Supplement 2.)

Adverbs

Another modifier is the **adverb,** a word that modifies anything except a noun or a pronoun. Most adverbs modify verbs (She walked *quickly.*). Other adverbs modify adjectives and other adverbs (The *very* old man walked *quite slowly*). Some adverbs modify whole sentences (*Consequently,* we refused the offer).

Adverbs tell certain things about the verb, the most common being:

1. **Manner:** John performed *well.* We worked *hard.* The child laughed *happily.* I would *gladly* change places with you.
2. **Time:** I must leave *now.* I'll see you *later. Soon* we shall meet *again.*
3. **Frequency:** We *often* go on picnics, *sometimes* at the lake but *usually* in the city park.
4. **Place:** *There* he sat, alone and silent. *Somewhere* we shall find peace and quiet.
5. **Direction:** The police officer turned *away.* I moved *forward* in the bus.
6. **Degree:** I could *barely* hear the speaker. I *absolutely* refuse to believe that story.

The most frequently used adverbs answer such questions as "How?" (manner or degree), "When?" (time or frequency), and "Where?" (place or direction).

Adverbs of a subclass called **intensifiers** modify adjectives or adverbs but not verbs. For example, a *very* good meal, his *quite* surprising reply, *too* often, *somewhat* reluctantly, and so on.

Many adverbs change form the way adjectives do, to show degree:

to drive *fast,* to drive *faster,* to drive *fastest*

to perform *satisfactorily,* to perform *more satisfactorily,* to perform *most satisfactorily*

See Supplement 2 for details on some common irregular intensifiers.

Prepositions

A **preposition** is a word that introduces a phrase and shows the relationship between the object of the phrase and some other word in the sentence. Notice that many prepositions show a relationship of space or time. Here are some common prepositions; those in the last column are called *group prepositions:*

about	beside	inside	through	according to
above	besides	into	throughout	because of
across	between	like	till	by way of
after	beyond	near	to	in addition to
against	by	of	toward	in front of
around	down	off	under	in place of
at	during	on	unfit	in regard to
before	except	out	up	in spite of
behind	for	outside	upon	instead of
below	from	over	with	on account of
beneath	in	since	without	out of

A preposition always has an object; with its object and any modifiers, the preposition makes a **prepositional phrase.** You can easily illustrate the function of prepositions by constructing sentences like the following:

After breakfast I walked *to* town *without* my friend. [Objects: *breakfast, town, friend.*]

On account of the rain, I canceled my plans *for* a game *of* tennis *at* the park *with* John. [Objects: *rain, game, tennis, park, John.*]

The trees *outside* the window *of* the kitchen are full *of* blossoms *during* the spring. [Objects: *window, kitchen, blossoms, spring.*]

Supplement 1

Besides what could be called true adjectives, there are other classes of words that modify nouns. If you concentrate on the *functions* of the various kinds of words, however, you can safely classify as adjectives all words that precede nouns and limit their meaning. Such adjectives include articles, numerals, and possessives (*an* apple, *the* weather, *my three* roommates); modifiers that can be used also as pronouns (*these* people, *some* friends, *all* workers); and nouns that modify other nouns (*basketball* players, *summer* days, *crop* failures).

Many words can be used as adjectives or as pronouns; the position of a word within the sentence determines which part of speech it is.

Several [*adj.*] classmates of mine [*pron.*] read this [*adj.*] report.
Several [*pron.*] of my [*adj.*] classmates read this [*pron.*].

Supplement 2

A few commonly used modifiers form their comparative and superlative degrees irregularly:

good *(adj.)*,	better,	best
well *(adv.)*,	better,	best
bad *(adj.)*,	worse,	worst

NAME _____ SCORE _____

Directions: In each space at the left, write one of the following numbers to identify the part of speech of each italicized word:

1. Noun	3. Verb	5. Adverb
2. Pronoun	4. Adjective	6. Preposition

———— 1. Far *below*, the people walked *slowly* down the sidewalk.
————

———— 2. *Few* of the new students ran the mile *within* the time limit.
————

———— 3. A *few* of the younger women responded *admirably* in the crisis.
————

———— 4. The professor's least *admirable* trait was chronic *grouchiness*.
————

———— 5. Marvin made a very *pointed* reference *to* Jan's late arrival.
————

———— 6. Then Jan referred *pointedly* to Marvin's hasty departure *yesterday*.
————

———— 7. Your great *haste* in our last session *spoiled* our report.
————

———— 8. My nephew *behaved* like a *spoiled* brat at dinner last night.
————

———— 9. Your brave response to Michael's *challenge* was *admirable*.
————

———— 10. "The *new* schedule changes my hours *considerably*," said Hester.
————

———— 11. Sam used *my* tennis racket rather than *yours*.
————

———— 12. *This* is my *most* difficult semester in years.
————

———— 13. "*Most of* you will laugh when you hear my story," said Maurice.
————

———— 14. The crowd was *mostly older* people in their late twenties and early thirties.
————

———— 15. My fiance waited for *me outside* the classroom door.
————

———— 16. *Outside*, the weather is simply *awful*.
————

———— 17. "Morgan, *that* was an *awfully* kind gesture," said my British cousin.
————

———— 18. Martha sings *quite* beautifully in *this* production.
————

_____ 19. Anyone could have thought of *such* a *simple* solution.
_____

_____ 20. I *simply* cannot find a replacement *for* Melanie in the quartet.
_____

_____ 21. *Nobody* stands *above* you on the promotion list.
_____

_____ 22. My brother *still* drives that *ancient* car.
_____

_____ 23. The manager *designated* Jim to find a new secretary *quickly*.
_____

_____ 24. Few of the *other* members consider Tom *dependable*.
_____

_____ 25. Constant *dependence* on the notes of other students caused Jim's problems
_____   *in* history class.

_____ 26. The meteorologists *depend* on the weather satellite to report changes
_____   *promptly*.

_____ 27. That *tasty* casserole appealed to the pickiest *eaters* in camp.
_____

_____ 28. The *taste* of the casserole appealed to the camp's *pickiest* eaters.
_____

_____ 29. *Kindness* is a most welcome *trait* in young children.
_____

_____ 30. The *kind* old woman gave the tired *hikers* a hot meal.
_____

_____ 31. Stand *up*, James, and speak *clearly*.
_____

_____ 32. *My* model works successfully; *yours* has failed.
_____

_____ 33. Of the three cars, the *oldest* one runs *best*.
_____

_____ 34. I get the *best* service *from* the oldest car.
_____

_____ 35. Henry's last paper *definitely pleased* his instructor.
_____

_____ 36. Lack of *definite* goals *quickly* doomed the latest reform movement.
_____

_____ 37. *Before* the coffee break Jane worked *slowly*.
_____

_____ 38. A *slow dance* is popular with some people.
_____

_____ 39. The *hard* pavement *scarcely* scuffed the new basketball.
_____

_____ 40. During the drought the farmer worked *hard* despite the *scarce* supply of
_____   water.

Exercise 2   *Parts of Speech*

NAME _____ SCORE _____

Directions: In each space at the left, write one of the following numbers to identify the part of speech of each italicized word:

1. Noun	3. Verb	5. Adverb
2. Pronoun	4. Adjective	6. Preposition

_____ 1. We might expect a *few* comments *from* the new manager.

_____ 2. The damage to the bridge was *quite extensive.*

_____ 3. The two fraternity skits *really amused* the crowd.

_____ 4. Her *great* amusement at the skits was *clear* to everyone.

_____ 5. "Your idea is *clearly* not *acceptable* to the group," said Al.

_____ 6. Barbara's *acceptance* to the Naval Academy came *yesterday.*

_____ 7. *Actually,* the *best* band in the contest was eliminated early.

_____ 8. Our new phone system is an *exact* duplicate of the system *at* headquarters.

_____ 9. We cannot *duplicate* the *noise* of that crowd.

_____ 10. A *few* of the first graders *found* arrowheads on the river bank.

_____ 11. *One* first grader put *his* in a small bag.

_____ 12. Last Saturday we *left early* for the drive to Canton.

_____ 13. Mack caught the *early* plane *to* Peoria.

_____ 14. *After* the movie last night, we went *out* for a pizza.

_____ 15. The students worked especially *hard* on *that* new project.

_____ 16. Their *hard* work was rewarded *with* an excellent evaluation.

_____ 17. Her *absence* was noted by all the staff *members.*

_____ 18. Mark was *absent* from class *yesterday.*

_____ 19. The committee selected *your* entry rather than *mine.*

_____ 20. *Selection* by the nominating committee is a *great* honor.

_____ 21. Beth's *enthusiasm* for her new job is *commendable.*

_____ 22. We *often commend* her for her enthusiastic attitude.

_____ 23. The *harshness* of the sergeant's voice startled *us.*

_____ 24. The supervisor *voiced* her displeasure *harshly.*

_____ 25. *This* is the only *usable* plan.

_____ 26. The lack of fan *support* had a *negative* effect on the team's performance.

_____ 27. The tornado *leveled* three *small* sheds on one farm in the area.

_____ 28. Those slender beams *support* the entire structure *of* the roof.

_____ 29. The *first* of the ripe peaches are *already* in the stores.

_____ 30. From far away came the mournful *notes* of a *bass* clarinet.

_____ 31. Three computers are *available* for the students in the *back* of the classroom.

_____ 32. *He* is the *most* talented of the rookie pitchers.

_____ 33. We all *admit* that she is a *likable* person.

_____ 34. *Several* of the lawyers in our office *think* that the testimony is inadmissible.

_____ 35. Your nephew made an *extremely* favorable *impression* on us.

_____ 36. The judges were not impressed *by* the *arguments* of the defense attorneys.

_____ 37. *Yours* was *probably* the best new novel on last year's list.

_____ 38. Loud *applause* from the crowd *echoed* through the vast auditorium.

_____ 39. We placed the new piano *against* the *inside* wall of the living room.

_____ 40. *Later,* Johnson became locally famous as a poet.

Directions: Each of these words is labeled as a noun, verb, adjective, or adverb. In the spaces following each word, write related words of the part of speech indicated. (Do not use adjectives ending in *ing* or *ed.*

Example: laugh (n.) ____*laughingly*____ (adv.) ____*laughs*____ (v.)

1. argument (n.) _____ (v.) _____ (adv.)

2. brave (v.) _____ (adv.) _____ (adj.)

3. bashfully (adv.) _____ (n.) _____ (adj.)

4. cancel (v.) _____ (n.) _____ (adj.)

5. dirty (v.) _____ (adj.) _____ (n.)

6. charitable (adj.) _____ (adv.) _____ (n.)

7. denial (n.) _____ (v.) _____ (adj.)

8. embarrass (v.) _____ (adv.) _____ (n.)

9. empathy (n.) _____ (v.) _____ (adv.)

10. fall (v.) _____ (n.) _____ (adj.)

11. free (adj.) _____ (adv.) _____ (n.)

12. gladness (n.) _____ (adj.) _____ (adv.)

13. injure (v.) _____ (n.) _____ (adj.)

14. luxurious (adj.) _____ (v.) _____ (adv.)

15. mystery (n.) _____ (adj.) _____ (adv.)

16. offend (v.) _____ (n.) _____ (adj.)

17. recognizable (adj.) _____ (v.) _____ (n.)

18. ridiculous (adj.) _____ (adv.) _____ (v.)

19. roughly (adv.) _____ (v.) _____ (adj.)

20. tame (adj.) _____ (adv.) _____ (v.)

NAME _____ SCORE _____

Directions: In the first space at the left, copy the subject of the sentence. In the second space, copy the verb. Many of the verbs consist of more than one word.

S. _____ 1. Yesterday three of my friends flew to Spain.
V. _____

S. _____ 2. With the opening of the new highway, we heard a great deal of
V. _____   traffic noise in our house.

S. _____ 3. A few of the visitors had recently come from Vancouver.
V. _____

S. _____ 4. A shortage of skilled workers in the shop has caused serious
V. _____   delays in production.

S. _____ 5. The recent graduates from boot camp will soon be departing for
V. _____   advanced training at other bases.

S. _____ 6. The real surprise in that game was Will, the designated hitter.
V. _____

S. _____ 7. The next arrival of a flight from Toronto will be tomorrow at
V. _____   noon.

S. _____ 8. Beside the books on that table were my car keys.
V. _____

S. _____ 9. By this time next week there will be no books on that subject in
V. _____   the library.

S. _____ 10. Behind the farmhouse stands a large grove of walnut trees.
V. _____

S. _____ 11. Monday is the first day of exams for this term.
V. _____

S. _____ 12. I've never heard a better performance from our local orchestra.
V. _____

S. _____ 13. My hardest course last term was calculus.
V. _____

S. _____ 14. In the attic behind the doorway into the storage room you'll find
V. _____   that trunk full of old papers.

S. _____ 15. Everybody in that building knows about the faulty air conditioner.
V. _____

S. _____ 16. Without that information we will need an entirely new method
V. _____   for determining our prices.

S. _____ 17. Neither of the people at the interview yesterday seemed familiar
V. _____   to me.

S. _____ 18. On the floor behind her running shoes, Marge located her lost
V. _____   belt.

S. _____ 19. Jan's the only member of our staff with a private office.
V. _____

S. _____ 20. Even with all that work in preparation for the exam, Jack still
V. _____   didn't make a good grade.

S. _____ 21. The company president, along with his new assistant, rode to the
V. _____   banquet in a limousine.

S. _____ 22. After two unsuccessful efforts, we finally reached an academic
V. _____   advisor.

S. _____ 23. My father, with two of his colleagues, is leaving for the conven-
V. _____   tion this morning.

S. _____ 24. One of Mary's friends had arrived on campus during that first
V. _____   class.

S. _____ 25. A brief stop for lunch became a tiresome experience because of
V. _____   a dead car battery.

S. _____ 26. A response to my letter of complaint came by return mail.
V. _____

S. _____ 27. Barb's interested in a major in art history.
V. _____

S. _____ 28. The team's quarterback, with a shy smile and a wave to the crowd,
V. _____   left the stage after his speech.

S. _____ 29. After the end of the winter semester many of the rooms in the
V. _____   dormitories are empty.

S. _____ 30. People from all over the valley come to that beautiful spring for
V. _____   their drinking water.

S. _____ 31. Good advice about course selection, along with ideas from for-
V. _____   mer students, appears in that short pamphlet.

S. _____ 32. Under the couch in the den the puppy has hidden one of my
V. _____   shoes.

S. _____ 33. That small stretch of sand is the most beautiful beach on this
V. _____   entire stretch of coastline.

S. _____ 34. Alongside the President walk his two Secret Service agents.
V. _____

S. _____ 35. Five staff members have worked for two weeks on that report.
V. _____

S. _____ 36. The arrival of Mickey Mouse at the theater inspired an excited
V. _____   cheer from all the children in the audience.

S. _____ 37. My father has owned that boat for ten years.
V. _____

S. _____ 38. Jane's excited about the prospects of the tennis team for the new
V. _____   season.

S. _____ 39. The new football coaches, along with their wives, will move to
V. _____   town next month.

S. _____ 40. There's little opportunity for practice on that particular course.
V. _____

Lesson 3 — *Basic Sentence Patterns with Intransitive Verbs*

As you know from Lesson 1, the sentence, a combination of subject and predicate arranged to make a statement, is the basic unit of written and oral communication. There are just five sentence types or patterns, and learning to recognize those five patterns can help you to become a more effective communicator. In this lesson and the following lesson, we will look at the five patterns so that you can learn to use them in your writing.

The nature of the verb is the key to recognizing sentence patterns. There are two types of verbs, transitive and intransitive. The prefix *trans* means across, and the letters *it* come from the Latin word meaning to *go,* so *transit* means to go across. The additional prefix *in* means *not,* so *intransit* means not to go across. (Don't confuse the Latin word with the colloquial *in-transit,* which means in the act of going somewhere.)

When an **intransitive verb** is used, the verb does not transfer its action to an object. In the sentence "John spoke softly," the action is *spoke* and the actor is *John.* The action does not "go across" to a noun that receives that action. The verb is intransitive. Some intransitive verbs do not express an action; they simply connect or link the subject to a noun that renames the subject or to an adjective that modifies the subject. These types of intransitive verbs are called **linking verbs.** In the following sentences there is no action:

> John is a *genius.*
> John is *brilliant.*

The subject *John* is simply linked by the verb to a word that identifies or modifies it.

In our system, Sentence Patterns 1 and 2 use intransitive verbs. Sentence Patterns 3, 4, and 5 use transitive verbs and are addressed in Lesson 4.

Sentence Pattern 1

Sentence Pattern 1 contains an intransitive verb and is the only sentence pattern that does not require a word to complete the sense of the action. Some activity takes place in each of these sentences, but no completer is needed because the action of the verb is not transferred to anything.

> The child *runs.*
> The tree *fell.*
> The customer *complained* loudly.
> The professor *walked* into the room unexpectedly.

The action of the verb is complete within itself. Pattern 1 sentences nearly always contain modifiers that tell how, when, and where the action occurred:

> Yesterday the neighborhood children played noisily in the vacant lot.

Notice that the material associated with the verb is all adverbial: "When?" *Yesterday.* "How?" *Noisily.* "Where?" *In the vacant lot.* The important characteristic of a Pattern 1 sentence is that there is no noun answering the question "What?" after the verb. The best way to recognize an intransitive verb is to spot the lack of a noun answering the question "What?" after the verb.

In some Pattern 1 sentences, the purpose of the statement is simply to say that the subject exists. Usually some adverbial material is added to show the place or the time of the existence:

> The glasses *are* in the cabinet.
> Flash floods often *occur* in the spring.
> There *were* several birds around the feeder.

Before you study the remaining sentence patterns, we need to define a term that identifies an important part of the sentences in the four remaining patterns. As you know, the two parts of any sentence are the subject and the predicate. The central core of the predicate is the verb, but the predicate also often includes words that complete the thought of the sentence. Words that follow the verb and complete the thought of the sentence are called **complements.** Complements can be nouns, pronouns, or adjectives, but all serve the same purpose in the sentence: they complete the idea or sense of the sentence.

Sentence Pattern 2

Pattern 2 includes two closely related kinds of sentences. The purpose of the first type of Pattern 2 sentence is to rename the subject, to say that the subject is the same as something else. In the sentence "John is a genius," the noun *genius* is called a **subjective complement** because it completes the verb and renames the subject. (See Supplement.) The intransitive linking verb used in Pattern 2 sentences is often a form of *be.*

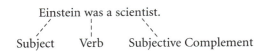

Note that both words, *Einstein* and *scientist,* refer to the same thing. There is no action; rather, a connection is established between the subject and the verb.

In the second type of Pattern 2 sentence, the subjective complement is an adjective, a word that describes rather than renames the subject. For example, in the sentence "The child is clever," the subject is joined by the verb to an adjective, again called a subjective complement. Comparatively few verbs serve the linking function. For convenience, you can think of them in three closely related groups:

1. *Be,* the most commonly used linking verb, and a few others meaning essentially the same thing: *seem, appear, prove, remain, continue,* and so forth

> John *is* a talented musician.
> The performer *seemed* nervous.
> He *remained* calm.
> His words *proved* meaningless.

2. *Become,* and a few others like it: *turn, grow, work, get, wear,* and so forth

   Later she *became* an accountant.
   Soon he *grew* tired of the game.
   Billy *turned* red from embarrassment.

3. A few verbs referring to the senses (*look, smell, taste, feel, sound*), which can be followed by adjective subjective complements that describe the condition of the subject

   The roses *look* beautiful in that vase.
   This milk *tastes* sour.

The ability to recognize Pattern 2 sentences will help you understand a few troublesome usage problems that will be examined in a later lesson—to understand why, for instance, careful writers use "feel bad" rather than "feel badly": "*I feel* bad about the election results."

Supplement

A note about grammatical terminology is needed here. A noun following a linking verb and renaming the subject is sometimes called a *predicate noun* or a *predicate nominative;* and an adjective following a linking verb and describing the subject is sometimes called a *predicate adjective.*

subjective complement (n.)	=	predicate noun
		predicate nominative
subjective complement (adj.)	=	predicate adjective

NAME _____   SCORE _____

Directions: Each of the following sentences is a Pattern 2 sentence containing a noun (or a pronoun) subjective complement. In the space at the left, copy the subjective complement.

_____ 1. Obviously, her efforts in that situation were a complete failure.

_____ 2. Her opponent in the next election will probably be an experienced politician.

_____ 3. With my uncle's help, my sister Nell has become an expert chess player.

_____ 4. The last-place finisher in yesterday's race was the early leader in today's race.

_____ 5. That small island was the location for our last picnic.

_____ 6. The conductor was the last person off the train after the accident.

_____ 7. Stolen items are an important part of any store's financial status.

_____ 8. This Saturday's game will be Jim's last appearance as a baseball player.

_____ 9. The source of that wild rumor will probably remain a mystery.

_____ 10. Two players from last year's team are now members of professional teams.

_____ 11. Mary and Hank have been a great help to me in this class.

_____ 12. The constant talking in the classroom next door became a distraction to the test takers.

_____ 13. My neighbor was a big winner in the state lottery last month.

_____ 14. During the absence of our team leader, Mike became a valuable source of information on our project.

_____ 15. Maybe this small success can be the first of many successful efforts.

_____ 16. That program has always been one of my favorites.

_____ 17. After several rounds of bidding on that chair, hers was the highest bid.

_____ 18. A car like that one might be a good choice for your sister.

_____ 19. We've always been close friends with the Johnsons.

_____ 20. Those early efforts at voter registration were the key to victory in the last election.

27

Directions: Each of the following sentences is a Pattern 2 sentence containing an adjective subjective complement. In the space at the left, copy the subjective complement.

_____ 1. By late yesterday afternoon, the stadium was full of fans.

_____ 2. Because of the weight of her pack, Julie grew very tired later in the afternoon.

_____ 3. In the bright sunlight, the milk on the porch quickly turned sour.

_____ 4. Midway through the roller coaster ride, Harry suddenly felt quite ill.

_____ 5. Martha will never become reconciled to the new political climate in Washington.

_____ 6. All of the committee's efforts toward a resolution of the conflict proved fruitless.

_____ 7. After months of training, I still did not feel ready for the expedition.

_____ 8. This batch of syrup tastes much sweeter than the previous batch.

_____ 9. By late afternoon the sky had turned quite dark.

_____ 10. The situation in the branch office in Rochester seemed totally unmanageable.

_____ 11. Valerie's not very flexible in her attitude toward new taxes.

_____ 12. That area of quiet water behind the big boulder looks attractive to fishermen.

_____ 13. She's excited by her new job in advertising.

_____ 14. The wind grew very cold later in the afternoon.

_____ 15. Those orchids look beautiful in that new display.

_____ 16. He'd always remained calm in the toughest situations.

_____ 17. On our project, help from anyone else seems unlikely.

_____ 18. Elaine was extremely happy with her grade on the calculus final.

_____ 19. Purchase of that tract of swamp land by The Nature Conservancy is probable under the new budget.

_____ 20. Your delight with that new car is obvious to everyone.

Exercise 3   *Sentence Patterns with Intransitive Verbs*

NAME _____ SCORE _____

Directions: Circle the subject and underline the verb in each of the following sentences. If the sentence is a Pattern 2 sentence, copy the subjective complement in the space at the left. If the sentence is a Pattern 1 sentence, leave the space blank.

_____ 1. Several trucks had already skidded off the highway.

_____ 2. Three of the cook's helpers argued noisily in the kitchen.

_____ 3. Grandfather has always been an extremely stubborn person.

_____ 4. The last of the buses has already left for the airport.

_____ 5. To us naive beginners, the whole process looked alarmingly complex.

_____ 6. With a smile on his face and laughter in his eyes, the old man walked quickly from the room.

_____ 7. In the hot weather, the butter out on the table turned soft very quickly.

_____ 8. This class looks unusually alert this morning.

_____ 9. Those sales figures can be, at best, only an educated guess at this time.

_____ 10. After the meeting with the president and his aide, Jim seemed very happy.

_____ 11. Here are your assignments for the next week.

_____ 12. The three dogs usually ride with Fred in the cab of the truck.

_____ 13. Early in the trial most of the jurors became convinced of the defendant's innocence.

_____ 14. The response to the appeal for money and canned goods for the storm's victims was surprisingly generous.

_____ 15. Some ice-cold lemonade will taste good after this long hike.

_____ 16. In next year's budget, the allotment for our department's budget is totally inadequate.

_____ 17. All of the students in my dorm studied hard for that test.

_____ 18. To most of my friends, the test seemed extremely hard.

_____ 19. The restoration of those historic buildings was a major project for the members of the Historical Society.

_____ 20. One of the suspects in the convenience store robbery has confessed to the crime.

_____ 21. About half of the students arrived late for class on Monday morning.

_____ 22. Margie's old car always looks spotlessly clean.

_____ 23. In spite of our efforts at friendship, the new neighbors remain unfriendly.

_____ 24. On the back cover of the book appears a picture of the author and his beautiful dog.

_____ 25. Monday will be the first day of the new president's term here at the college.

_____ 26. After the game most of the students remained in the stadium for about an hour.

_____ 27. In his call to his parents last night, Alex seemed delighted with his new schedule.

_____ 28. On the platform at the front of the room sat the four judges.

_____ 29. After a short rest and a big meal, we all felt quite refreshed.

_____ 30. That's Ginny's new car, the one next to the red truck in the parking lot.

_____ 31. Serious brush fires have broken out in the lower part of the valley.

_____ 32. The people at the front desk have been busy all morning long.

_____ 33. The first thing on my list for today is a strong cup of coffee.

_____ 34. The group's next big project will be a trip to Trinidad during spring break.

_____ 35. The river below that factory was once highly polluted.

_____ 36. Jack's success in that course seemed unlikely after his poor performance in the previous semester.

_____ 37. Dr. Johnson's speech at commencement was blessedly short.

_____ 38. Two beautiful Siamese cats lay on the floor in front of the fireplace.

_____ 39. Next Tuesday will probably be our only chance for an afternoon off in the next two weeks.

_____ 40. At the end of the last class, all of us left immediately for the lake.

Lesson 4   *Basic Sentence Patterns with Transitive Verbs*

In Sentence Pattern 2, the intransitive verb links the subject to a noun or adjective that completes the idea of the sentence: "Maria is our pitcher"; "Maria is brilliant." When a **transitive verb** is used, the action expressed by the verb "goes across" to some noun that receives the action. That noun is called the **direct object** and is the receiver of the action expressed in the verb. In the sentence "John watched a movie," the action (the verb) is *watched,* and the actor (the subject) is *John.* The receiver of the action (the direct object) is *movie.* The direct object can be found by asking the question What? after the subject and verb have been found. "John watched what? John watched a movie."

Sentence Pattern 3

In Pattern 3 sentences, the verb is a transitive verb. It does not link or connect; instead, it identifies an action and transfers that action to a receiver or object of the action (the direct object). The subject–verb combination of the sentence does not complete a thought unless there is an object to receive the action named in the verb. For example, in the sentence "The child hits the ball," the subject–verb combination (*child hits*) does not make a complete statement. A complete statement requires that the child hit *something.*

The direct object is always a noun or a noun equivalent, such as a pronoun:

I broke my glasses. What names the activity? *Broke* is the verb. Who broke? *I* is the subject. I broke what? *Glasses.* Thus, *glasses* is the direct object.

Someone saw us. What names the activity? *Saw.* Who saw? *Someone* saw. Someone saw what? *Us* is the direct object.

We need to draw a contrast between a Pattern 2 sentence and a Pattern 3 sentence. Although both patterns require a complement, in a Pattern 2 sentence such as "The child is a genius," the subject is either renamed or modified by the subjective complement. In the sentence "Someone saw us," it is clear that *someone* and *us* are not the same. *Us* is the receiver of the action *saw* and simply cannot be taken to be the same as the *someone* who saw. In both Pattern 2 and Pattern 3 sentences, the thought of the sentence is not complete without a complement, but in Pattern 3 the subject acts upon the complement, the direct object.

Sentence Pattern 4

Pattern 4 sentences also contain a direct object. But because Pattern 4 sentences use verbs such as *give* or *show,* the sentences need a **second** complement to complete their thought. After a transitive verb such as *shows, gives,* or *tells,* the direct object (the receiver of the action) answers the question Who? or What? and an **indirect object** answers the question To whom? or For whom? Thus, "She sang a lullaby," is a Pattern 3 sentence, but "She gave the children a gift," is a Pattern 4 sentence.

In the sentence "The parents give the child a present," you can easily see that two complements are used. The sentence mentions the thing that is given (*present*, the direct object) and the person to whom the direct object is given (*child*, the indirect object). Although the indirect object usually names a person, it can name a nonhuman thing, as in "We gave your *application* a careful reading."

Other verbs that are commonly used this way and therefore produce a Pattern 4 structure are *allow, assign, ask, tell, write, send, pay, grant,* and so on. Nearly all sentences using such verbs can make essentially the same statement by using a prepositional phrase, usually beginning with the preposition *to* or *for*. When the prepositional phrase is present in the sentence, it is a Pattern 3 sentence.

> The postman brought me a letter. [Pattern 4; *me* is an indirect object.]
>
> The postman brought a letter to me. [Pattern 3; *me* is the object of a preposition.]
>
> Mother bought us some candy. [Pattern 4]
>
> Mother bought some candy for us. [Pattern 3]

Sentence Pattern 5

Pattern 5 sentences regularly use verbs such as *consider, call, think, find, make, elect, appoint,* and *name*. There are two closely related types of Pattern 5 sentences. Each type starts out like a Pattern 3 sentence:

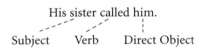

His sister called him.

Subject   Verb   Direct Object

But the nature of the verb *called* allows the use of a second complement answering the question "What?" after *called him*. His sister called him what?

> His sister called him a genius.

The reference of the two nouns following the verb is a key to the difference between this type of sentence and a Pattern 4 sentence. In a Pattern 4 sentence the two noun complements refer to different things, but in a Pattern 5 sentence they refer to the same thing.

> Mother made us some fudge. [Pattern 4; *us* and *fudge* refer to different things.]
>
> This experience made John an activist. [Pattern 5; *John* and *activist* are the same thing.]

Thus there are two complements in Pattern 5 sentences. The one closer to the verb is the direct object. The second complement is called the **objective complement**. In the first type of Pattern 5 sentence the objective complement is a noun that *renames* the direct object. In the second type of Pattern 5 sentence, the objective complement is an adjective that *describes* the direct object.

> His sister called him a genius.
> His sister called him brilliant.

Because the objective complement renames or describes the direct object, we can use a handy test to help us recognize Pattern 5: The insertion of *to be* between the complements will give us an acceptable English wording.

We appointed Jones [to be] our representative.
I thought this action [to be] unnecessary.

Sometimes the word *as* is used between the direct object and the objective complement in Pattern 5 sentences:

We appointed Jones as our representative.

Some adjective objective complements are very important to the meaning of the verb. Thus, it is sometimes effective to place these objective complements immediately after the verb and before the direct object:

Usual order: He set the caged animals [D.O.] free [O.C.].
Variation: He set free [O.C.] the caged animals [D.O.].

Supplement

With one special kind of verb, there is a problem of distinguishing between a direct object and the object of a preposition. Here are two examples:

Harry jumped off the box.
Harry took off his raincoat.

The first sentence is Pattern 1. *Off* is a preposition, *box* is the object of the preposition, and the prepositional phrase is used as an adverbial modifier, because it tells *where* Harry jumped. The second sentence is Pattern 3. The verb, with its adverbial modifier *off*, is the equivalent of the transitive verb *remove*. *Raincoat* is the direct object.

There is another way to distinguish between the adverbial use and the prepositional use of such a word as *off* in the preceding examples. When the word is a vital adverbial modifier of the verb, it can be used in either of two positions: following the verb or following the direct object.

Harry took off his raincoat.
Harry took his raincoat off.

When the word is a preposition, the alternate position is not possible: "Harry jumped the box off" is not an English sentence. Here are some other examples of verbs with adverbial modifiers. Notice that in each case you can easily find a transitive verb synonym for the combination:

Give up [*relinquish*] her rights.
Leave out [*omit*] the second chapter.
Put out [*extinguish*] the fire.
Make over [*alter*] an old dress.
Make up [*invent*] an excuse.

SUMMARY OF VERBS USED IN DIFFERENT SENTENCE PATTERNS

1. **Verbs that serve a linking function and commonly form Pattern 2 sentences:**
   be, seem, appear, prove, remain, continue, become, turn, grow, work, get, wear, look, smell, taste, feel, sound

2. **Verbs that commonly produce Pattern 4 sentences:**
   allow, assign, ask, tell, write, send, pay, grant

3. **Verbs that commonly produce Pattern 5 sentences:**
   consider, call, think, find, make, elect, appoint, name

NAME _____   SCORE _____

Directions: Each of these sentences is a Pattern 3 sentence. Circle the subject and underline each verb. In the space at the left, copy the direct object.

_____ 1. The boys sampled nearly every one of the prize-winning cookies.

_____ 2. Your sister made an excellent impression on the interviewing committee.

_____ 3. Richard has not read any of that assignment in the textbook.

_____ 4. I will bookmark that site on the Internet.

_____ 5. Last night on television we watched the first half of a very exciting movie.

_____ 6. Bob found one of those coins in the parking lot.

_____ 7. Because of her long years of experience, my Aunt Martha plays a mean game of tennis.

_____ 8. The next test will cover the material in the first three chapters in the textbook.

_____ 9. Dozens of people cleaned up the vacant lot on the corner of Fourth Avenue and High Street.

_____ 10. Our club appreciates your generous gift to that charity.

_____ 11. At last night's rodeo, we watched exciting bull-riding by some very brave cowboys.

_____ 12. As part of your new assignment, you will count the money at the end of the night shift.

_____ 13. Mrs. Rawlings always enjoys her students' short stories.

_____ 14. The three men crossed the makeshift bridge very cautiously.

_____ 15. The senator pointed out some significant changes in the tax law.

_____ 16. On my way home from work tonight, I'll pick up a couple of pizzas.

_____ 17. Bob's wife bought the largest SUV on the market.

_____ 18. The windstorm last night knocked down several trees at the back of our yard.

_____ 19. Jack hit the best serve of the match on that last point.

_____ 20. Yesterday Pam cut up the vegetables for the stew long before lunch time.

Directions: The following are Pattern 3, 4, or 5 sentences. Identify the italicized complement by writing one of the following in the space at the left:

    D.O. [direct object]   I.O. [indirect object]   O.C. [objective complement]

_____ 1. Marsha has usually completed *all* of her deliveries before noon.

_____ 2. The carpenter made the opening for the window *larger*.

_____ 3. The crowd-control ropes will keep out the curious *spectators*.

_____ 4. The new air conditioner will keep the room perfectly *cool*.

_____ 5. The judge gave the youthful first *offender* one more chance.

_____ 6. In yesterday's meeting the boss paid *Trisha* a great compliment.

_____ 7. The young politician has not yet paid off *all* of his campaign debts.

_____ 8. Next week I'll give *myself* a day off.

_____ 9. June's father found *her* an inexpensive used car.

_____ 10. The jury has found her *guilty* of taking a bribe.

_____ 11. Jackson found a few days' *work* at the local hat factory.

_____ 12. The new zoning regulation allows *either* of those businesses in this area.

_____ 13. Alice brought *Mom* some grape jelly from a farm down the valley.

_____ 14. The recruits consider the obstacle course extremely *difficult*.

_____ 15. The four of us thought up several new *projects* for the department.

_____ 16. The most recent storm left the farms in the valley *devastated*.

_____ 17. The company president's clear directive left no *room* for debate.

_____ 18. Uncle Roger's will left each *child* a small trust fund.

_____ 19. The angry child called her friend a *liar*.

_____ 20. This morning's crossword puzzle gave *us* three hours of amusing frustration.

Exercise 4   *Complements*

NAME _____   SCORE _____

Directions: Circle the subject and underline the verb in each of the following sentences. Identify the italicized complement by writing one of the following in the spaces at the left:

    S.C. [subjective complement]   D.O. [direct object]
    I.O. [indirect object]   O.C. [objective complement]

_____ 1. The President has made Ms. Sharpe his *chief of staff.*

_____ 2. The inventor suggested a new *product* for the company.

_____ 3. The book reviewer paid the *author* a very high compliment.

_____ 4. Hal offered *me* $150 for that pair of skis.

_____ 5. The television sportscaster called our team the *underdog* in the tournament.

_____ 6. The exhausted elderly man called a *taxi.*

_____ 7. The team gave *Freeman* a huge bonus for signing the contract.

_____ 8. To the people from Alaska, the humidity in Louisiana seemed extremely *high.*

_____ 9. June's nephew colored the wallpaper *blue.*

_____ 10. In response to my explanation, the teacher granted me an *extension* on the paper.

_____ 11. The stylist left Mary's hair very *curly.*

_____ 12. Uncle Sal told the *officer* a very lame story.

_____ 13. He's *one* of the best teachers in the entire college.

_____ 14. The boss called Mike's *departure* a great loss to our department.

_____ 15. Bob sang the school fight *song* off-key.

_____ 16. The cinnamon buns in the oven smell *spicy.*

_____ 17. All afternoon Helen has searched for her lost car *keys.*

_____ 18. Mrs. Cooper promised the kindergarten *children* a special dessert for tomorrow's lunch.

_____ 19. That brief shower was a welcome *relief* from the heat.

_____ 20. Every child recited the *poem* perfectly.

37

Directions: Using appropriate forms of the verb indicated, write twenty original sentences illustrating the following patterns:

       Sentences 1–5: Pattern 2
       Sentences 6–10: Pattern 3
       Sentences 11–15: Pattern 4
       Sentences 16–20: Pattern 5

1. be _____

2. become _____

3. remain _____

4. turn _____

5. grow _____

6. grow _____

7. repair _____

8. tear _____

9. cancel _____

10. spend _____

11. tell _____

12. give _____

13. read _____

14. show _____

15. assign _____

16. appoint _____

17. elect _____

18. color _____

19. find _____

20. leave _____

Lesson 5 *Forms of the Verb; Auxiliary Verbs*

In this lesson you will examine a few more forms and uses of verbs, including some additional auxiliary verbs. With these forms and those that you have already examined, you will be acquainted with nearly all of verb forms that the average speaker and writer will ever use.

In Lesson 2 you examined the partial conjugation of three verbs, *earn, grow,* and *be.* You may want to refer to that conjugation (pages 9–10) as we discuss a few more points about changes in verb form.

Third-person singular verbs in the present tense end in *s* (or *es*): *earns, teaches, is, has.* Notice that on nouns, the *s* (*es*) ending shows a plural form, whereas on verbs it shows a singular form:

> *dogs, noses*   (plural nouns)
> *wags, sniffs*   (singular verbs)

If you review the conjugation of the verb *be* in Lesson 2, you will notice the verb is completely irregular. Unlike any other verb in the language, it has three forms (*am, is,* and *are*) in the present tense and two forms (*was* and *were*) in the past tense.

In general, the tenses are used as follows:

Present: Action occurring at the present moment.
             He *earns* a good salary.

Past: Action occurring at a definite time before the present moment.
             Last year he *earned* a good salary.

Future: Action occurring at some time beyond the present moment.
             Next year he *will earn* a good salary.

Present perfect: Action continuing up to the present moment.
             So far this year he *has earned* ten thousand dollars.

Past perfect: Action continuing to a fixed moment in the past.
             Before leaving for college, he *had earned* ten thousand dollars.

Future perfect: Action continuing to a fixed moment in the future.
             By next Christmas he *will have earned* ten thousand dollars.

In Lesson 21 you will be reminded of a few usage problems involving tenses.

Principal Parts

We noted in Lesson 2 that *earn* is a regular verb and *grow* is an irregular verb. We customarily make use of three distinctive forms, called the **principal parts** of the verb, to show the difference between regular and irregular verbs. The principal parts are the:

- *Base* or infinitive, the "name" of the verb, used in the present tense with *s* (*es*) added in the third-person singular
- *Past,* the form used in the simple past tense
- *Past participle,* the form used in the three perfect tenses

In all regular verbs, the past and the past participle are alike, formed simply by the addition of *ed* to the base form (or only *d* if the base word ends in *e*). Thus, *earn* becomes *earned.* Irregular verbs are more complicated, because for nearly all of them the past tense and the past participle are not spelled alike. Thus, the past tense of *grow* is *grew* and the past participle of *grow* is *grown.* Following are the three forms of some irregular verbs, illustrating spelling changes and endings that are found.

Base	Past	Past Participle
be	was, were	been
become	became	become
bite	bit	bitten
break	broke	broken
catch	caught	caught
do	did	done
eat	ate	eaten
put	put	put
ring	rang	rung
run	ran	run
see	saw	seen

(You will study more principal parts of verbs and the usage problems associated with them in Lesson 21.) Both regular and irregular verbs add *ing* to their base form to produce the **present participle.** The present participle is often used with auxiliary verbs.

Auxiliary Verbs

In the sample conjugation in Lesson 2, you observed the use of *shall/will* and *have* as auxiliary verbs in the future tense and the perfect tenses. Another important auxiliary is *be,* used with the present participle (the *ing*) form of the main verb to produce what is called the **progressive form.** As an example of its use, suppose someone asks you what you are doing in your English class. You probably would not reply, "Right now, we *review* parts of speech." Instead, you probably would say, "Right now, we *are reviewing* parts of speech," to show that the action is not fixed in an exact moment of time but is a continuing activity. This very useful type of verb occurs in all six tenses:

We are reviewing.
We were reviewing.
We shall be reviewing.
We have been reviewing.
We had been reviewing.
We shall have been reviewing.

Another type of auxiliary verb includes *may, might, must, can, could, would,* and *should. May, can,* and *might* are used to suggest possibility. *Can* sometimes also suggests capability.

I may go to town tomorrow   (If certain conditions exist.)
I might go to town tomorrow. (If certain conditions exist.)
I can go to town tomorrow.   (I am able to go.)

Must indicates an obligation.

I must go to town.

Could is used to indicate ability, possibility, or permission in the past tense.

I could have gone to town.   (If I had wanted to go.)

These words are called **modal auxiliaries,** and they are used the way *will* and *shall* are used:

I *should study* this weekend.
I *should have studied* last weekend.

Occasionally *do* acts as a modal auxiliary and combines with the base form of a main verb to make an "emphatic" form (But I *did* pay that bill last month). In Lesson 6 you will examine the much more common use of the *do* auxiliary, in questions and negatives.

Other variations of some modals and "time" auxiliaries make use of *to* in the verb phrase.

Mr. Nelson *has to retire* [must retire] early.
You *ought to eat* [should eat] more vegetables.
I *used to be* a secretary.
Jim *was supposed to be here* at ten o'clock.
I *am to depart* for Miami early in the morning.
I *am going to depart* for Miami early in the morning.
We *meant to leave* much earlier today.

Here are a few other points to remember about auxiliary verbs:

1. *Have, be,* and *do* are not used exclusively as auxiliaries; they are three of the most commonly used main verbs:

   I *have* a brown pen. [Main verb]
   I *have* lost my brown pen. [Auxiliary]
   He *is* a good speaker. [Main verb]
   He *is* becoming a good speaker. [Auxiliary]
   He *did* a good job for us. [Main verb]
   Yes, I *did embellish* the story somewhat. [Auxiliary]

2. When the verb unit contains auxiliaries, there may be short adverbial modifiers separating parts of the whole verb phrase:

We *have* occasionally *been* sailing.
He *has,* of course, *been telling* the truth.

3. In a few set expressions following introductory adverbs, usually adverbs of time, the subject is placed within the verb phrase between an auxiliary and the main verb:

Only lately *have* I *learned* to drive.
Rarely *do* we *turn on* the television set.

NAME _____ SCORE _____

Directions: Each of these sentences contains at least one auxiliary verb. (Some have two; some have three.) Copy the auxiliary verb(s) in the first space at the left. In the second space, write **1, 2, 3, 4,** or **5** to identify the sentence pattern.

_____ _____   1. Marilyn has just mailed that contest entry to the television station.

_____ _____   2. Next we must find a new location for the graduation ceremony.

_____ _____   3. We should leave tomorrow at about five o'clock.

_____ _____   4. Careful preparations might give us more confidence during that important test next week.

_____ _____   5. A week in that beautiful setting on the lake would be extremely restful.

_____ _____   6. The new schedule at work will offer us an opportunity for a three-day weekend once a month.

_____ _____   7. By noon Professor Johnson had been walking briskly for about an hour.

_____ _____   8. There should have been a greater effort toward reconstruction in the wake of the tornado.

_____ _____   9. Her lack of cooperation on this project has made our work very difficult.

_____ _____   10. Often you can see those large cranes out on the prairie.

_____ _____   11. My uncle has sent the kids several interesting videos.

_____ _____   12. For days we have been finding small pieces of glass in the carpets on the second floor.

_____ _____   13. Someone should tell the reporters the new departure time.

_____ _____   14. The president is keeping her hopes high.

_____ _____   15. In the darkness I could barely see the pathway down to the dock.

_____ _____   16. By the end of the semester I will have completed all my required courses.

_____ _____   17. The transmission in Jane's new car has been giving her some trouble.

_____ _____   18. There must be some other, simpler solution to this problem.

43

_____ 19. Interest in that new computer program has been increasing every
_____   day.
_____ 20. The semifinal match between Harris and Conley could be the
_____   most competitive match in the tournament.
_____ 21. The sales clerk must not have been showing you the cheaper
_____   models of that computer.
_____ 22. Only later did the girls become aware of the threat of a flood.
_____
_____ 23. Nearly every person in the company had received that memo-
_____   randum.
_____ 24. The temperature down in the valley has been rising rapidly for
_____   the past few hours.
_____ 25. Many in that department had never felt certain about the com-
_____   pany's goals.
_____ 26. We should finish up that paper as quickly as possible.
_____
_____ 27. The change in the examination date had left us poorly prepared
_____   for the math questions.
_____ 28. She's still being quite negative about that new proposal.
_____
_____ 29. By next month we will have completed the first ten houses in the
_____   subdivision.
_____ 30. The secretary might have already sent each committee a copy of
_____   the minutes of the last meeting.
_____ 31. Every one of us should have been training for that marathon for
_____   the past three months.
_____ 32. The other students have given us several suggestions for fund-
_____   raising projects.
_____ 33. A few of you could have been gathering firewood for the bonfire.
_____
_____ 34. Next time I will paint the barn a bright red.
_____
_____ 35. Mike's comments might give some people the wrong impression.
_____
_____ 36. I must get approval for my extra day of vacation.
_____
_____ 37. More careful preparations would have made that paint job better.
_____
_____ 38. Robert did not show the Boy Scouts the movie about snakes.
_____
_____ 39. No teacher should ever tolerate sloppy work on chemistry exper-
_____   iments.
_____ 40. Very seldom does one get an opportunity such as this one.
_____

Exercise 5 — *Complements*

NAME _____ SCORE _____

Directions: In the space at the left, write one of the following to identify the italicized word:
    S.C. [subjective complement]   I.O. [indirect object]
    D.O. [direct object]   O.C. [objective complement]

If the italicized word is not used as a complement, leave the space blank. Circle every auxiliary verb.

_____ 1. The coaches felt very *good* about the results of their recruiting efforts.

_____ 2. At last Jim remembered the former coach's *name*.

_____ 3. Mr. Wilson bought a *few* of those old books in Europe.

_____ 4. The office manager recently gave *Beth* a new computer for her office.

_____ 5. She's always been one of our most effective *hitters*.

_____ 6. The workers on the night shift elected Max their *representative* to the Grievance Committee.

_____ 7. That apple pie on the shelf in the kitchen smells *wonderful.*

_____ 8. The personnel manager offered the *secretaries* a change in their work schedule.

_____ 9. Marie bought *one* of the puppies in that new litter for her little brother.

_____ 10. Some change from this hot, dry weather would surely be *welcome.*

_____ 11. We did not meet many of the *people* on the soccer team at the first team meeting.

_____ 12. After the thunderstorm there were several small *fires* in the valley.

_____ 13. Tomorrow Jorge will show the *class* slides of his trip to Rocky Mountain National Park.

_____ 14. The long delay in the traffic jam left Marge *short* of time.

_____ 15. The noise from the chickens in my neighbor's yard has become a major *annoyance* to all of us.

_____ 16. The guide pointed out *several* of the historic buildings in the downtown area.

_____ 17. Eventually Mark's efforts for reform of the campus election rules will become *successful.*

_____ 18. Most runners consider high-quality shoes an absolute *necessity* for good performance.

_____ 19. We need to give *ourselves* more time for that committee meeting.

_____ 20. The team leader bought *each* of the team members lunch yesterday.

_____ 21. Here is the answer *key* to yesterday's crossword puzzle.

_____ 22. Teachers should allow us more *time* for essay tests.

_____ 23. To a few of the managers, the long workshop on employee relations seemed *unnecessary.*

_____ 24. Perhaps I should cut out those *articles* on house painting.

_____ 25. The reporter called the court's decision a *milestone* in the history of the First Amendment.

_____ 26. Out of the water, the brilliantly colored fish turned a dull gray *color.*

_____ 27. After a few hundred feet the path heads *south* along the river bank.

_____ 28. The cook quickly flipped over the *steak* on the grill.

_____ 29. The leader ran over the *top* of the hill and down the other side.

_____ 30. The girls told *us* a wonderfully funny story about their ski trip.

_____ 31. Last semester Tim played in the college jazz *band.*

_____ 32. Usually he played the *trumpet.*

_____ 33. Unfortunately, Tommy could not back up his *story* about the unicorn in the garden.

_____ 34. Jill's parents were certainly *supportive* during her problems with that history course.

_____ 35. I'll probably show *them* the entire downtown area on our tour.

_____ 36. The club has elected Marge *treasurer* for the next year.

_____ 37. Seldom does anyone get an *opportunity* such as the new job at Acme Corporation.

_____ 38. Her resignation made the entire staff a little *sad.*

_____ 39. Mr. Thurman has made *us* a better offer for that antique painting.

_____ 40. The new financial officer has made some real *improvements* in our accounting system.

Lesson 6   *Alterations of Basic Sentence Patterns*

Any long piece of writing made up exclusively of basic sentences would be too monotonous to read. You should think of the basic sentences not as models for your writing but as elementary units, important because they are the structures from which more effective sentences develop. In this lesson, we shall look at two alterations of basic sentence patterns:

1. Sentences that use passive verbs
2. Sentences in the form of a question

Lessons 7 through 11 will then show how basic sentences can be combined and certain elements can be reduced to subordinate clauses and phrases to produce varied, well-developed sentences.

Passive Voice

In Lesson 2, you examined a partial conjugation of the verb *earn*. The forms listed there are in the active voice, which means that the subject is the doer of the action. A more complete conjugation would include the passive voice. In the passive voice, the subject is not the doer of the action, but the verb is always transitive. Passive verb forms make use of the auxiliary verb *be* combined with the past participle of the verb, as shown in the following illustration of the third-person singular in the six tenses:

> This amount is earned.
> This amount was earned.
> This amount will be earned.
> This amount has been earned.
> This amount had been earned.
> This amount will have been earned.

The present and past tenses of progressive verbs can also be shifted to the passive voice, giving us forms in which *be* is used in two auxiliary capacities in the same verb form:

> These cars *are being sold* at a loss.
> These cars *were being sold* at a loss.

Because only transitive verbs have passive forms, only sentence patterns 3, 4, and 5 can be altered to the passive voice. When the idea of a Pattern 3 sentence in the active voice is expressed with a passive verb, there is no direct object (complement) in the sentence:

Active Voice: Children play games.

Passive Voice: Games are played [by children].

If the doer of the verb's action is expressed in a sentence using a passive verb, the doer must occur as the object of the preposition *by*. When a Pattern 4 sentence is altered to form a passive construction, the indirect object that follows the active verb becomes the subject of the passive verb:

Active Voice: John gave Allen a model plane.

Passive Voice: Allen was given a model plane [by John].

Here the passive verb is followed by a complement, *plane,* which we continue to call a direct object in spite of the fact that it follows a passive verb.

Notice also how a Pattern 5 sentence can be given a different kind of expression by means of a passive verb:

Active Voice: The parents consider the child a genius.
                  The parents consider the child clever.

Passive Voice: The child is considered a genius [by the parents].
                  The child is considered clever [by the parents].

In these sentences, the direct object becomes the subject but the passive verb requires a complement (*genius, clever*). Because the complement renames or describes the subject, it is called a subjective complement.

The passive voice serves a real purpose in effective communication: It should be used when the *doer* of the action is unknown or is of secondary interest in the statement. In such a situation, the writer, wishing to focus attention on the *receiver* of the action, places that unit in the emphatic subject position. The passive verb form makes this arrangement possible. Thus, instead of some vague expression such as "Somebody should wash these windows," we can say, "These windows *should be washed.*"

Sometimes the passive voice is described as "weak." Admittedly some writers do get into the habit of using the passive form when there is little justification for it. In most narrative writing, the doer of the action is logically the subject of the verb. "The fullback crossed the goal line" would certainly be preferred to "The goal line was crossed by the fullback," a version that gives the same information but tends to stop any action suggested by the sentence. The passive voice also lends itself to a kind of muddied, heavy-footed writing that produces prose like this:

> It *is now rumored* that the secretary of defense *has been informed* that contingent plans *have been made to.* . . .

The writer of such a sentence, however, probably finds the passive voice effectively hides the identity of the person who is spreading the rumor, who has informed the secretary of defense, or who has made the plans. This use of the passive voice creates an impersonal, bureaucratic language very popular in many institutions.

You should practice with passive constructions so you can use this important device when it is called for. Equally important, if a criticism of your writing mentions doubtful uses of the passive, you need to be able to recognize passive verbs in order to change them when it is necessary.

Questions

In the sentence types you examined in earlier lessons, you noted the normal positioning of the main sentence parts: the subject first, followed by the verb, followed by the complement, if any. In questions, however, other arrangements are possible. As we study these new structures, we must first recognize the fact that there are two kinds of questions:

1. Questions answered by "Yes" or "No"
2. Questions answered by information

Questions Answered by "Yes" or "No"

In the following paired sentences, the first sentence is a statement and the second sentence a related question. These sentences demonstrate how the structure of a Yes/No question differs from that of a statement.

1. John is happy.   Is John happy?
2. You were there.   Were you there?
3. You see Ms. Locke often.   Do you see Ms. Locke often?
4. You heard the announcement.   Did you hear the announcement?

Notice from these examples that if the verb is *be* in the present or past tense, the subject and the *be* form (*am, are, is, was,* or *were*) reverse positions. With other one-word verbs in the present or past tense, the proper form of the auxiliary *do* is used, followed by the subject and the base form of the main verb.

   If the verb already has an auxiliary, the subject follows the auxiliary verb. If there are two or more auxiliaries, the subject follows the first one.

5. You have seen the movie.   Have you seen the movie?
6. They will arrive later.   Will they arrive later?
7. The house is being painted.   Is the house being painted?
8. He should have been told.   Should he have been told?

When the verb is *have* in the present tense, two versions of the question are possible: the subject–verb reversal and the *do* auxiliary. (See Supplement 1.)

9. You have enough money.   Have you enough money?
10. You have enough money.   Do you have enough money?

Questions Answered by Information

Some questions ask for information rather than for a "Yes" or "No" response. These questions make use of words called **interrogatives,** words that stand for unknown persons, things, or descriptive qualities. The most commonly used interrogatives are these:

pronouns: *who (whom), which, what*
adjectives: *whose, which, what*
adverbs: *when, where, why, how*

The interrogative pronoun *who,* which stands for an unknown person or persons, has three forms:

1. *Who,* when it is used as a subject or a subjective complement
2. *Whose,* when it is used as a possessive modifier of a noun
3. *Whom,* when it is used as an object

(In a later lesson you will learn that these three forms of *who* have another important use in subordinate clauses. And the choice between *who* and *whom* as a problem of usage is discussed more extensively in Lesson 24.)

In questions using these interrogatives, the normal arrangement of the main sentence parts is retained only when the interrogative is the subject or a modifier of the subject. (Here again we shall use paired statements and related questions to demonstrate these structures.)

1. *My brother* [S.] paid the bill.   *Who* [S.] paid the bill?
2. *Five cars* [S.] were damaged.   *How* many cars [S.] were damaged?

In all other situations the subject–verb position is altered as it is with Yes/No questions. The interrogative word, or the unit containing the interrogative word, stands at the beginning of the sentence to signal that a question, not a statement, is forthcoming:

I studied *geometry* [D.O.] last night.
What [D.O.] did you study last night?

You saw *Jim* [D.O.] at the party.
Whom [D.O.] did you see at the party?

She is Mother's *cousin* [S.C.].
Who [S.C.] is she?

We can use Bill's *car* [D.O.].
Whose car [D.O.] can we use?

You spent fifteen *dollars* [D.O.].
How much money [D.O.] did you spend?

You [S.] called *Bob* [D.O.] a *thief* [O.C.].
Who [S.] called Bob a thief?
Whom [D.O.] did you call a thief?
What [O.C.] did you call Bob?

When the interrogative unit is the object of a preposition, two arrangements of the question are often possible:

1. The entire prepositional phrase may stand at the beginning.
2. The interrogative may stand at the beginning with the preposition in its usual position.

The speaker was referring *to the mayor.*
To whom was the speaker referring?
Whom was the speaker referring to?

(See Supplement 2.)

Supplement 1

The type of verb also determines the structuring of sentences that are negative rather than positive. The positioning of the negator *not* (or its contraction *n't*) depends on the presence or absence of an auxiliary verb. Sentences using *be* or *have* must be considered special cases.

1. If the verb is *be* in the present tense or in the past tense, used either as the main verb or as an auxiliary verb, the *not* follows the *be* form:

   I *am not* pleased with the report.
   He *was not* [wasn't] available.
   They *were not* [weren't] invited.

2. With other one-word verbs in the present or past tense, the proper form of the auxiliary *do* is used, followed by the negator and the base form of the main verb:

   I *do not* [don't] expect a reward.
   He *does not* [doesn't] attend regularly.
   We *did not* [didn't] respond.

3. If the verb already has an auxiliary, the negator follows the auxiliary. When there are two or more auxiliaries, the *not* follows the first one:

   We *could not* [couldn't] see very well.
   I *may not* have understood him.
   They *will not* [won't] refund my money.
   This cake *ought not* to have been baked so long.

4. When *have* in the present tense is the main verb, two negative forms are possible:

   I *have not* [haven't] enough time to play.
   I *do not* [don't] have enough time to play.

Supplement 2

At the informal language level, another version—"*Who* was the speaker referring to?"—is often found, despite the traditional demand for the objective case for the object of a preposition. The formal level of both spoken and written English would call for: "*To whom* was the speaker referring?"

Alterations of Basic Sentence Patterns:
Passive Verbs; Questions

NAME _____ SCORE _____

Directions: These are Pattern 3, 4, or 5 sentences. In the first space at the left, write the pattern number. In the second space at the left, write the passive verb form that is used when the italicized word in the sentence is made the subject.

Example:

___4___
___will be sent___   Soon they will send *you* a copy of that proposal.

_____
_____   1. People on the neighboring farm could see the *flames*.

_____
_____   2. We will allow *you* another chance.

_____
_____   3. Someone has already met the *candidate* at the airport.

_____
_____   4. Some senators are considering a tax *cut*.

_____
_____   5. The commission has kept those *results* secret for some time now.

_____
_____   6. The commission will give *us* those results tomorrow.

_____
_____   7. We would appreciate your *cooperation* in this matter.

_____
_____   8. The store will send *you* a new catalogue.

_____
_____   9. Some people might consider your *actions* unwise.

_____
_____   10. You should have paid the *speaker* before the program.

Directions: The purpose of this exercise is to contrast the structure of a question with that of a statement. In the space at the left, copy the word from the question that serves the function of the italicized word in the statement.

_____ 1. How many cookies did she bake?
She baked 100 *cookies.*

_____ 2. How many copies are ready for the meeting?
Ten *copies* are ready for the meeting.

_____ 3. What are you concerned about in this situation?
I am concerned about tomorrow's *weather.*

_____ 4. Whose proposal did you select?
I selected Tom's *proposal.*

_____ 5. Whose car did you drive?
I drove Martin's *car.*

_____ 6. Whose car is that?
That is Martin's *car.*

_____ 7. How many errors did you find on that page?
I found three *errors* on that page.

_____ 8. Whom should the president choose as her assistant?
The president should choose *Robert* as her assistant.

_____ 9. Who will be the president's assistant?
Robert will be the president's assistant.

_____ 10. Who will the president's assistant be?
The president's assistant will be *Robert.*

_____ 11. To whom was that message sent?
That message was sent to *Mr. Worth.*

_____ 12. What color did she paint her room?
She painted her room a soft *pink.*

_____ 13. Who sang Charley that corny love song?
Anne sang Charley that corny love song.

_____ 14. What did Anne sing to Charley?
Anne sang a corny love *song* to Charley.

_____ 15. To whom did Anne sing that corny love song?
Anne sang that corny love song to *Charley.*

Alterations of Basic Sentence Patterns:
Passive Verbs; Questions

Directions: Each of the following sentences uses a passive verb. Underline the verb. Rewrite each sentence using an active form of the verb. (You will have to supply a logical subject of the active verb if the passive verb does not provide one.) If your rewrites are correctly done, your first four sentences will be Pattern 3, your next three will be Pattern 4, and your final three will be Pattern 5.

1. By noon all the autographed baseballs had been bought up by eager collectors.

   _____

2. The edges of those wooden planks must be sanded very carefully.

   _____

3. That house was built by Mark's grandfather in 1903.

   _____

4. This new vaccine was developed by a medical researcher in a small laboratory in Maine.

   _____

5. We should have been given a copy of the format long before the due date for our papers.

   _____

6. A mature dog is usually given only one meal a day.

   _____

7. Each of us was told a different story by the children.

   _____

8. That poor fellow should not have been judged competent to stand trial.

   _____

9. That answer is considered correct by only a few scholars in the field.

   _____

10. Marie was voted "Most Likely to Succeed" by her classmates.

    _____

55

Directions: The italicized word in each of the following questions is a complement or the object of a preposition. In the space at the left, write one of the following to identify the italicized word:

    D.O. [direct object]   O.C. [objective complement]
    S.C. [subjective complement]   O.P. [object of preposition]
    I.O. [indirect object]

_____ 1. To whom did you first tell the good *news*?

_____ 2. To *whom* did you first tell the good news?

_____ 3. *What* did the company give Tom?

_____ 4. What did the company give *Tom*?

_____ 5. How *happy* were you with that decision?

_____ 6. *Whom* did the class elect as president?

_____ 7. Whom did the class elect as *president*?

_____ 8. How *short* has the supply of medicine become?

_____ 9. How *exciting* was last night's movie?

_____ 10. How many *arrowheads* did you find on your walk?

_____ 11. *Which* of the two questions did you find most difficult?

_____ 12. How much did you show the *audience* about that magic trick?

_____ 13. To *whom* should we give this last rose?

_____ 14. *What* were you two talking about out in the hall?

_____ 15. How much credit do you give the advertising *campaign* for our successful sales effort?

_____ 16. *What* will the interest on your car loan be?

_____ 17. *What* will the interest on your car loan amount to?

_____ 18. How *large* has the crowd become?

_____ 19. Whose *candidacy* do you favor in the election?

_____ 20. *Whom* should we select as our representative?

_____ 21. Whom should we select as our *representative*?

_____ 22. *Who* will our new representative be?

_____ 23. Why did you keep that talent *hidden* for all these years?

_____ 24. What *player* did the team make that offer to?

_____ 25. What *offer* did the team make to the player?

Clauses and Phrases

Lessons, Practice Sheets, and Exercises

Lesson 7 — *Coordination: Compound Sentences*

To begin to study sentences that build on the simple patterns discussed in the previous lessons, let's examine a student writer's description of a snowstorm. Each sentence is numbered for later reference.

(1) The first really serious snowfall began at dusk and had already spread a treacherous powdering over the roads by the time the homeward-bound crowds reached their peak. (2) As the evening deepened, porch and street lights glowed in tight circles through semisolid air. (3) The snow did not fall in a mass of fat, jovial flakes; it squatted in a writhing mist of tiny particles and seemed less snow than a dense, animated fog. (4) Through the night the wind rose, worrying the trees as a puppy shakes a slipper. (5) It rushed round the corners of buildings and tumbled over roofs, from which it snatched armfuls of snow to scatter in the streets. (6) Save for the occasional grumble of a sanitation truck sullenly pushing its plow, all sound stopped. (7) Even the wind was more felt than heard. (8) Day did not dawn. (9) The world changed from charcoal gray to lead between six and seven, but the change was one from night to lesser night. (10) The snow still whirled. (11) Drifts had altered the neat symmetry of peaked roofs into irregular mountain ranges ending in sheer cliffs four or five feet above the leeward eaves. (12) The downwind side of every solid object cast a snow shadow that tapered away from a sharp hump until it merged into the surrounding flat pallor. (13) Along the street, windshield wipers, odd bits of chrome, startling blanks of black glass, and isolated headlights decorated large white mounds. (14) Men and women shut off their alarm clocks, stretched, yawned, looked out of their windows, paused in a moment of guilt, and went back to bed. (15) Snow had taken the day for its own, and there was no point in arguing with it.

The fifteen sentences of this paragraph are all made up of groups of related words called clauses. A **clause** is a group of words that always contains a subject and a verb in combination. Recalling the scenes, actions, and responses associated with the event, the author has created a series of clauses (subject-verb combinations): the snowfall began, the snowfall had spread a powdering, the homeward-bound crowds reached their peak, the evening deepened, lights glowed, and so on.

Although it may not be apparent when you first read the paragraph, the entire passage is based on short, simple sentences of the patterns studied in the preceding lessons. The writer's problem was to combine or alter these short statements in order to put them into their most pleasing and effective form. Presenting all of them as basic sentences would communicate the author's ideas but in a form that, in addition to being monotonous, would not give proper emphasis to the most important ideas. Only two sentences (8 and 10) are retained as one-subject, one-verb basic sentences. Some of the sentences (3, 9, and 15) combine two basic sentences, giving each clause equal force. Two sentences (1 and 5) join more than one verb to the same subject. Sentence 13 joins four subjects to the same verb, and Sentence 14 has two subjects joined to six verbs.

In the next several lessons we shall be examining the word groups—independent clauses, subordinate clauses, and phrases—that are the language tools allowing a writer to apply various strategies to produce effective sentences.

Compounding Sentences

A sentence, as you learned in Lesson 1, is a word group containing a subject and a verb. From this definition, and from the one already given for a clause, it would seem that a sentence and a clause are identical. And this is true for one kind of clause, the **independent clause** (also called the *main clause* or *principal clause*). The independent clause can stand by itself as a sentence. Every example sentence and every exercise sentence that you have worked with thus far in this book has been made up of one independent clause. We call a sentence consisting of only one independent clause a **simple sentence.**

One means of combining or altering short, simple sentences is called *compounding*, joining grammatically equal parts so that they function together. We can join two or more subjects, verbs, complements, or modifiers by using a **coordinating conjunction.** (**Conjunctions** are words that join words, phrases, or clauses; conjunctions that join grammatically equal units are called *coordinating*.) The three common coordinating conjunctions are *and, but,* and *or;* other coordinators are *nor, for, yet,* and *so.* With the use of a coordinating conjunction, we can join two very short sentences and create a longer, more readable sentence.

Dad read the notice. I read the notice.
Dad *and* I read the notice. [Compound subjects]

Marge enjoys golf. Marge enjoys tennis.
She enjoys golf *and* tennis. [Compound direct objects]

I studied very hard. I failed the test.
I studied very hard *but* failed the test. [Compound verbs]

I found the lecture interesting. I found the lecture instructive.
I found the lecture interesting and instructive. [Compound objective complements]

I can see you during your lunch hour. I can see you after five.
I can see you during your lunch hour or after five o'clock. [Compound prepositional phrases]

Compounding is often used with two (sometimes more than two) independent clauses; the result is a common type of sentence called the **compound sentence.** We can create compound sentences in two ways.

Clauses Joined by a Coordinating Conjunction

Any of the coordinating conjunctions already mentioned can be used to join two independent clauses. The normal punctuation is a comma before the conjunction:

> I had reviewed the material, and I did well on the test.

It is important to distinguish this sentence from a nearly synonymous version using a compound verb:

> I had reviewed the material and did well on the test.

In this version, the sentence is not a compound sentence because there is no separate subject for the second verb. It is a simple sentence with a compound verb and should be written without a comma.

Clauses Joined by a Semicolon

Sometimes the two independent clauses stand side by side with no word tying them together:

> No one was in sight; I was alone in the huge auditorium.

Often the second of the two clauses joined by a semicolon begins with an adverbial unit that serves as a kind of tie between the clauses. This adverbial unit may be:

1. A simple adverb

> Currently we are renting an apartment; later we hope to buy a house.
> These were last year's highlights; now we must look at plans for next year.

2. A short phrase

> I cannot comment on the whole concert; in fact, I slept through the last part of it.

3. A conjunctive adverb

> Your arguments were well presented; *however,* we feel that the plan is too expensive.

The most common conjunctive adverbs are *therefore, however, nevertheless, consequently, moreover, otherwise, besides, furthermore,* and *accordingly.* These words, often followed by a comma, should be used cautiously; they usually contribute to a heavy, formal tone. To lessen this effect, writers often place them, set off by commas, within the second clause:

> Your arguments were well presented; we feel, *however,* that the plan is too expensive.

Because adverbial units like *later* and *therefore* are *not* coordinating conjunctions, the use of a comma to join the two clauses is inappropriate. This error is often called a *comma splice* or a *comma fault.* The important thing to remember is that when independent clauses are joined by a coordinating conjunction, the use of a comma is the custom. When there is no coordinating conjunction, the comma will not suffice; the customary mark is the semicolon. We will study these punctuation rules thoroughly in Lesson 17.

NAME _____ SCORE _____

Directions: The following twenty-five sentences illustrate three types of sentences:

Type 1. The sentence is a simple sentence with the subject having two verbs joined by a coordinating conjunction. Normal punctuation: none.

We worked on the car all day but could not find the trouble.

Type 2. The sentence is a compound sentence with the two independent clauses joined by a coordinating conjunction: *and, but, or, nor, for, yet,* or *so.* Normal punctuation: a comma before the conjunction.

We worked all day on the car, and now it runs well.

Type 3. The sentence is a compound sentence without one of the coordinating conjunctions joining the independent clauses. (The second clause often begins with an adverbial unit.) Normal punctuation: a semicolon.

We worked all day on the car; now it runs well.

In each of the following sentences, the ∧ symbol marks a point of coordination. Indicate the correct punctuation by writing **C** for comma, **S** for semicolon, and **0** for no punctuation.

_____C_____ 1. Jenny pumped on the gas pedal and pulled out the choke on that old car ∧ yet the motor still would not start.

_____0_____ 2. My friends know how badly I need help ∧ and will certainly come to my rescue.

_____S_____ 3. My friends will certainly come to my rescue ∧ they know how badly I need help.

_____C_____ 4. My friends will certainly come to my rescue ∧ for they know how badly I need help.

_____S_____ 5. The flash fire could have turned into a disaster ∧ there was only one guard on duty that night.

_____C_____ 6. The report from the laboratory arrived the next day ∧ and the results of the tests were very encouraging.

_____0_____ 7. Riverside Park does a huge business in the late fall ∧ but is closed from Thanksgiving until the beginning of spring.

_____S_____ 8. The dress rehearsal went strictly according to form ∧ everything was chaotic.

61

_____ 9. The base price for that camera is $750 ∧ with the 80–200 Macro Zoom lens included, the package costs $1,100.

_____ 10. The base price for that camera is $750 ∧ but it will cost $1,100 with the 80–200 Macro Zoom lens included.

_____ 11. The lens and the camera base are $1,100 ∧ however, without the lens the base is $750.

_____ 12. Stay tuned to this channel ∧ in one hour we will show the final heat of the Funny Car race.

_____ 13. Stay tuned to this channel ∧ and in one hour we will show the final heat of the Funny Car race.

_____ 14. For the students the new schedule means an extra holiday ∧ for the faculty, it means the loss of one day of teaching.

_____ 15. George must have completed the renovations on his shop ∧ for the sign says he will open for business next Monday.

_____ 16. "Please don't try to help me," said Mary ∧ "you'll only make things more confusing."

_____ 17. Members of that religious group don't use tractors ∧ they rely on horse-drawn plows instead.

_____ 18. Many students have registered for Professor Zorn's class ∧ for he is a very entertaining lecturer.

_____ 19. Many students have registered for Professor Zorn's class ∧ for several reasons he is a very popular teacher.

_____ 20. We would have stopped for groceries on the way home ∧ but the store was very crowded at the time.

_____ 21. Alicia will probably move to Oregon after graduation ∧ but perhaps she will remain here for graduate school.

_____ 22. The left-hander swung hard at the first pitch ∧ but the ball cracked noisily into the catcher's mitt.

_____ 23. Theresa bought a raincoat and a pair of new gloves ∧ but she did not buy any boots for the cold weather ahead.

_____ 24. The dean's announcement must have been very interesting ∧ for people have been talking about it all afternoon.

_____ 25. Maria's car is a 1966 model ∧ for a car so old, it is in amazingly good shape.

NAME _____ SCORE _____

Directions: The following twenty-five sentences illustrate three types of sentences:

Type 1. The sentence is a simple sentence with the subject having two verbs joined by a coordinating conjunction. Normal punctuation: none.

We worked on the car all day but could not find the trouble.

Type 2. The sentence is a compound sentence with the two independent clauses joined by a coordinating conjunction: *and, but, or, nor, for, yet,* or *so.* Normal punctuation: a comma before the conjunction.

We worked all day on the car, and now it runs well.

Type 3. The sentence is a compound sentence without one of the coordinating conjunctions joining the independent clauses. (The second clause often begins with an adverbial unit.) Normal punctuation: a semicolon.

We worked all day on the car; now it runs well.

In each of the following sentences, the ∧ symbol marks a point of coordination. Indicate the correct punctuation by writing **C** for comma, **S** for semicolon, and **0** for no punctuation.

_____ 1. Yesterday the men finished that project ∧ therefore they stayed home today.

_____ 2. The shortstop dove for the ball ∧ but was not quite able to field it cleanly.

_____ 3. That politician made promises to every group in the county ∧ thus she has assured herself of major conflicts in the future.

_____ 4. Usually Jim takes his vacation in August ∧ he's never been to the mountains in October before.

_____ 5. The service in this restaurant has always been excellent ∧ last night, however, our waiter was very slow.

_____ 6. I enrolled yesterday in History 211 ∧ several of my friends enjoyed the course very much last semester.

_____ 7. The secretary is searching everywhere for that lost file ∧ for we need it desperately for this afternoon's meeting.

_____ 8. The people in the stands whistled and stamped their feet ∧ for them only a victory would be satisfactory.

_____ 9. "We need to get to the station early today," said Tom ∧ "that train always leaves exactly on time."

_____ 10. I looked for that book for an hour ∧ it is definitely not on the shelves in our library.

_____ 11. Maria will either take that job in Los Angeles ∧ or take a tour of Europe immediately after graduation.

_____ 12. Maria will either take that job in Los Angeles ∧ or she will take a tour of Europe immediately after graduation.

_____ 13. Mark studied hard for that test ∧ yet everyone else in the class made a better grade.

_____ 14. I wanted to go to last night's game ∧ but I had not finished my report for today's meeting.

_____ 15. Laura came late to class today ∧ she shut off her alarm clock by mistake this morning.

_____ 16. Anna made an appointment with an advisor today ∧ for she wants to change her major to computer science.

_____ 17. Anna wants to change her major to computer science ∧ for some reason she no longer enjoys music courses.

_____ 18. You can print out seven copies of that report ∧ or take the original to the Copy Center for the extra copies.

_____ 19. Several people left the movie early ∧ the talkative audience made them very angry.

_____ 20. "Please help me look for my contact lens," begged Robert ∧ "I've already lost one this week."

_____ 21. Radar was first used in World War II for tracking enemy planes ∧ now it has many uses in civilian life.

_____ 22. We need to pay close attention to that map ∧ several people have gotten lost on that road in the last few days.

_____ 23. We need to pay close attention to that map ∧ for several people have gotten lost on that road in the last few days.

_____ 24. Check your work on that problem very carefully ∧ for that problem the answer in the key is incorrect.

_____ 25. The two girls had looked everywhere for that jacket ∧ therefore they were surprised to find it in the trunk of the car.

Directions: Combine the short sentences in each numbered item into one longer sentence.

1. Jim loves detective stories.
    He also reads poetry occasionally.

    _____

2. A few students arrived a little early for class.
    Most, however, hurried into class at the bell.

    _____

3. We went to the auto show last week.
    There we saw an interesting display of futuristic cars.

    _____

4. The people in the audience cheered loudly.
    For them, the beauty of the music made the evening complete.

    _____

5. Alicia looked everywhere for that book.
    She needed another quick look at Chapter 7 before the test.

    _____

6. The boys worked very hard on the lawn all morning.
    They finally finished their work a little after noon.

    _____

7. Alec made careful preparations for the raft trip.
    Thus he started without any delay the next morning.

    _____

8. The boys ran quickly down the hill.
    Then they crossed the creek at the edge of the pasture.

    _____

9. We looked for John in every shop along Main Street.
    Apparently he had gone back to the campus earlier in the morning.

    _____

10. The whole team was exhausted from the long bus trip.
    They all slept until almost eleven o'clock this morning.

    _____

Lesson 8 — *Subordination: Adverb Clauses*

To this point you have had practice with the simple sentence (one independent clause) and the compound sentence (two or more independent clauses). Basic as these sentences are to your thinking and writing, you need to move beyond these structures in order to make your writing flexible and effective. Often you can improve the precision of your statements if you use slightly more complex structures.

"Rain began to fall, and we stopped our ball game" is a perfectly correct sentence. But notice these slightly altered versions of that sentence:

> When rain began to fall, we stopped our ball game.
> After rain began to fall, we stopped our ball game.
> Because rain began to fall, we stopped our ball game.

These three, in addition to lessening the singsong tone of the compound sentence, are more informative. The first two tell the time at which the game was stopped—and notice that *when* and *after* point out slightly different time frames. The third version gives a different relation between the two statements; it tells not the time of, but the reason for, stopping the game.

If, instead of writing the compound sentence, "Rain was falling, and we continued our ball game," you write "Although rain was falling, we continued our ball game," you have refined your thinking and your expression. Your readers now interpret the sentence exactly as you want them to: They now know that the ball game was continued in spite of the fact that rain was falling.

The process by which a statement is reduced to a secondary form to show its relation to the main idea is called **subordination.** The grammatical unit that expresses a secondary idea as it affects a main idea is the **subordinate,** or **dependent, clause,** which we define as a subject–verb combination that cannot stand alone as a sentence. A subordinate clause works in a sentence in the same way that a single part of speech—an adverb, an adjective, or a noun works. Instead of a single word—quickly, quick, quickness—used as an adverb, an adjective, or a noun, a group of words is used. A sentence made up of one independent clause and at least one dependent clause is a **complex sentence.**

Adverb Clause

The **adverb clause** works in exactly the same way a one-word adverb works; it provides information by modifying a verb, an adjective, or another adverb. The most common types of adverb clauses modify verbs. In fact, they answer direct questions about the action: When? (time); Where? (place); Why? (cause); and How? (manner). The role of the adverb clause is shown by the conjunction that introduces the adverb clause. The conjunction—the structural signal of subordination—is not an isolated word standing between the two clauses. It is part of the subordinate clause. In such a sentence as, "We left the house after the rain stopped," the unit "the rain stopped" could stand alone as an independent clause.

But the clause is made dependent by the inclusion of the conjunction *after*. The dependent clause "after the rain stopped" establishes the time when "we left the house." Thus, the clause works as an adverb of time in the same way that the one-word adverbs work in the following sentences:

> We left the house *early.*
> We left the house *late.*
> We left the house *yesterday.*

Various types of adverb clauses and their most common conjunctions are listed here with examples.

Time (*when, whenever, before, after, since, while, until, as, as soon as*):

> The baby cried *when the telephone rang.*
> The cat ran out *before Lou could shut the door.*
> *After the bell rings,* no one can enter.
> I've known Palmer *since he was in high school.*
> You should not whisper *while Dr. Fuller is lecturing.*
> You may leave *as soon as your replacement arrives.*

Place (*where, wherever*):

> We parted *where the paths separated.*
> I shall meet you *wherever you want me to.*

Cause (or **Reason**) (*because, since, as*):

> I walk to work every day *because I need the exercise.*
> *Since she could not pay the fine,* she could not drive the car.
> *As you are the senior member,* you should lead the procession.

Purpose (*so that, that, in order that*):

> We left early *so that we could catch the last bus.*
> They died *that their nation might live.*
> They came to America *in order that they might find freedom.*

Manner (*as, as if, as though*):

> Stan acted *as if the party was boring him.*
> Please do the work *as you have been instructed.*

Result (*so . . . that, such . . . that*):

> Jerry arrived *so late that he missed the concert.*
> The workmen made *such a racket that I got a headache.*

Condition (*if, unless, provided that, on condition that*). This kind of adverb clause gives a condition under which the main clause is true:

Sit down and chat *if you are not in a hurry.*
He will not give his talk *unless we pay his expenses.*
She will sign the contract *provided that we pay her a bonus.*
If I were you, I would accept the offer.
If you had told me earlier, I could have helped.

There is an alternate arrangement for certain kinds of conditional clauses. In this arrangement *if* is not used; instead, a subject–verb inversion signals the subordination. Sentences like the last two preceding examples sometimes take this form:

Were I you, I would accept the offer.
Had you told me earlier, I could have helped.

Concession (*although, though, even if, even though, since*). This clause states a fact in spite of which the main idea is true:

Although she is only nine years old, she plays chess.
Our car is dependable *even though it is old.*

Comparison (*than, as*). Two distinctive characteristics of the adverb clause of comparison should be noted. First, part or all of the verb, although it is needed grammatically, is usually not expressed. Second, when an action verb is not expressed in the subordinate clause, the appropriate form of the auxiliary *do* is often used even though the *do* does not occur in the main clause:

Gold is heavier *than iron* [is].
Your computer is not as new *as mine* [is].
Her theme was better *than any other student's in the class* [was].
Ellen earned more bonus points *than her brother* [did].

Adverb clauses may also modify verbs, adjectives, and adverbs. In this type of clause, the conjunction *that* is sometimes unexpressed.

Jim slept *as late as possible.* [Modifies the verb *slept*]
We are sorry *that you must leave early.* [Modifies the adjective *sorry*]
I am sure *(that) he meant no harm.* [Modifies the adjective *sure*]
The car is running better *than it did last week.* [Modifies the adverb *better*]

Elliptical Clause

Ellipsis means *omission,* to *leave something out.* A clause that leaves some parts understood or unexpressed is called an **elliptical clause.** There are many types of elliptical clauses. You should be aware of them because they can lend variety to your writing. In the following examples, brackets enclose the parts of the clauses that may be unexpressed. (See Supplement.) Note that all the types of adverb phrases (time, place, cause, purpose, manner, result, condition, concession, and comparison) may be elliptical.

While [I was] *walking home,* I met Mr. Jones.
When [he is] *in Cleveland,* he stays with us.
Call your office *as soon as* [it is] *possible.*
Adjustments will be made *whenever* [they are] *necessary.*

Mary, *although* [she is] *a talented girl,* is quite lazy.
If [you are] *delayed,* call my secretary.
Your ticket, *unless* [it is] *stamped,* is invalid.

A Note on Sentence Variety

Although some adverb clauses—those of comparison, for instance—have a fixed position within the sentence, many adverb clauses may be placed before, inside, or following the main clause:

When they deal with the unknown, Greek myths are usually somber.
Greek myths, *when they deal with the unknown,* are usually somber.
Greek myths are usually somber *when they deal with the unknown.*

Notice that no comma is used in the third example above. Usually a comma is not needed when the adverbial clause is the final element of the sentence, as the third example below also illustrates.

Although he did not have authority from Congress, President Theodore Roosevelt ordered construction of the Panama Canal.

President Theodore Roosevelt, *although he did not have authority from Congress,* ordered construction of the Panama Canal.

President Theodore Roosevelt ordered construction of the Panama Canal *although he did not have authority from Congress.*

You should practice various arrangements to relieve the monotony that comes from reliance on too many "main-subject-plus-main-verb" sentences.

Supplement

Occasionally an elliptical adverb clause of comparison must be recast because the exact meaning is unclear when parts of the clause are unexpressed. Here are two sentences that are ambiguous in the shortened forms of the clauses:

Mr. Alton will pay you more *than Stan.*

Probable Meaning: Mr. Alton will pay you more than [he will pay] Stan.
Possible Meaning: Mr. Alton will pay you more than Stan [will pay you].

Parents dislike homework as much *as their offspring.*

Probable Meaning: Parents dislike homework as much as their offspring [dislike homework].
Possible Meaning: Parents dislike homework as much as [they dislike] their offspring.

SUMMARY OF ADVERB CLAUSES

1. Function: to modify a verb, an adjective, or an adverb
2. Position: fixed for some types (She sold more tickets *than I did*); others may be at the beginning, in the interior, or at the end of main clause
3. Subordinators: conjunctions, most of which show adverbial relationships such as time (*when, since, while*), cause (*because, as*), and so on
4. Special structures:
   a. An adverb clause modifying an adjective subjective complement and subordinated by *that* sometimes has the subordinator *that* unexpressed:

   I'm sure *(that) you are wrong.*

   b. Elliptical clauses:

   Mary is older than I (am).
   If (you are) unable to attend, call me.
   While (she was) preparing lunch, Mary cut her finger.

NAME _____   SCORE _____

Directions: Identify each of the italicized adverb clauses by writing one of the following numbers in the space at the left:

1. Time	4. Purpose	7. Condition	10. Modification of an
2. Place	5. Manner	8. Concession	adjective or adverb
3. Cause	6. Result	9. Comparison	

__6__ 1. Bryan slept so late this morning *that he missed class.*

__5__ 2. Julia studies *as if she is afraid she will flunk every test.*

__7__ 3. We will go on the hike tomorrow only *under the condition that we will not start out very early in the morning.*

__8__ 4. The politician's speech, *although cleverly written,* was not well received by the audience.

__4__ 5. "I worked hard yesterday *so that I could take today off,*" said Ken.

__3__ 6. Arline is studying math *because she intends to major in computer science.*

__7__ 7. *Unless Julie begins to come to class every day,* the instructor will drop her from the roll.

__10__ 8. I'm sure *that Terry will be back soon with our sandwiches.*

__5__ 9. Martha sometimes works *as if she is bored with her job.*

__1__ 10. Automobiles have been generally affordable *since Henry Ford developed the assembly line.*

_____ 11. *Since Roberta got free tickets for us,* we are all going to the concert.

_____ 12. Please finish those spreadsheets *as soon as you can.*

_____ 13. Tonight's audience is slightly larger *than last night's.*

_____ 14. *Although I had seen the movie several months ago,* I remembered that scene very clearly.

_____ 15. That engine will not start *unless you close the choke.*

_____ 16. *If you are unhappy* with your new office, you should tell the office manager.

_____ 17. I'm afraid *that my answer is incorrect.*

_____ 18. In that situation, you should get help *wherever you can find it.*

_____ 19. Yesterday Lewis slept *until the phone rang at noon.*

_____ 20. My little brother read more books *than anyone else in his class.*

_____ 21. *"Although I am dieting faithfully,* I'm not losing much weight," complained Walt.

_____ 22. Read the script *exactly as it is written.*

_____ 23. The broker is not sure *that this mutual fund is the best choice for us.*

_____ 24. *After she finishes her run each day,* Ellie always stretches very carefully.

_____ 25. *As we had no firm plans for the afternoon,* we watched football practice for a few minutes.

_____ 26. *As we left the station,* rain began to fall.

_____ 27. Is Jim as tall *as Harry?*

_____ 28. *Even though I have used it for years,* I still like my old computer very much.

_____ 29. Good pitchers always act *as though they don't hear the crowd.*

_____ 30. The class is certainly glad *that the teacher has returned from her illness.*

_____ 31. Print that sign very legibly *so that everyone can read it.*

_____ 32. *Before you check that suitcase,* be sure to put an address label on it.

_____ 33. Only one sales person sold more cars *than Martha.*

_____ 34. Tamara can pass this course *if she passes the last two tests.*

_____ 35. We're glad *that you have enrolled in the karate class.*

_____ 36. Nellie has written us two letters *since she left for Canada.*

_____ 37. We left earlier than usual *because the roads were quite foggy.*

_____ 38. *When you find the answer to that question,* please call me.

_____ 39. *Although there were a few people present,* the band had not arrived for the concert.

_____ 40. Sam ate a big breakfast *after he returned from band practice.*

Exercise 8   *Adverb Clauses*

NAME _____   SCORE _____

Directions: Each sentence contains one adverb clause. Underline each adverb clause. In the space at the left, write one of the following numbers to identify the type of clause:

1. Time	4. Purpose	7. Condition	10. Modification of an
2. Place	5. Manner	8. Concession	adjective or adverb
3. Cause	6. Result	9. Comparison	

_____ 1. Whenever Tim arrives, please call my secretary.

_____ 2. Although we had not heard any noise, the books had fallen off the shelf in the library.

_____ 3. Jamie's GPA is slightly higher than mine.

_____ 4. That fishing license, if it contains a trout stamp, will allow you to catch three trout a day during the season.

_____ 5. My mother was convinced that we should leave early in the morning.

_____ 6. The three little kids ran as if their lives were in danger.

_____ 7. Because the test covers so much material, I started studying early yesterday morning.

_____ 8. How can we plan if there is no established goal for our work?

_____ 9. Please fax your answer to us so that we can begin work immediately.

_____ 10. Please make a check mark wherever you find an error in computation.

_____ 11. If I were you, I would take the introductory course first.

_____ 12. The boys walked so fast that they left the rest of us far behind.

_____ 13. Jim is confident that he can get an interesting summer job.

_____ 14. The contractor says that this old house is built better than most newer houses.

_____ 15. That blue shirt, although old, is still very comfortable.

_____ 16. The boss hired eight new workers in order that we might finish the work on time.

_____ 17. The children acted as if they did not want to leave the zoo.

_____ 18. Since we added a voice mail system, communication in the office has been much improved.

_____ 19. Since she has lost her driver's license, Mary has been taking the bus to work.

_____ 20. The men are making preparations as quickly as they can.

_____ 21. I'm not sure that I understand that first problem in the textbook.

_____ 22. That bill won't leave the committee unless Senator Jackson votes for it.

_____ 23. Even though Julia presented a convincing argument, the class voted against her proposal.

_____ 24. The cross-country team is certainly glad that the heat wave has broken.

_____ 25. Please do not line up until your group has been called.

_____ 26. You must provide a cover sheet for your paper exactly as you were instructed.

_____ 27. Bob has taken a course in Spanish so that he can talk to people on his vacation in Costa Rica.

_____ 28. The people in the back of the room chanted so loudly that we could not hear the speaker.

_____ 29. If I had known about that mixed doubles tournament, Jennifer and I would have entered.

_____ 30. My little brother is now taller than I am.

_____ 31. As he was walking toward our table, the waiter dropped our entire order.

_____ 32. We found a place to pick blueberries where the bushes are high and the ground is not steep.

_____ 33. Jim usually watches television while doing his homework.

_____ 34. I'll play ball with you after I finish my dessert.

_____ 35. Although dark clouds have moved in from the west, it has not yet begun to rain.

_____ 36. If you want to see the birds, you have to get up early in the morning.

_____ 37. Little Billy hits the baseball farther than his older friends do.

_____ 38. Jessica is pleased that she won a full scholarship to the university.

_____ 39. Her mouth puckered as if she had eaten something very sour.

_____ 40. Because the blizzard had felled so many trees, we were unable to drive up our driveway.

Directions: Rewrite the sentence or sentences in each numbered item as a complex sentence using an adverbial clause; use the subordinating conjunction that properly establishes the relationship between the two sentences or clauses. Note that certain coordinating conjunctions have direct equivalents in subordinating conjunctions.

1. We were late for the opening of the concert, for we encountered two massive traffic jams on the way. (Cause)

   _____

2. We already had thirty copies of the book, but we did not have enough for all the members of the class. (Concession)

   _____

3. Jan set her alarm clock for very early yesterday morning, for she wanted to watch the sun rise over the ocean. (Cause)

   _____

4. You need to leave by 4:00 P.M., or you will get caught in the traffic leaving town. (Condition)

   _____

5. Marge studied for several hours yesterday, but she still did not make a very high grade on the test. (Concession)

   _____

6. The alarm rang at 6:30 A.M., and everyone woke up. (Time)

   _____

7. You need to finish that paper soon.
   If you don't, you won't be able to turn it in on time. (Condition)

   _____

8. We turned left at a certain place.
   The road came to a dead-end. (Place)

   _____

9. Barbara had worked hard and saved money for several months; thus she was able to pay all her college bills at the beginning of the term. (Cause)

   _____

10. On Monday Al went to several card shops to find an Alex Rodriguez baseball card for his little brother. (Purpose)

   _____

Lesson 9   *Subordination: Adjective Clauses*

Just as a single-word adjective modifies a noun or pronoun, clauses that begin with *who, whom, whose, which,* or *that* can modify nouns or pronouns. A clause that modifies a noun or pronoun is called an **adjective** or **relative clause.** An adjective clause gives information about the noun in the same way that the one-word adjectives do. Both one-word adjectives and adjective clauses can be seen as basic sentences that have been worked into a main clause.

> I looked into the sky. The sky was blue.
> I looked into the blue sky.

> I looked into the sky. The sky was filled with towering cumulous clouds.
> I looked into the sky, which was filled with towering cumulous clouds.

In Item 1 the sentence, "The sky was blue," becomes the one-word adjective *blue* and modifies the noun *sky.* In Item 2 the sentence, "The sky was filled with towering cumulous clouds," cannot become a one-word adjective; therefore, the sentence becomes an adjective or relative clause opened by the word *which.* The clause modifies the word *sky* in the sense that it provides us with information about the sky.

Adjective Clauses

Nearly all of the adjective clauses you read, write, or speak use *who, whose, whom, which,* or *that* to tie the adjective clause to the noun it modifies. These words, in spite of the fact that they join one clause to a word in another clause, are not conjunctions. They are pronouns that have a connective or *relating* function; thus they are called **relative pronouns.** (See Supplement.) Relatives can function *within* the adjective clause as subjects, direct objects, or objects of prepositions.

It is helpful to think of an adjective clause as a simple sentence that is incorporated within another sentence. The relative pronoun, by substituting for a noun, refers ("relates") the clause directly to the word being modified. Because the relative pronoun is the word signaling the subordination, the pronoun, sometimes preceded by a preposition, always begins the adjective clause.

Examine the following paired units. Every "A" unit has two simple sentences; the second repeats a noun from the first sentence. The "B" sentence shows how the second idea has been reduced to an adjective clause and has become part of the first sentence. Notice that the normal position of an adjective clause is immediately following the noun or the pronoun it modifies.

A. This is a well-built truck. *The truck* will save you money.
B. This is a well-built truck *that* will save you money.
   [The clause modifies *truck. That* is the subject in the adjective clause.]

A. Alice has a new boyfriend. *The new boyfriend* [or *He*] sings in a rock group.
B. Alice has a new boyfriend *who* sings in a rock group.
   [*Who* is the subject in the clause that modifies *boyfriend*.]

A. Here is the book. I borrowed *the book* [or *it*] yesterday.
B. Here is the book *that* I borrowed yesterday.
   [*That* is the direct object in the adjective clause.]

A. The firm hired Chet Brown. The boss had known *Chet Brown* [or *him*] in Omaha.
B. The firm hired Chet Brown, *whom* the boss had known in Omaha.
   [*Whom* is the direct object in the adjective clause.]

A. May I introduce Dick Hart? I went to college *with Dick Hart* [or *him*].
B. May I introduce Dick Hart, with *whom* I went to college?
   [The clause modifies *Dick Hart*. Notice that the preposition *with* stands at the beginning of the clause with its object *whom*. At the informal level of language usage, the preposition in this structure is sometimes found at the end of the clause. See Supplement 2 of Lesson 6 on page 51.]

A. She is a young artist. I admire the young *artist's* [or *her*] work.
B. She is a young artist *whose* work I admire.
   [*Work* is in this position because, although it is the direct object of *admire*, it cannot be separated from its modifier, the relative adjective *whose*, which must be placed at the beginning of the adjective clause.]

We also use the adverbs *when* and *where* as relatives. *When* and *where* introduce adjective clauses in combinations meaning "time when" and "place where." The following examples show that the subordinator is really the equivalent of an adverbial prepositional phrase. (The "B" sentences are complex sentences combining the material of the two "A" sentences.)

A. Beth and I recalled the time. We considered ourselves rebels *at that time*.
B. Beth and I recalled the time *when* we considered ourselves rebels.

A. This is the spot. The explorers came ashore at this spot.
B. This is the spot *where* the explorers came ashore.

These clauses are logically considered adjective clauses because they immediately follow nouns that require identification, and the clauses give the identifying material. If you remember "time-when" and "place-where," you will not confuse this type of adjective clause with other subordinate clauses that may use the same subordinators.

Note: In certain adjective clauses the relative word is unexpressed; the meaning is instantly clear without it: the food *(that) we eat*, the house *(that) he lived in*, the man *(whom) you saw*, the time *(when) you fell down*, and so on.

Restrictive and Nonrestrictive Adjective Clauses

Depending on their role in a sentence, adjective clauses are restrictive or nonrestrictive. A **restrictive clause** provides identification of the noun it modifies. A **nonrestrictive clause** provides information that is not essential for identification. Thus, in the sentence "The man who owns that car just walked up," the man is identified by the clause *who owns that car*. But in the sentence "John Williams, who owns that car, just walked up," the clause *who* *owns that car* does not identify John Williams (he is identified by his name); the clause tells us something additional, it adds information about John Williams.

Restrictive Clauses

The restrictive adjective clause is not set off by commas because it is essential to the identification of the word being modified.

> The grade *that I received on my report* pleased me.
> Anyone *who saw the accident* should call the police.

Without the modifying clauses (*that I received on my test; who saw the accident*) the nouns are not identified. What grade and what anyone are we talking about? But when we add the modifiers, we identify the *particular* grade and the *particular* anyone. In other words, this kind of clause restricts the meaning of a general noun to one specific member of its class.

Nonrestrictive Adjective Clauses

The nonrestrictive adjective clause does require commas. Although the clause supplies additional or incidental information about the word that it modifies, the information is not needed for identifying the noun. (Don't, however, get into the habit of thinking that a nonrestrictive clause is unimportant; unless it has some importance to the meaning of the sentence, it has no right to be in the sentence.) Nonrestrictive modifiers are usually found following proper nouns (*Mount Everest, Philadelphia, Mr. Frank Smith*); nouns already identified (the oldest *boy* in her class, her only *grandchild*); and one-of-a-kind nouns (Alice's *mother*, the *provost* of the college, the *writer* of the editorial).

The following examples contrast restrictive and nonrestrictive adjective clauses. (See Supplement.)

> I visited an old friend *who is retiring soon.* [Restrictive]
> I visited my oldest and closest friend, *who is retiring soon.* [Nonrestrictive]

> The man *whose car had been wrecked* asked us for a ride. [Restrictive]
> Mr. Ash, *whose car had been wrecked,* asked us for a ride. [Nonrestrictive]

> A small stream *that flows through the property* supplies an occasional trout. [Restrictive]
> Caldwell Creek, *which flows through the property,* supplies an occasional trout. [Nonrestrictive]

> She wants to retire to a place *where freezing weather is unknown.* [Restrictive]
> She wants to retire to Panama City, *where freezing weather is unknown.* [Nonrestrictive]

Supplement

A few distinctions in the use of *who, which,* and *that* in adjective clauses are generally observed. *Which* refers only to things; *who* refers to people; and *that* refers to things or people. *That* is used only in restrictive clauses; in other words, a "that" adjective clause is not set off by commas. Because *which* is the relative pronoun that must be used in a nonrestrictive clause modifying a thing, there is a convention that *which* should not introduce a restrictive adjective clause. This convention is generally, but by no means always, observed. People tend to use *which* in their writing when *that* would be better.

SUMMARY OF ADJECTIVE CLAUSES

1. Function: to modify a noun or a pronoun
2. Position: follows the noun or pronoun that it modifies
3. Subordinators:
   a. relative pronouns (*who, whom, which, that*), which function within the adjective clause as subjects, direct objects, or objects of prepositions
   b. relative adjectives (*whose, which*)
   c. relative adverbs (*when, where*)
4. Special problem: Adjective clauses that are vital to the identification of the nouns being modified are restrictive and do not require commas. Clauses not necessary for identification are nonrestrictive and are set off by commas.

Practice Sheet 9

Adjective Clauses

NAME _____ SCORE _____

Directions: Each italicized unit is an adjective clause. In the space at the left, copy the word the adjective clause modifies. Be prepared to explain why some of the clauses are set off by commas and some are not.

books   1. Our history teacher will be satisfied only if we read both books *that she assigned to us.*

high school   2. Joyce took her cousin to see the local high school, *where she had played volleyball when she was a senior.*

flight   3. Jim changed his plans because the flight *on which he had reservations was canceled.*

watch   4. Andy still carries the watch *his grandfather gave him when he graduated from high school.*

Dick Lee   5. I have never trusted Dick Lee, *who probably gave the story to the reporters.*

road   6. Since the road *we usually took to the farm* was closed, we had to take a long detour.

someone   7. The police are certain that they will find someone *who witnessed the altercation.*

Dallas   8. Jerry spent his vacation in Dallas, *where his cousin manages a theater.*

mystery   9. Last week I read a mystery *that was better than anything I read last summer.*

spot   10. If you can find the spot *where the money is hidden,* you'll be a very rich person.

_____ 11. When I was a girl, I always envied Julie Ross, *whose hair was longer and silkier than mine.*

_____ 12. Ms. Treadwell looked at Tim's theme, *one page of which was stained with grease and ketchup.*

_____ 13. If the report *the sergeant gave us* is true, heads will roll.

_____ 14. I revisited the house *where I roomed when I was in college.*

_____ 15. This trip took place in 1938, *when rural roads were not maintained as well as they are today.*

83

Directions: Each sentence contains one adjective clause. Underline the adjective clause and copy the word it modifies in the space at the left.

_____ 1. The usher stopped a woman who was trying to slip into her seat after the performance started.

_____ 2. When the fellow whose car I had borrowed reappeared, I was mightily embarrassed.

_____ 3. I am sure that those who arrive late will not be seated until intermission.

_____ 4. Our new neighbor has a dog that barks whenever anyone walks down the street.

_____ 5. Lou is the only one of my close friends who is older than I.

_____ 6. Janice's car alarm went off so often last weekend that the man who lives downstairs called the police.

_____ 7. The dean is still angry because he cannot identify the person who wrote that funny satire on college life.

_____ 8. My advisor enrolled me in Speech 301, which is not a required course.

_____ 9. After George pitched the no-hitter, he heard from scouts who hadn't called him since he was in the tenth grade.

_____ 10. Although Grandma's sofa, where I was lying, was so short that I could not stretch out, I soon fell asleep anyway.

_____ 11. I reminded Terry of the time our boat ran out of gas in the middle of the lake.

_____ 12. Nearly everything Dad read in the paper this morning upset him.

_____ 13. James, whose car was parked next to mine, had left his lights on.

_____ 14. Robert probably left that book on the table where he was sitting when he ate his lunch.

_____ 15. Beth was upset because the term-paper subject she was assigned seemed very dull.

Directions: The two sentences in each item can be combined into one sentence by changing the second sentence into an adjective clause. Be sure to punctuate the adjective clauses correctly.

1. I moved my car to a covered garage. There it will not have to stand out in the snow all the time.

   _____

2. Wilbur and Orville Wright were inventors. Their first powered airplane opened the aviation age.

   _____

3. Lydia was wearing a beautiful dress. Her mother had been married in it.

   _____

4. Not many people will vote for Jim Blackstone. He was soundly defeated in the last three elections.

   _____

5. That turn in the walk is the very spot. Aunt Alice slipped and hurt her ankle there.

   _____

6. Have you met Alex Garcia? He is the new head of Business Information Systems for the company.

   _____

7. That red convertible has been carefully maintained. It once belonged to my Uncle Ben.

   _____

8. That small farm makes a wonderful weekend retreat. It is about fifty miles outside of town.

   _____

9. The letter of recommendation has never arrived. Mr. Johnson promised to send it last week.

   _____

10. The salesperson no longer works for the store. I sent my letter of complaint to her.

    _____

Lesson 10   *Subordination: Noun Clauses*

An adverbial clause such as *after the rain stopped* can work to set the time of the main verb just as the single-word adverb *yesterday* does. The adjective clause *whom I knew well* can modify our understanding of a noun in the same way the single-word adjective *tall* does. **A noun clause works in a similar way: It does the work of a regular noun.**

Noun Clauses

A **noun clause** is a group of words containing a subject–verb combination and a subordinating word. The subordinating words that serve to introduce noun clauses are conjunctions (*that, if, whether*); pronouns (*who, whom, what, which, whoever, whatever, whichever*); adjectives (*whose, which, what*); and adverbs (*when, where, why, how*). Remember that the subordinating word is part of the clause and always stands at or near the beginning of the clause.

Jill now wonders *if her answer was the correct one.*
[Noun clause subordinated by the conjunction *if.*]

All of us hope *that you'll return soon.*
[Noun clause subordinated by the conjunction *that.*]

I do not know *who he is.*
[Noun clause subordinated by the pronoun *who* used as the subjective complement within the clause.]

I know *what I would do with the extra money.*
[Noun clause subordinated by the pronoun *what* used as the direct object within the clause.]

Tell me *whom Mary is feuding with now.*
[Noun clause subordinated by the pronoun *whom* used as the object of the preposition *with.*]

You must decide *which car you will use today.*
[Noun clause subordinated by the adjective *which* modifying the direct object *car.*]

Why Morton left school still puzzles his friends.
[Noun clause subordinated by the adverb *why.*]

As you can see from these examples, a noun clause, like a noun, can be a subject, direct object, subjective complement, object of a preposition, or appositive (see page 91). You can understand the uses of the noun clause if you think of it as a clause equivalent to a "something" or a "someone" in one of these noun slots:

Subject (S)

The *girl* opened the window. [Single-word noun as S.]
Whoever came in first opened the window. [Noun clause as S.]
His *story* is very convincing. [Noun as S.]
What he told us is very convincing. [Noun clause as S.]

Subjective Complement (S.C.)

This is his *story.* [Single-word as S.C.]
This is *what he told us.* [Noun clause as S.C.]

Direct Object (D.O.)

Mr. Allen announced *his resignation.* [D.O. with adj.]
Mr. Allen announced *that he would resign.* [Noun clause as D.O.]
Can you tell me your *time* of arrival? [Single-word as D.O.]
Can you tell me *when you will arrive?* [Noun clause as D.O.]

Object of a Preposition (O.P.)

Give the package to the *man.* [Single-word as O.P.]
Give the package to *whoever opens the door.* [Noun clause as O.P.]

Note that the choice between *who/whoever* and *whom/whomever* depends on its use in the clause. This rule creates apparently awkward and sometimes tricky choices:

Give the book to whomever you see first. [*whomever* is the object of the verb see]
Give the book to whoever answers the door. [*whoever* is the subject of the verb answers]

(See Supplement 1.)

In noun clauses used as direct objects, the conjunction *that* is often unexpressed because the meaning is usually clear without it.

I know *that you will be happy here.*
[Noun clause subordinated by the conjunction *that.*]

I know *you will be happy here.*
[Noun clause with subordinating word omitted.]

This omission of the subordinating word creates an ellipsis, a construction similar to an elliptical adverbial clause. In adverbial clauses, the subject and part of the verb (the auxiliaries) are omitted. In this construction, only the subordinating word is omitted.

Most of the noun clauses that you read and write will be used as subjects, direct objects (the most common use), subjective complements, or objects of prepositions. However, two rather special uses should be noted, the *delayed* noun clause and the *appositive* noun clause.

Delayed Noun Clause

One common use of a noun clause is as a delayed subject. The signal for this construction is the word *it* standing in the subject position, with the meaningful subject being a noun clause following the verb:

It is unfortunate *that you were delayed.*

Although the sentence begins with "It" and the clause follows the verb, the clause is the real subject. The meaning of the sentence is "That you were delayed is unfortunate."

A related noun clause use puts the word *it* in the direct object slot with a noun clause following an objective complement. This use, which is encountered less frequently than the delayed subject, gives us a clause that we can call a delayed direct object:

We think it unlikely *that Jones will be reelected.*

Appositive Noun Clause

To understand the other special noun clause, you must know what an appositive is. An **appositive** is a noun unit inserted into a sentence to rename another noun that usually immediately precedes the appositive. A simple example occurs in the following sentence:

Senator Jones, a dedicated environmentalist, objected.

Because any noun unit can be used as an appositive, noun clauses sometimes function in this position. Some noun clause appositives are separated from the noun they are renaming by at least a comma, sometimes by a heavier mark:

There still remains one mystery: *how the thief knew your name.* [The noun clause renames the preceding noun, *mystery.*]

A rather special type of appositive noun clause, subordinated by *that* and following such nouns as *fact, belief, hope, statement, news,* and *argument,* is usually not set off by any mark of punctuation:

You cannot deny the fact *that you lied under oath.*
Your statement *that the boss is stupid* was undiplomatic.

(See Supplement 2.)

Supplement 1

You have probably already noticed that the pronouns, adjectives, and adverbs that subordinate noun clauses are essentially the same words that are used in questions (Lesson 6). The two uses are alike in the important respect that they always stand at the beginning of the clause. The two uses differ in that, as interrogatives, the words bring about the subject–verb inversion, whereas in noun clauses the subject–verb position is the normal one:

Whom will the mayor appoint?
[This sentence is a direct question; it calls for an answer. *Whom* is the D.O. of the main verb.]

I wonder whom the mayor will appoint.
[This sentence is a statement, not a direct question. Notice that a question mark is not required. *Whom* is the D.O. within the noun clause.]

Supplement 2

Because an appositive is a renamer, it represents a reduced form of a Pattern 2 sentence in which the subject and a noun subjective complement are joined by a form of *be.* The writer of the sentence "Senator Jones, a dedicated environmentalist, objected" could have written two simple sentences, the second one repeating a noun used in the first:

Senator Jones objected.
Senator Jones [or He] is a dedicated environmentalist.

The adjective clause offers the writer one device for compressing this information into one sentence:

> Senator Jones, who is a dedicated environmentalist, objected.

The appositive represents a further compression:

> Senator Jones, a dedicated environmentalist, objected.

If you think of the appositive as a renamer of the preceding noun (the two nouns could be joined by a form of *be*), you have a handy test to help you recognize any noun clause appositive use:

> There still remains one mystery: *how the thief knew your name.*
> [Test: The mystery *is* how the thief knew your name.]

> You can't deny the fact *that she has real talent.*
> [Test: The fact *is* that she has real talent.]

> Your contention *that the witness lied* has some merit.
> [Test: The contention *is* that the witness lied.]

If you remember a few points about the form, function, and positioning of adjective and noun clauses, you should have little difficulty in distinguishing between them. Although certain kinds of noun clauses in apposition may, at first glance, look like adjective clauses, a few simple tests clearly show the difference:

> The news *that you brought us* is welcome. [Adjective clause]
> The news *that Bob has recovered* is welcome. [Noun clause]

If you remember that an adjective clause is a describer and that an appositive noun clause is a renamer, you can see that in the first sentence the clause describes—in fact, identifies— the noun *news,* but it does not tell us what the news is. In the second sentence the clause does more: It tells us what the news is. Remember the *be* test. "The news is *that you brought us* . . ." does not make sense, but "The news is *that Bob has recovered* . . ." does; therefore the second clause is a noun clause in apposition.

Another test that can be applied to these two types of sentences is based on the fact that in adjective clauses, but not in noun clauses, *which* can be substituted for *that.* "The news *which* you brought us . . ." is acceptable English; the clause, in this case, is an adjective clause. But because we can't say "The news *which* Bob has recovered . . ." the clause is a noun clause; it cannot be an adjective clause.

SUMMARY OF NOUN CLAUSES

1. Function: to work as a noun within the main clause
2. Positions: subject (or delayed subject), renaming subjective complement, direct object (or delayed direct object), object of preposition, or appositive
3. Subordinators:
   a. conjunctions: *that, if, whether*
   b. pronouns: *who, whom, which, what,* and . . . *ever* forms, standing for unknown persons or things
   c. adjectives: *whose, which, what*
   d. adverbs: *when, where, why, how*
4. Special problem: Some noun appositive clauses closely resemble adjective clauses. They differ in that, in addition to describing the noun, the appositive clause renames the noun:

   The remark *that Jim made* [adjective clause] was unwise.
   The remark *that Mr. Smith cannot be trusted* [appositive noun clause] was unwise.

Practice
Sheet 10   *Noun Clauses*

NAME _____   SCORE _____

Directions: Identify the use of each italicized noun clause by writing one of the following abbreviations in the space at the left:

    S.   [subject or delayed subject]   S.C. [subjective complement]
    D.O. [direct object or delayed   O.P. [object of preposition]
          direct object]   Ap. [appositive]

_____ 1. And that is *why I have always tried to avoid cold weather.*

_____ 2. *Whoever did this* must have had a key to the office.

_____ 3. Can you explain to me *how I might improve my golf swing?*

_____ 4. I hope *you'll feel better soon.*

_____ 5. It's a foregone conclusion *that our football coach will be replaced soon.*

_____ 6. *How he became a skilled photographer* is a long story.

_____ 7. We were amazed at *how cheerful Uncle Norm was.*

_____ 8. Thatcher's main objection to the lease is *that the rent on the warehouse is too high.*

_____ 9. It's a pity *that the lecture series did not receive more publicity.*

_____ 10. It really distresses me *that you doubt my story.*

_____ 11. Do you think it possible *that Schaeffer might be elected?*

_____ 12. The belief *that milk sours during a severe thunderstorm* was once popular.

_____ 13. Your statement *that the legislators are a bunch of crooks* will earn you few votes.

_____ 14. Your advisor will tell you *where your first class meets.*

_____ 15. I agree with your contention *that the bankruptcy laws should be simplified.*

_____ 16. I sometimes wonder *if this rain will ever cease.*

_____ 17. Have the police revealed *whose fingerprints were found on the knife.*

_____ 18. I think *I'm ready for the exam.*

_____ 19. This spot is *where the first settlers from Norway landed.*

_____ 20. Why have the newspapers printed nothing about *what really happened?*

Directions: Each of the following sentences contains a noun clause. Put parentheses around each noun clause and identify its use by writing one of the following in the space at the left:

    S.   [subject or delayed subject]   S.C.   [subjective complement]
    D.O. [direct object or delayed   O.P.   [object of preposition]
            direct object]   Ap.   [appositive]

Note: In some of the following sentences the noun clause is within another subordinate clause. In others the noun clause contains a subordinate clause.

_____   1. Martha chuckled softly while Jim tried to remember where he had left his keys.

_____   2. Jack's contention was that the price we had paid was too high.

_____   3. Although the old man could not tell me where the county courthouse is, we had an interesting conversation.

_____   4. Her friends think it unlikely that Fran will ever marry again.

_____   5. Part of Paul's problem is that he resists those who try to help him.

_____   6. Since the item that was delivered to my apartment was not what I had purchased at the store, I returned it the next day.

_____   7. It's true that I should have studied harder for the exam.

_____   8. I must admit that I should have studied harder for the exam.

_____   9. My admission that I should have studied harder for the exam surprised my roommates.

_____   10. I suspect that voters who live in farming areas will defeat the referendum.

_____   11. Why didn't you object if you knew that you were being overcharged?

_____   12. The truth of the matter is that Jackson could not pay the initiation fee.

_____   13. Whoever owns the Buick that is blocking my driveway needs to move it immediately.

_____   14. It is quite possible that the report you got the figures from is out of date.

_____   15. Don't you ever worry about how you will pay for these luxuries?

_____   16. Why Ann works when she could retire with a good pension puzzles me.

_____   17. I know that the receptionist was surprised by the request I made.

_____   18. Most people think it a crime that the bond issue for schools was defeated.

_____   19. One reporter asked the candidate if he had any inherited wealth.

_____   20. Frankly, I was shocked when Al admitted he had never voted.

Exercise 10   *Noun Clauses*

NAME _____   SCORE _____

Directions: Each of the following sentences contains one noun clause. Put parentheses around each noun clause and identify its use by writing one of the following in the space at the left:

S.	[subject or delayed subject]	S.C.	[subjective complement]
D.O.	[direct object or delayed direct object]	O.P.	[object of preposition]
		Ap.	[appositive]

_____ 1. What John said immediately after the robbery was not reported.

_____ 2. The explanation that Marian gave was that she did not receive the announcement about the meeting.

_____ 3. Marian's explanation that she did not receive the announcement about the meeting provoked a good deal of laughter.

_____ 4. By the third game it became clear that our expectations for the basketball team had been unrealistically high.

_____ 5. Last night I heard Senator Rogers tell about how she and two other senators tried to propose campaign reforms.

_____ 6. Most employees suspect that the president of the company will be leaving soon for another job.

_____ 7. A widespread suspicion among the employees is that the president of the company will be leaving soon for another job.

_____ 8. Among the employees it is suspected that the president of the company will be leaving soon for another job.

_____ 9. If the book in the bookstore is not what you need, order something else from the publisher.

_____ 10. The reason for last week's increase in sales was that many more spectators than we expected came out to the race.

_____ 11. What we drafted yesterday should be given to the Public Relations Department for immediate release to the newspapers.

_____ 12. We were delighted when we discovered that much of the work on the second project had already been done by another group.

_____ 13. Whoever finishes the problem first should write it out on the chalkboard.

_____ 14. The class will give a brief round of applause to whoever finishes that problem first.

_____ 15. The President should have known that any legislation on that issue would meet resistance from special interest groups.

Directions: Combine the following pairs of word groups into a single sentence by joining the second to the first as a noun clause.

1. The instructor told Michael (something).
   He would very likely pass the course.

   _____

2. Some players think (something) is possible.
   The rules will be changed next year.

   _____

3. Did you know (something)?
   We were only two miles away at the time.

   _____

4. The announcement did not come as a surprise to anyone.
   (The announcement was that) Jackson has resigned as head coach.

   _____

5. (Someone) should be at least a little embarrassed.
   Whoever missed those errors on the magazine's title page.

   _____

6. (Something) was very fortunate.
   There was an open parking space right in the front row.

   _____

7. (Something) was not clear from our last conversation.
   Whether you are planning to stay through Monday morning.

   _____

8. Please give this message to (someone).
   Whomever you see in the main office.

   _____

9. The only question is (something).
   Why James took that difficult class in the first place.

   _____

10. His friends had only one question.
    Why James took that difficult class in the first place.

    _____

Exercise 10A

Subordinate Clauses

NAME _____ SCORE _____

Directions: The italicized material in each of these sentences is a subordinate clause. In the space at the left, write one of the following to identify the clause:

    Adv. [adverb clause]   Adj. [adjective clause]   N. [noun clause]

_____ 1. I hope you will remember *why I offered you that other position.*

_____ 2. *How this new rule will change the practice of law* is not clear at this time.

_____ 3. The person *who wrote me that letter* is a very skilled writer.

_____ 4. The important concepts in today's lecture became less clear *as I became more fatigued.*

_____ 5. *Because the voters found those two amendments confusing,* they refused to pass either of them.

_____ 6. We all laughed at Allan because he said *that the last history test was not very difficult.*

_____ 7. James was amused when the children were surprised by *what they saw at the end of the movie.*

_____ 8. Larry was able to use the book *I sent him* as a source for his research paper.

_____ 9. A student *who considered the prerequisites for the chemistry course too demanding* took her case to the dean.

_____ 10. No one in the administration knows *whom the President will nominate for that cabinet position.*

_____ 11. No one in the administration knows *who the President's cabinet nominee will be.*

_____ 12. That movie, *because it is quite suspenseful,* became very popular.

_____ 13. I heard *that the last two miles of that race left Becky exhausted.*

_____ 14. Martha is new to politics; she believes everything *the candidates tell her.*

_____ 15. Martha is new to politics; she believes *whatever the candidates tell her.*

_____ 16. When our class toured the city's new aquarium, we saw aquatic species *that we had never seen before.*

_____ 17. *If you can keep your feet dry,* you may be able to avoid blisters during the long hike.

_____ 18. Jack refused to show any of us *what he paid for his new car.*

_____ 19. The only advice *the coach could give us* was that we need to try harder next time.

_____ 20. The only advice that the coach could give us was *that we need to try harder next time.*

_____ 21. *What we sent you yesterday* should be a pleasant surprise.

_____ 22. The package *we sent you yesterday* should be a pleasant surprise.

_____ 23. The old man *whom I met on the plane* was a very talkative person.

_____ 24. Somehow the instructor got the idea *that I am not interested in this class.*

_____ 25. The band at the party down the street was so loud *that my father became angry and called the police.*

Directions: In each pair of word groups, use the first group as a main clause and add the second to the first by making it an adjective clause, an adverb clause, or a noun clause. Rewrite enough of the two word groups to make the new sentence clear. Identify the subordinate clause you have created by writing one of the following in the space at the left:

      Adv. [adverb clause]   Adj. [adjective clause]   N. [noun clause]

_____ 1. Jean was pleased.
       Her new car arrived yesterday.

_____

_____ 2. Not everyone in the class knew (something).
       The due date for the paper had been postponed.

_____

_____ 3. Alec likes to go back to that spot in the lake.
       (The spot is) where he caught his trophy bass.

_____

_____ 4. By that time (something) was certain.
       We had made enough money to pay for the trip.

_____

_____ 5. The block was so heavy that (something) happened.
       I dropped it on the new floor.

_____

_____ 6. You need to follow these instructions (in a certain way).
       Exactly as they are written.

_____

_____ 7. Give your report to (someone).
       Whoever is running tomorrow's meeting.

_____

_____ 8. The fact was not known to anyone in the office.
       The network crashed last night during the storm.

_____

_____ 9. We might need to cut down that tree.
       Lightning struck it last night.

_____

_____ 10. The person is sitting at the first desk on your right.
        The person can help you with that problem.

_____

Directions: In place of the *someone* or *something* in the first sentence, put a noun clause formed from the idea of the second sentence or phrase. The suggested subordinating word is provided in parentheses.

> *Example:*   *Someone* should turn on the heat. (whoever)
> The person who gets to the cabin first.
>
> *Whoever gets to the cabin first should turn on the heat.*

1. I know *something*. (what)
   The thing that needs to be done to solve that problem.

   _____

2. They all hope *something*. (that)
   We can finish this project by Friday.

   _____

3. Jim understands *something*. (how)
   How that program works.

   _____

4. Have you decided *something*? (where)
   The place you want to spend your vacation.

   _____

5. We need to tell Dad *something*. (when)
   The time he should pick us up at the airport.

   _____

6. You should have *something* by tomorrow morning. (whatever)
   The things you need to finish the new cabinets.

   _____

7. *Someone* should move that car. (whoever)
   The person who left it in my driveway.

   _____

8. They think *something* is unlikely. (that)
   Jim will arrive in time for the meeting.

   _____

9. *Someone* should return my textbook and lecture notes. (whoever)
   The person who picked them up by mistake.

   _____

10. I just figured *something* out. (how)
    The way to print my article in three columns per page.

    _____

Lesson 11   *Subordination: Gerund and Infinitive Phrases*

A **phrase** is a group of related words that does *not* contain a subject and a verb in combination. Like the subordinate clause, the phrase is used in a sentence as a single part of speech. Many of the sentences that you have studied so far have contained a prepositional phrase, which consists of a preposition, a noun or a pronoun used as its object, and any modifiers of the object. Most prepositional phrases are used as adjectives or adverbs:

> Most *of my friends* live *in the East.*
> [The first phrase is used as an adjective to modify the pronoun *most;* the second is used as an adverb to modify the verb *live.*]

Much less commonly, a prepositional phrase is used as a noun:

> *Before lunch* is the best time for the meeting.
> [The phrase is the subject of the verb *is.*]

> She waved to us from *inside the phone booth.*
> [The phrase is the object of the preposition *from.*]

Another very important kind of phrase makes use of a verbal. A **verbal** is a word formed from a verb but used as a different part of speech. There are three kinds of verbals: the gerund, the infinitive, and the participle.

Gerunds

A **gerund** is a noun formed by adding *-ing* either to the base of the verb *(studying)* or to an auxiliary *(having studied, being studied, having been studied).* You might think of the gerund phrase as the equivalent of a noun. It can appear in any place in a sentence where a noun might appear: subject, direct object, renaming subjective complement, object of preposition, or (rarely) appositive.

> *Studying* demands most of my time. [Subject]
> I usually enjoy *studying.* [Direct object]
> My main activity is *studying.* [Renaming subjective complement]
> You won't pass the course without *studying.* [Object of preposition]
> Might I suggest to you another activity: *studying?* [Appositive]

These single-word gerund uses are uncomplicated. "He enjoys *studying*" and "He enjoys football" are alike in their structure; the only difference is that in one the direct object is a word formed from a verb and in the other it is a regular noun. Because they are formed from verbs, are "verbal nouns," gerunds can have a direct object or a subjective complement. The following examples will help to clarify this important point.

He enjoys *walking in the snow.*
[The gerund has no complement. Compare "He walks in the snow."]

She enjoys building model airplanes.
[*Airplanes* is the direct object of the gerund *building.* Compare "She builds model airplanes."]

He enjoys *being helpful.* He enjoyed *being elected treasurer.*
[*Helpful* is the subjective complement of the gerund *being; treasurer* is the subjective complement of the passive gerund *being elected.* Compare "He is helpful." and "He was elected treasurer."]

She enjoyed *telling us the good news.*
[*Us* is the indirect object and *news* is the direct object of the gerund *telling.* Compare "She told us the good news."]

He enjoyed *making our vacation pleasant.*
[*Vacation* is the direct object of the gerund *making* and *pleasant* the objective complement of *vacation.* Compare "He made our vacation pleasant."]

Infinitives

An **infinitive** is a verbal consisting of the base of the verb, usually preceded by *to* (*to* is called the sign of the infinitive). The infinitive uses auxiliaries to show tense and voice: *to study, to have studied, to be studying, to have been studying, to be studied, to have been studied.* An **infinitive phrase** consists of an infinitive plus its modifiers and/or complements. Infinitive units are used as nouns, as adjectives, and as adverbs:

To attend the party without an invitation would be tactless.
[The infinitive phrase is used as the subject of the sentence. Within the phrase, *party* is the direct object.]

It would be tactless *to attend the party without an invitation.*
[In this pattern the infinitive phrase is called a delayed subject; hence it serves a noun use. The signal word is *it;* although *it* stands in subject position, the infinitive phrase is the meaningful subject. Sometimes the *it* is in the direct object slot with the delayed infinitive phrase following as an objective complement: I would consider it tactless *to attend the party without an invitation.* Compare a similar noun clause use in Lesson 10.]

I wanted *to give Charles another chance.*
[The infinitive phrase is the direct object of *wanted.* Within the phrase, *Charles* is the indirect object and *chance* the direct object of the infinitive. Compare "I gave Charles another chance."]

My plan is *to become an active precinct worker.*
[The infinitive phrase is used as a noun; it is a subjective complement that renames the subject *plan.* Within the phrase, *worker* is the subjective complement of the infinitive. Compare "I became an active precinct worker."]

The test *to be taken next Friday* is an important one.
[The infinitive phrase is used as an adjective modifying *test.*]

I am happy *to meet you.*
[The infinitive phrase is used as an adverb modifying the adjective *happy.*]

To be sure of a good seat, you should arrive early.
[The infinitive phrase is used as an adverb modifying *should arrive.*]

Infinitive phrases sometimes include their own subjects. Notice that when a pronoun is used as the subject of an infinitive, the pronoun is in the objective case (see Lesson 24).

> We wanted *her to resign.*
> We know *him to be a good referee.*

In a rather common sentence type, the subject of an infinitive is preceded by *for,* which in this case is considered part of the phrase.

> *For us to leave now* would be impolite.
> It's silly *for you to feel neglected.*

The infinitive without *to* may form a phrase that is used as the direct object of such verbs as *let, help, make, see, hear,* and *watch:*

> The teacher let *us leave early.*
> Martha watched *her son score the winning touchdown.*

The infinitive without *to* is also sometimes used as the object of a preposition, such as *except, but,* or *besides:*

> He could do nothing except *resign gracefully.*
> He did everything but *write the paper for me.*

Supplement 1

In Lesson 6 you learned that an interrogative unit in a direct question stands at the beginning of the sentence. Notice how this positioning can affect the internal makeup of a gerund phrase or an infinitive phrase:

> *How many natives* did the missionaries succeed in *converting*?
> [*Converting* is the gerund form of a transitive verb and therefore requires a direct object, in this case *natives.*]

> *Which car* did you finally decide *to buy*?
> [*Car* is the direct object of the infinitive *to buy.*]

Supplement 2

When the gerund is preceded by a pronoun, the pronoun should be in the prossessive case.

> The audience *enjoyed Maria's dancing in the first act.*
> [Compare "The audience enjoyed Maria's dance in the first act."]

> We appreciated *your helping the class with that project.*
> [Compare "We appreciated your help with that project."]

SUMMARY OF GERUND PHRASES; INFINITIVE PHRASES

Gerund Phrases

1. Forms: *studying, having studied, being studied, having been studied*
2. Function: as a noun within the larger unit
3. Positions: subject, renaming subjective complement, direct object, object of preposition, and (rarely) appositive

Infinitive Phrases

1. Forms: *to study, to have studied, to be studying, to have been studying, to be studied, to have been studied.* Some infinitive phrases have subjects (We wanted her to run for office) in the objective case.
2. Function: as adjective (Here are the letters *to be mailed today*), as adverb (I am happy *to meet you*), or as noun (*To leave* now would be unwise)
3. Positions: subject (or delayed subject), direct object (or delayed direct object), renaming subjective complement, and (rarely) object of preposition.
4. Special structures:
   a. *For* sometimes introduces an infinitive phrase that has a subject.

      For you to criticize his work would be presumptuous.

   b. A phrase with a subject but without the marker *to* is often used as a direct object following one of these verbs: *let, help, make, see, hear, watch*:

      Mother let *us mix the cookie dough.*
      Ms. Jones heard *the man threaten the cashier.*

   c. The infinitive without *to* is used as object of prepositions *except, but, besides.*

      He could do nothing but *leave quietly.*

NAME _____ SCORE _____

Directions: In the space at the left, copy one of the following abbreviations to identify the use of the italicized gerund phrase:

    S.   [subject]   S.C. [subjective complement]
    D.O. [direct object]   O.P. [object of preposition]

_____ 1. Have you ever considered *becoming a volunteer?*

_____ 2. When did you start *parking your car in that expensive garage?*

_____ 3. How did you feel about *passing that difficult test?*

_____ 4. *Being subjected to telephone sales calls* annoys my father very much.

_____ 5. My most unpleasant job was *pouring concrete in the heat of summer.*

_____ 6. Does *being an only child* mean that you get more expensive presents on your birthday?

_____ 7. It's impossible to ask that question without *appearing insensitive.*

_____ 8. The repair crew should stop *making that horrible racket* by tomorrow.

_____ 9. Dr. Johnson's toughest job is *convincing people that they should exercise regularly.*

_____ 10. Since *entering med school,* Jill has done nothing but study.

_____ 11. Does *installing air conditioning in schools* really improve student performance?

_____ 12 You can become eligible to win this jackpot by *subscribing to five magazines you probably don't want.*

_____ 13. My grandmother's hobby is *writing letters to the editor of the local paper.*

_____ 14. I barely have time for a cup of coffee before *leaving for my first class.*

_____ 15. Last summer Janice tried *selling kitchen products by telephone.*

_____ 16. *Mowing the lawn* has always been my least favorite job around the house.

_____ 17. *Delivering pizzas to college dorms* is a pretty thankless job.

_____ 18. After *hearing the good news about the lottery,* Phil walked in and quit his job.

_____ 19. The suspect denied *being in the area on the night of the crime.*

_____ 20. My fondest memory of my grandfather's farm is *jumping into the cool pond on a hot summer's day.*

Directions: In the space at the left, write one of the following abbreviations to identify the use within the sentence of the italicized infinitive phrase:

N. [noun (subject, delayed subject,   Adj. [adjective]
     direct object, subjective complement,   Adv. [adverb]
     object of preposition)]

_____ 1. *To find the area of a rectangle,* multiply the length times the width.

_____ 2. The reporters made a great effort *to uncover the facts in that case.*

_____ 3. "Please help me *make this cake,*" said Marcie.

_____ 4. They could do nothing except *close up the shop for the day.*

_____ 5. "We need to find a way *to save money on paper supplies,*" said the office manager.

_____ 6. I think it would be easier *to start over again from the beginning.*

_____ 7. The proctor let *us work on the test a few minutes after the end of the period.*

_____ 8. Can you teach me *to operate that drill press?*

_____ 9. Mrs. Lambert bought a new car this month *to avoid a price increase at the beginning of the year.*

_____ 10. "We need *to find some other route through the mountains,*" said Becky.

_____ 11. I saw *you carry that book out of the library yesterday.*

_____ 12. It would be impolite *to decline the invitation at this late date.*

_____ 13. The plan was *to leave early in the morning so that we could avoid the traffic.*

_____ 14. *To improve her speed over short distances,* Julie runs a series of short sprints after practice each day.

_____ 15. The bank is willing *to postpone the closing on our new house.*

_____ 16. As a new student, you will need *to learn the location of the library and the bookstore as soon as possible.*

_____ 17. After a short nap, my father was ready *to begin the yard work.*

_____ 18. His sisters always accused Larry of trying *to avoid washing dishes.*

_____ 19. Just before we left the stadium we made one last attempt *to find Jan's lost purse.*

_____ 20. *To discover a new route to India* was the reason Columbus set out from Spain.

Exercise 11 — *Gerund and Infinitive Phrases*

NAME _____ SCORE _____

Directions: Each sentence contains one gerund phrase. Underline it. In the space at the left, write one of the following abbreviations to identify the use of the gerund phrase:

    S.   [subject]   S.C. [subjective complement]
    D.O. [direct object]   O.P. [object of preposition]

_____ 1. You can learn basic CPR by attending one seminar on a Saturday.

_____ 2. My brother says that he will always remember watching his college team win the conference championship.

_____ 3. Sara enjoyed working as an athletic trainer last semester.

_____ 4. The hardest part of the project was finding twenty people who were willing to answer our long questionnaire.

_____ 5. Running a public relations campaign for an inexperienced candidate is a big challenge.

_____ 6. It is important to type rapidly without making any mistakes.

_____ 7. Could we try interviewing two or three more people before we make a decision?

_____ 8. Jerry is considering buying a new computer with a very large hard drive capacity.

_____ 9. Alice's favorite sport is flying sailplanes through the mountains.

_____ 10. I believe that we could improve the team's image by establishing a dress code for our trips.

_____ 11. Sleeping until noon is one of the luxuries Carol allows herself on weekends.

_____ 12. Before leaving school for the holiday, please be sure to remove all the trash from your room.

_____ 13. To our surprise, the easiest job on the yearbook staff was selling ads.

_____ 14. For that reason, finding people to sell ads for the yearbook was not very difficult.

_____ 15. People with a knack for selling were quite successful in their efforts to find buyers for yearbook ads.

_____ 16. Many people enjoyed selling ads for a popular project such as the yearbook.

_____ 17. We were able to reduce the cost of the yearbook by selling more ads this year than ever before.

_____ 18. The biggest challenge for the Athletic Department is finding a coach to replace Doug Wilson, a very successful coach.

_____ 19. At last night's meeting a highly vocal minority argued for removing several books from the shelves in the local library.

_____ 20. Learning to tie three or four basic knots is important for a beginning sailor.

Directions: Each sentence contains one infinitive phrase (some with subjects). Underline each infinitive phrase. In the space at the left, write one of the following abbreviations to identify the use of the phrase in the sentence:

N. [noun]   Adj. [adjective]   Adv. [adverb]

——————— 1. Karen promised to return the book early Monday morning.

——————— 2. Those new purchasing procedures have done nothing but make our work more complicated.

——————— 3. The jury was not able to reach a verdict today, and so they must return again tomorrow.

——————— 4. The hospitality committee did not find enough money to pay for the band for the next party.

——————— 5. When you come for the exam, remember to bring at least two Number 2 pencils.

——————— 6. The ecstatic fans watched the ball sail over the fence for a home run.

——————— 7. To improve the team's chances for winning the pennant, the general manager traded for a new outfielder.

——————— 8. I think that we should let the class go home early because it is the day before a holiday.

——————— 9. Was it difficult to learn that new program for your computer?

——————— 10. The usher will help you find your seat in the darkened auditorium.

——————— 11. Because I registered on the last day, I had no chance to enroll in that special math class.

——————— 12. When Mary was only twelve, her grandfather taught her to drive the tractor on his farm.

——————— 13. That new computer program should make it easier for you to balance your checkbook.

——————— 14. Abby was not strong enough to lift the spare tire out of the trunk.

——————— 15. "I have 500 pages of reading to do before the next test," groaned Mark.

——————— 16. A good coach knows how to inspire a team when it faces a tough game.

——————— 17. "I'm not ready to get up yet," whispered Becky, pulling the covers back over her head.

——————— 18. The new manager's first goal is to restore morale in the accounting department.

——————— 19. To reach the base of mountain is our goal for the first day.

——————— 20. The police officer ordered me to pull over to the curb.

Directions: Combine the two sentences in each item into a single sentence by resolving one sentence into a gerund phrase or an infinitive phrase to replace the italicized word(s) in the other sentence.

1. Alice washes her new car twice a week.
   She enjoys doing *that job.*

   _____

2. Mark wants to become a computer programmer.
   At this time *this* is his goal.

   _____

3. When Shirley first came to town, she needed to find a job.
   Finding one was her first important task.

   _____

4. When she was young, Caroline studied karate.
   Doing this gave her great powers of concentration.

   _____

5. Tammy did not say goodbye to her friends.
   Without *doing something,* Tammy left the restaurant.

   _____

6. If you ask your advisor, perhaps she will be able *to do something.*
   She will be able to help you select a course.

   _____

7. Your best option at this point is *something.*
   You should study the material and take the test again.

   _____

8. You can register for next term by telephone.
   It is a fairly simple thing *to do something.*

   _____

9. Painting the walls and the trim in that room is our job for today.
   Our job for today is *to do something.*

   _____

10. Studying for the test was easy.
    It was easy *to do something* once I outlined the chapters in the text.

    _____

Lesson 12 *Subordination: Participial and Absolute Phrases*

A participle is an adjective formed from a verb by adding *ing* or *ed* to the base form of the verb (*studying, studied*) or to an auxiliary (*having studied, being studied, having been studied*). (Note that many verbs have irregular past participles. See pages 204–205 for lists of such verbs.) By itself, a participle works exactly as any one-word adjective works:

> The *injured* bird clung to the *swaying* branch.
> [The past participle *injured* modifies the noun *bird;* the present participle *swaying* modifies the noun *branch.*]

Often, however, the participle is combined with other words to form a **participial phrase** that modifies a noun.

> The taxi driver, *being a war veteran,* signed the petition.
> [The participial phrase modifies the noun *taxi driver.* Within the phrase, *veteran* is a subjective complement.]

> *Calling the bomb threat a hoax,* the authorities did nothing.
> [The participial phrase modifies the noun *authorities.* Within the phrase, *threat* is a direct object and *hoax* is an objective complement.]

Participial Phrases

The similarity between an adjective clause and a participial phrase is obvious:

1. A man grabbed the microphone. The man [*or* He] was wearing a black mask.
   [Two independent clauses]

   a. A man *who was wearing a black mask* grabbed the microphone.
      [Adjective clause. *Mask* is a direct object of the verb.]
   b. A man *wearing a black mask* grabbed the microphone.
      [Participial phrase. *Mask* is a direct object of the participle.]

2. Jo's parents left the concert early. They found the music uncomfortably loud.
   [Two independent clauses]

   a. Jo's parents, *who found the music uncomfortably loud,* left the concert early.
      [Adjective clause. *Music* is a direct object and *loud* an objective complement of the verb.]
   b. Jo's parents, *finding the music uncomfortably loud,* left the concert early.
      [Participial phrase. *Music* is a direct object and *loud* an objective complement of the participle.]

These two examples point out another similarity: Like the adjective clause, the participial phrase can be either restrictive or nonrestrictive. The phrase in the first example identifies the man; it is restrictive and is not set off by commas. The phrase in the second example is not needed to identify parents; it requires commas because it is nonrestrictive.

113

Like adjective clauses, participial phrases must be very close to the noun they modify. An adjective clause must follow the noun it modifies. A restrictive (identifying) participial phrase normally follows the noun it modifies, as in the example, "A man wearing a black mask. . . ." Unlike a nonrestrictive adjective clause, however, a nonrestrictive participial phrase can move into another position in the sentence. Observe the positions of the participial phrase in the following sentences:

> Steve, having passed the test with flying colors, decided to celebrate.
> Having passed the test with flying colors, Steve decided to celebrate.

Occasionally, the participial phrase can be moved to the end of the clause:

> Steve decided to celebrate, having passed the test with flying colors.

Because a participle is an adjective formed from a verb and thus suggests an action, the participial phrase can be used to relieve the monotony of a series of short, independent clauses:

> Pam wanted desperately to hear the rock concert, but she was temporarily short of funds, and she knew that her cousin Alice had an extra ticket, and so she decided to call her. [Four independent clauses]
>
> Wanting desperately to hear the rock concert but being temporarily short of funds, Pam decided to call her cousin Alice, knowing that she had an extra ticket. [One independent clause and three participial phrases]
>
> Jensen stood at home plate. He waggled his bat. He eyed the pitcher coldly. He took a mighty swing at the first pitch. He hit the ball out of the park. [Five independent clauses]
>
> Standing at home plate, waggling his bat and eyeing the pitcher coldly, Jensen took a mighty swing at the first pitch, hitting the ball out of the park. [One independent clause and four participial phrases]

Absolute Phrases

The **absolute phrase** is a special kind of phrase, different from the standard participial phrase in both form and function. Within the absolute phrase, the participle follows a noun or a pronoun that is part of the phrase. The phrase adds to the meaning of the whole sentence, but it does not directly modify any noun or pronoun in the sentence. The absolute phrase is a versatile structure capable of many variations and widely used in modern writing to point out subtle relationships underlying the ideas within a sentence:

> *All things being equal,* Mary should easily win the race.
>
> *The storm having passed,* the ball game resumed.
>
> The police recovered eight of the paintings, *three of them badly damaged.*
>
> The mob reached the palace gates, *the leader (being) a burly, red-haired sailor.*
> [Occasionally an absolute phrase having a noun and a complement appears with the participle unexpressed.]

A special kind of phrase using *with* to introduce the absolute phrase can add subtle modifying and narrative coloring to a sentence:

With the band playing and the crowd applauding furiously, Jim Kinman was obviously uncomfortable as he stood on the stage.

They held the funeral on the second day, *with the town coming to look at Miss Emily beneath a mass of bought flowers, with the crayon face of her father musing profoundly above the bier.* . . . (William Faulkner)

But we can't possibly have a garden party *with a dead man just outside the front gate.* (Katherine Mansfield)

The face was a curious mixture of sensibility, *with some elements very hard and others very pretty*—perhaps it was in the mouth. (Katherine Anne Porter)

Notice that the *with* in this construction is quite unlike *with* in its common prepositional use:

The acquitted woman left the courtroom *with her* lawyer.
[*with* used as a preposition]

The acquitted woman left the courtroom *with her head held high.*
[*with* used to introduce the absolute phrase]

SUMMARY OF PARTICIPIAL PHRASES; ABSOLUTE PHRASES

Participial Phrases

1. Forms: *studying, studied, having studied, being studied, having been studied, having been studying*
2. Function: to modify a noun or pronoun. Those that identify the noun or pronoun are restrictive and require no punctuation; others are nonrestrictive and are set off by commas.
3. Position: if restrictive, always following the word it modifies. Nonrestrictive phrases may stand after the noun, at the beginning of the sentence, and occasionally at the end of the sentence.

Absolute Phrases

1. Form: a noun or pronoun followed by a participle

   The crops having failed, Grandfather sold the farm.

2. Function: adds to the meaning of the entire sentence but does not modify a word or fill a noun "slot"
3. Position: at the beginning, in the interior, or at the end of the larger unit; always set off by commas
4. Special structures:
   a. The participle *being* is sometimes unexpressed.

      Its chairman [being] a retired military person, the committee is well disciplined.

   b. The phrase sometimes begins with the word *with.*

      With its supply of ammunition exhausted, the garrison surrendered.

NAME _____   SCORE _____

Directions: The italicized unit in each sentence is either a participial phrase or an absolute phrase. If the unit is a participial phrase, copy in the space at the left the noun or pronoun that the phrase modifies. If the unit is an absolute phrase, leave the space blank. Be prepared to discuss in class the complements, if any, within the phrases.

Note: Review also the other verbal phrases. Of the following sentences, five contain gerund phrases and six contain infinitive phrases.

_____ 1. *His application having been accepted,* Will began organizing himself for college.

_____ 2. Ms. Wood, *knowing that program very thoroughly,* was able to correct my errors very quickly.

_____ 3. All my winter clothes, *stored in the basement,* were damaged by the flood.

_____ 4. Books *left on the tables* will be reshelved by the clerks.

_____ 5. *Dr. Collins having retired,* the college began the search for a new department head.

_____ 6. *Time being very short,* we let the others help us with the work.

_____ 7. My brother walked home from school today, *having locked his keys in the car.*

_____ 8. Martha, *being new to the area,* was often confused by directions from local people.

_____ 9. *Martha being new to the area,* directions from local people were often quite confusing.

_____ 10. *With eyes burning and minds stuffed with information,* the boys were tired from studying for the exam.

_____ 11. My grandmother often told us wild stories *based on her life on the frontier.*

_____ 12. "I'll make a contribution," said the old man, *quietly handing the Girl Scout a dollar bill.*

_____ 13. Jim's first mistake was choosing a summer job *paying a low hourly wage and a small sales commission.*

_____ 14. The loggers looked for other work, *the lumber mill having gone out of business.*

_____ 15. *Waving their carefully lettered signs,* the fans looked around for the television cameras.

_____ 16. "Anyone *finding and returning my diamond bracelet* will receive a cash reward," said the desperate woman.

_____ 17. *The weather having cleared up,* I intend to leave early in the morning.

_____ 18. We will need to order more franks and buns, *today's crowd being far larger than yesterday's.*

_____ 19. *Asking everyone to rise,* the singer began the national anthem.

_____ 20. *All the others having left for the day,* Tom helped Mr. Johnson by locking up all the supply cabinets.

_____ 21. *Arriving home well after midnight,* the Harris family slept until about ten o'clock.

_____ 22. The bridge, *covered with a thin coat of ice,* was extremely dangerous this morning.

_____ 23. *Quickly pulling on a jacket,* the reporter went quietly out the door without saying goodbye.

_____ 24. We moved the party to Ellen's house, *my apartment being only a tiny efficiency.*

_____ 25. The top student in the class won a scholarship *funded by two local businesses.*

_____ 26. Into the hall walked the two small girls, *tracking mud on the new white carpet.*

_____ 27. We saw the two boys out in the rain, *trying to start the old jalopy.*

_____ 28. The little boy clapped his hands, *clearly delighted with the birthday cake.*

_____ 29. The girls left the garage at noon, *the flat tire finally repaired.*

_____ 30. *Impressed by the high school player's high batting average,* the team decided to offer him a large bonus.

Exercise 12 | *Participial and Absolute Phrases*

NAME _____ SCORE _____

Directions: Each of the following sentences contains one participial phrase or one absolute phrase. Underline the phrase. If it is a participial phrase, copy in the space at the left the noun or pronoun that the phrase modifies. If it is an absolute phrase, leave the space blank.

_____ 1. Having passed the bar exam, Marie began searching for a job with a small law firm.

_____ 2. With only one day remaining before vacation, I gave my important cases to a colleague.

_____ 3. All the people standing in line now must be registered before we start closing for the night.

_____ 4. The report containing all the important figures for this year will be available soon.

_____ 5. Several of us intend to go to the mountains next week, exams being over for this term.

_____ 6. The last of the glasses having been packed for shipment, we took all the boxes to the post office.

_____ 7. Everyone holding a ticket for tonight's game needs to read the policy on rain-outs.

_____ 8. My friend Lisa, her degree finally finished, is going to Europe this summer.

_____ 9. The arrival of the new computers stopped our work for today, giving us a much-needed break.

_____ 10. My replacement having just arrived, I think I will go home now.

_____ 11. Having found two good sources for her short paper, Tammy copied the articles and went out for a pizza.

_____ 12. The audience left the auditorium, laughing together at the speaker's closing story.

_____ 13. For Mike, the term ended on a high note, two Bs and an A being the best grades he had ever made.

_____ 14. "Those of you needing rooms for the convention should sign up with Marcia now," said Alex.

_____ 15. Those books are old and tattered, their titles covered with green mold.

_____ 16. Running ahead of schedule on their project, the team members took a long lunch hour today.

_____ 17. The team having scored three touchdowns early, the coach put in the second-string players in the second half.

_____ 18. Encouraged by her success in calculus class, Tina considered registering for another math course.

_____ 19. At 6:00 P.M. the registrar closed the doors, all the classes for next term being filled.

_____ 20. Those boots ought to work well out on the trail, having a stout lug sole to prevent slipping.

_____ 21. Having already run four miles earlier, Melissa declined our invitation to run down to the river and back.

_____ 22. Interest rates being reasonably low now, prospects for buying a house are excellent.

_____ 23. Taking everything into account, I think that a pontoon boat is a great idea.

_____ 24. Totally captivated by the young children's singing and dancing, Jo spent a wonderful afternoon in the theater.

_____ 25. Johnson having been transferred to Cleveland, Ms. Amato is now handling all those accounts.

_____ 26. The School Board, having convened at 1:00 P.M., finally adjourned at 8:30 P.M. last night.

_____ 27. Jenny's paper, with a large B written on the top of the first page, was returned yesterday afternoon.

_____ 28. Having overslept almost an hour, Max rushed into work late and missed an important meeting.

_____ 29. The chicken, having been in the smoker for several hours, looked and tasted delicious.

_____ 30. The last student having finished the exam, the teacher picked up the papers and left the room.

Exercise 12A

Verbal Phrases; Complements in Phrases

NAME _____ SCORE _____

Directions: In the first space at the left, write one of the following letters to identify the italicized verbal phrase:

    G. [gerund phrase]   P. [participial phrase]
    I. [infinitive phrase]   A. [absolute phrase]

In the second space, write one of the following abbreviations to identify the complement printed in boldfaced type within the phrase:

    S.C. [subjective complement]   I.O. [indirect object]
    D.O. [direct object]   O.C. [objective complement]

_____   1. It's nearly impossible *to navigate these **roads** during the rainy season.*
_____

_____   2. The opposing lawyer could do nothing *except voice his **disapproval**.*
_____

_____   3. Robert's lawyer called her first witness, *the judge having made her job **difficult**
_____   by refusing her request for adjournment.*

_____   4. The homeowner and the decorator discussed *painting the fence a bright **red.***
_____

_____   5. Have you ever heard Jenny *singing those beautiful Irish **folksongs**?*
_____

_____   6. *Being a kind and gentle **person**,* my aunt was only too glad to lend us her car.
_____

_____   7. It was Mrs. Stuart's custom *to read the **class** her favorite sonnets by Shake-
_____   speare.*

_____   8. The spies secretly watched *the coach give the **players** two special plays for the
_____   next game.*

_____   9. Jack began *to look **happy*** when he heard his name read on the list of prize
_____   winners.

_____ 10. On our next trip, we should try *to visit **Jim and Martha**.*
_____

———————   11. *With the race not half **over,*** the storm broke and the rain drenched the
———————   unhappy runners.

———————   12. *After leaving the **office,*** please lock the door to the building.
———————

———————   13. Danny turned off the computer, *leaving the last two pages of his paper*
———————   ***unwritten.***

———————   14. Danny turned off the computer, *the last two pages of his paper finally **finished.***
———————

———————   15. Marge was delighted *to show **us*** her collection of baseball cards.
———————

———————   16. *Reading all that **material** for the test* kept me busy well into the night.
———————

———————   17. Try *staying **awake*** during Dr. Johnson's lectures.
———————

———————   18. The best thing to do now is *to put **everything** back on the shelf and start the*
———————   *project over again tomorrow.*

———————   19. *The teacher being very **late,*** the class dismissed itself and went to the coffee
———————   shop.

———————   20. *Handing **Marcia** the ticket,* the officer said, "Have a nice day and please drive
———————   more carefully."

Directions: Combine the two sentences in each item into a single sentence by converting the second sentence into a participial phrase or an absolute phrase.

1. The students stood in the stadium.
   They shouted the words to the college's fight song.

   _____

2. Five hundred students camped out in front of the ticket office.
   Tickets for the tournament were going on sale the next morning.

   _____

3. The entire staff left the office.
   They hurried to the parking lot and drove away.

   _____

4. The two small boys walked forlornly down the road.
   They looked everywhere for their lost dog.

   _____

5. We all packed up and went home for the holidays.
   The last exam was finally finished.

   _____

6. Miss Jackson told us the name of the book's author immediately.
   She had read the book just last week.

   _____

7. We decided to rent a van for the trip.
   The only available cars were small, cramped sedans.

   _____

8. John was able to recommend two hotels in London.
   He had recently spent two weeks there.

   _____

9. The police recovered the stolen cars.
   Three of them were badly burned.

   _____

10. Tom and Mike left the game in the eighth inning.
    Their team's ten-run lead seemed quite safe at that point.

    _____

3 Sentence Building

Lessons, Practice Sheets, and Exercises

Lesson 13 *Completeness*

To be complete, a sentence must

1. Contain a subject and a verb.

2. Be able to stand alone as an independent unit.

A group of words without both a subject and a verb cannot be a complete sentence. A group of words containing both a subject and a verb but opening with a subordinating conjunction cannot be a complete sentence. The subordinating conjunction makes the clause dependent instead of independent.

Sentence Fragments

A group of words that does not have a subject and a verb and cannot stand alone is called an incomplete sentence, or **sentence fragment.** Sometimes a sentence fragment is punctuated as if it were a sentence. This mistake of punctuation is called a **period fault.** Sentence fragments almost always fit one of the following patterns:

1. A subordinate clause standing as a sentence. (But remember that *and, but, for, or,* and *nor* do not subordinate. A clause introduced by one of these words may stand as a sentence.)

    Fragments: The clerk finally let us see the contract. *Although she clearly hated to reveal its contents.*

                   Bob tried to start the old lawn mower. *Which never seemed to work properly for him.*

2. A verbal phrase punctuated as a sentence:

    Fragments: The delegates agreed on a compromise wage scale. *Realizing that the strike could not go on indefinitely.*

                   Nell had ordered her tickets a month ago. *To be sure of getting good seats.*

3. A noun followed by a phrase or a subordinate clause but lacking a main verb:

> **Fragments:** The committee should include Ms. Jones. *A tireless worker with many constructive ideas.*
>
> The mayor asked Bentley to take the job. *Bentley being the only available person with field experience.*
>
> The coach thinks our prospects are good. *A chance, perhaps, to win back the conference championship.*
>
> Junior will require a special kind of tutor. *Someone who will realize how sensitive the child really is.*

You should learn to avoid using fragments in your writing. Usually a close reading of anything you have written will reveal sentence fragments so that you can correct them. You can improve your skill at identifying fragments by using the following strategy: When you check what you have written, read the sentences in a paragraph in reverse order. Start with your last sentence and work back to your first. This process, which breaks the tie between a fragment and the sentence that it depends on, makes any grammatically incomplete sentence stand out.

Correcting Sentence Fragments

When you have discovered a fragment in your writing, any one of several possible corrections is easy to make.

- You can attach the fragment to the preceding sentence by doing away with the fragment's capital letter and supplying the right punctuation.
- You can change the fragment to a subordinate clause and attach it to the appropriate main clause by means of the right connective.
- You can change the fragment to an independent clause by supplying a subject or a verb or both.

Consider the following corrected sentences:

> The clerk finally let us see the contract, *although she clearly hated to reveal its contents.*
>
> Bob tried to start the old lawn mower, *which never seemed to work properly for him.*
>
> The delegates agreed on a compromise wage scale *because they realized that the strike could not go on indefinitely.*
>
> *To be sure of getting good seats,* Nell had ordered her tickets a month ago.
>
> The committee should include Ms. Jones, *a tireless worker with many constructive ideas.*
>
> The mayor asked Bentley to take the job, *Bentley being the only available person with field experience.*
>
> The coach thinks our prospects are good; *we have a chance, perhaps, to win back the league championship.*

Junior will require a special kind of tutor. *He or she must be someone who will realize how sensitive the child really is.*

There are a few types of word groups that are not considered fragments. Although they lack a complete subject–verb combination, these types of word groups are accepted as legitimate language patterns. They are

1. **Commands,** in which the subject *you* is understood:

   Please be seated. Put your name on a slip of paper. Pass the papers to the left aisle. [See Lesson 21, Supplement.]

2. **Exclamations:**

   What excitement! Only two minutes to go! Good Heavens, not a fumble? How terrible!

3. **Bits of dialogue:**

   "New car?" she asked. "Had it long?"
   "Picked it up last week," he replied.

4. **Occasional transitions between units of thought:**

   On with the story.
   And now to conclude.

You have very likely observed in your reading that experienced writers sometimes use sentence fragments, especially in narrative and descriptive writing. But these writers are skilled workers who know how to use fragments to achieve particular stylistic effects. You should first master the fundamental forms of the sentence. Once you have learned to write clear, correct sentences without faltering, there will be plenty of time for experimenting.

Practice Sheet 13

Completeness

NAME _____ SCORE _____

Directions: Study these word groups for completeness. In the space at the left, write **S** if the word group is a grammatically complete sentence. Write **F** if the word group is a fragment.

___F___   1. Although we had worked very hard for several hours and checked the results of our work thoroughly.

___S___   2. In addition, my back hurts.

___F___   3. Yellowstone Park, a most beautiful and exciting place, which I first visited with my parents several years ago.

___F___   4. The work in that course being much more difficult than any I had encountered earlier.

___S___   5. Try to read slowly and pronounce the words distinctly.

___F___   6. John Bishop, the new computer programmer whose job is to take the bugs out of all our old programs.

___S___   7. But that story doesn't explain why we moved to Connecticut.

___F___   8. A good performance, certainly, but not strong enough to suggest that she has a great future in acting.

___F___   9. A problem that few administrators on this campus even recognize.

___S___   10. Seeing the car on the side of the road, Bob stopped to help out.

___F___   11. And now, after an entire semester, the end of a long difficult course of study.

___S___   12. No, that is not what I meant to say.

___F___   13. A movie enjoyed by almost everyone who saw it.

___F___   14. Bats, balls, gloves, a chest protector, bases—all sitting in the trunk of the car, ready for any game that might come up.

___S___   15. Only a few still live in the city who remember the great fire.

F ___ 16. Sifting the sand and gravel carefully through the screen and discovering a beautiful ruby.

S ___ 17. Sitting in the bottom of the pan with the sand and gravel was a beautiful ruby.

F ___ 18. The instructor's dress shirt looking as though she had slept in it.

F ___ 19. A funny book, to be sure, but hardly a literary masterpiece.

F ___ 20. Because I think that I have already studied enough history.

S ___ 21. Walk this way, please.

F ___ 22. To be able, whenever you are asked, to respond to questions that come from the textbook.

S ___ 23. As for your statement that little is accomplished through argument, I certainly agree.

F ___ 24. Turning this way and that, tipping his hat and waving to the crowd, never realizing that everyone was laughing at him.

S ___ 25. Next time, he promised, he would be thoroughly prepared for any quiz that might come his way.

F ___ 26. Wilma's dedication to the work, which brought her back to the theater time and time again.

F ___ 27. A strange comment for a trained mechanic to make.

S ___ 28. What opportunities do you see here for making a profit?

F ___ 29. Having just completed a complicated design project, a task she finished well ahead of schedule.

S ___ 30. But I hope that you will try harder next time.

NAME _____ SCORE _____

Directions: Each numbered unit consists of a sentence and a fragment. In the space provided, rewrite enough of the material to show how you would correct the error, either by attaching the fragment, properly punctuated, to the sentence or by recasting the fragment so that it becomes an independent clause or a complete sentence.

1. The inheritance gave Julie an opportunity to work full time on her novel. Allowing her to quit her job on the tugboat.

   _____

2. The movie surprises all the viewers. Although the same twist occurs in earlier movies by this director.

   _____

3. The morning's practice was a complete disaster. The curtain refusing to open and the lights failing to operate.

   _____

4. My next book will be divided into three parts. One part dealing with the past, one the present, and one the future.

   _____

5. Choosing a winner proved to be a difficult job. Eventually causing a noisy dispute among the judges.

   _____

6. My little sister is an avid collector of baseball cards. Some of which are surprisingly valuable.

   _____

7. The advertising campaign has brought many new students to the college. Some who have come from islands in the South Pacific.

   _____

8. The special diet helped Jim gain back the weight he lost. By giving him a precise list of foods to eat each day.

   _____

9. Making their coach extremely proud. Two girls on the softball team have been selected for the All-Conference Team.

   _____

10. The town's police force recently bought two horses. Although no one on the force knows anything about horsemanship.

_____

11. The football team lost a heartbreaker last night. Our quarterback throwing an interception that was returned for a touchdown.

_____

12. The television anchor wore a bright orange scarf last night. A scarf that clashed with the jacket of her co-anchor.

_____

13. Martin enjoys painting watercolors in his spare time. Developing these skills while he was in the submarine service.

_____

14. Our history professor recently traveled to Scotland. Supposedly to locate records of his father's family.

_____

15. Jane's father went to school with Mary Allison. A successful lawyer who was recently appointed to the State Supreme Court.

_____

16. My brother recently bought a beautiful sailboat. Because he wants to get away from the noise and confusion of the city.

_____

17. Many medical advances were discovered quite by accident. Fleming, for example, having discovered penicillin when he failed to clean a petri dish.

_____

18. The guide divided us into two groups. One with experience at rafting and one with no experience at all.

_____

19. The college recently hired a new president. A man who has extensive experience in fundraising.

_____

20. Joan went back to school to study computer programming. After her job in the steel mill was phased out.

_____

NAME _____ SCORE _____

Directions: Each numbered unit consists of a sentence and a fragment. In the space provided, rewrite enough of the material to show how you would correct the error, either by attaching the fragment, properly punctuated, to the sentence or by recasting the fragment so that it becomes a complete sentence.

1. Morgan began a new program for improving his grades. Including regular study sessions, library work, and some tutoring in one difficult class.

   _____

2. Maria spends every night reading romance novels. Although her friends want her to go out with them.

   _____

3. The men definitely worked hard in that last hour. Thinking the whole time that it was necessary to finish the job before they left.

   _____

4. Even the most dedicated students need some recreation. Perhaps taking up the guitar or listening to music.

   _____

5. Mr. Nash's son is learning to program computers. A bright, inquisitive boy of ten who is quite skilled for his age.

   _____

6. Martha had soon made several new friends. Spending all her time outside of class in the Student Union or the Recreation Center.

   _____

7. My sister Ella has a large collection of recordings by great blues singers. Including all the records of the great Muddy Waters.

   _____

8. Jason read the fine print on that contract for almost two hours. Giving him a pounding headache.

   _____

9. Angela is trying to raise her GPA to 3.1. A possibility if she makes all As this term.

   _____

10. We have a full tank of gas and $20 cash. Which is enough for us to get safely home for the weekend.

   _____

11. Paul has postponed graduation for one more term. Hoping to be here for one more football season.

   _____

12. We have ordered several additional pieces of equipment. A new lathe, for example, and a fine new milling machine.

   _____

13. The company continues the search for a new marketing director. A search that has been going on for five months.

   _____

14. The football team has signed a blue-chip prospect as quarterback. Thought by some to be a future Heisman Trophy winner.

   _____

15. The dean offered Barbara two possible strategies. Improving her grades or finding a job after this semester.

   _____

16. The college makes great efforts to help students with academic difficulties. Providing tutors and offering review classes before exams.

   _____

17. The coach has scheduled cross-country practice at 6:00 A.M. Temperatures in mid-afternoon often reaching 100 degrees at this time of year.

   _____

18. That novel has been read by most people on campus. A suspense thriller that frightens almost everyone who reads it.

   _____

19. We need to paint the house in the near future. But not until after the winter storms.

   _____

20. My advisor suggested that I take an introductory computer course. A useful class and one that might lead me to study computer science.

   _____

Lesson 14 *Misplaced Modifiers; Dangling Modifiers*

Proper arrangement of the parts of your sentence will help make your meaning clear. Ordinarily the main parts—the subjects, the verbs, the complements—cause no problems. Modifying words and phrases and subordinate clauses can cause problems if they are not located carefully. Here we shall consider five possible trouble spots in the placing of modifiers.

1. Although we sometimes use a rather loose placement for some common adverbs, such as *only, nearly, almost,* and *hardly,* we can write precise sentences only when such adverbs are placed close to the words they modify:

Loose:	This will *only* take five minutes.
	Jill *nearly* saw ninety movies last year.
Better:	This will take *only* five minutes.
	Jill saw *nearly* ninety movies last year.

2. Words and phrases that attach themselves to the wrong word can confuse the reader:

Loose:	I wish every person in this class could know the man I'm going to talk about *personally.*
Better:	I wish every person in this class could know *personally* the man I'm going to talk about.
Loose:	It was reported that the Italian premier had died *on the eight o'clock newscast.*
Better:	*On the eight o'clock newscast,* it was reported that the Italian premier had died.
Loose:	The police department will be notified of all reported obscene phone calls *by the telephone company.*
Better:	The police department will be notified *by the telephone company* of all reported obscene phone calls.

3. The **squinting modifier** is one that is placed between two units, either of which it could modify:

Loose:	Students who can already type *normally* are put into an advanced class.
Better:	Students who can already type are *normally* put into an advanced class.
Loose:	He said *after the dinner* some color slides would be shown.
Better:	He said some color slides would be shown *after the dinner.*

4. The **split infinitive** results from the placing of an adverbial modifier between the *to* and the verb stem of an infinitive. Although greatly overemphasized by some as an error, the split infinitive, particularly with a modifier consisting of more than one word, is usually avoided by careful writers:

Loose:	Dad likes to *once in a while* plan and cook a dinner.
Better:	*Once in a while,* Dad likes to plan and cook a dinner.

5. The conjunctions *both . . . and, not only . . . but also, either . . . or,* and *neither . . . nor* are used in pairs and are called **correlatives.** Because they point out the equal relationship between units, they should be placed immediately before the parallel units that they connect:

Loose: We sent invitations *both* to Webster *and* Jenkins.
Better: We sent invitations to *both* Webster *and* Jenkins.
           [The parallel words are *Webster* and *Jenkins.*]

Loose: This woman *not only* can get along with young people *but also* with their parents.
Better: This woman can get along *not only* with young people *but also* with their parents.

Loose: You must *either* promise me that you will come *or* send a substitute.
Better: You must promise me that you will *either* come *or* send a substitute.

Dangling Modifiers

There should be a clear relationship between a word being modified and the modifying phrase. Any modifying phrase that does not attach itself clearly to the word it is supposed to modify is called a **dangling modifier.** A dangling modifier can create a confusing sentence. Participial phrases are especially apt to float free in a sentence.

> *Stepping into the boat,* my camera fell into the water.

This sentence contains a participial phrase and a main clause, but the phrase does not actually modify any word in the main clause. The sentence is made up of two thoughts that can be expressed as

> I stepped into the boat.
> My camera fell into the water.

We can make the two sentences into a compound sentence:

> I stepped into the boat, and my camera fell into the water.

Or we can make the first clause an introductory adverbial element:

> As I stepped into the boat, my camera fell into the water.

But we cannot convert the first sentence into a participial phrase because the only noun the phrase could modify is *camera,* and the camera did not step into the boat. The sentence, if read literally, becomes nonsense. We could rework the sentence by changing the subject of the second clause in a way that allows the participial phrase to modify the new subject:

> Stepping into the boat, I dropped my camera into the water.

Because the person who dropped the camera and the person who is stepping into the boat are the same, *I,* the sentence is now correct.

Gerund Phrases and Infinitive Phrases

Gerund phrases and infinitive phrases can also cause problems when they are randomly inserted into sentences:

> *After studying all morning,* a nap was Mary's only goal for the afternoon.

The intended meaning of the sentence is clear, but the literal meaning is that the nap studied all morning; the phrase attaches itself to the first available noun, in this case, a noun that produces a nonsense statement.

> *To qualify for that job,* good typing skills are a necessity.

Again, the intended meaning is clear, but the literal meaning is nonsense: good typing skills are not qualifying for that job; a person with good typing skills is qualifying for that job. Remember the phrase that contains the verbal must have a word to refer to, and that word must be close enough to the phrase so that the reader does not associate the phrase with the wrong word.

Correcting Danglers

The easiest way to correct a dangler is to supply the word that the phrase should modify and to place the phrase next to that word. Another way is to change the dangling phrase to a subordinate clause with a subject and verb expressed.

1. Participial phrase at the beginning of a sentence

   Dangler: *Burned to a cinder, I* could not eat the toast.
   [The sentence sounds as if I were burned to a cinder. The word that the dangler should modify is *toast,* but this word is too far from the phrase immediately associated with it.]

   Better: Burned to a cinder, the toast could not be eaten.
   I could not eat the toast because it was burned to a cinder.

2. Gerund following a preposition

   Dangler: Before *making a final decision,* other cars should be driven.
   [Are the other cars making a final decision? That is not what is meant, and yet that is what the sentence states.]

   On graduating from high school, my father let me work in his office.
   [The sentence says that your father let you work in his office when he, not you, graduated from high school.]

   Since *breaking my leg,* my neighbors have helped with my farm chores.
   [A logical sentence only if the neighbors broke your leg.]

   Better: Before making a final decision, drive other cars.
   Before you make a final decision, you should drive other cars.

On graduating from high school, I went to work in my father's office.
After I had graduated from high school, my father let me work in his office.

Since breaking my leg, I have been helped with my farm chores by my neighbors.
My neighbors have helped with my farm chores since I broke my leg.

3. Elliptical "time" clause (see Lesson 8), usually introduced by *when* or *while*

Dangler:	*When ten years old,* my father sold the farm and moved to Dallas.
	While weeding my vegetable garden, a garter snake startled me.
	[The understood subject of the adverb clause is different from the subject of the main clause, but the reader assumes that both clauses have the same subject. The result is a ridiculous meaning that the writer never intended.]
Better:	When ten years old, I moved to Dallas after my father sold the farm.
	When I was ten years old, my father sold the farm and we moved to Dallas.
	While weeding my vegetable garden, I was startled by a garter snake.
	While I was weeding my vegetable garden, a garter snake startled me.

4. Introductory infinitive phrase naming a specific action

Dangler:	*To enter the contest,* a box top must be sent with your slogan.
	[*box top* is not entering the contest. To avoid this problem, be sure that the word that the phrase attaches to names the logical doer of that action.]
Better:	To enter the contest, you must send a box top with your slogan.
	If you want to enter the contest, a box top must be sent with your slogan.
	When you enter the contest, send a box top with your slogan.

NAME _____ SCORE _____

Directions: From each of the following pairs of sentences, select the one that is more precise and write its letter in the space at the left. Be prepared to explain your choice.

_A_   1. a. That tree is almost twice as tall as the house.
      b. That tree almost is twice as tall as the house.

_A_   2. a. In its report the committee established the need for radical new approaches to the problem.
      b. The committee established the need for radical new approaches to the problem in its report.

_B_   3. a. After your registration, you may either pay for your textbooks by check or by credit card.
      b. After your registration, you may pay for your textbooks either by check or by credit card.

_A_   4. a. This morning on a walk down the road I saw five turtles.
      b. This morning I saw five turtles on a walk down the road.

_B_   5. a. I am trying to not only improve my typing speed but also my accuracy.
      b. I am trying to improve not only my typing speed but also my accuracy.

_B_   6. a. Fred observed several people jogging down the road from his vantage point in the tree.
      b. From his vantage point in the tree, Fred observed several people jogging down the road.

_B_   7. a. You only can hear the band in that concert next Friday.
      b. You can hear the band only in that concert next Friday.

_B_   8. a. We need to, in spite of the problems involved, get the business on a sound financial footing.
      b. In spite of the problems involved, we need to get the business on a sound financial footing.

_A_   9. a. People who run long distances may suffer occasionally from shinsplints, a problem caused by overuse.
      b. People who occasionally run long distances may suffer from shinsplints, a problem caused by overuse.

_B_ 10. a. Either you make the repair now, or you run the risk of a major breakdown later.
      b. You either make the repair now, or you run the risk of a major breakdown later on.

139

Directions: In the space at the left, write **A** or **B** to indicate the logical place for the italicized modifier.

Note: In some sentences, both choices create a meaningful sentence. Be prepared to explain the exact meaning created by your choice.

A ___ 1. (*only*) **A** Jim Martin can **B** repair that computer successfully.

A or B ___ 2. (*usually*) Staff members who **A** enjoy softball are **B** invited to try out for the company team.

B ___ 3. (*almost*) Marsha has **A** found **B** all the books related to her research project.

A ___ 4. (*in my biology class*) Yesterday there was a presentation **A** about the importance of careful disposal techniques for nuclear waste **B**.

A ___ 5. (*walking out of the library*) **A** the two girls saw a huge spider **B**.

A ___ 6. (*not*) Please recognize that **A** every adult is **B** as interested in physical fitness as you are.

B ___ 7. (*either*) **A** they have **B** shipped the package, or they will bring it when they come.

B ___ 8. (*often*) Students who do not **A** go to the computer lab **B** have difficulty with their programming.

B ___ 9. (*under pressure*) My boss has all the characteristics of a man who is able to **A** perform well **B**.

A ___ 10. (*in my locker at the gym*) **A** I have a terrific novel about counter-intelligence work **B**.

A ___ 11. (*at the team meeting*) I heard **A** that our star quarterback was injured **B**.

A ___ 12. (*eagerly*) The puppy jumped **A** to **B** get the bone.

A or B ___ 13. (*by the advance scouts*) The general sent word **A** that no enemy troops had been seen **B**.

A or B ___ 14. (*quietly*) Jim said **A** that Marge had left the room **B**.

B ___ 15. (*almost*) Loretta and her two friends **A** ate **B** two hot fudge sundaes apiece yesterday at the party.

NAME _____   SCORE _____

Directions: In each of the following sentences there is a poorly positioned word or phrase. Rewrite each sentence to position the modifier more precisely.

1. "I neither admire your professional activities nor your choice of friends," said the judge.

   _____

   _____

2. Estelle is a partner in a company that makes and sells knitted clothing for women based in Dallas.

   _____

   _____

3. Dad always remembers to on special occasions display Old Glory on the flagpole.

   _____

   _____

4. The first patient said that for fifteen years he had only smoked filtered cigarettes.

   _____

   _____

5. The artist tells of his first clumsy attempts to paint in the first chapters of his book.

   _____

   _____

6. The delegate who had seconded the motion quickly left the room.

   _____

   _____

7. I read three essays written by Emerson at the suggestion of my teacher.

   _____

   _____

8. In her speech opposing the amendment, the junior senator from Idaho nearly talked two hours.

   _____

   _____

9. I remember the neighborhood well, with it's rusting cars perched on cement blocks and mangy noisy dogs.

   _____

   _____

10. Students who can type sixty words a minute automatically are put into a special class.

   _____

   _____

Directions: In the space at the left, write **A** or **B** to indicate the logical place for the italicized modifier.

_____ 1. (*with a smile on her face*) **A** the delighted child told her mother about the new doll **B**.

_____ 2. (*not*) We know that **A** all our members will **B** get involved in the fund drive.

_____ 3. (*from the crowd*) Smith's arrival at home plate brought forth **A** loud boos **B**.

_____ 4. (*diligently*) Janet's intention is to **A** work **B** on her law degree for the next three years.

_____ 5. (*not only*) Learning to play bridge will **A** give you **B** an interesting hobby but also allow you to make new friends.

_____ 6. (*not only*) Learning to play bridge **A** will give you **B** a new hobby but also new friends.

_____ 7. (*every morning*) **A** Jill tries to check **B** the Dow Jones Industrial Average and the prices of her stocks.

_____ 8. (*as an assignment for history class*) **A** I studied two historical novels written in the eighteenth century **B**.

_____ 9. (*nearly*) Yesterday my little brother **A** fell **B** ten feet from the roof of our garage.

_____ 10. (*after several telephone calls*) **A** the store agreed to **B** credit my account for the shirts mistakenly charged last month.

_____ 11. (*not only*) On the first day of class Jim **A** had to buy **B** several expensive text-books but also a new dictionary.

_____ 12. (*not only*) On the first day of class Jim **A** had **B** to buy several expensive text-books but also to locate his new dictionary.

_____ 13. (*after taking a short nap*) **A** Jim was rested enough to mow the lawn **B**.

_____ 14. (*eagerly*) The woman who had won the prize **A** walked **B** to the front of the auditorium to receive it.

_____ 15. (*only*) We should have known that a chance to go to Australia probably **A** comes **B** once in a lifetime.

NAME _____   SCORE _____

Directions: One sentence of each pair contains a dangling modifier. In the space at the left, write the letter that identifies the correct sentence.

_____A_____ 1. a. While walking outside to pick up the newspaper, Mike saw a brightly colored bird sitting in a nearby tree.
              b. Mike saw a brightly colored bird sitting in a nearby tree while walking outside to pick up the newspaper.

_____B_____ 2. a. To find the distance from Chicago to Philadelphia, the chart on page five of the road atlas should be checked.
              b. To find the distance from Chicago to Philadelphia, check the chart on page five of the road atlas.

_____B_____ 3. a. Living on a dry, dusty road, my car needs to be washed almost every week.
              b. Living on a dry, dusty road, I need to get my car washed almost every week.

_____A_____ 4. a. Working in an office without windows, I am always surprised by the weather when I leave work.
              b. Working in an office without windows, the weather almost always surprises me when I leave work.

_____A_____ 5. a. When my sister was twenty and a student at NYU, she became very interested in film making.
              b. At the age of twenty, as a student at NYU, film making began to interest my sister.

_____A_____ 6. a. Viewed from the top row of the upper deck, the baseball players look about the size of ants.
              b. Viewing them from the top row of the upper deck, the baseball players look about the size of ants.

_____B_____ 7. a. Sprained very severely, a cast will probably be necessary for Myra's ankle.
              b. Sprained very seriously, Myra's ankle will probably need a cast.

_____B_____ 8. a. Having dropped the glass and broken it, my young niece's eyes filled with tears.
              b. After my young niece dropped the glass and broke it, her eyes filled with tears.

_____A_____ 9. a. Quietly opening the door, the young teacher faced the class, a tentative smile on her face.
              b. Quietly opening the door, the class faced the young teacher, a tentative smile on her face.

_____ 10. a. Having thawed out completely, that hamburger meat should not be frozen again.
     b. Having thawed out completely, we should not freeze that hamburger meat again.

_____ 11. a. The rowboat rocking wildly and leaking like a sieve, the two boys decided to hurry to shore.
     b. Rocking wildly and leaking like a sieve, the two boys decided to hurry to shore in the rowboat.

_____ 12. a. By adding a little more water to the batter, your cookies can be thinner and crisper.
     b. If you add more water to the batter, you can make thinner, crisper cookies.

_____ 13. a. While still in her last year in law school, Margaret was offered a job with a large firm in Los Angeles.
     b. While still in her last year of law school, a large law firm in Los Angeles offered Margaret a job.

_____ 14. a. You could improve your grade by reviewing between tests, trying to work regularly and consistently.
     b. Your grade could be improved by reviewing between tests, trying to work regularly and consistently.

_____ 15. a. Although he was already in college, Max's parents insisted on selecting his courses each term.
     b. Although already in college, Max's parents insisted on selecting his courses each term.

_____ 16. a. This morning my car ran out of gas while I was driving down the freeway.
     b. This morning my car ran out of gas while driving down the freeway.

_____ 17. a. After adding the items on my deposit slip, I found an error of twenty dollars.
     b. After adding the items on my deposit slip, an error of twenty dollars was discovered.

_____ 18. a. The lightning struck across the street while I was entering the house.
     b. The lightning struck across the street while entering the house.

_____ 19. a. To find your room assignment, check the list posted in the lobby.
     b. To find your room assignment, the list posted in the lobby should be checked.

_____ 20. a. Finding Mary in the cafeteria, we made plans to go to the football game together.
     b. When I found Mary in the cafeteria, we made plans to go to the football game together.

NAME _____ SCORE _____

Directions: Rewrite each of the following sentences twice. In the first rewrite, change the dangling modifier to a complete clause with subject and verb. In the second, retain the phrase but begin the clause with a word the phrase can logically modify.

1. Having worked the first equation incorrectly, the rest of Jim's work on that problem was also incorrect.

   a. _____

   b. _____

2. After working in the fields on a hot day, a swim in the cold creek is very refreshing.

   a. _____

   b. _____

3. To find your way down that trail at night, a good flashlight is necessary.

   a. _____

   b. _____

4. When almost finished with the survey, the computer lost all our data.

   a. _____

   b. _____

5. Having practiced that formation every day for a month, it seemed easy to the members of the band.

   a. _____

   b. _____

6. Before buying a house, it is wise to have an inspector check it thoroughly.

   a. _____

   b. _____

7. To qualify for that position, two years as an assistant manager are necessary.

    a. _____

    b. _____

8. Crawling under the table to retrieve my shoes, my head hit the underside of the table with a loud crack.

    a. _____

    b. _____

9. At the age of twelve, my grandfather took me on a fishing trip to New Zealand.

    a. _____

    b. _____

10. Entering the building, the code for the burglar alarm must be entered into the keypad.

    a. _____

    b. _____

Lesson 15 *Subordination*

Beginning writers sometimes string together too many short sentences, or they tie clauses together with conjunctions—*and, but, or*—that fail to establish precise relations between the clauses.

> **Poor:** Sally usually attends each concert. She missed this one. She went to the airport to meet her cousin Ellen. Ellen was arriving from Atlanta.
>
> I rode around town for three days, but I couldn't find a place to stay, and then I located this apartment, and so I am comfortable.

If you use the methods of creating and combining sentences that we have studied, you will make your writing more precise, more economical, and more meaningful:

> **Improved:** Although Sally usually attends each concert, she missed this one because she went to the airport to meet her cousin Ellen, who was arriving from Atlanta.
>
> After riding around town for three days without finding a place to stay, I finally located this apartment, where I am comfortable.

Get into the habit of trying different methods of subordinating material. Notice in the following sentences how an idea can be expressed in a variety of ways:

Two Sentences:	The small car was inexpensive to drive. It had only four cylinders.
Compound Verb:	The small car had only four cylinders and was inexpensive to drive.
Compound Sentence:	The small car was inexpensive to drive, for it had only four cylinders.
Adverbial Clause:	Because the small car had only four cylinders, it was inexpensive to drive.
Adjective Clause:	The small car, which had only four cylinders, was inexpensive to drive.
Participial Phrase:	The small car, having only four cylinders, was inexpensive to drive.
	Having only four cylinders, the small car was inexpensive to drive.
	The small car was inexpensive to drive, having only four cylinders.
Absolute Phrase:	The small car having only four cylinders, it was inexpensive to drive.
Prepositional Phrase:	The small car with only four cylinders was inexpensive to drive.
Appositive:	The small car, a four-cylinder model, was inexpensive to drive.
Adjective Modifier:	The small four-cylinder car was inexpensive to drive.

The use of subordination produces more than a pleasing sound in writing. It makes a crucial contribution to meaning by eliminating uncertainty about what is most important in a message. Consider the following string of simple sentences:

> The management and union representatives announced an agreement. A strike had been threatened but was averted. The employees of Grantex Company reported for work today. They were relieved.

There is no way of knowing from these sentences which fact is most significant: The agreement? The avoidance of a strike? The workers' reporting for work? Their relief? Rewritten with proper subordination, the news reveals what the writer believes is most significant:

> The relieved employees of Grantex Company reported for work today after the management and union representatives announced an agreement that averted a threatened strike.

The only independent clause in the sentence concerns the workers' return to work. That is the important message. A writer more interested in strikes and their effect on the general economy might report the event thus:

> The threatened strike was averted at Grantex Company when the management and union representatives announced an agreement, after which the relieved employees reported for work today.

A Note on Sentence Variety

Preceding lessons have demonstrated how subordinate clauses and phrases, by compressing material, help the writer avoid tiresome strings of independent clauses. You have also seen that certain subordinate units—adverbial clauses and participial phrases in particular—can be put in several places within the sentence, thus helping to prevent monotony in your sentences.

Another unit useful for achieving compression and variety is the appositive. (See Lesson 10.) As noun renamers, appositives closely resemble—they might be called the final reduction of—Pattern 2 clause and phrase modifiers of nouns:

> Ted could explain the trick to us. Ted [or He] is an amateur magician. [Two independent clauses]
> Ted, *who is an amateur magician,* could explain the trick to us. [Adjective clause]
> Ted, *being an amateur magician,* could explain the trick to us. [Participial phrase]
> Ted, *an amateur magician,* could explain the trick to us. [Appositive]

Although the usual position of an appositive is immediately following the noun it renames, many appositives, like many nonrestrictive participial phrases, can precede the main noun (in which case they are called *pre-positional appositives*); sometimes they are effectively placed at the end of the clause:

> Lawyer Somers, *a master of wit and guile,* cajoles and browbeats in the courtroom.
> *A master of wit and guile,* Lawyer Somers cajoles and browbeats in the courtroom.
> Lawyer Somers cajoles and browbeats in the courtroom, *a master of wit and guile.*

As a final example of language tools for renaming and modifying nouns, study this tightly constructed sentence:

> One of the five largest towns in Roman England, home of King Arthur's legendary Round Table, seat of Alfred the Great, whose statue looks down its main street, early capital of England, and victim of Cromwell's destructive forces, Winchester is an enchanting cathedral city in which layer after layer of history is visibly present.
>
> Elisabeth Lambert Ortiz, "Exploring Winchester,"
> *Gourmet,* March 1978, p. 21

This sentence is made up of one independent clause, which includes an adjective clause, and five pre-positional appositives, the third of which contains an adjective clause. The statements underlying this sentence might be charted as follows:

> [Winchester was] one of the five largest towns in Roman England.
> [Winchester was] the home of King Arthur's legendary Round Table.
> [Winchester was] the seat of Alfred the Great.
> [Alfred the Great's] statue looks down its main street.
> [Winchester was] the early capital of England.
> [Winchester was] the victim of Cromwell's destructive forces.
> Winchester is an enchanting cathedral city.
> [In this city] layer after layer of history is visibly present.

We see here that eight statements—enough to make up a paragraph of clear but unrelieved simple sentences—have been shortened into one complex sentence. The layering of appositives and adjective clauses produces compression, sentence variety, and proper emphasis.

NAME _____ SCORE _____

Directions: In each sentence you will find a subordinate unit in italics. In the space at the left, write one of the following numbers to identify the italicized subordinate unit:

     1. Adverbial clause   4. Gerund phrase   7. Infinitive phrase
     2. Adjective clause   5. Absolute phrase
     3. Participial phrase   6. Appositive

_____   1. *Although the bread was dry and crumbly,* the hungry boy ate it eagerly.

_____   2. The hungry boy eagerly ate the bread, *which was dry and crumbly.*

_____   3. *Using special materials ordered from a catalogue,* Mario built a doghouse for his collie.

_____   4. Uncle Johnny, *who was one of the original settlers,* told us a story about the early years in this city.

_____   5. Uncle Johnny, *one of the original settlers,* told us a story about the early years in this city.

_____   6. That wonderful old leather jacket has always kept me very warm *since my brother gave it to me years ago.*

_____   7. *Beautifully cared for all these years,* that old Cadillac runs very well.

_____   8. *Because that old Cadillac has been beautifully cared for all these years,* it runs very well.

_____   9. *After spending four years in the Air Force,* Jack went to law school.

_____   10. *Although our return man fumbled the punt at the twenty-yard line,* one of our blockers fell on the ball.

_____   11. *Increasing the amount of water* will thin the batter.

_____   12. Martha Johnson, *who is the new librarian,* presented a book review.

_____   13. Martha Johnson, *the new librarian,* presented a book review.

_____   14. *Because I could not decide between the two books,* my uncle gave me both of them.

_____   15. *The boys being unable to complete the project,* the group leader postponed the presentation.

Directions: Change the italicized sentence to the structure indicated in the parentheses and write the two sentences as one.

1. Yesterday I met Charles Atwood. *He is our new computer programmer.* (appositive)

   _____

   _____

2. Yesterday I met Charles Atwood. *He is our new computer programmer.* (adjective clause)

   _____

   _____

3. *The technician checked all the printed circuits.* He replaced one defective circuit. (preposition plus gerund phrase)

   _____

   _____

4. *Spray some lubricant on the drawer slides.* It will stop the squeaking. (gerund phrase)

   _____

   _____

5. *Spray some lubricant on the drawer slides.* It will stop the squeaking. (infinitive phrase)

   _____

   _____

6. *The team selected a new coach.* The public relations department prepared a press release. (absolute phrase)

   _____

   _____

7. *The team selected a new coach.* The public relations department prepared a press release. (adverbial clause of time)

   _____

   _____

8. *I finished the paint job on my car.* I put all the paints in the paint locker. (participial phrase)

   _____

   _____

9. *Jim sent out ten resumes last month.* He has received no replies yet. (adverbial clause of concession)

   _____

   _____

10. *Jim received no replies to the ten resumes.* He will send out twenty this month. (adverbial clause of reason)

    _____

    _____

Exercise 15   *Subordination*

NAME _____ SCORE _____

Directions: Rewrite each sentence by removing the coordinating conjunction and changing the italicized material to the construction indicated in the parentheses.

1. *The budget is finished,* and April is leaving on vacation tomorrow. (absolute phrase)

   _____

   _____

2. The painting has soft colors, *and that's something I usually appreciate in a work of art.* (appositive plus adjective clause)

   _____

   _____

3. *Stack those cans very carefully,* or you will cause a minor catastrophe. (adverbial clause of condition)

   _____

   _____

4. *Stack those cans very carefully,* and you will avoid a minor catastrophe. (adverbial clause of condition)

   _____

   _____

5. The boss wrote a short memo, and *it contained two new policies.* (adjective clause)

   _____

   _____

6. *The car windows were open,* and the seats are soaked with rain. (absolute phrase)

   _____

   _____

7. *The car windows were open,* and the seats are soaked with rain. (adverbial clause of reason)

   _____

   _____

8. *Carl had never played golf before,* but his first lesson was very successful. (adverbial clause of concession)

   _____

   _____

9. *Carl had never played golf before,* and his first lesson was not very successful. (adverbial clause of reason)

   _____

   _____

10. *Carl had never played golf before,* and his first lesson was not very successful. (absolute phrase)

    _____

    _____

11. On the street corner I saw two little girls, *and they were trying to sell lemonade.* (adjective clause)

    _____

    _____

12. On the street corner I saw two little girls, and *they were trying to sell lemonade.* (participial phrase)

    _____

    _____

13. *Order a copy of that book for me,* and I will pick it up next week. (adverbial clause of condition)

    _____

    _____

14. *Marcie left for class at about nine o'clock,* and she was carrying a copy of her term paper. (adverbial clause of time)

    _____

    _____

15. Marcie left for class at about nine o'clock, and *she was carrying a copy of her term paper.* (participial phrase)

    _____

    _____

16. *I have been to several of her concerts,* but I've never learned to enjoy her music. (adverbial clause of concession)

    _____

    _____

17. *The tennis match ended early,* and we all went to a movie. (absolute phrase)

    _____

    _____

18. *Find some time to study tomorrow,* or you probably won't pass that test. (adverbial clause of condition)

    _____

    _____

19. *Jim had driven almost all the way to work,* and he returned home to pick up his briefcase. (participial phrase)

    _____

    _____

20. I met the new physics instructor, and *she encouraged me to sign up for a class.* (adjective clause)

    _____

    _____

Lesson 16   *Parallel Structure; Comparisons*

There are two other situations in which the underlying logic of the sentence requires the writer to select very carefully the structure and position of the sentence units.

Parallel Structure

When two or more parts of a sentence are similar in function, they should be expressed in the same grammatical construction; in other words, they should be **parallel.** The principle of parallelism implies that, in a series, nouns should be balanced with nouns, adjectives with adjectives, prepositional phrases with prepositional phrases, clauses with clauses, and so forth. The following sentence owes much of its clarity and effectiveness to its careful parallel arrangement: Two adjective clauses are joined with *and,* two adverbs with *but,* and three noun direct objects with *and.*

> Anyone who studies world affairs *and* who remembers our last three wars will realize, sadly *but* inevitably, that another conflict will endanger the economic strength of our nation, the complacency of our political institutions, *and* the moral fiber of our people.

Anyone ‖ who studies world affairs *and*
    who remembers our last three wars will realize, ‖ sadly *but*
        inevitably,
    that another conflict will endanger ‖ the economic strength of our nation,
        the complacency of our political institutions,
        and the moral fiber of our people.

Two types of errors, the false series and the *and who* construction, work to destroy parallelism by using coordinate conjunctions to join grammatical units that are not alike.

1. The false or shifted series

Weak:	Most people play golf for exercise, pleasure, and so they can meet others.
	[The *and* ties an adverb clause to two nouns.]
Better:	Most people play golf for exercise, for pleasure, and for social contacts.
Weak:	Our new teacher was young, tall, slender, and with red hair.
	[The *and* suggests that it will be followed by a fourth adjective, not a prepositional phrase.]
Better:	Our new teacher was young, tall, slender, and red-haired.
Weak:	Mr. Little's speech was tiresome, inaccurate, and should have been omitted.
Better:	Mr. Little's speech was tiresome, inaccurate, and unnecessary.

155

2. The *and who* or *and which* construction

Weak: Their son is an athlete with great talent *and who* will soon be well known.
Better: Their son is an athlete who has great talent and who will soon be well known.
Their son is a greatly talented athlete who will soon be well known.
[Here the unbalanced modification is avoided.]

Weak: I am taking Physics 388, a difficult course *and which* demands much time.
Better: I am taking Physics 388, which is a difficult course and demands much time.
I am taking Physics 388, which is difficult and demands much time.

Comparisons

When you write sentences that make comparisons or contrasts, you need to observe certain forms if your writing is to be clear and precise.

1. Be sure that you compare only those things that are capable of being compared:

Faulty: The storage capacity of this computer is much greater than our old one.
[*One* refers to computer; thus, two unlike things, storage capacity and the computer, are being compared.]
Improved: The storage capacity of this computer is much greater than *the storage capacity of* our old one.
The storage capacity of this computer is much greater than *that of* our old one.

Faulty: The influence of the political leader is more ephemeral than the artist.
[Here, *influence,* an abstract quality, is being compared to a person, the artist.]
Improved: The influence of the political leader is more ephemeral than *the influence of* the artist.
The influence of the political leader is more ephemeral than *that of* the artist.
The political leader's influence is more ephemeral than *the artist's.*

2. When you use the comparative form of an adjective in a comparison, use *any other* when it is necessary to exclude the subject of the comparison from the group:

Faulty: Wilson, the first-string center, is heavier than any man on the team.
[In this version the writer is comparing Wilson to the members of a group that includes Wilson.]
Improved: Wilson, the first-string center, is heavier than *any other* man on the team.

3. When your sentence contains a double comparison, be sure to include all the words necessary to make the idiom complete:

Faulty: He is now as tall as his mother, if not taller.
Improved: He is now as tall *as,* if not taller *than,* his mother.

Faulty: She is one of the best runners in the club, if not the best.
Improved: She is one of the best *runners,* if not the best *runner,* in the club.

Double comparisons may create sentences that sound somewhat awkward even though they form the comparison correctly and completely. You may want to recast the sentence to make it read more smoothly.

1. Try forming two sentences:

    He is now as tall as his mother. He may, indeed, be taller than she.
    She is one of the best runners in the club. She may even be the best runner in the club.

2. Try writing two independent clauses:

    He is now as tall as his mother, and he may be even taller than she is.
    She is one of the best runners in the club, and she may be the best runner in the club.

(See Supplement for more details on sentences used to compare and contrast.)

Supplement

In addition to requiring the structural units already mentioned, comparison–contrast sentences place a few constraints on the form of the adjective or adverb.

1. When your comparison is limited to two things, use the comparative degree:

    Both Jane and Laura sing well, but Jane has the *better* voice.
    Which takes more time, your studies or your job?

2. Use the superlative for more than two things:

    January is the *worst* month of the year.

You learned in Lesson 2 that there are two ways of forming the comparative and superlative degrees. In general, *er* and *est* are used with short words, and *more* and *most* with longer words.

    When I was *younger,* I was *more apprehensive* about thunder and lightning.
    This encyclopedia is the *newest* and the *most comprehensive.*
    Maria works *faster* than I and also *more accurately.*

Remember that in present-day standard English, *er* or *est* is not combined with *more* or *most* in the same word. We don't say, for example, *more pleasanter, most loveliest,* or *more faster.*

Practice Sheet 16   *Parallel Structure; Comparisons*

NAME _____   SCORE _____

Directions: In the space at the left, copy the letter of the sentence in each pair that is logically structured.

_____   1. a. Joanna fought for the promotion not simply for the money but also for the challenge.
            b. Joanna fought for the promotion not simply for the money but also because she wanted a challenge.

_____   2. a. The new policy encourages us to take sick leave rather than coming to work with minor ailments.
            b. The new policy encourages us to take sick leave rather than come to work with minor ailments.

_____   3. a. Our company is looking for a person who has high intelligence and works creatively.
            b. Our company is looking for a person who has high intelligence and with great creativity.

_____   4. a. Our tennis team is well trained, carefully conditioned, and extraordinarily dedicated to winning.
            b. Our tennis team is well trained, staying carefully conditioned, and dedicating itself extraordinarily to winning.

_____   5. a. Amanda Hightower is a politician whose education is outstanding and possesses great political savvy.
            b. Amanda Hightower is a politician who has an outstanding education and great political savvy.

_____   6. a. After fighting for years for environmental causes, Mirta Lopez is disliked by industry and feared by politicians.
            b. After fighting for years for environmental causes, Mirta Lopez is disliked by industry and bringing fear to politicians.

_____   7. a. I intend to change my lifestyle by going on a diet and exercises every day.
            b. I intend to change my lifestyle by going on a diet and exercising every day.

_____   8. a. Joe forgets that his proposal needs the support of every club in school and approval by the two deans.
            b. Joe forgets that his proposal needs to be supported by every club in school and approval by the two deans.

_____   9. a. Look at Mary Lou, perspiring daintily and trying to look ladylike while throwing the discus.
            b. Look at Mary Lou, perspiring daintily and tries to look ladylike while throwing the discus.

_____   10. a. Many people think that committees produce more confusion than constructive work.
            b. Many people think that committees are more confusing than constructive work.

159

Directions: From each of the following pairs of sentences, select the one that states the comparison correctly and copy its letter in the space at the left.

_B_ 1. a. The climate and geography of the Gulf Coast are different from the Great Lakes area.
   b. The climate and geography of the Gulf Coast are different from those of the Great Lakes area.

_A_ 2. a. A good suntan oil allows the skin to tan rather than to burn.
   b. A good suntan oil allows the skin to tan rather than burning.

_A_ 3. a. One executive looked old and fat, had a thick beard, and wore a scowl all the time.
   b. One executive looked old and fat with a thick beard, and wore a scowl all the time.

_A_ 4. a. I always like a band that has plenty of enthusiasm and tries to please its audience.
   b. I always like a band with plenty of enthusiasm and that tries to please its audience.

_B_ 5. a. Mrs. Powers is a teacher whose ability is unquestioned and has great rapport with the students.
   b. Mrs. Powers is a teacher who has unquestioned ability and great rapport with the students.

_B_ 6. a. Having worked for years as a police dispatcher, she speaks slowly, distinctly, and with great precision.
   b. Having worked as a police dispatcher for years, she speaks slowly, distinctly, and very precisely.

_B_ 7. a. Mr. Selig anticipates making a quick profit on his stocks and get out of the market before a downturn.
   b. Mr. Selig anticipates making a quick profit on his stocks and getting out of the market before a downturn.

_B_ 8. a. A good politician should smile broadly, shaking hands firmly, and have a good memory for names.
   b. A good politician should smile broadly, shake hands firmly, and have a good memory for names.

_A_ 9. a. On the front step stood Cousin Lem, wearing a straw hat, chewing on a straw, and looking like he just got off the farm.
   b. On the front step stood Cousin Lem, wearing a straw hat, chewed on a straw, and looked like he just got off the farm.

_A_ 10. a. The crowd thought that Dawson was more a clown than a ballplayer.
   b. The crowd thought that Dawson was more a clown than being a good ballplayer.

NAME _____   SCORE _____

Directions: Rewrite each sentence to correct the faulty parallelism.

1. Fred's old car was rusty, dented, and had bald tires.

_____

2. My Uncle Roy avidly pursues three hobbies: playing golf, collects stamps, and reading mystery stories.

_____

3. Professor Yellin is strict, demanding, and who gives fairly low grades.

_____

4. I enjoy tennis for the exercise, the competition, and because it takes my mind off school work.

_____

5. A notebook computer will be lightweight, compact, and have a fast operating speed.

_____

6. The workshop on spreadsheets taught me several useful techniques and which was quite entertaining.

_____

7. It is a fine school, with an excellent library, new laboratories, and has a fairly small student body.

_____

8. The instructional manual for the computer was somewhat useful, but one in which most of the information was far too technical for me.

_____

9. That particular drill improved my play at the net, and my stamina increased also.

_____

10. The three men took up skydiving for the excitement and so they could brag to their friends about their courage.

_____

Directions: Rewrite each sentence to correct the faulty comparison.

1. You forgot to tell me weather conditions here are different from home.

   _____

2. Mark is stronger than any boy in his class.

   _____

3. My qualifications for the job are as good as, if not better than, Mr. Stack.

   _____

4. Watching the rocket launch was one of the greatest, if not the greatest, thrill of my life.

   _____

5. Who earns the most, you or your brother?

   _____

6. Our state university has a better school of pharmacy than any university in the state.

   _____

7. The area's temperatures are usually much higher than the nearby mountainous region.

   _____

8. It's clear that Rosemary dislikes music as much as her sister.

   _____

9. The safecracker was tall and lanky, and he had slender fingers like a surgeon.

   _____

10. Jill's boat is one of the fastest, if not the fastest, boat in its class.

   _____

Punctuation
Lessons, Practice Sheets, and Exercises

Lesson 17 *Commas to Separate*

As your writing grows more precise and more economical, you will need to use commas to separate certain parts of the sentence so that your work cannot be misunderstood. There are five rules that cover the occasions when commas are used to separate parts of a sentence.

The Five Rules for Commas to Separate

1. Use commas before *and, but, for, or, nor, yet,* and *so* when they join the clauses of a compound sentence:

   I placed the typed sheet on his desk, and he read it slowly.

   His face turned red, but he did not say a word.

   I knew he was angry, for he rose and stomped out of the room. [Note that no comma is used before the conjunction in a compound predicate.]

At this point, you might reread Lesson 7. Remember that a semicolon rather than a comma is usually required in a compound sentence when no coordinating conjunction is present.

2. Use a comma between the items of a series.

   The land looked brown, parched, lifeless, and ominous. [Four adjectives]

   Volunteers may be students, office workers, housewives, or retirees. [Four nouns]

   The dog charged through the door, down the steps, and into the garage. [Three phrases]

   He understands what he must do, when he must do it, and why it must be done. [Three subordinate clauses]

   Larry brought the wood, Mark built the fire, and I got the steaks ready. [Three independent clauses]

A series is composed of three or more words, phrases, or clauses of equal grammatical rank. A series usually takes the form of *a, b, **and** c;* sometimes it may be *a, b, **or** c.* Although commas may be used to separate a series of short clauses, the punctuation must change if the clauses have commas within them.

163

Larry, who has a pickup truck, brought the wood, Mark, who was once a Boy Scout, built the fire, and I got the steaks ready.

Obviously commas do not effectively separate the independent clauses in this sentence, so we need to use a mark with greater strength, in this case the semicolon.

Larry, who has a pickup truck, brought the wood; Mark, who was once a Boy Scout, made the fire; and I got the steaks ready.

In journalism, writers often omit the comma before the final conjunction. It is easier to remember the rule if you develop a consistent pattern of using the comma before the final conjunction.

3. Use a comma between coordinate adjectives preceding a noun.

the harsh, cold wind

When applied to adjectives, the word **coordinate** indicates that two adjectives modify a single noun with equal force. We usually separate coordinate adjectives with a comma. Sometimes it is difficult to know whether or not two adjectives are equal. Consider the following:

the harsh cold wind
the difficult final exam

Two tests will help you to decide if the adjectives are equal.

First, if you can use the word *and* instead of a comma between the two words and still produce a correct statement, the adjectives are equal, and a comma should be used to separate them. *The harsh and cold wind* makes perfect sense in English, demonstrating that the adjectives are equal in force and need a comma. But you would never say *the difficult and final exam;* thus the adjectives are not coordinate, and the comma is not needed.

Second, if the adjectives sound natural in reversed position, they are equal and can be separated by a comma if the word *and* is not used. The phrase, *the cold, harsh wind* is just as readable as *the harsh, cold wind,* again demonstrating that the adjectives are equal.

When you use more than two adjectives before a noun, you should use the *and* test, checking the adjectives by pairs, the first with the second, the second with the third, and so on to determine the need for commas. It may help you to know that we usually do not use commas before adjectives denoting size or age. And remember that you never use a comma between the last adjective and the noun.

Observe how use of these tests determines punctuation like the following:

a neat, courteous little boy
a hot, steamy summer day

Because we don't say, "a neat and courteous and little boy," we would place a comma between neat and courteous, but not between courteous and little. We could say *a hot, steamy summer day* or *a steamy, hot summer day,* but not *a hot and steamy and summer day.*

4. Use a comma after most introductory modifiers. The following specific applications of this rule will help you to use it correctly.

   a. Put commas after introductory adverbial clauses:

   Unless the flood water recedes soon, we're in trouble.
   If we can prove that the signature was forged, we will win the case.
   Before sophomores will be admitted to courses numbered 300 or above, they must have official permission.
   Before I answer you, I want to ask another question.
   When he arrived, he seemed distraught.

   b. Put commas after introductory verbal-phrase modifiers:

   Having climbed the steep trail up Cougar Mountain, Bob decided to take some pictures.
   To get the best view of the valley, he walked to the edge of the cliff.
   After opening his backpack, he searched for his new telephoto lens.

   c. Put a comma after an introductory absolute element, such as a phrase, an adverb modifying the whole sentence, a mild exclamation, and *yes* and *no.*

   In fact, there was no way to keep the front door closed.
   Certainly, I'll be glad to help you.
   Well, what are we to do now?
   No, we are not in danger.

   d. Ordinarily, do not put a comma after a single prepositional phrase at the beginning of a sentence. If the opening element contains two or more phrases, use a comma to separate the phrases from the main clause. A long introductory prepositional phrase is not followed by a comma when the subject and verb are reversed.

   After a heavy dinner we usually went for a short walk.
   In early summer many birds nested there.
   In spite of the very heavy wind and the pelting hailstones, the third race was completed.
   In the name of justice, please help these people.
   After school, or during the evening, teachers were expected to find time for grading papers and preparing lessons.
   Between the dusty night table and the unmade bed were all the magazines that I wanted to read.

5. Use a comma between any two words that might be mistakenly read together:

   Before, he had been industrious and sober. [Not *before he had been*]
   Once inside, the dog scampered all over the furniture. [Not *inside the dog*]
   While we were eating, the table collapsed. [Not *eating the table*]
   After we had washed, Mother prepared breakfast. [Not *washed Mother*]
   Ever since, he has been afraid of deep water. [Not *ever since he has been*]
   Shortly after ten, thirty new recruits appeared. [Not *shortly after ten thirty*]

NAME _____ SCORE _____

Directions: Each of the following sentences has two commas missing. Add the commas where they are necessary. In the spaces at the left, write the numbers of the following rules that apply to the commas you have added:

1. Before a coordinating conjunction in a compound sentence
2. In a series
3. Between coordinate adjectives
4. After an introductory modifier
5. To prevent misreading

_____
_____   1. A band, two singers and several comedians appeared on stage at the same time and the announcer had to stop the show to restore order.

_____
_____   2. Looking carefully on all the shelves I finally found that colorful interesting history of World War II.

_____
_____   3. My brother tripped, fell forward and dropped the tall cumbersome stack of books onto the library floor.

_____
_____   4. After we had walked two hours in that cold icy wind we finally came to the top of the mountain and the comfort of the restaurant.

_____
_____   5. Marge owns a drill press a lathe, and a sheet metal brake but we will have to borrow an air compressor from someone else.

_____
_____   6. Instead of leaving the men set to work immediately on repairing the windows, the locks and the venetian blinds.

_____
_____   7. Excited by the wailing mournful howls of the wolves on the distant hills the sled dogs tugged at their chains and barked loudly.

_____
_____   8. Arthur once tried valiantly to learn the intricate demanding rules of bridge; ever since he has played only hearts and rummy.

_____
_____   9. Although the three girls had studied engineering at different schools they nevertheless had developed an interest in bridges, tunnels and highways.

_____
_____   10. Ellison attempted to program the VCR but his valiant efforts were thwarted by the obscure badly written directions in the manual.

_____
_____   11. Having located my car keys after a long search in the grass I made a hasty embarrassed exit from the party.

_____ 12. Roberta had once worked for a few days on a television crew; after that
_____ shooting an award-winning television program had been her passionate all-
consuming goal.

_____ 13. After applauding the audience in that dark dimly lit theater settled back for
_____ an entertaining evening of country and western music.

_____ 14. Since we can't find a new part for the broken movie projector we will use
_____ slides snapshots, and simple sketches in our program.

_____ 15. The team could take an expensive charter flight to the play-offs or they could
_____ take a cheaper less convenient commercial flight.

_____ 16. The lightning destroyed the computer most of the data files, and two televi-
_____ sion sets but the insurance will pay all but $200 of the loss.

_____ 17. Looking carefully for a certain leather jacket Mark spent a long tiring day at
_____ the local shopping mall.

_____ 18. The bearded scowling pitcher shook his head at the catcher, whirled quickly
_____ and threw out the runner leading off first base.

_____ 19. After Jennie had warmed up for a few minutes in the infield she took her
_____ place at the starting blocks in the last race of the long difficult season.

_____ 20. Morris has already taken Spanish, French and two years of Russian but he
_____ wants to switch his major from foreign languages to engineering.

Exercise 17 *Commas to Separate*

NAME _____ SCORE _____

Directions: Each of the following sentences has two commas missing. Add the commas where they are necessary. In the spaces at the left, write the numbers of the following rules that apply to the commas you have added:

1. Before a coordinating conjunction in a compound sentence
2. In a series
3. Between coordinate adjectives
4. After an introductory modifier
5. To prevent misreading

_____   1. Jim's father, mother and brother all have engineering degrees but his mother
_____   is the only one who works as an engineer.

_____   2. Looking quickly around the stadium the two boys found seats near a kindly
_____   smiling old gentleman.

_____   3. The television hissed loudly, showered sparks all over the room and then
_____   lapsed into a strange angry silence.

_____   4. By the time we had found our happy tired colleagues they had picked
_____   enough blueberries for two pies.

_____   5. My brother used to sell all sorts of equipment but now he specializes in lawn-
_____   mowers, edgers and other lawn tools.

_____   6. After losing the players went to the locker room and packed up their bats
_____   gloves, and uniforms.

_____   7. Promising an end to the hot unendurably long drought the weather fore-
_____   casters predicted thunderstorms and cooler temperatures.

_____   8. When I refinished the antique table the humidity was very high; later on the
_____   top of the table developed bubbles and blisters.

_____   9. The suave polished ambassador graciously welcomed the envoys, members
_____   of parliament and other local dignitaries.

_____   10. The warm gooey chocolate syrup spread across the cold vanilla ice cream and
_____   I watched expectantly as the walnut chunks sank deeper under the surface of
              the syrup.

Directions: Under each rule, write two sentences of your own composition to illustrate the punctuation to be used. Bring your work to class for discussion. The purpose of this exercise is to help you recognize punctuation situations in your own writing.

1. Comma used before a coordinating conjunction in a compound sentence.

   a.

   b.

2. Commas used in a series (one series of single words and one series of phrases).

   a.

   b.

3. Comma used after an introductory modifier (one adverbial clause and one verbal phrase).

   a.

   b.

4. Comma used between coordinate adjectives.

   a.

   b.

5. Comma used to prevent misreading.

   a.

   b.

NAME _____ SCORE _____

Directions: The following sentences contain numbered spots where punctuation might be needed. In the correspondingly numbered spaces at the left, write **C** if a comma is needed, **S** if a semicolon is needed, or **0** if no punctuation is needed.

1. _____   (1) Racing down the street, jumping from the truck and hooking up the
                        ¹
2. _____   hoses the firefighters had the blaze extinguished immediately.
                        ²
3. _____   (2) The two couples rose from their table and walked to the dance floor the
                        ³   ⁴
4. _____   band stopped playing when they stepped onto the floor.

5. _____   (3) After all the people believe in our election process; it seems clumsy but
                        ⁵   ⁶
6. _____   it works pretty well most of the time.

7. _____   (4) In most detective stories the hero is a fast-talking gum-chewing tough
                        ⁷   ⁸
8. _____   guy with a dumb blonde girlfriend.

9. _____   (5) About 3:00 P.M. we all left the office and went to the park for a swim
                        ⁹
10. _____   in the cool refreshing waters of the lake.
                        ¹⁰
11. _____   (6) While leaving Mr. Kittle stopped at the desk and made a reservation
                        ¹¹   ¹²
12. _____   for his next stop.

13. _____   (7) Before beginning to write, the woman set two pens, a ruler and a
                                                                              ¹³
14. _____   yellow legal pad precisely in the middle of her desk.
                        ¹⁴
15. _____   (8) After walking through most of the theater I finally found seats on the
                        ¹⁵
16. _____   very first row there, I was in the middle of the action.
                        ¹⁶
17. _____   (9) Jim chose not to return to his previous job instead he entered a technical
                        ¹⁷   ¹⁸
18. _____   school to study computer repair.

19. _____ (10) Although they had never sailed anything larger than a pram the three

20. _____ women chartered a forty-foot sloop and went for a three-week island

cruise.

Just as there are times when you need to use commas to separate items, there are times when you need to use commas to enclose items. Use commas to enclose **interrupters,** those words, phrases, or clauses that interrupt the normal word order of a sentence.

Common Interrupters

The most common types of interrupters are discussed below.

1. Nonrestrictive adjective clauses and phrases

   The coach's Awards Banquet speech, *which was one of her best,* should be printed. [Nonrestrictive adjective clause]

   Jan's mother, *holding a winning ticket,* went to the desk. [Nonrestrictive participial phrase]

   Professor Angela Cheney, *at the far end of the head table,* summoned a waiter. [Nonrestrictive prepositional phrase]

Clauses and phrases not essential to identify a noun are set off by commas. (See Lesson 9 to review restrictive and nonrestrictive clauses and phrases.) Note that, in some cases, the meaning of the sentence depends on whether a clause is taken as restrictive or nonrestrictive.

   My brother-in-law *who lives in Akron* is a chemist.
   [The writer has more than one brother-in-law. The restrictive clause is needed to distinguish this brother-in-law from other brothers-in-law.]

   My brother-in-law, *who lives in Akron,* is a chemist.
   [The writer is telling us that he or she has only one brother-in-law. Identification is not explicit.]

2. Most appositives

   One comedian, *the one with the the lisp,* was booed.
   The major, *a veteran of three wars,* accepted the award.
   Mr. Tate, *our head counselor,* will speak.
   Our head counselor, *Mr. Tate,* will speak.

As you learned in Lesson 10, the most common type of appositive immediately follows the noun or pronoun that it renames. Appositives like these are called loose or nonrestrictive appositives and are set off. Sometimes, however, an appositive functions in the same way that a restrictive adjective clause functions: It identifies a preceding noun that, without the appositive, could refer to any member of a class. An appositive of this sort is not set off:

   my brother Jack
   the poet Keats

173

the apostle Paul
the preposition *to*

3. Absolute phrases

Today being a holiday, I plan to loaf and relax.

Her replacement having arrived early, Bea had time to shop.

He sat there in silence, *his left cheek twitching as usual.*

He stood in the doorway, *his wet cloak dripping water on the rug,* and waited for some sign of recognition.

An absolute phrase, which consists of a noun or a pronoun and a verbal (see Lesson 12), modifies the sentence as a whole, not any special part of it. Because the phrase is not restricted to any special part of the sentence, the phrase should be set off.

4. Parenthetical expressions

The text, *moreover,* had not been carefully proofread.
You will find, *for example,* that the format is not attractive.
The meal, *to tell the truth,* was quite unappetizing.
His appearance, *I must admit,* would startle anyone.

These are words, phrases, or clauses that break into the sentence to explain, to emphasize, to qualify, or to point the direction of the thought and should be set off.

5. Words used in direct address

"Remember, *Jimmy,* that we like your work," he said.
"*Henry,*" said the teacher, "you made an A on your paper."
"I believe, *sir,* that you have been misinformed," she replied.
"And now, *dear friends and neighbors,* let's eat," said Father Jamison.

6. Expressions designating the speaker in direct quotations

"With your permission," *Tom replied,* "I'll go home for the day."
"That will have to do," *said Mrs. Garcia,* "until we think of something better."

Other punctuation marks may be used instead of the comma if the sentence justifies their use.

"How shall I tell him?" asked Mary timidly. [Question mark after question]

"Silence!" he shouted. "Get to work at once!" [Exclamation point]

"Two of the buildings are firetraps," replied the inspector; "moreover, the library needs a new roof." [Semicolon required to avoid a comma fault between independent clauses]

7. Negative insertions used for emphasis, units out of their position, and tag questions (short interrogative clauses combined with statements)

Our plane was an old propeller model, *not the 747 we had expected.*
Tired and footsore, the hikers finally reached camp.
The hikers finally reached camp, *tired and footsore.*
Her answer was a good one, *don't you think?*
You remember, *don't you,* Dr. Wade's eloquent eulogy?

8. Degrees, titles, and the like when they follow names

Helen Lyle, *Ph.D.,* gave the opening address.
The new ambassador is Peter Jones, *Esq.*

9. In dates and addresses

On July 14, *1904,* in a little cottage at 316 High Street, *Mayville, Illinois,* the wedding took place.

When a year follows a month, rather than a day of the month, the year is usually not set off. No comma is needed before a ZIP code number:

As of March 1985 his mailing address was 1675 East Union Street, Seattle, WA 98122.

Practice Sheet 18

Commas to Enclose

NAME _____ SCORE _____

Directions: Insert commas where they are necessary in the following sentences. Then, before each sentence, write one of the following numbers to indicate the rule that governs the punctuation of the sentence:

1. A nonrestrictive clause or phrase
2. An appositive
3. A noun in direct address
4. A parenthetical element
5. The speaker in dialogue
6. An absolute phrase

_____ 1. The wild ponies live on Assateague Island an island off the coast of Virginia and Maryland.

_____ 2. That package in my opinion should have been wrapped more carefully.

_____ 3. The blizzard having arrived earlier than expected we were all trapped in the gymnasium for two days.

_____ 4. "I need to pay some bills today" said Mike.

_____ 5. Jim March easily the best athlete in the school broke his ankle yesterday in a skiing accident.

_____ 6. Yolanda her interest in playing bridge having died dropped out of the neighborhood bridge club.

_____ 7. Take the other children Mary to see the puppies in the barn.

_____ 8. Alma looking very tired from the drive arrived about midnight last night.

_____ 9. Ms. Marshall the most experienced teacher in the department is also very popular with the students.

_____ 10. I heard the news from Mel who always seems to know what's going on in the office.

_____ 11. My last class for today economic geography was canceled.

_____ 12. My sister left for Seattle yesterday her car loaded with luggage and her collection of teddy bears.

_____ 13. Richard who usually works with great accuracy made three errors on that last set of problems.

_____ 14. My cousin recently moved to New York City where he hopes to find a job in the television industry.

_____ 15. My brother's children who watched "Sesame Street" learned to count at an early age.

Directions: Each of the following sentences contains either an adjective clause or a participial phrase in italics. Insert commas where they are needed. In the space at the left of each sentence write **R** if the clause or phrase is restrictive, **N** if the clause or phrase is nonrestrictive.

_____ 1. Every student *who buys at least $50 worth of books* will receive a free backpack from the bookstore.

_____ 2. That baseball glove *faded and worn from years of use* is still my brother's most prized possession.

_____ 3. Students in the Lofton Building *where the air conditioning is being replaced* will find the heat very difficult to bear.

_____ 4. John Johnson *desperately trying to finish an overdue paper* was the last student out of the library today.

_____ 5. Some students *desperately trying to finish overdue papers* worked late in the library last night.

_____ 6. The new long-lasting paint *which was developed in our university's laboratories* will surely revolutionize building maintenance.

_____ 7. June wants to buy a word-processing program *that can correct her grammatical mistakes.*

_____ 8. Bob's cousin Rhoda *who recently moved here from Texas* is studying hotel management.

_____ 9. Dr. Lamont's first article *which was published five years ago* is still considered a definitive study on diabetes.

_____ 10. In fact, all the articles *that Dr. Lamont has written* have made major contributions in that area.

_____ 11. A family friend *who is an accountant* does my income tax for me every year.

_____ 12. Jim Travers *who is an accountant* does my income tax for me every year.

_____ 13. Students *already enrolled in the aviation program* need not attend tomorrow's meeting.

_____ 14. Marsha *who is already enrolled in the aviation program* does not need to attend tomorrow's meeting.

_____ 15. Everyone *needing a student ID card* should report to the dean's office on Tuesday morning.

Exercise 18   *Commas to Enclose*

NAME _____   SCORE _____

Directions: Recognizing typical punctuation situations in your own writing is a very important skill. In the spaces provided, write two sentences to illustrate each of the rules indicated. Be sure to include all necessary punctuation.

1. Two sentences with nonrestrictive adjective clauses.

a.

b.

2. Two sentences with nonrestrictive participial phrases.

a.

b.

3. Two sentences with appositives.

a.

b.

4. Two sentences with nouns used in direct address.

a.

b.

5. Two sentences with parenthetical elements.

a.

b.

6. Two sentences with absolute phrases.

a.

b.

Directions: Each of the following sentences contains one adjective clause or one participial phrase. Underline the phrase or clause. Insert commas where they are needed. In the space at the left of each sentence write **R** if the clause or phrase is restrictive, **N** if the clause or phrase is nonrestrictive.

_____ 1. James is one of those people who never lose their optimistic outlook on life.

_____ 2. How many feet long is that plank lying on the workbench?

_____ 3. Janice Moore who attended college here last year has gone to England to study.

_____ 4. Our apartment complex needs to hire someone who can do minor repairs in the apartments.

_____ 5. Our apartment complex hired Ron Jones who can do minor repairs in the apartments.

_____ 6. The girl standing at the end of the front row in that picture is my brother's daughter.

_____ 7. Marlene running down the street missed the bus by about thirty seconds.

_____ 8. The new junior class treasurer is a girl who is majoring in anthropology.

_____ 9. The new junior class treasurer is Arline Rollins who is majoring in anthropology.

_____ 10. Two students standing in the back of the room left class before the end of the lecture.

_____ 11. How old is that child standing at the end of the line?

_____ 12. My old jacket which Dad gave me for my sixteenth birthday has finally gotten too torn to wear.

_____ 13. A man wearing a gray coat and old, scuffed boots walked up the path.

_____ 14. My grandfather wearing a gray coat and old, scuffed boots walked up the path.

_____ 15. My little brother is one of those people who will always need extra tutoring in math.

_____ 16. Marsha Richmond who graduated from law school last year has joined the FBI.

_____ 17. A woman who graduated from the law school last year joined the FBI.

_____ 18. I always enjoy movies that are set in the old west.

_____ 19. My father loves the movie *Stagecoach* which is set in the old west.

_____ 20. Rosie standing on a chair to reach a book on a high shelf fell and hurt her ankle.

NAME _____ SCORE _____

Directions: The following sentences contain forty numbered spots, some with punctuation and some with no punctuation. In the correspondingly numbered spaces at the left, write C if the punctuation is correct and W if the punctuation is wrong.

1. _____ (1) When the team left about 1,500 avid, football fans stood beside the
2. _____ road and cheered.
3. __C__ (2) Ed Lindsay left Nebraska on April 20, 1991, he arrived in Seattle two
4. __W__ days later.
5. _____ (3) I had a wonderful day yesterday; I slept late, went out for a delicious
6. _____ breakfast and spent the day watching football.
7. __W__ (4) After Joan left the meeting was adjourned, and all the new, club members
8. __W__ went to lunch together.
9. _____ (5) That old building once a restaurant, has been purchased by a
10. _____ company that wants to put a bank in it.
11. __W__ (6) The race course was long, hilly and extremely steep but Maria ran her
12. __W__ best time for the season.
13. _____ (7) The computers were down for the whole weekend, no accounts, I
14. _____ guess, were updated or corrected.
15. __W__ (8) Arnold Russell, who moved here from upstate has opened a shop, that
16. __W__ specializes in repairing old musical instruments.
17. _____ (9) The ski trip we scheduled for next week has been postponed, the
18. _____ weather has been unseasonably warm for three weeks.

181

19. _____ (10) The easiest way to Ruston is to drive up Highway 18, turn north onto
19

20. _____ Rutledge Road and then take Weston Lane into town.
20

21. _____ (11) The test was difficult, but I'm certain that a take-home test would have
21   22

22. _____ been far more difficult.

23. _____ (12) After that grouchy, older man moved next door; we kids never could
23   24

24. _____ play ball in the street again.

25. _____ (13) When the lightning struck the old water tower toppled into the city
25   26

26. _____ square.

27. _____ (14) Cynthia did not know that we had left the room, she was drowsing
27   28

28. _____ peacefully on the couch.

29. _____ (15) The lecture having ended we wearily closed our notebooks and walked
29   30

30. _____ out of the room.

31. _____ (16) Wilma's favorite food is pasta, she tries to go to a different Italian
31   32

32. _____ restaurant every weekend.

33. _____ (17) The biggest house on Main Street, the old Spencer house, has been
33

34. _____ sold; the new owner is an architect.
34

35. _____ (18) "For most of you in the room rent is a major item in your budget,"
35   36

36. _____ said the speaker.

37. _____ (19) In this morning's mail I received a large envelope containing a copy
37   38

38. _____ of an article about a friend of mine.

39. _____ (20) Since Al is the person who holds the school record for the 100-meter
39

40. _____ dash he is expected to do well at every track meet.
40

Lesson 19 *Tricky Punctuation Marks*

This lesson covers a number of tricky punctuation marks.

Apostrophe

The apostrophe (') has three uses:

1. To form the possessive of nouns and indefinite pronouns
2. To mark the omitted material in contractions
3. To form certain plurals, such as those of letters and abbreviations

Forming Possessives

Any noun, whether singular or plural, that does not end in *s* shows ownership by adding an apostrophe and *s:*

> a boy's hat [the hat belongs to the boy], the horse's tail, Carol's car, men's shoes, children's toys

Plural nouns that end in *s* form possessives by adding an apostrophe after the *s:*

> boys' hats, horses' tails, the Smiths' home, ladies' dresses

Singular nouns ending in *s* or *z* form the possessive by adding 's.

> *the countess's castle*   *Frances's reply*   *Mr. Gomez's report*

On rare occasions, if the pronunciation of the word with the additional s-sound would be awkward, it is permissible to form the possessive with an apostrophe alone.

> *for goodness' sake*

For the sake of uniformity, the exercises on possessives will ask that you use the 's after singular nouns ending in *s*.

The indefinite pronouns, but not the personal pronouns, form the possessive with the aid of the apostrophe:

> somebody's sweater, anyone's opinion, anybody's game [But note the possessive forms of pronouns: *his, hers, its, theirs, ours, yours, whose.*]

Compound words and word groups form the possessive by adding an apostrophe and *s* to the last word of the group:

> My sister-in-law's last visit was in December.
> Did you get anyone else's opinion of your paper?

Note that establishing ownership of two or more items requires careful attention. For individual ownership, add an apostrophe and *s* at the end of both owners.

Oliver Stone*'s* and Alfred Hitchcock*'s* movies [indicating that each owned certain movies]

For joint ownership of two or more items, add an apostrophe and *s* at the end of the second owner's name:

Rogers and Hammerstein*'s* musicals [indicating that they wrote the musicals as joint projects]

Omitted Material

The apostrophe is also used to stand for the omitted material in contractions:

doesn't [does not], won't [will not], she's [she is, she has], o'clock [of the clock], rock 'n' roll [rock and roll]

You must learn to distinguish carefully between the following pairs of contractions and possessives:

Contraction	*Possessive*
it's [it is, it has]	its
there's [there is, there has]	theirs
they're [they are]	their
who's [who is, who has]	whose
you're [you are]	your

Unusual Plurals

Use an apostrophe to form the plural of letters and words that are treated as words.

the three *R*'s; mostly *A*'s and *B*'s; too many *and*'s; no *if*'s, *and*'s, or *but*'s about it.

Although usage is divided, many authorities no longer require the formation of the plurals of numbers and symbols with an apostrophe.

Btus, CPAs, 1980s, scores in the 80s and 90s

Many writers need to be reminded regularly of an important related fact: An apostrophe is never used in forming the plural of either a common or a proper noun.

There are two Kathys in the class. Two grandmas attended.

Colon

The colon (:) is a formal mark announcing an explanation, a list, or a quotation to follow.

My fellow Americans: My speech tonight will examine. . . .
All hikers must bring the following: a flashlight, a small ax, and a waterproof tarpaulin.
Mr. Rankin stood and addressed the group: "I don't intend to take much of your time today."

The colon is used in formal papers to begin a quotation of four or more lines. The text of the quotation is indented from both margins and is not set off by quotation marks.

In cases where the colon sets off a quotation, the identifying tag should appear in the independent clause.

Colons are also used as a mark of separation in certain special constructions:

Hours, minutes, and seconds
    1:14:10 P.M.

Biblical chapters and verses
    I Kings 2:1

Titles and Subtitles
    Conversations: Famous Women Speak Out

Note that after a colon it is permissible to have an initial capital letter if the text following the colon is a complete sentence. Do not use a colon to separate a verb from its complement or a preposition from its object.

Faulty: All hikers must bring: a flashlight, a small ax, and a waterproof tarpaulin.
Faulty: The things a hiker must bring are: a flashlight, a small ax, and a waterproof tarpaulin.
Faulty: The hiker's equipment should consist of: a flashlight, a small ax, and a waterproof tarpaulin.

Dash

The dash (—) is used to show an abrupt change in thought in the sentence. It must be used sparingly and never as a substitute for other marks.

Superior students—notice that I said *superior*—will not have to take the test.
New surroundings, new friends, a challenging new job—all these helped Eugene overcome his grief.

Hyphen

The hyphen (-) is used to divide a word at the end of a line and to join words to form various types of compounds. Divide a word only between syllables. With words having a prefix or a suffix, divide the word after the prefix and before the suffix. Avoid dividing a word so that a single letter ends or begins a line. (Consult your dictionary for problems of syllabic division.)

mathe-matics *not* mathem-atics
inter-collegiate *not* intercol-legiate
govern-ess *not* gov-erness
enough *not* e-nough
many *not* man-y

Use hyphens to join the parts of compound modifiers preceding nouns.

Observe his well-kept lawn. His lawn is well kept.
We deplore your devil-may-care attitude.

This use of a hyphen sometimes determines an exact meaning:

> a roll of twenty-dollar bills; a roll of twenty dollar bills
> all-American boys; all American boys

Use hyphens with compound numbers from twenty-one to ninety-nine and with fractions:

> Twenty-two people claimed the one-third share of the reward money but received only one-eighth.

Use hyphens, particularly with prefixes and suffixes, to avoid awkward combinations of letters or to distinguish between two meanings of a word:

> anti-intellectual
> pre-Aztec
> her doll-like face
> re-cover a couch [not recover the money]

Quotation Marks

Quotation marks should be used to enclose quoted material and words you may use in some special way. Use double quotation marks (" ") to enclose the exact words of a quoted speech. Quotation marks always come in pairs. The marks show the beginning and the end of a speech, whether it is part of a sentence, one sentence, or several sentences. If a speech is interrupted by material showing who said it, quotation marks set off the quoted material from the explanatory material. Use quotation marks where the directly quoted material begins and where it ends or is interrupted. Indirect quotations are *not* set off by quotation marks:

> "I admit," said Ralph, "that I was mistaken."
> [Note that the explanatory material is set off from the direct quotation.]
> Peg answered, "I didn't attend. I wasn't in town." [More than one sentence.]
> Peg answered that she hadn't attended because she hadn't been in town.
> [This is an indirect quotation. Words not directly quoted do not need quotation marks.]

Use double quotation marks to set off the subdivisions of books, names of songs, and titles of units of less than book length, such as short stories, short poems, essays, and articles:

> The second chapter of *Moby Dick* is entitled "The Carpet-Bag."
> Eva Peron sings "Don't Cry for Me Argentina" in the musical, *Evita*.
> Our anthology includes "Threes," a poem from Sandburg's *Smoke and Steel*.
> The first article I read for my research paper was William Calvin's "The Great Climate Flip-flop" in the *Atlantic Monthly*.

Titles of books, magazines, long poems, newspapers, motion pictures, and radio and television series are not set in double quotation marks. In printed material, these items are set in italic type (*type like this*). Other special uses of italics are for foreign words and phrases and for names of ships, planes, and spacecraft. In handwritten or typewritten papers, underlining (<u>typescript like this</u>) is the equivalent of italics in printed material. Word-processors can produce effects such as bold (**bold**) and italic, which gives students a capability previously not available except through typesetting.

Double quotation marks are also used to set off slang words used in serious writing. Sometimes double quotation marks are used to set off words when they are referred to as words:

> The witness had only recently been released from the "slammer."
> Words like "seize" and "siege" are often misspelled.

Usage is divided on these uses of quotation marks. The two words in the second example would almost certainly appear in italics in printed material. Student writers of handwritten or typed material should either underline such words or set them off by quotation marks, the first method being the more common practice.

Double Quotation Marks with Other Punctuation

Follow this usage in the placing of quotation marks in relation to other marks:

1. Commas and periods always go inside quotation marks.
2. Semicolons and colons always go outside quotation marks.
3. Question marks and exclamation points go inside if they belong to the quoted part, outside if they do not.

> "Come in," said my uncle, "and take off your coats." [Comma and period]
>
> Mr. Lowe said, "I heartily endorse this candidate"; unfortunately most of the audience thought he said *hardly* instead of *heartily*. [Semicolon outside]
>
> "Heavens!" he exclaimed. "Is this the best you can do?" [Exclamation point and question mark]
>
> Mother asked, "Where were you last night?" [No double punctuation]
>
> Did she say, "I came home early"?
> [Question mark belongs to the whole sentence, not to the quoted part]
>
> Did Mother ask, "Where were you last night?"
> [Note that there is only one question mark after a double question like this]

Single Quotation Marks

Use single quotation marks to enclose a speech within a speech:

> "I wonder what he meant," said Betty, "when he said, 'There are wheels within wheels.' "

You may not write many sentences like this one, but just the same, you should note that when you have quotes within quotes, the period comes inside both the single and double quotation marks.

NAME _____   SCORE _____

Directions: In the spaces at the left, write C if the punctuation is correct and W if it is wrong. Within the incorrect sentences, correct the faulty punctuation by adding, removing, or changing marks.

_____ 1. It's amazing, isn't it, that another persons' name and major are exactly the same as your's?

_____ 2. You've balanced all the shareholder's accounts, haven't you?

_____ 3. "Where's the list of new subscribers?" asked the manager. "I can't find it in anybody's folder."

_____ 4. Joan Cross' final words to her staff were a trifle unusual: "Folks, Im begging you to work harder. Theyre going to fire me if you don't."

_____ 5. On her twenty-first birthday Gina's parents gave her twenty-one hundred-dollar bills to help her buy a new car.

_____ 6. "This morning I'd like to begin with a report—but we covered that yesterday, didn't we?" said the lecturer.

_____ 7. Our local television stations' evening news always contains certain items: a list of robberies, reports of auto accidents, and any other strange stories that draw immediate attention.

_____ 8. "There's my dog running through Mr. Thomas' yard," shouted Rhoda. Your's must still be in the house."

_____ 9. The last finisher's are struggling past the finish line in threes and fours; they all ask immediately for their running time, their T-shirt prize, and a glass of water.

_____ 10. I think it is Kellys First Law that says: Whatever can go wrong will go wrong, usually when you least expect it.

_____ 11. "Everyone whos' going should line up now," said Myrtle. "The bus's *buses* are leaving at ten o'clock sharp from in front of the school's cafeteria."

_____ 12. Even earning all A's won't get you into their School of Marine Science; you've got to be recommended by a faculty member also.

_____ 13. One of the kids showed me her prizes from the show: one of Elvis' shoestrings, sheet music from a top band's recording session, and a lock of hair snipped from a popular singer's bangs.

_____ 14. "Amos' AnchorClankers" was our boat crew's nickname; we didn't win any prizes, but we did take a lot of eighth and ninth place's.

_____ 15. One of the founders' sons is now the president; some think—but other's disagree—that he really earned the job through hard work.

Directions: Sentences 1–5 are indirect quotations. In the space provided, rewrite each sentence as a direct quotation. Sentences 6–10 are direct quotations. Rewrite each as an indirect quotation. You will have to alter some verb forms and some pronoun forms as well as the punctuation.

1. The mayor said that she has ordered a new car phone.

   _____
   _____

2. General Steiner answered that he did not intend to dispatch any more messages during the maneuvers.

   _____
   _____

3. Ramona Rice replied that she had never met the stranger before.

   _____
   _____

4. Mrs. Overholt asked why the bridge club had skipped its regular meeting.

   _____
   _____

5. Did you tell me that the new map shows a detour between here and Baltimore?

   _____
   _____

6. The announcement clearly stated, "Only members of the graduate's immediate family will be admitted to the auditorium."

   _____
   _____

7. The moderator of the debate said, "The reporter from the Washington Post will ask the first question."

   _____
   _____

8. The first graders said in chorus, "Every time we plan to go on a picnic, it rains and we can't go."

   _____
   _____

9. Why didn't I see the little sign that said, "Instructions for assembly are taped to the bottom of the carton"?

   _____
   _____

10. Captain Manley came over to our group and asked, "Will anyone who knows how to operate a computer come over and help us?"

    _____
    _____

NAME _____ SCORE _____

Directions: In the spaces at the left, write C if the punctuation is correct or W if it is wrong. Within the incorrect sentences, correct the faulty punctuation by adding, removing, or changing marks.

_____ 1. My replacement—he signed a contract yesterday—has experience thats sure to be valuable in the coming months.

_____ 2. I have always admired George Washington's honest response to his father: Yes, I cut down your cherry tree.

_____ 3. Yesterday my roommate got a package filled with: cookies, popcorn, and several cans of macadamia nuts.

_____ 4. Is this your racket? Mines at home, and I need to use your's during PE class.

_____ 5. "How will we know who's supposed to bring the donuts for the study session tonight?" asked Al.

_____ 6. Last nights practice session was canceled: the drama teacher was out of town.

_____ 7. Thats a difficult job, but we can do it. All it takes is time—hours and hours of time.

_____ 8. Its not clear to me why our cars time in the quarter mile is so much slower than all the others times.

_____ 9. My grandmother had an interesting definition of "luck": hard work and preparation meeting an opportunity for achievement.

_____ 10. "I was amazed," said Ramona; "I had never seen thirty one hundred dollar bills before."

_____ 11. "I read Irwin Shaw's short story, 'The Eighty-Yard Run,' and I found it just a little depressing," said Shane.

_____ 12. "I always misspell the word 'independent,' " said Marcie; "I put an 'A' in the last syllable instead of an 'E.' "

_____ 13. My list for the canoe trip includes: duct tape, candles, and waterproof matches. What's on your's?

_____ 14. The Jones' left for town early this morning: they needed to drop Mrs. Jones' car off at the repair shop.

_____ 15. A lawyers work must be perfect, with all the t's crossed and all the i's dotted.

Directions: Sentences 1–5 are indirect quotations. In the space provided, rewrite each sentence as a direct quotation. Sentences 6–10 are direct quotations. Rewrite each as an indirect quotation. You will have to alter some verb forms and some pronoun forms as well as the punctuation.

1. Tom said that he had just opened his book and started to read when the fire alarm rang.

2. The teacher said that she would cover the answers to those questions in the next class.

3. The boss reminded Harry that he had agreed to work on Saturday night for the next four weeks.

4. Fifteen minutes after we began to work, June asked when we would stop for lunch.

5. Art told Shelly that he wanted to read her paper after she had finished typing it.

6. The technician said, "I think I will check the fuses before I do anything else."

7. When the bell rang, Rick told Tom, "We should get lunch before we go to our next class."

8. Wilma said, "I won't be home until after eight o'clock tonight."

9. The students asked, "Can we have another day to study for the test?"

10. As soon as the plane took off, the two small children sitting next to me asked, "Will you read us a story?"

Lesson 20 — *End Marks; Summary of Punctuation Rules*

This lesson discusses end marks and summarizes all the punctuation rules presented in this book.

Period

The **period** is used after a complete declarative sentence and after ordinary abbreviations. Its use as end punctuation after sentences needs no examples. Its use after abbreviations is a little more complicated.

Personal Titles

A period is used in the following abbreviations: *Mr., Mrs., Ms., Messrs., Mmes.,* and *Dr.* These abbreviations appear before the name. Periods are also used for *Jr., Sr., Esq., D.D., Ph.D.,* and so forth, which are used after names. Miss does not require a period. *Ms.,* used instead of *Miss* or *Mrs.* when marital status is not indicated, is usually considered an abbreviation and uses a period, although some modern dictionaries have entries for it either with or without a period.

Latin-Based Terms

The following initials and abbreviations, used only in documentation pages and tabulations but not in ordinary writing, require periods: *e.g. (for example), etc. (and so forth), i.e. (that is), p., pp. (page, pages),* and *vol. (volume).* A.D., B.C., A.M., and P.M. (usually set in small caps in printed material) are used only with figures and where necessary for clearness. Note: A.D. should precede the year (A.D. 37); B.C., however, should follow the year (31 B.C.).

Addresses

The following abbreviations require periods and are acceptable in addresses but should be spelled out in ordinary writing: *St. (Street), Ave. (Avenue), Blvd. (Boulevard), Dr. (Drive), Rd. (Road), Co. (Company),* and *Inc. (Incorporated).* Conventionally, periods have been used with abbreviations of the states *(Mass., Minn., Tex., W. Va.).* However, the two-letter capitalized symbols authorized by the U.S. Postal Service *(MA, MN, TX, WV)* do not require periods.

Poor: Last Mon. P.M. I visited my two older bros., who live in N.Y. Chas. works for a mfg. co. there. Thos. attends NYU, preparing himself for a gov't. job. He's coming home for Xmas.

Right: Last Monday afternoon I visited my two older brothers, who live in New York. Charles works for a manufacturing company there. Thomas attends New York University, preparing himself for a government job. He's coming home for Christmas.

193

Acronyms and Measurements

In modern usage, the "alphabet" name forms, or acronyms, of various governmental or intergovernmental agencies, social or professional organizations, and units of measurement used in scientific contexts are usually not followed by periods: *ACLU, CARE, CBS, CIA, NAACP, NCAA, NATO, PTA, SEC, UNESCO, Btu* (British thermal unit), *mpg, mph, rpm.* New acronyms and abbreviated forms spring into existence nowadays with regularity. The following examples contain some that have gained common acceptance fairly recently: *AIDS* (acquired immune deficiency syndrome), *CAT scan* (computerized axial tomography), *CATV* (community antenna television), *CD* (certificate of deposit), *CEO* (chief executive officer), *COLA* (cost-of-living adjustment), *CPR* (cardiopulmonary resuscitation), *DWI* (driving while intoxicated), *IRA* (individual retirement account), *MIA* (missing in action), *MRI* (magnetic resonance imaging), *OPEC* (Organization of Petroleum Exporting Countries), *PC* (personal computer), *STOL* (short takeoff and landing), *VCR* (videocassette recorder). Refer to your dictionary when in doubt about the meaning of an abbreviated form or the possibility of using periods. Be prepared to find apparent inconsistencies and divided usage.

Question Mark

The **question mark** is used after a *direct question,* which is an utterance that calls for an answer. (See Lesson 6.) A question mark is not used after an *indirect question,* which is a statement giving the substance of a question but not the words that would be used in a direct question.

Direct: Who goes there? Is that you? When do we eat? How much do I owe you? "Who goes there?" he demanded. [In dialogue]
Indirect: She asked me how old I was. I wondered why she would ask such a question. [Note that these are statements, not direct questions.]

Refer to page 187 to review the use of question marks with quotation marks.

Exclamation Point

The **exclamation point** is used sparingly in modern writing and should be reserved for statements of strong feeling. Mild exclamations, such as *oh, goodness, well, yes,* and *no,* are followed by commas, not exclamation points. Be sure to place the exclamation mark after the exclamation itself.

"Help! I'm slipping!" he shouted. [Note the period after *shouted.*]
"Stop that!" she screamed. [Do not put the exclamation point after *screamed.*]
"Well, it was exciting, wasn't it?" "Oh, I had a pleasant time."

SUMMARY OF PUNCTUATION RULES

This summary provides the indispensable punctuation rules for anything you write. Colons, commas, periods, and even question marks and exclamation points do have other uses for special occasions or effects, but these occasional applications rarely cause problems for most writers.

Commas to Separate: Five Rules

1. Compound sentences
2. Items in a series
3. Coordinate adjectives
4. Introductory modifiers
5. Words that may be misread together

Colon: Two Rules

1. Use a colon to announce a list, an explanation, or a long quotation.
   a. If the text following a colon is a complete sentence, use an initial capital letter.
   b. Do not use a colon to separate a verb from its complement or a preposition from its object.
2. Use a colon to separate hours, minutes, and seconds; Biblical chapters and verses; titles and subtitles.

Apostrophe: Two Rules

1. With possessives
2. With contractions

Period: Two Rules

1. After declarative sentences
2. After most abbreviations

Commas to Enclose: Eight Rules

1. Nonrestrictive clauses and phrases
2. Appositives
3. Absolute phrases
4. Parenthetical expressions
5. Words in direct address
6. The speaker in dialogue
7. Negative insertions
8. Dates, addresses, degrees, and titles

Semicolon: Two Rules

1. In compound sentences without a conjunction joining the independent clauses
2. To separate items in a series when commas occur within items

Quotation Marks: Three Rules

1. Enclose direct quotations
2. Set off titles
3. Set off words used in some special way

Question Mark: One Rule

1. After direct questions

NAME _____   SCORE _____

Directions: In the space at the left, write C if the punctuation in the sentence is correct and W if it is wrong. Within the incorrect sentences, correct the faulty punctuation by adding, removing, or changing marks.

_____   1. Jim's address at his new job is 1 W. Warrington Dr., Hallmark, PA 10070.

_____   2. Last semester Ms Johanssen worked as an intern for HEW in Washington, DC

_____   3. A PAC is a political action committee, but the PAC-10 is a football conference.

_____   4. Juanita Peterson is a systems analyst for N.A.S.A; she is working on a new LEM for future moon shots.

_____   5. The sign in the western saloon read, "Check all knives, guns, brass knuckles, etc at the door."

_____   6. Leonardo da Vinci drew out the first concept for a helicopter in c. A.D. 1490, about 450 years before Igor Sikorsky built the first one for military use in the USA.

_____   7. "Look at the ticker tape," she screamed! "The market is taking off."

_____   8. Do you think the JD degree or the M. B. A. degree will be more valuable in the future?

_____   9. Just before they leave for the day, Mrs. Allmand, Ms. Roland, and Mr Scarborough download their data to Cleveland for processing.

_____   10. I found that article in Volume 39, No. 3., p. 101,.

_____   11. "How do we get to Smith Creek W. Va.," asked Martin?

_____   12. "Holy cow!" shouted the Cubs announcer. "It's a triple play!"

_____   13. Ms Morton asked when the new supplies would arrive?

_____   14. "HO! HO! HO!" shouted Melinda, strapping a pillow to her waist. "I'm going to work as a department store Santa."

_____   15. Will they be here, do you think, by 11:00 P.M. tonight?

Directions: In the following sentences correct every error in punctuation. Then, in the column at the left, circle every number that represents an error in that sentence:

1. Comma omitted
2. Apostrophe omitted or misused

3. Comma misused for semicolon
4. Semicolon misused for comma

1 2 3 4   (1) For people looking for an exciting canoe trip; we have a ten-day trek departing next week from Olden, Maine covering 750 miles of lakes and whitewater rivers.

1 2 3 4   (2) Towering high over the western section of the city is a beautiful glass-walled skyscraper it's walls reflecting the mountains far across the valley.

1 2 3 4   (3) Lostman's River the location for that movie, can't be navigated at this time of year because the water is too low.

1 2 3 4   (4) Smiling grimly the coach looked at the team and said, "I don't believe in all my years of coaching that I've seen a weaker performance than your's in the first half of this game."

1 2 3 4   (5) Since you are in a hurry to get back to that store where you left your watch; take my car and go ahead of the rest of us.

1 2 3 4   (6) That's a great idea, let's try to finish by nine oclock and then we can go for a late supper at Charleys Diner.

1 2 3 4   (7) "My car is not nearly as new and fancy as their's," laughed Ron "but it starts every time and runs very dependably."

1 2 3 4   (8) The Foster's, our new neighbors moved here from Southern California; a place where they never saw snow and never owned winter clothes.

1 2 3 4   (9) Jim decided to leave for home a little early, the road down the mountain, he reminded us is very dangerous in the fog.

1 2 3 4   (10) For those of you who want to know our present financial situation; we have $450.12 in the clubs checking account and we have $12 in savings.

NAME _____ SCORE _____

Directions: The following sentences contain forty numbered spots, some with punctuation and some with no punctuation. In the correspondingly numbered spaces at the left, write **C** if the punctuation is correct or **W** if it is wrong.

1. _____ (1) The most useful tools for college students are: a computer, a good
                                                             1

2. _____   dictionary and the ability to stay awake.
                         2

3. _____ (2) Maria, who recently graduated from nursing school, said, "I worked
                                                            3   4

4. _____   at two jobs when I was in school."

5. _____ (3) "Can you tell me the name of the architect who designed the Empire
                                                            5

6. _____   State Building?" asked Miss. Marcus.
                                       6

7. _____ (4) I have read several good mysteries lately, there are several highly
                                                    7

8. _____   skilled new writers on the market.
                         8

9. _____ (5) The map says the town is five miles away, if we don't reach it in a
                                                    9

10. _____   few minutes, we must be lost.
                         10

11. _____ (6) Whenever my little brother goes away to camp, he complains about
                                                                 11

12. _____   the horrible tasteless food served in the cafeteria.
                         12

13. _____ (7) I went to the book store yesterday, I tried to find a backpack exactly
                                                    13

14. _____   like your's.
                    14

15. _____ (8) "When will you be ready to leave?" asked Robert, who was standing
                                                    15   16

16. _____   impatiently in the doorway.

17. _____ (9) Her books, her stereo, two pairs of new jeans—all were in her car
                              17   18

18. _____   when it was stolen.

19. _____ (10) The smiling mischievous little boys pushed the two pretty girls into
                    19

20. _____   the sloppy mud puddle.
                    20

21. _____ (11) "Have you ever read 'The Pit and the Pendulum'," asked Donna, who
                                                                        21

22. _____   is a fan of Edgar Allen Poe?
                    22

23. _____ (12) We finished eating the cats got the scraps, and we cleared the table and
                    23   24

24. _____   washed the dishes.

25. _____ (13) The room was painted a deep blue; the only light came from a large
                    25

26. _____   window, that overlooked a parking lot.
                    26

27. _____ (14) The young law students all want one thing; to get a job with a big
                    27   28

28. _____   firm in a large city.

29. _____ (15) "After all my friends," said the president, "we've just begun to evaluate
                    29   30

30. _____   the impact of those changes on operating costs."

31. _____ (16) Al doesnt think he will leave tomorrow, his car needs some work before
                    31   32

32. _____   he can go.

33. _____ (17) A stack of twenty dollar bills sat in front of the teller and he handed ten
                    33   34

34. _____   to a customer needing two hundred dollars.

35. _____ (18) Tony asked Cary why she had not returned the librarys copy of the new
                                                                          35

36. _____   sports magazine?
                    36

37. _____ (19) The staff needs some special equipment for the new project; a
                                                                          37

38. _____   microscope, two new computers and a scanner.
                    38

39. _____ (20) If properly maintained tents can be used for many camping
                    39

40. _____   seasons, without any problems.
                    40

NAME _____ SCORE _____

Directions: The following sentences contain forty numbered spots, some with punctuation and some with no punctuation. In the correspondingly numbered spaces at the left, write **C** if the punctuation is correct or **W** if it is wrong.

1. _____   (1) "I think its time for lunch," said Yolanda, "but Barb hasn't come—ah,
                       ¹   ²

2. _____   there she is now."

3. _____   (2) The nursery sold us three small oak trees, a red maple tree, and several
                                                                ³

4. _____   small shrubs planted in fancy pots.
                                       ⁴

5. _____   (3) As we started to walk down the trail along came three laughing kids on
                                                         ⁵

6. _____   fancy mountain bikes.
                               ⁶

7. _____   (4) Ms. Jacksons novel is extremely exciting and seems destined to make
                          ⁷   ⁸

8. _____   the best-seller list very soon.

9. _____   (5) Marcia Wilson, our most experienced player came in to pinch-hit in
                                                               ⁹

10. _____   the ninth inning; unfortunately, she struck out.
                                 ¹⁰

11. _____   (6) Since Saturday was a cold damp day; we could not paint the trim on
                                              ¹¹   ¹²

12. _____   the outside of the house.

13. _____   (7) Janice Thompson, our sales manager, joined the company on May 17,
                                                        ¹³

14. _____   1992, sales have increased dramatically since then.
                    ¹⁴

15. _____   (8) The book I just finished has all the important qualities; suspense, a
                                                                             ¹⁵

16. _____   little comedy, and a fast-paced tricky climax.
                             ¹⁶

17. _____   (9) The shoes I found in my locker in the gym are not mine; I wonder
                                                                          ¹⁷

18. _____   who's they are?
                    ¹⁷   ¹⁸

19. _____ (10) "My life," said Harold, "has only three parts to it: going to class,
   ₁₉

20. _____ studying, and going to work.
   ₂₀

21. _____ (11) After Alma gave her speech about student government; the usually
   ₂₁

22. _____ sullen drowsy class gave her a round of applause.
   ₂₂

23. _____ (12) The two children, while rummaging in the basement, discovered an old
   ₂₃

24. _____ sword, a pair of boots and a couple of medals.
   ₂₄

25. _____ (13) "Anyone who is interested in a tour of the local planetarium should
   ₂₅

26. _____ pick up a ticket from my office," said Professor Hall.
   ₂₆

27. _____ (14) The parts are all stored in this box, to begin the assembly, check the
   ₂₇   ₂₈

28. _____ parts list to be sure they're all there.

29. _____ (15) Uncle Will's tractor, which is his pride and joy, seems to be
   ₂₉

30. _____ perfectly-maintained.
   ₃₀

31. _____ (16) Almost as soon as I stopped the policeman signaled me to get out of
   ₃₁

32. _____ the car and walk toward him.
   ₃₂

33. _____ (17) Janice left on vacation yesterday, taking with her: two novels, a
   ₃₃   ₃₄

34. _____ supply of sunscreen, and a big umbrella.

35. _____ (18) We decided not to go fishing this morning, the water being disturbed
   ₃₅

36. _____ and cloudy because of the storm.
   ₃₆

37. _____ (19) A beautiful horse, a palomino, I believe, ran across the pasture with
   ₃₇

38. _____ its golden mane shimmering in the sunlight.
   ₃₈

39. _____ (20) In the opinion of some researchers tend to concentrate too much on
   ₃₉

40. _____ basic research and not enough on practical matters.
   ₄₀

5 Usage

Lessons, Practice Sheets, and Exercises

In Lesson 2 you learned that some verbs are regular and others are irregular. Regular verbs add an *ed* ending in the past tense (earn, earned), but irregular verbs change their form (grow, grew). Since verb forms change to indicate changes in tense and voice, it is necessary to pay close attention to the forms of all verbs. We shall now review certain places where incorrect forms sometimes appear because of confusion in the use of the principal parts (the base, past tense, and past participle) of verbs. (See Supplement.)

Verb Forms

To gain assurance in your use of verbs, you must remember how the past tense and the past participle are used. The **past tense** is always a single-word verb; it is never used with an auxiliary:

> I *ate* my lunch. [Not: I *have ate* my lunch.]

The **past participle**, when it is used as a verb, is *never* a single word; it is used with the auxiliary *have* (in the correct tense) to form the perfect tenses or the auxiliary *be* (in the correct tense) to form the passive voice:

> I *have done* the work. [Not: I *done* the work.]
> The work *was done.* [Not: I the work *was did.*]

(The past participle is, of course, used as a single word when it is a modifier of a noun: the *broken* toy, the *worried* parents, some *known* criminals.)

There are four groups of verbs that often cause confusion. Each group contains verbs that have similar trouble spots. The basic solution for the problem in each group is to master the principal parts of the verbs. The principal parts are listed in this lesson in the customary order: base form, past tense, and past participle (P.P.).

Past Tense versus Past Participle

Sometimes errors occur because the past tense of a verb is confused with the past participle of the verb.

	Verb	Past tense	P.P.
Later they *became* [not *become*] more friendly.	become	became	become
They *began* [not *begun*] to laugh at us.	begin	began	begun
He had never *broken* [not *broke*] the law.	break	broke	broken
I should have *chosen* [not *chose*] a larger car.	choose	chose	chosen
Yesterday the child *came* [not *come*] home.	come	came	come
I *did* [not *done*] what she told me to do.	do	did	done
He *drank* [not *drunk*] some water.	drink	drank	drunk
I had *driven* [not *drove*] all day.	drive	drove	driven
The lamp had *fallen* [not *fell*] over.	fall	fell	fallen
The bird has *flown* [not *flew*] away.	fly	flew	flown
Small puddles have *frozen* [not *froze*] on the sidewalks.	freeze	froze	frozen
Dad has *given* [not *gave*] me a car.	give	gave	given
Theresa has *gone* [not *went*] to school.	go	went	gone
I've never *ridden* [not *rode*] a horse.	ride	rode	ridden
We ran out when the fire alarm *rang* [not *rung*].	ring	rang	rung
Lenny has *run* [not *ran*] in two marathons.	run	ran	run
I *saw* [not *seen*] your nephew yesterday.	see	saw	seen
It must have *sunk* [not *sank*] in deep water.	sink	sank	sunk
She should have *spoken* [not *spoke*] louder.	speak	spoke	spoken
The car had been *stolen* [not *stole*].	steal	stole	stolen
The witness was *sworn* [not *swore*] in.	swear	swore	sworn
John has *swum* [not *swam*] across the lake.	swim	swam	swum
Someone had *torn* [not *tore*] the dollar bill.	tear	tore	torn
You should have *worn* [not *wore*] a hat.	wear	wore	worn
I have already *written* [not *wrote*] my essay.	write	wrote	written

Regular versus Irregular

Sometimes errors occur because an irregular verb is thought to be regular.

	Verb	Past tense	P.P.
The wind *blew* [not *blowed*] steadily all day.	blow	blew	blown
John *brought* [not *bringed*] Mary some flowers.	bring	brought	brought
This house was *built* [not *builded*] in 1795.	build	built	built
Barbara *caught* [not *catched*] two trout.	catch	caught	caught
Slowly they *crept* [not *creeped*] up the stairs.	creep	crept	crept
He *dealt* [not *dealed*] me a good hand.	deal	dealt	dealt
The men quickly *dug* [not *digged*] a pit.	dig	dug	dug
She *drew* [not *drawed*] a caricature of me.	draw	drew	drawn
All the men *grew* [not *growed*] long beards.	grow	grew	grown
Ben *hung* [not *hanged*] his cap on the hook.	hang	hung	hung
I *knew* [not *knowed*] him at college.	know	knew	known
I have never *lent* [not *lended*] him money.	lend	lent	lent
We *sought* [not *seeked*] shelter from the rain.	seek	sought	sought
The sun *shone* [not *shined*] all day yesterday.	shine	shone	shone
The prince *slew* [not *slayed*] the fierce dragon.	slay	slew	slain
I soon *spent* [not *spended*] the money.	spend	spent	spent
Ms. Andrews *taught* [not *teached*] us algebra.	teach	taught	taught

	throw	threw	thrown
	weep	wept	wept

Lou *threw* [not *throwed*] the receipt away.
The old man *wept* [not *weeped*] piteously.

Obsolete or Dialectal Forms

A third type of error results from the use of an obsolete or dialectal form of the verb, a form not considered standard now:

	Verb	Past Tense	P.P.
I *am* [not *be*] working regularly.	be*	was, were	been
I *have been* [not *been*] working regularly.			
The child *burst* [not *busted*] out crying.	burst	burst	burst
I've *bought* [not *boughten*] a car.	buy	bought	bought
I *climbed* [not *clumb*] a tree for a better view.	climb	climbed	climbed
The women *clung* [not *clang*] to the raft.	cling	clung	clung
The dog *dragged* [not *drug*] the old shoe home.	drag	dragged	dragged
The boy was nearly *drowned* [not *drownded*].	drown	drowned	drowned
At the picnic I *ate* [not *et*] too many hot dogs.	eat	ate	eaten
Betty *flung* [not *flang*] the stick away.	fling	flung	flung
You *paid* [not *payed*] too much for it.	pay	paid	paid
It had been *shaken* [not *shooken*] to pieces.	shake	shook	shaken
He had never *skinned* [not *skun*] an animal.	skin	skinned	skinned
A bee *stung* [not *stang*] me as I stood there.	sting	stung	stung
The girl *swung* [not *swang*] at the ball.	swing	swung	swung
I wonder who could have *taken* [not *tooken*] it.	take	took	taken

Confusing Verb Forms

A fourth type of verb error results from a confusion of forms of certain verbs that look or sound almost alike but are actually quite different in meaning, such as *lie, lay; sit, set;* and *rise, raise.* Note that three of these troublesome verbs—*lay, set,* and *raise*—in their ordinary uses take an object. The other three—*lie, sit, rise*—do not take an object.

	Verb	Past Tense	P.P.
Please *lay* your books [D.O.] on the table.	lay	laid	laid
Mary *laid* several logs [D.O.] on the fire.			
The men have *laid* some boards [D.O.] over the puddle.			
Our cat often *lies* [not *lays*] on the couch.	lie	lay	lain
Yesterday our cat *lay* [not *laid*] on the couch.			
Our cat has *lain* [not *laid*] on the couch all morning.			
She *sets* the plate [D.O.] in front of me.	set	set	set
An hour ago Tom *set* out some food [D.O.] for the birds.			
I had *set* the camera [D.O.] at a full second.			

*As you learned in Lesson 2, the irregular verb *be* has three forms (*am, are, is*) in the present tense, and two forms (*was, were*) in the past tense.

I usually *sit* in that chair. Yesterday he *sat* in my chair. I have *sat* at my desk all morning.	sit	sat	sat
At her command they *raise* the flag [D.O.]. The boy quickly *raised* his hand [D.O.]. He had *raised* the price [D.O.] of his old car.	raise	raised	raised
He *rises* when we enter the room. Everyone *rose* as the speaker entered the room. The water has *risen* a foot since midnight.	rise	rose	risen

Exceptions

The rules and illustrations given here will serve as a guide in most situations. They show the importance of knowing the principal parts of these verbs. Note, however, that there are a few exceptions, such as the intransitive uses of *set:*

A *setting* [not *sitting*] hen *sets*. [of course, a hen, like a rooster, may be said to *sit* when that is what is meant.]

The sun *sets* in the west.

Cement or dye *sets*.

A jacket *sets (fits)* well.

With a few verbs, special meanings demand different principal parts. For example, the past tense and the past participle of *shine,* when the verb is used as a transitive verb, are *shined:*

This morning I *shined* [not *shone*] my shoes.

The verb *hang* with the meaning "to execute by suspending by the neck until dead" uses *hanged,* not *hung,* for the past tense and the past participle. When in doubt, always refer to your dictionary.

Sequence of Tenses

In Lesson 2 you studied a partial conjugation showing the forms of three sample verbs as they occur in six tenses. In Lesson 5 you were told the basic uses of the six tenses. Although most student writers usually have little difficulty in establishing and maintaining logical time relationships in their sentences, there are a few situations that sometimes cause confusion.

Subordinate Clauses

The tense in a subordinate clause is normally the same as that in the main clause unless a different time for the subordinate statement is clearly indicated.

We think that Mary studies hard all the time.
We think that Mary studied hard for the last test.
We think that Mary will study hard for the next test.
We think that Mary has studied hard for all her tests.
We think that Mary had studied hard before last week's test.

We thought that Mary studied hard all the time.
We thought that Mary studied hard in the past.
We thought that Mary would study hard for the next test.
We thought that Mary has studied hard all year.
We thought that Mary had studied hard last semester.

Universally True Statements

The present tense is used for a statement that is universally true.

The dietitian reminded us that whipped cream *is* (not *was*) fattening.
I wonder who first discovered that oysters *are* (not *were*) edible.

Shifting Tenses

In narrative writing a shift from past tense to present tense, a device sometimes used effectively by skilled writers, should be used cautiously.

The library *was* silent except for an occasional whisper, when suddenly a side door *opened* [not *opens*] and a disheveled young man *dashed* [not *dashes*] in and *started* [not *starts*] yelling "Man the lifeboats!" After the librarians *had managed* to restore order . . .

Present Perfect Tense

The perfect form of an infinitive should not be used when the controlling verb is in the present perfect tense.

Correct: I would have liked to see that performance.
Incorrect: I would have liked to have seen that performance.

In the indicative mood, there is rarely any confusion over the correct form of the infinitive.

Correct: I have wanted to run that marathon for years.

Supplement

When a sentence makes a statement or asks a question, the verb is said to be in the **indicative mood** or **mode** (see Lesson 2). Two other moods indicate a different purpose in the sentence.

Imperative Mood
When the sentence gives a direction or command, the verb is in the **imperative mood.** The imperative of all regular verbs simply uses the base form of the verb without a subject.

Please *give* me the ball.
Take out your pen and paper.

Even the verb *to be,* irregular in most formations, uses the base to form the imperative.

Be careful; the steps are slippery.
Please *be* on time; the bus will depart promptly.

Subjunctive Mood

The present subjunctive uses the base form of the verb, regardless of the subject.

The catalogue recommends that she *study* accounting in the first semester.

The past subjunctive takes the same form as the past tense of the verb. (The auxiliary *be* is always *were* regardless of the number or person of the subject.)

I wish I *were* at home today.

The past perfect subjunctive has the same form as the past perfect.

I wish I *had gone* home earlier.

We also use the subjunctive in these special ways:

1. In clauses beginning with *that* when they follow words such as *ask, suggest, require, recommend,* and *demand.*

   The policy requires that we *submit* our requests in writing.
   The manager insisted that we *be* present for the ceremony.

2. In clauses beginning with *if* when the clause makes a statement that is clearly and unmistakably contrary to fact.

   If I *were* able to sing, I would try out for the Met.
   If he were young again, he would live life differently.

NAME _____ SCORE _____

Directions: In the space at the left, write the correct form of the verb shown in parentheses. Do not use *ing* forms.

___begun___
___paid___
1. Janice has (begin) to regret having (pay) in advance for the full-year membership at the gym.

_____
_____
2. You (do) a good deed when you (give) your computer to the retirement home.

___written___
___taken___
3. So far this term we have (write) four papers and (take) two tests.

_____
_____
4. The accountant took the witness stand and (swear) that he had not (break) the law.

___swum___
___lay___
5. After she had (swim) fifty laps, Betsy (lie) on the pool deck and rested for thirty minutes.

_____
_____
6. I have (ride) this bike for a whole month now and never (fall) once.

___frozen___
___drank___
7. Safely aboard the ship again, the half-(freeze) sailor eagerly (drink) a hot cup of coffee.

_____
_____
8. "I've (grow) tired of this coat," said Jenny; "after all, I have (wear) it for three years now.

___seen___
___became___
9. After he had (see) only half the movie, Lee (become) quite restless and left the theater.

_____
_____
10. The crowd applauded wildly when a student (climb) the fence and (tear) down the sign.

___spent___
___eaten___
11. I've (spend) years searching for a perfect piece of apple pie, but I've never (eat) a better one than this.

_____
_____
12. You could have (go) with us in our car if you had (speak) to me earlier.

___chosen___
___driven___
13. "You've (choose) wisely," said the salesman. "This car has been (drive) only a few thousand miles."

_____
_____
14. I (fling) open the door, and there I saw two men I had never (see) before in my life.

_____
_____
15. "I've (run) in several marathons, but I've never (come) close to winning," said Jack.

_____
_____
16. As Martha (stand) at the bus stop, a man (creep) up behind her and stole her purse.

_____
_____
17. Jean (set) her book aside and said, "This silly story should never have been (tell).

_____
_____
18. Ted has probably already (spend) the money you (lend) him yesterday.

_____
_____
19. This morning the cat (lie) in the sun for two hours and never even (raise) her head when the dog walked by.

_____
_____
20. The child (swing) high into the tree and (cling) precariously to a small branch.

Directions: Each sentence has two italicized verb units. If the verb form is correct, write C in the space at the left. If it is incorrect, write the correct form in the space.

—————————— 1. The sun hasn't *shined* for two weeks, but shortly after noon today
—————————— it *burst* through the clouds.

—————————— 2. Sharon admitted that she had *taken* the dress back to the store
—————————— after she had *wore* it to a party.

—————————— 3. Early this morning my grouchy neighbor *come* over and *flung* the
—————————— newspaper down on my desk.

—————————— 4. Marilyn was upset when she *tore* the dress because she had *wore*
—————————— it only three times.

—————————— 5. "Come in, my friend," said the host; *lay* your packages on the
—————————— table, *set* down, and take a rest.

—————————— 6. It would have been wiser to *have taken* the other road; this one is
—————————— all *tore* up.

—————————— 7. You should have *known* that on a holiday Stan would still be *lying*
—————————— in bed at noon.

—————————— 8. The lifeguard had often *spoke* to us about the dangers of *drownd-*
—————————— *ing* in the heavy surf.

—————————— 9. I'm sure you have *been told* many times that Pluto *was* the far-
—————————— thest planet from the sun.

—————————— 10. "Your overcoat is *lying* in the hallway, exactly where you *laid* it
—————————— yesterday," said Mother.

—————————— 11. By the time I got to school, the ten o'clock bell had *rang* and the
—————————— class had already *began*.

—————————— 12. "I *been* living on this street for three months and have not *saw*
—————————— the trash collectors once," said my neighbor.

—————————— 13. I have not *spoke* to Jim since last Friday when I *seen* him in class.

—————————— 14. The champion looks a little nervous. Her hands *shook* when she
—————————— *was sinking* that last putt.

—————————— 15. We had intended *to have left* Toledo before the sun *rose* this
—————————— morning.

_____ 16. Jackson rushed into the room and *yells,* "The wind just *blew*
_____ down that big tree in the pasture."

_____ 17. The book I was *given* to read was not one I would have *chose* for
_____ myself.

_____ 18. "After *setting* in that fishing boat all morning, I was nearly *froze,*"
_____ said Alice.

_____ 19. After June had *drunk* the hot tea, she *begun* to feel a little better.
_____

_____ 20. "The doctor ordered me to *lay* down and rest after I've *ate* my
_____ lunch," said Aunt Martha.

NAME _____   SCORE _____

Directions: In the space at the left, write the correct form of the verb shown in parentheses. Do not use *ing* forms.

_____   1. As the clock struck ten, the elderly lady (rise) from her chair and
_____   (blow) out the candle.

_____   2. "I have (know) Jerry for many years and have often (lend) him
_____   money," said Mrs. Jolley.

_____   3. Our annual sale has just (begin); you couldn't have (choose) a
_____   better time to buy a new suit.

_____   4. I (see) your son yesterday, and I commented on how tall he has
_____   (grow).

_____   5. Yesterday the sun (shine), and we (lie) on the deck all afternoon.
_____

_____   6. The shipwrecked sailors (spend) three days on the raft; fortu-
_____   nately none of them (drown).

_____   7. The price of the stock has (rise) sharply; now many people wish
_____   they had (buy) more.

_____   8. "I've never (fly) before," she said; "in the past I've always (take)
_____   the train."

_____   9. "No, thank you; I've already (eat) too many hot dogs and (drink)
_____   too much root beer," said Hal.

_____   10. After lunch a boy (come) into the nurse's office and said, "While
_____   I was on the playground, a bee (sting) me."

_____   11. Larry came into the kitchen, (lay) his books on the table, and said
_____   wearily, "I've (write) two exams today."

_____   12. After being (swear) in, the witness said, " I have never (see) that
_____   man before in my life."

_____ 13. Sandy had just (lie) down to rest when her son called out, "Mom,
_____ a truck just (drive) into our driveway."

_____ 14. The man (dive) into the water, (swim) to boat, and dragged him-
_____ self aboard it.

_____ 15. Soon the police (become) convinced that the truck had been
_____ (steal) in Albany last week.

_____ 16. Jane (sink) the long putt, and her opponent rushed over and
_____ (shake) her hand.

_____ 17. "I (tear) this shirt a month ago and haven't (wear) it since," said
_____ Mike.

_____ 18. "You (do) a brave thing when you (run) after that robber," said
_____ the detective.

_____ 19. Manny sighed deeply, (climb) onto the horse, and (cling) to its
_____ mane with both hands.

_____ 20. My little brother (burst) into the room, climbed on the bed, and
_____ asked, "Are you going to (lie) there all day?"

Directions: Each sentence has two italicized verb units. If the verb form is correct, write C in the corresponding space at the left. If the verb form is incorrect, write the correct form in the space.

_____   1. Jack said to his sister, "I've *wrote* two long reports since the last
_____   time I *saw* you."

_____   2. "All of us have *ate* breakfast, and the two of you are still *lying* in
_____   bed," said Granddad.

_____   3. Centuries ago a thief could be *hanged* if he had *stole* even one loaf
_____   of bread.

_____   4. Paul walked home from the store, sat down wearily, and *says,* "It's
_____   the hottest day of the year, and I've *wore* this tie for eight long
                          hours."

_____   5. Charles *done* a kind thing when he *brought* the hungry dog home
_____   for a meal.

_____   6. Uncle Ray has often *spoke* of the time he *threw* the javelin in
_____   the Olympic tryouts.

_____   7. "I could have *swore* that my keys were not *laying* on that table ear-
_____   lier this morning," said Mother.

_____   8. I *pay* for the shirt, but I must have *forgot* to pick it up off the
_____   counter.

_____   9. Were you *taught* in astronomy class that the diameter of Mars
_____   *was* 4,200 miles?

_____   10. Last year an airline *give* the museum a DC-3 that had *flown* over
_____   sixteen million miles.

_____   11. In last week's adventure race, the contestants *swimmed* one mile
_____   and *run* five miles.

_____   12. "I *been* living in this county for twenty years," said the farmer,
_____   "and the creek has never *froze* this early in the winter."

_____   13. You've always *known,* haven't you, that a rolling stone *gathered* no
_____   moss?

_____   14. Frank *hung* up his coat and then *begun* to take off his tie.

—————————— 15. The soldiers all *shoned* their shoes until the tips *shined* like stars.
——————————

—————————— 16. My family first *set* foot in this county 100 years ago, and we *been* living here ever since.
——————————

—————————— 17. The earliest we have ever *swum* in the river was the first of May, but this year warm weather *come* earlier.
——————————

—————————— 18. My father has *flown* so often recently that he wishes someone *had give* him a train ticket.
——————————

—————————— 19. When the seller *raised* the price of the car, I should have *rose* from my chair and canceled the deal.
——————————

—————————— 20. That book has *lain* on the table for three days, but no one can tell me who *laid* it there originally.
——————————

Lesson 22 *Using Verbs Correctly: Subject–Verb Agreement*

Examine the following conjugation. Note that in the present tense, the third-person singular *(he, she, it)* verb form differs from the third-person plural *(they)* verb form.

I earn	We earn
You earn	You earn
He, She, It *earns*	They *earn*

We refer to this change as a change in number. As noted in Lesson 2, **singular number** refers to only one thing; **plural number** refers to more than one thing. Notice how verbs and nouns differ in this respect: The *s* ending on nouns is a plural marker, but on verbs it designates the singular form.

The following examples show how the number of the subject (one or more than one) affects the form of the verb. (See Supplement.) The verbs *have, do,* and *be* are important because they have auxiliary uses as well as main-verb uses. *Be* is an exceptional verb; it changes form in the past tense as well as in the present tense.

Singular	*Plural*
She *walks* slowly.	They *walk* slowly.
Mother *seems* pleased.	My parents *seem* pleased.
Mary *has* a new dress.	All of the girls *have* new dresses.
He *has traveled* widely.	They *have traveled* widely.
She *does* her work easily.	They *do* their work easily.
Does he *have* enough time?	*Do* they *have* enough time?
He *is* a friend of mine.	They *are* friends of mine.
My brother *is coming* home.	My brothers *are coming* home.
His camera *was taken* from him.	Their cameras *were taken* from them.

Verb Agrees in Number

The relation of verb form to subject follows an important principle of usage: **The verb always agrees in number with its subject.** Although the principle is simple, some of the situations in which it applies are not. You will avoid some common writing errors if you keep in mind the following seven extensions of the principle. The first is probably the most important.

1. The number of the verb is not affected by material that comes between the verb and the subject.

    Immediate *settlement* of these problems *is* [not *are*] vital. [The subject is *settlement. Problems,* being here the object of the preposition *of,* cannot be a subject.]

    The *cost* of replacing the asbestos shingles with cedar shakes *was* [not *were*] considerable.

    Tact, as well as patience, *is* [not *are*] required.

    Mr. Sheldon, together with several other division heads, *has* [not *have*] left.

217

Each of the plans *has* [not *have*] its good points.
Is [not *Are*] *either* of the contestants ready?

Determine the *real* subject of the verb; watch out for intervening words that might mislead you. The number of the verb is not altered when other nouns are attached to the subject by means of prepositions such as *in addition to, together with, as well as, with, along with.* Remember that indefinite pronoun subjects like *either, neither, each, one, everyone, no one, somebody* take singular verbs. *None* may take either a singular or a plural verb, depending on whether the writer wishes to emphasize "not one" or "no members" of the group.

None of us *is* [or *are*] perfect.

2. A verb agrees with its subject even when the subject follows the verb.

On the wall *hangs* a *portrait* of his father. [*portrait hangs*]
On the wall *hang portraits* of his parents. [*portraits hang*]
He handed us a piece of paper on which *was scribbled* a *warning.* [*warning was scribbled*]
There *was* barely enough *time* remaining.
There *were* only ten *minutes* remaining.
There *seems* to be one *problem* remaining.
There *seem* to be a few *problems* remaining.
Here *is* a free *ticket* to the game.
Here *are* some free *tickets* to the game.

Be especially careful to find the real subject in sentences starting with *there* or *here.*

3. Compound subjects joined by *and* take a plural verb.

A little *boy* and his *dog were* playing in the yard.
On the platform *were* a *table* and four *chairs.*

But the verb should be singular if the subjects joined by *and* are thought of as a single thing, or if the subjects are considered separately, as when they are modified by *every* or *each:*

Plain *vinegar* and *oil is* all the dressing my salad needs. [One thing]
Every *man* and every *woman is* asked to help. [Considered separately]

4. Singular subjects joined by *or* or *nor* take singular verbs.

Either a *check* or a money *order is* required.
Neither the *manager* nor his *assistant has* arrived yet.
Was Mr. Phelps or his *son* put on the committee?

In some sentences of this pattern, especially in questions like the last example, a plural verb is sometimes used, both in casual conversation and in writing. In serious and formal writing, the singular verb is considered appropriate. If the subjects joined by *or* or *nor* differ in number, the verb agrees with the subject nearer to it:

Neither the *mother* nor the two *boys were* able to identify him.
Either the *players* or the *coach is* responsible for the defeat.

5. Plural nouns of amount, distance, and so on, when they are used as singular units of measurement, take singular verbs.

   A hundred *dollars was* once paid for a single tulip bulb.
   Thirty *miles seems* like a long walk to me.
   Seven *years* in prison *was* the penalty that he had to pay.

6. A collective noun is considered singular when the group is regarded as a unit; it is plural when the individuals of the group are referred to.

   The *audience is* very enthusiastic tonight.
   The *audience are* returning to their seats. [Notice pronoun *their.*]
   The *band is* playing a rousing march.
   Now the *band are* putting away their instruments. [Again note *their.*]
   Most of the book *is* blatant propaganda.
   Most of her novels *are* now out of print.
   The *rest* of the fortune *was* soon gone.
   The *rest* of his debts *were* left unpaid.
   The *number* of bank failures *is* increasing.
   A *number* of these bank failures *are* being investigated.

Words like *number, all, rest, part, some, more, most, half* are singular or plural, depending on the meaning intended. A word of this type is often accompanied by a modifier or referred to by a pronoun, either of which gives a clue to the number intended. When the word *number* is a subject, it is considered singular if it is preceded by *the* and plural if it is preceded by *a.*

7. When the subject is a relative pronoun, the antecedent of the pronoun determines the number (and person) of the verb. (See Lesson 23, page 225.)

   He told a joke *that was* pointless. [*joke was*]
   He told several jokes *that were* pointless. [*jokes were*]
   I paid the expenses of the trip, *which were* minimal. [*expenses were*]
   Jack is one of those boys *who enjoy* fierce competition. [*boys enjoy*]

The last example, sometimes called the "one of those . . . who" sentence, is particularly troublesome. Often a plural verb is used. If we recast the sentence to read "Of those boys who enjoy fierce competition, Jack is one," however, it becomes clear that the logical antecedent of *who* is the plural noun *boys.* However, usage is divided. And notice that a singular verb must be used when the pattern is altered slightly:

   Jack is the only *one* of my friends *who enjoys* fierce competition.

Because a relative pronoun subject nearly always has an antecedent that is third-person singular or third-person plural, we are accustomed to pronoun–verb combinations like these:

   A boy *who is* . . .
   Boys *who are* . . .

A woman *who knows* . . .
Women *who know* . . .

But in those occasional sentences in which a relative pronoun subject has an antecedent that is in the first or second person, meticulously correct usage calls for subject–verb combinations like the following:

I, *who am* in charge here, should pay the bill. [*I . . . am*]
They should ask me, *who know* all the answers. [*I . . . know*]

You, *who are* in charge here, should pay the bill. [*You . . . are*]
They should ask you, *who know* all the answers. [*you . . . know*]

Supplement

One particular error of subject–verb agreement warrants special attention. The third-person singular present tense form of the verb *do* is *does.* The plural form is *do.* The misuse of the negative contraction *don't* (instead of *doesn't*) with a third-person singular subject is quite often encountered in spoken English. Many people, justly or unjustly, look on the "it-don't" misuse as an important marker of grossly substandard English. Such forms as the following should be avoided in all spoken and written English:

Faulty: My father *don't* like broccoli.
Faulty: It really *don't* matter.
Faulty: Jack Johnson *don't* live here now.
Faulty: One of her teachers *don't* like her.
Faulty: This fudge tastes good, *don't* it?
Faulty: The fact that the bill is overdue *don't* bother him.

SUMMARY OF CORRECT VERB USE

1. The principal parts of a verb are the present, the past, and the past participle. Avoid confusing the principal parts of irregular verbs (*run, ran, run; eat, ate, eaten; fly, flew, flown*) with those of regular verbs (*study, studied, studied*). Be especially careful with the often confused principal parts of *lie* and *lay, sit* and *set.*
2. Singular verbs are used with singular subjects; plural verbs are used with plural subjects.
    a. Nouns intervening between the subject and the verb do not determine the number of the verb. (Resistance to the actions of these government agencies *is* [not *are*] growing.)
    b. Singular subjects joined by *and* normally take plural verbs. Singular subjects joined by *or* or *nor* normally take singular verbs.
    c. Some nouns and pronouns (collective nouns, and words like *number, all, half,* etc.) are singular in some meanings, plural in others.

NAME _____ SCORE _____

Directions: These sentences are examples of structures that often lead to errors in subject–verb agreement. In the space at the left, copy the correct verb in the parentheses. In each sentence the subject of the verb is printed in bold type.

_____Were_____ 1. Left behind in the closet (was, were) only a **sweater and three old shirts.**

_____ 2. The **connection** between time spent watching television and poor academic performance (is, are) becoming quite clear.

_____sit_____ 3. There in the outer office (sits, sit) **a detective and two uniformed officers.**

_____ 4. We worked very hard on that project, but the **results** of our work (is, are) still in doubt.

_____is_____ 5. In our college library, unrestricted **access** to books in the stacks (is, are) not permitted.

_____ 6. **Tom Wilson,** in addition to three other people, (has, have) verified that a school holiday has been declared.

_____has_____ 7. A **lack** of chain saws and other power equipment (has, have) slowed the clearing of that lot.

_____ 8. Mike said that the **number** of high grades on the final exam (has, have) set a new record.

_____have_____ 9. A **number** of people (has, have) come by the office to ask about concert tickets.

_____ 10. By early evening there (was, were) about a dozen **people** gathered in the lobby of the television station.

_____is_____ 11. Neither **Wayne nor Martha** _{the boys} (is, are) prepared for a pop quiz this morning.

_____ 12. The **value** of the tapes and compact disks lost in the fire (is, are) a subject for debate.

_____enjoy_____ 13. Alice is one of those people **who** (enjoys, enjoy) both classical and rock music.

_____ 14. The **rest** of the money in the entertainment fund (has, have) been donated to the Children's Home Society.

_____were_____ 15. The **rest** of the books (was, were) returned to the shelves by the library aides.

Directions: If you find an error in subject–verb agreement, underline the incorrect verb and write the correct form in the space at the left. Circle the subject of every verb you change. Some of the sentences may be correct.

_____ 1. The social and political implications of the reductions in the defense budget often becomes overwhelming.

_____ 2. The quality of the repairs done on my computer are open to question.

_____ 3. Packed into that small closet, in addition to some clothes and books, was the rest of my record collection.

_____ 4. I wonder why the memory of my last efforts at writing a paper late at night have made no change in my study habits.

_____ 5. It seems that neither color coordination nor comfort are a consideration when selecting clothes for class.

_____ 6. Also included in the sale price are a two-year warranty, floor mats, and dinner for two at the Pizzarama.

_____ 7. "I wonder if chocolate cake and a diet cola is a good choice for breakfast," said Howard.

_____ 8. Long hours spent in aerobic workouts has enabled Laura to reduce her body-fat content by five percent.

_____ 9. "In my opinion," said Jeremy, "there's few experiences as unpleasant as root canal work."

_____ 10. Has any of the engineers been able to explain the problems in that air conditioning system?

_____ 11. One item we forgot to include in our list of camping equipment are lightweight tents.

_____ 12. Neither the dean nor the vice president were able to tell us where the class meets.

_____ 13. There is, I suspect, two or three ways to solve that problem without calling in outside help.

_____ 14. Some managers mistakenly think that continued criticism of small mistakes is a good way to improve performance.

_____ 15. "Eight weeks are not a sufficiently long time to master all of European history," observed Professor Jones.

NAME _____ SCORE _____

Directions: If you find an error in subject–verb agreement, underline the incorrect verb and write the correct form in the space at the left. Circle the subject of every verb you change. Some of the sentences may be correct.

three days
seems,_____ 1. "Three days seem to me to be enough time for us to build that deck," said Walt.

box, has been taken
box, has been_____ 2. The box with three computers and a laser printer inside have been taken to the loading dock.

are, canoes
____are, canoes___ 3. In addition to the small rowboat, there is three fine wooden canoes in the boathouse.

_____C_____ 4. Usually a list of your expenses and a folder containing your receipts are included with your monthly report.

are, meetings
__are, meetings__ 5. When you begin to teach, the first day's meetings with the new students is going to be unforgettable.

is, discussion
is, discussion____ 6. Monday afternoon's discussion of all the errors from the previous two games are extremely dreary.

_____ 7. The lecturer told several stories that were quite funny, and the laughter helped the audience to relax.

_____ 8. My friend Jerry is one of those people who seems to be naturally talented in music.

_____ 9. A large number of the books in our library is old and should be replaced.

_____ 10. Were either Jim or Yolanda in that group that left on the first bus?

_____ 11. Immediate solutions to the large number of problems plaguing our computer network are vital.

_____ 12. The twins and their sister Amy are arriving tonight on the ten o'clock plane.

_____ 13. Ten thousand dollars were paid as a reward for information leading to the capture of that embezzler.

_____ 14. A large part of the student body don't know who the student government president is.

_____ 15. The baseball team is picking up their bats and gloves and walking slowly to the clubhouse.

_____ 16. There is a billiard table and a bowling alley in the basement of the student union.

_____ 17. We received a letter in which there was directions to the hotel and a picture of its entrance.

_____ 18. Ms. Rogers, along with all the division directors, is taking the plane to Charlotte tonight.

_____ 19. All the division directors and Ms. Rogers is taking the plane to Charlotte tonight.

_____ 20. Everyone who read that book has been asked to give some kind of opinion of it to the class.

_____ 21. Neither of the two children were able to find an article on dog training.

_____ 22. In that one picture is an All-American and three all-conference players.

_____ 23. Each manager and each assistant director was asked for an opinion on the new vacation policy.

_____ 24. Neither the two sisters nor their mother were able to attend the first meeting of the fund-raising committee.

_____ 25. Most of the people who asked about the reform program know very little about its details.

_____ 26. Most of the information on those programs are very confusing.

_____ 27. Lance is the only member of that group who enjoy horror movies as much as I do.

_____ 28. Mark London, along with several co-workers, are organizing a trip to the Orient.

_____ 29. One of the first things Jon did when he started the project were to interview the police chief.

_____ 30. The chance to win a small fortune and a good deal of fame lead many to play the lottery.

Lesson 23 *Using Pronouns Correctly: Reference; Agreement*

As you learned in Lesson 1, a pronoun is a word that substitutes for a noun or another pronoun. The word for which a pronoun stands is called the pronoun's **antecedent**:

> I called *Harry,* but *he* didn't answer. [*He* substitutes for *Harry. Harry* is the antecedent of *he.*]
>
> My *cap and scarf* were where I had left *them.* [The antecedent of *them* is the plural unit *cap and scarf.*]
>
> *I* will wash *my* car tomorrow.
>
> *One* of my friends is painting *his* house.
>
> *Three* of my friends are painting *their* houses.

To use pronouns effectively and without confusing your reader, you must follow two basic principles:

1. Establish a clear, easily identified relationship between a pronoun and its antecedent.
2. Make the pronoun and its antecedent agree in person, number, and gender.

Let us examine these requirements more fully.

Role of Antecedents

Personal pronouns should have definite antecedents and should be placed as near their antecedents as possible. Your readers should know exactly what a pronoun stands for. They should not be made to look through several sentences for a pronoun's antecedent, nor should they be asked to manufacture an antecedent for a pronoun. When you discover in your writing a pronoun with no clear and unmistakable antecedent, your revision, as many of the following examples demonstrate, will often require rewriting to remove the faulty pronoun from your sentence.

Faulty:	A strange car followed us closely, and *he* kept blinking his lights at us.
Improved:	A strange car followed us closely, and the driver kept blinking his lights at us.

Faulty:	Although Jenny was a real sports fan, her brother never became interested in *them.*
Improved:	Although Jenny really liked sports, her brother never became interested in them.

Faulty:	Mike is an excellent typist, although he never took a course in *it.*
Improved:	Mike is an excellent typist, although he never took a course in typing.

The indefinite *you* or *they* is quite common in speech and in chatty, informal writing, but one should avoid using either in serious writing:

Faulty:	In Alaska *they* catch huge king crabs.
Improved:	In Alaska huge king crabs are caught. [Often the best way to correct an indefinite *they* or *you* sentence is to use a passive verb.]

225

Faulty: Before the reform measures were passed, *you* had few rights.
Improved: Before the reform measures were passed, people had few rights.
               Before the reform measures were passed, one had few rights.

Faulty: At the employment office *they* gave me an application form.
Improved: A clerk at the employment office gave me an application form.
               At the employment office I was given an application form.

A pronoun should not appear to refer equally well to either of two antecedents:

Faulty: Frank told Bill that *he* needed a haircut. [Which one needed a haircut?]
Improved: "You need a haircut," said Frank to Bill. [In sentences of this type, the direct quotation is sometimes the only possible correction.]

Avoid the Indefinite It

The "it says" or "it said" introduction to statements, although common in informal language, is objectionable in serious writing because the "it" has no antecedent. (See Supplement.)

Faulty: *It* says in the directions that the powder will dissolve in hot water.
Improved: The directions say that the powder will dissolve in hot water.

Faulty: *It* said on the morning news program that a bad storm is coming.
Improved: According to the morning news program, a bad storm is coming.

Avoid Unclear References

Avoid vague or ambiguous reference of relative and demonstrative pronouns.

Faulty: Only twenty people attended the lecture, *which* was due to poor publicity.
Improved: Because of poor publicity, only twenty people attended the lecture.

Faulty: Good writers usually have large vocabularies, and *this* is why I get poor grades on my papers.
Improved: I get poor grades on my papers because my vocabulary is inadequate; good writers usually have large vocabularies.

Special Cases: Which, This, That

Sometimes the antecedent of the pronouns *which, this,* and *that* is an idea rather than the expressed noun. In a sentence such as "The children giggled, *which* annoyed the teacher" or "The children giggled, and *this* annoyed the teacher," what annoyed the teacher is not the *children* but "the giggling of the children" or "the fact that the children giggled." This kind of reference to a preceding idea rather than to an expressed noun is unobjectionable provided that the meaning is instantly and unmistakably clear. But you should avoid sentences like those shown below. In the first example readers would be hard pressed to discover exactly what the *which* means, and in the second they must decide whether the antecedent is the preceding idea or the noun immediately preceding the *which*:

Faulty: Hathaway's application was rejected because he spells poorly, *which* is very important in an application letter.
Improved: Hathaway's application was rejected because he spells poorly; correct spelling is very important in an application letter.

Faulty: The defense attorney did not object to the judge's concluding remark, *which* surprised me.

Improved: I was surprised that the defense attorney did not object to the judge's concluding remark.

Pronoun Agreement

Pronouns should agree with their antecedents in person, number, and gender. The following chart classifies for you the three forms of each personal pronoun on the basis of person, number, and gender:

	Singular	*Plural*
1st Person	*I, my, me*	*we, our, us*
2nd Person	*you, your, you*	*you, your, you*
3rd Person	*he, his, him*	
	she, her, her	*they, their, them*
	it, its, it	

A singular antecedent is referred to by a singular pronoun; a plural antecedent is referred to by a plural pronoun.

> Dad says that *he* is sure that *his* new friend will visit *him* soon.
> Dad and Mother say that *they* are sure that *their* new friend will visit *them* soon.

This principle of logical pronoun agreement is not as simple as these two examples might suggest. Recent language practices have given rise to two situations for which it is impossible to make rules that apply in every instance. Student writers must, first, be aware of certain changing ideas about pronoun usage; they must then prepare themselves to make decisions among the choices available.

Indefinite Pronouns

The first of these two troublesome situations relates to some of the indefinite pronouns: *one, everyone, someone, no one, anyone, anybody, everybody, somebody, nobody, each, either,* and *neither.* These words have generally been felt to be singular; hence pronouns referring to them have customarily been singular and, unless the antecedent specifies otherwise, masculine. Singular pronouns have also been used in formal writing and speaking to refer to noun antecedents modified by singular qualifiers such as *each* and *every.* The four following examples illustrate the traditional, formal practice:

> Everybody has *his* faults and *his* virtues.
> Each of the sons is doing what *he* thinks is best.
> England expects every man to do *his* duty.
> No one succeeds in this firm if Dobbins doesn't like *him.*

The principal difficulty with this usage is that these indefinites, although regarded by strict grammarians as singular in form, carry with them a group or plural sense, with the result that people are often unsure whether pronouns referring to them should be singular or plural. Despite traditional pronouncements, every day we hear sentences of the "Everyone-will-do-*their*-best" type. Beginning writers, however, would do well to follow the established practice until they feel relatively secure about recognizing the occasional sentence in which a singular pronoun referring to an indefinite produces a strained or unnatural effect even though it agrees in form with its antecedent.

Gender Issues

Closely related to this troublesome matter of pronoun agreement is the second problem, gender. What reference words should be used to refer to such a word as *student*? Obviously there are female students, and there are male students. With plural nouns there is no problem; *they*, *their*, and *them* refer to both masculine and feminine. For singular nouns there is *she*, *hers*, *her* and *he*, *his*, *him*, but there is not a pronoun to refer to third-person singular words that contain both male and female members.

Here again, as with the reference to third-person singular indefinites, the traditional practice has been to use masculine singular pronouns. Eighty or so years ago Henry James wrote the following sentence: "We must grant the artist his subject, his idea, his *donné*; our criticism is applied only to what he makes of it." In James's day that sentence was undoubtedly looked upon as unexceptionable; the pronouns followed what was then standard practice. But attitudes have changed. In the 1990s, if that sentence got past the eyes of an editor and appeared on the printed page, its implication that artists are exclusively male would make the sentence unacceptably discriminatory to many readers.

Reliance on the *he or she* pronoun forms is an increasingly popular solution to some of these worrisome problems of pronoun reference. The *he or she* forms agree in number with the third-person singular indefinites. And the use of these forms obviates any possible charge of gender preference. However, excessive use of *he or she*, *his or her*, and *him or her* is undesirable. (Notice the cumbersome result, for instance, if a *he or she* form is substituted for all four of the third-person singular masculine pronouns in the Henry James sentence.)

Here is a very important point for you to remember: When you are worried about a third-person singular masculine pronoun you have written, either because its reference to an indefinite antecedent does not sound quite right to you or because it shows an undesirable gender preference, you can remove the awkwardness, in nearly every instance that arises, by changing the antecedent to a **plural** noun, to which you then refer by using *they*, *their*, and *them*.

By way of summary, study these four versions of a sentence as they relate to the two problems just discussed:

Every member of the graduating class, if *he* wishes, may have *his* diploma mailed to *him* after August 15. [This usage reflects traditional practice that is still quite widely followed. The objection to it is that the reference words are exclusively masculine.]

Every member of the graduating class, if *he or she* wishes, may have *his or her* diploma mailed to *him or her* after August 15. [The singular reference is satisfactory, but the avoidance of masculine reference has resulted in clumsy wordiness.]

Every member of the graduating class, if *they* wish, may have *their* diplomas mailed to *them* after August 15. [This version, particularly if used in spoken English, would probably not offend many people, but the lack of proper number agreement between the pronouns and the antecedent would rule out its appearance in edited material.]

Members of the graduating class, if *they* wish, may have *their* diplomas mailed to *them* after August 15. [In this version the pronouns are logical and correct in both number and gender.]

A few other matters of pronoun reference, mercifully quite uncomplicated, should be called to your attention. If a pronoun refers to a compound unit or to a noun that may be either singular or plural, the pronoun agrees in number with the antecedent. (See Lesson 22, Rule 6.)

Wilson and his wife arrived in *their* new car.
Neither Jill nor Martha has finished *her* term paper.
The rest of the lecture had somehow lost *its* point.
The rest of the workers will receive *their* money soon.
The eight-o'clock class has *its* test tomorrow.
The ten-o'clock class finished writing *their* themes.

Beware of "You"

An antecedent in the third person should not be referred to by the second person *you*. This misuse develops when writers, forgetting that they have established the third person in the sentence, shift the structure and begin to talk directly to the reader:

Faulty: In a large university a *freshman* can feel lost if *you* have grown up in a small town.
Improved: In a large university a freshman can feel lost if he or she has grown up in a small town.

Faulty: If a *person* really wants to become an expert golfer, *you* must practice everyday.
Improved: If a person really wants to become an expert golfer, she or he must practice every day.

Supplement

At this point you should be reminded that *it* without an antecedent has some uses that are completely acceptable in both formal and informal English. One of these is in the delayed subject or object pattern. (See Lesson 10.) Another is its use as a kind of filler word in expressions having to do with weather, time, distance, and so forth.

It is fortunate that you had a spare tire.
I find *it* difficult to believe Ted's story.
It is cold today; *it* snowed last night.
It is twelve o'clock; *it* is almost time for lunch.
How far is *it* to Phoenix?

Using Pronouns Correctly: Reference; Agreement

NAME _____ SCORE _____

Directions: One sentence in each of the following pairs is correct, and the other contains at least one reference word that is poorly used. In the space at the left, write the letter that identifies the correct sentence. In the other sentence, circle the pronoun or pronouns that have vague or incorrect reference.

_____ 1. a. Many people dream of winning a vast fortune, but for most it's only a dream that can never come true.
　　　　　 b. Many people dream of winning a vast fortune, but for most such a fortune is only a dream that can never come true.

_____ 2. a. All those who want to play in the slow-pitch softball league should pay their fees before Tuesday night's practice.
　　　　　 b. Everyone who wants to play in the slow-pitch softball league should pay their fees before Tuesday night's practice.

_____ 3. a. The company president told Maurine that she was going to be assigned to the new committee on relocation.
　　　　　 b. The company president told Maurine, "You are going to be assigned to the new committee on relocation."

_____ 4. a. "I don't think anyone could pass that course without working himself half to death," said Marvin.
　　　　　 b. "I don't think anyone could pass that course without working themself half to death," said Marvin.

_____ 5. a. It said over the loudspeaker that those who have reserved seats would be admitted to the stadium first.
　　　　　 b. Over the loudspeaker the announcer said that those who have reserved seats would be admitted to the stadium first.

_____ 6. a. As a kid Marlene always wanted to study acting, but in college she decided not to become one.
　　　　　 b. As a kid Marlene always wanted to study acting, but in college she decided not to become a drama major.

_____ 7. a. According to the registrar's office, all applicants for the freshman class must complete their applications before June 1.
　　　　　 b. According to the registrar's office, everyone applying for the freshman class must complete their applications before June 1.

_____ 8. a. The note in the catalogue suggests that you should take typing before you take a computer course.
　　　　　 b. The note in the catalogue suggests that students should take typing before they take a computer course.

231

_____ 9. a. When the students finished with the tools, not any of them were returned to the toolbox.
   b. When the students finished with the tools, they did not return any of the tools to the toolbox.

_____ 10. a. *Laugh With Us,* a new program, will replace *Guess Again,* which surprised many viewers.
   b. Many viewers were surprised to learn that *Laugh With Us,* a new program, will replace *Guess Again.*

_____ 11. a. As a student registered for chemistry, you need to get some tutoring if you start to fall behind.
   b. A student registered for chemistry needs to get some tutoring if you start to fall behind.

_____ 12. a. The FBI sent out a brochure advertising openings for jobs in their organization.
   b. The FBI sent out a brochure advertising openings for jobs in its organization.

_____ 13. a. All the members of the Brain Bowl team received new blue blazers, and they gave the old blazers to Goodwill.
   b. Every member of the Brain Bowl team received a new blue blazer, and they gave the old blazers to Goodwill.

_____ 14. a. The newscaster reported that the local school board will soon hold elections by districts for the first time.
   b. It said on the news that the local school board will soon hold elections by districts for the first time.

_____ 15. a. The board of directors announced that they will soon offer the company's stock for sale to the public.
   b. The board of directors announced that it will soon offer the company's stock for sale to the public.

Exercise 23   *Using Pronouns Correctly: Reference; Agreement*

NAME _____   SCORE _____

Directions: In the space at the left, copy the correct pronoun or pronoun–verb combination given in parentheses. Circle the antecedent of the pronoun.

one, he or she 1. Not (one) of the older employees feels that (he or she owes, they owe) any loyalty to the new managers.

_____ 2. Has Jane's group finished (its, it's, their) part of the project yet?

student, he or she 3. By the time the average student graduates, (he or she, they) should have spent many hours learning how to use computers.

_____ 4. Before students can enroll for a scuba diving course, (he or she, you, they) must swim 100 yards under water.

citizens, their 5. The citizens of our county registered (its, their) opinion of county government by electing a new mayor.

_____ 6. Anyone who buys an older car must prepare (himself or herself, themselves) for some expensive repairs.

few, their 7. Out of the students surveyed, only a few knew (his or her, their) exact GPA.

_____ 8. People who intend to take that cruise will want to get (his or her, their) immunization shots early.

each, its 9. Did you know that each of those clubs has (its, their) own representative on the Interclub Council?

_____ 10. The members of the clubs elect (its, their) representatives annually.

Jim nor Walt, his 11. Neither Jim nor Walt has worked very much on (his, their) speech for next week's election.

_____ 12. Barbara, Marge, and Roberta will each bring in (her, their) report on Monday.

brothers, their 13. My brothers, Jim, Rob, and Harry, intend to show (his, their) old Ford at the next classic car show.

_____ 14. Some seniors find it difficult to remember how strange college was when (he or she was, they were) freshman.

bookstore, its 15. The local bookstore is holding a sale; all (its, their) book prices have been reduced by twenty-five percent.

233

Directions: Each sentence contains at least one reference word that is poorly used. In the space at the left, copy the pronoun or pronouns that have vague or incorrect reference. In the space below each sentence, rewrite enough of the sentence to make the meaning clear.

_____ 1. When someone tries to call that phone number, they usually get two of the digits reversed.

_____

_____ 2. After Max had waited in line for an hour, they told him that the class he wanted was already closed.

_____

_____ 3. My dad told George that he needed to invest a little money from each paycheck to pay for his retirement.

_____

_____ 4. The announcer said that anyone who is not completely happy with a purchase can get their money back.

_____

_____ 5. The ten o'clock class will have their test tomorrow, and they must turn in their projects on Friday.

_____

_____ 6. In the town of Wilder, they strictly enforce the speed limits, and you can get a ticket if you speed.

_____

_____ 7. Connie wants to be an artist, although you have a hard time getting started and most don't make much money.

_____

_____ 8. If anyone enjoys hard work, they might consider studying accounting.

_____

_____ 9. Sue does not enjoy tennis because she does not serve well, which is a basic requirement of the game.

_____

_____ 10. On my birthday each one of my relatives sent me a card they thought I might enjoy.

_____

Lesson 24　*Using Pronouns Correctly: Case*

In Lesson 23 the chart on page 227 classifies the personal pronouns on the basis of person, number, and gender. The three forms that are listed there for each person—first, second, and third, singular and plural—illustrate the three cases nouns and pronouns fall into: nominative, possessive, and objective. *I* and *they* are nominative, *my* and *their* are possessive, and *me* and *them* are objective, for example.

The way you use these pronouns in everyday language, in sentences such as "Two of *my* books have disappeared; *they* cost *me* twenty dollars, and *I* must find *them*," demonstrates that the case form you choose depends on how the word is used within the sentence. In this lesson we shall examine instances where the wrong choice of pronoun form is possible.

The only words in modern English that retain distinctions between nominative and objective case forms are the first- and third-person personal pronouns and the relative pronouns *who* and *whoever*. In nouns the nominative and objective forms are identical, and the correct use of the one distinctive form, the possessive, requires essentially only a knowledge of how the apostrophe is used. (See Lesson 19.)

Here are the pronouns arranged according to their case forms. The first eight are the personal pronouns; notice that the only distinctive form of *you* and *it* is the possessive. The last three pronouns, which we shall examine separately from the personal pronouns, are used only in questions and in subordinate clauses. (See Supplement for a discussion of *which* in the possessive case.)

Nominative	Possessive	Objective
I	my, mine	me
you	your, yours	you
he	his, his	him
she	her, hers	her
it	its, its	it
we	our, ours	us
you	your, yours	you
they	their, theirs	them
which	———	which
who	whose	whom
whoever	whosever	whomever

Personal Pronouns in the Possessive Case

The **possessive case** is used to show possession. Review carefully the following three possible trouble spots.

Modifiers and Nominals

The preceding chart shows two possessive forms for the personal pronouns. The first form for each pronoun is used as a *modifier* of a noun. The second form is used as a nominal;

235

in other words, it fills a noun slot, such as the subject, the complement, or the object of a preposition:

> This is *your* seat; *mine* is in the next row.
> Jane preferred *my* cookies; some of *hers* were burned.
> *Their* product is good, but the public prefers *ours*.

Indefinite Pronouns

The indefinite pronouns use an apostrophe to form the possessive case: *everybody's* duty, *one's* lifetime, *everyone's* hopes, someone *else's* car. But the personal pronouns do not:

> These seats are *ours* [not *our's*]. *Yours* [not *Your's*] are in the next row.

Learn to distinguish carefully between the following possessives and contractions that are pronounced alike; *its* (possessive), *it's* (it is, it has); *theirs* (possessive), *there's* (there is, there has); *their* (possessive), *they're* (they are); *whose* (possessive), *who's* (who is, who has); *your* (possessive), *you're* (you are):

> *It's* obvious that the car has outworn *its* usefulness.
> *There's* new evidence that *they're* changing *their* tactics.

Possessive Pronouns with Gerunds

Formal usage prefers the possessive form of pronouns (occasionally of nouns also) preceding gerunds in constructions like the following:

> He was unhappy about *my* [not *me*] voting for the bill.
> Her report led to *our* [not *us*] buying additional stock.
> Chad boasted about his *son's* [not *son*] having won the scholarship.

Personal Pronouns in the Nominative and Objective Cases

The rules governing the uses of the other two cases are very simple. A pronoun is in the **nominative case** when it is used

1. As a subject: *They* suspected that *he* was lying.
2. As a subjective complement: This is *she* speaking.
3. As an appositive of a nominative noun: *We* editors help young writers.

A pronoun is in the **objective case** when it is used

1. As an object of a verb or verbal: Ted told *her* the news. We enjoyed meeting *them*.
2. As an object of a preposition: Everyone except *me* had left the room.
3. As the subject of an infinitive: The police officer ordered *me* to halt.
4. As an appositive of an objective noun: Three of *us* truck drivers stopped to help.

We need not examine in detail every one of these applications. As people become more adept at using the English language, they learn that such usages as "*Them* arrived late" and

"I spoke to *she*" do not conform to the system of the language. Instead, we should examine the trouble spots where confusion may arise.

When you use the nominative and objective personal pronouns, exercise care in the following situations.

Pronoun Part of Compound Unit

When the pronoun follows *and* (sometimes *or*) as part of a compound unit, determine its use in the sentence and choose the appropriate case form. The temptation here is usually to use the nominative, although the last example in the following list shows a trouble spot where the objective case is sometimes misused. If you test these troublesome constructions by using the pronoun by itself, you will often discover which form is the correct one:

The man gave Sue and *me* some candy. [Not: Sue and *I*. Both words are indirect objects. Apply the test. Notice how strange "The man gave . . . *I* some candy" sounds.]

Send your check to either my lawyer or *me*. [Not: to . . . *I*.]

Have you seen Bob or *her* lately? [Direct objects require the objective case.]

Just between you and *me*, the lecture was a bore. [Never say "between you and I." Both pronouns are objects of the preposition *between*. If this set phrase is a problem for you, find the correct form by reversing the pronouns: You would never say "between I and you."]

Ms. Estes took *him* and *me* to school.
[Not *he* and *I* or *him* and *I*. Both pronouns are direct objects.]

Will my sister and *I* be invited? [Not *me*. The subject is *sister* and *I*.]

Comparisons after As and Than

In comparisons after *as* and *than*, when the pronoun is the subject of an understood verb, use the nominative form:

He is taller than *I* [*am*]. I am older than *he* [*is*].
Can you talk as fast as *she* [*can talk*]? No one knew more about art than *he* [*did*].

Sentences like these nearly always call for nominative case subjects. Occasionally the meaning of a sentence may demand an objective pronoun. Both of the following sentences are correct; notice the difference in meaning:

You trust Mr. Alton more than *I*. [Meaning ". . . more than I (trust Mr. Alton")."]
You trust Mr. Alton more than *me*. [Meaning ". . . more than (you trust) me."]

"It is" Expressions

Ordinarily, use the nominative form for the subjective complement. The specific problem here concerns such expressions as *It's me, It is I, It was they,* or *It was them.* Many people say *It's me,* but they would hesitate to say *It was her, It was him,* or *It was them,* instead of

It was she, It was he, or *It was they.* However, this is a problem that does not arise often in the writing of students. The following are examples of correct formal usage:

It is *I.*
It could have been *he.*
Was it *she*?
Was it *they* who called?

"We" versus "Us" and "I" versus "Me"

An appositive should be in the same case as the word that it refers to. Notice particularly the first three examples that follow. This usage employing *we* and *us* as an appositive modifier preceding a noun is a real trouble spot:

We boys were hired. [The unit *We boys* is the subject and requires the nominative.]
Two of *us* boys were hired. [The object of a preposition requires the objective case.]
Mr. Elder hired *us* boys. [Not *we boys* for a direct object.]
Two boys—you and *I*—will be hired. [In apposition with the subject.]
Mr. Elder will hire two boys—you and *me.* [In apposition with the object.]

Problems with Who and Whom

The only other pronouns in standard modern English that have distinctive nominative, possessive, and objective forms are *who/whose/whom* and *whoever/whosever/whomever.* (See Supplement.) The rules that apply to the personal pronouns apply to these words as well: In the subject position *who/whoever* should be used, in the direct object position *whom/whomever* should be used, and so forth. (These pronouns, it should be noted, are never used as appositives.)

The special problem in the application of the case rules to these words comes from their use as interrogatives and as subordinating words. As you learned in Lessons 6, 9, and 10, these words, because they serve as signal words, always stand at the beginning of their clauses. To locate the grammatical function of the pronoun within its clause, you must examine the clause to determine the normal subject–verb–complement positioning.

Direct Object or Object of a Preposition

In formal usage, *whom* is required when it is a direct object or the object of a preposition, even though it stands ahead of its subject and verb:

Whom did Mr. Long hire?
[If you are troubled by this sort of construction, try substituting a personal pronoun and placing it after the verb, where it normally comes: "Did Mr. Long hire *him*?" You would never say "Did Mr. Long hire *he*?" The transitive verb *hire* requires a direct object pronoun in the objective case.]

He is a boy *whom* everyone can like. [*Whom* is the object of *can like.*]

Wilson was the man *whom* everybody trusted. [Everybody trusted *whom.*]

She is the girl *whom* Mother wants me to marry. [Object of the verbal *to marry.*]

Whom was she speaking to just then? [To *whom* was she speaking?]

Beginning a Subordinate Clause

When *who(m)* or *who(m)ever* begins a subordinate clause that follows a verb or a preposition, the use of the pronoun *within its own clause* determines its case form:

> We do not know *who* broke the window.
> [*Who* is the subject of *broke*, not the direct object of *do know*.]

> No one knows *who* the intruder was.
> [*Who* is the subjective complement in the noun clause.]

> We do not know *whom* the police have arrested.
> [The objective form *whom* is used because it is the direct object of *have arrested*. The direct object of *do know* is the whole noun clause.]

> I will sell the car to *whoever* offers the best price.
> [The whole clause, *whoever offers the best price*, is the object of the preposition *to*. Whoever is the subject of *offers*. The subject of a verb must be in the nominative case.]

After a Parenthetical Insertion

When the pronoun subject is followed by a parenthetical insertion like *do you think, I suspect, everyone believes*, or *we know*, the nominative case form must be used:

> *Who* do you think *has* the best chance of winning?
> [*Who* is the subject of *has*. The *do you think* is a parenthetical insertion.]

> Jenkins is the one *who* I suspect *will make* the best impression.
> [Determine the verb that goes with the pronoun. If you are puzzled by this type of sentence, try reading it this way: "Jenkins is the one *who will make* the best impression—I suspect."]

But if the pronoun is not the subject of the verb, the objective form should be used:

> He is an achiever *whom* I suspect you will eventually envy.
> [*Whom* is the direct object of *will envy*.]

Supplement

The chart on page 235 shows that the pronoun *which* has no possessive case form, a situation that brings about a minor problem of word choice. As you learned when you studied the adjective clause, *who(m)* normally refers to persons, and *which* to things. But *whose* may be used in an adjective clause as the possessive form of *which* to refer to a nonhuman antecedent:

> It is a disease *whose* long-term effects are minor.

If *whose* is not used in such a sentence, the "of-which" form must be used, producing a perfectly correct but cumbersome sentence:

> It is a disease the long-term effects *of which* are minor.

SUMMARY OF CORRECT PRONOUN USE

1. A pronoun should have a clearly identified antecedent, with which it agrees in person, number, and gender.
2. Be aware of the special problem of pronoun reference to third-person singular antecedents that include both masculine and feminine members—pronouns like *everybody* and *someone* and nouns like *person, student, employee,* and so on.
   NOTE: Using a plural rather than a singular antecedent is one obvious way of avoiding this problem.
3. Use nominative forms of pronouns for subjects, subjective complements, and appositives that rename nominative nouns. Use objective forms of pronouns for objects of verbs or prepositions, subjects of infinitives, and appositives that rename objective nouns.
4. Be aware of a particular pronoun problem when a personal pronoun is tied to a noun or another pronoun by *and* or *or:*

   Mickey and I [not *Mickey and me*] were sent to the principal's office.
   Mr. Case sent *Mickey and me* [not *Mickey and I*] to the principal's office.
   And so, neighbors, please vote for *Ms. Stone and me* [not *Ms. Stone and I*].

5. Remember that the case of *who* is determined by its use in its own clause. It may be a direct object that precedes the subject [*Whom* has your wife invited?] or a subject immediately following a verb or a preposition [We wonder *who* will win. Our dog is friendly with *whoever* pets it.].

NAME _____ SCORE _____

Directions: Each italicized pronoun in these sentences is correctly used. In the space at the left, write one of the following numbers to identify the use of the pronoun:

1. Subject
2. Subjective complement
3. Appositive modifier of nominative noun

4. Direct or indirect object
5. Object of preposition
6. Appositive modifier of objective noun

_____ 1. Yesterday Professor Jones asked both Tom and *me* to make a speech next week.

_____ 2. *We* players don't resent hard work because it helps us to improve our performance.

_____ 3. None of *us* employees received that memorandum.

_____ 4. Do you think that Marge is a better speaker than *I*?

_____ 5. That letter should be sent to *whoever* is responsible for handling such insurance claims.

_____ 6. I'd like to keep this information a secret between you and *me*.

_____ 7. That candidate is a woman *who*, according to her biography, has no prior experience in politics.

_____ 8. The clerk handed Jane and *me* new registration packets.

_____ 9. Martin seems puzzled; it could have been *he* who was outside when the instructions were read.

_____ 10. *Whom* do you think we should appoint as Arthur's replacement?

_____ 11. *Who* do you think should be Arthur's replacement?

_____ 12. Every one of *us* programmers can do that simple work.

_____ 13. Maria asked *who* the coach was in 1987.

_____ 14. Diligent students like you and *me* can always be counted on to take thorough notes.

_____ 15. The letter writer, *whoever* she is, failed to do any significant research on that problem.

_____ 16. The new officers are Ray, Alice, and *I*.

_____ 17. The list of new officers includes Ray, Alice, and *me*.

_____ 18. Roger thought the assignment was for Barbara, Jack, and *him*.

_____ 19. The girls didn't know *whom* the garage was sending to pick up the car.

_____ 20. The girls didn't know *who* was being sent to pick up the car.

Directions: In the space at the left, copy the correct pronoun from within the parentheses.

_____Whom_____ 1. (Who, Whom) do you think the department will send as its representative at the conference in London?

_____who_____ 2. Will you tell me (who, whom) your assistant was on that project last year?

_____us_____ 3. The men's basketball coach recruited three of (us, we) tallest intramural players for the varsity.

_____me_____ 4. Every worker on that shift, including James and (I, me), worked overtime last night.

_____she_____ 5. When Marie was in elementary school, the three best spellers were Alex, Tammie, and (her, she).

_____ 6. Are you sure that the black umbrella is (yours, your's) and not Nancy's?

_____ 7. The general public needs to be informed about politicians as corrupt as (he, him) and his colleagues.

_____ 8. The business students will support (whoever, whomever) the Business Council selects.

_____ 9. The business students will vote for (whoever, whomever) gets the approval of the Business Council.

_____ 10. Most people say that only good math students like you and (her, she) should take that course in the summer.

_____ 11. "I don't think making coffee in the morning is actually (anybodies, anybody's) job," said Edwina.

_____ 12. "A few of (us, we) players would like to practice Saturday morning," said Wanda.

_____ 13. The manager (whose, who's) in charge of that new project is in town today.

_____ 14. Those who work as slowly as Rick and (I, me) don't belong in this advanced class.

_____ 15. Annabelle is a person (who, whom) creates a very good first impression on people she meets.

_____ 16. "I can predict (who, whom) the coach will choose as captain in the fall," said Alan.

_____ 17. Almost everyone, except, of course, for Robin and (I, me), was on time this morning.

_____ 18. If you can't type that paper for me, (who, whom) do you think can do it?

_____ 19. When we went to San Francisco, my aunt took my sister and (I, me) to a very famous restaurant.

_____ 20. The prize goes to (whoever, whomever) solves that problem first.

Exercise 24 *Using Pronouns Correctly: Case*

NAME _____ SCORE _____

Directions: If you find an incorrectly used pronoun, underline it and write the correct form in the space at the left. If a sentence is correct, leave the space blank.

_____ 1. I told Marta that, if I were she, I would study for tomorrow's test.

_____ 2. Except for she and Ellen, all the women on the committee voted to meet tomorrow night at eight o'clock.

_____ 3. Would you please send all of we members of the nominating committee a list of your previous elected offices?

_____ 4. Does the coach know about my leaving practice early yesterday?

_____ 5. How will the detectives find who the thief is?

_____ 6. I think the detectives should look for whomever they think has the missing file folders.

_____ 7. "That plan was proposed by the class president, but it was not accepted by us," said Bob.

_____ 8. Joanna bought a new car last week; it's stereo system includes a compact disk changer.

_____ 9. John and Tom are back for the summer; it could have been they whom you saw in the mall today.

_____ 10. Standing all together at the front of the room were the president, the treasurer, and us department heads.

_____ 11. Betsy said, "Keep this news between you and I, but I heard that next Tuesday is going to be a holiday."

_____ 12. The receptionist answered the phone and asked, "And whom may I say is calling?"

_____ 13. Who is the president expecting to call on today?

_____ 14. Someone else's application arrived earlier than those submitted by Joyce and I.

_____ 15. Janice wants to call her sister, whom she thinks will want to join us for dinner.

_____ 16. I think Paul might need help; a beginner like he might have trouble installing that program.

_____ 17. Everyone except us new workers will be covered by the new benefits package.

_____ 18. "Whose going to tell the boss that the hard disk crashed last night?" asked Raymond.

_____ 19. "And can you guess whose job it will be to restore the data to that disk?" groaned Meryl.

_____ 20. Every rookie, whoever he is, has to endure practical jokes played by the veterans.

_____ 21. The office manager promised to give my brother and I good references for our work this past summer.

_____ 22. Who do you think we should choose as our advisor for next semester?

_____ 23. Dr. Magnusen is one man who's opinion I value.

_____ 24. I'd like to use your computer; our's is in the repair shop.

_____ 25. Roberta just hired a new secretary who, she learned, cannot operate a computer.

NAME _____   SCORE _____

Directions: Whenever you find an incorrectly used pronoun, copy it in the space at the left. Then in the space below the sentence, write enough of the sentence to show how you would make it clear and correct. No sentence contains more than two poorly used pronouns; some sentences may be correct.

_____   1. The director told we students that they've decided not to use any students as extras in the movie.

_____

_____   2. Ask Jenny if that book on the back seat of my car is hers; it's not mine or yours.

_____

_____   3. The clerk told Ed that you have to have your registration form signed by someone in the dean's office.

_____

_____   4. Give this note to whoever you can find downstairs and tell them to take it to the coach's office, please.

_____

_____   5. Mary asked Sue if her sister had brought back her clean laundry when she came for the weekend.

_____

_____   6. It says in the handbook that March first is the last day you can withdraw from a course.

_____

_____   7. "You can select whoever you wish for a partner; its your choice," said the teacher.

_____

_____   8. The boss called earlier; she wants to know who we've hired and how we located them.

_____

_____   9. Uncle Walt, who is a scuba diver, says he can teach us to dive if we are interested in it.

_____

_____   10. Each student should have their own computer and they should give each one individual instructions.

_____

_____ 11. Jane Roberts, whom most of us think should be the next manager, has better credentials for it than anyone else.

_____ 12. I lost yesterday's lecture notes, but John and Anne, who sit next to me, will lend me their's.

_____ 13. On the television last night they announced that people who use well water should boil it before drinking it.

_____ 14. Every entering freshman must attend orientation before they can sign up for their courses.

_____ 15. My parents, who both attended a local college, allowed my sister and I to choose an out-of-state school.

_____ 16. The guides gave each hiker a picnic lunch, but they had eaten everything well before noon.

_____ 17. "The climax of that movie was so frightening it made you forget how funny you thought the opening was," said Tom.

_____ 18. I wonder if our leaving the party early angered anyone who was there.

_____ 19. Everyone who my father employed last summer has returned to college to pursue their degree.

_____ 20. Please send copies of the schedule to all we freshmen so we can pick out our classes early.

Lesson 25   *Using Modifiers and Prepositions Correctly*

In Lesson 2 you learned that an adjective is a word that describes or limits a noun or a pronoun. You also learned that an adverb modifies a verb, an adjective, or another adverb. Many adverbs end in *ly,* such as *happily, beautifully,* and *extremely.* (But some adjectives—*lovely, likely, deadly, neighborly,* and *homely,* for instance—also end in *ly.*). Some adverbs do not end in *ly,* and these happen to be among the most frequently used words in speech and writing: *after, always, before, far, forever, here, not, now, often, quite, rather, soon, then, there, too, very.* Some words can be used either as adjectives or as adverbs, as the following examples show:

Adverbs	*Adjectives*
He came *close.*	That was a *close* call.
She talks too *fast.*	She's a *fast* thinker.
Hit it *hard.*	That was a *hard* blow.
She usually arrives *late.*	She arrived at a *late* hour.
He went *straight* to bed.	I can't draw a *straight* line.

Some adverbs have two forms, one without and one with the *ly: cheap, cheaply; close, closely; deep, deeply; hard, hardly; high, highly; late, lately; loud, loudly; quick, quickly; right, rightly; slow, slowly.* In some of these pairs the words are interchangeable; in most they are not. The idiomatic use of adverbs is a rather complex matter; no rules can be made that govern every situation. We can, however, make a few generalizations that reflect present-day practice.

1. The shorter form of a few of these—*late, hard,* and *near,* for example—fills most adverbial functions because the corresponding *ly* forms have acquired special meanings:

We must not stay *late.*	I have not seen him *lately* [recently].
I studied *hard* last night.	I *hardly* [scarcely] know him.
Winter is drawing *near.*	I *nearly* [almost] missed the last flight.

2. The *ly* form tends toward the formal, with the short form lending itself to more casual, informal speech and writing:

Informal	*Formal*
It fell *close* to the target.	You must watch him *closely.*
They ate *high* off the hog.	She was *highly* respected.
Drive *slow*!	Please drive more *slowly.*
Must you sing so *loud*?	He *loudly* denied the charges.
We searched far and *wide.*	She is *widely* known as an artist.

3. Because the short form seems more direct and forceful, it is often used in imperative sentences:

   Hold *firm* to this railing.
   "Come *quick*," yelled the officer.

4. The short form is often the one used when combined with an adjective to make a compound modifier preceding a noun:

a *wide*-ranging species	The species ranges *widely.*
a *slow*-moving truck	The truck moved *slowly.*

Typical Adverb/Adjective Trouble Spots

For the sake of simplifying the problem of the right use of adverbs and adjectives, we may say that there are three main trouble spots.

Misusing an Adjective for an Adverb

A word is an adverb if it modifies a verb, an adjective, or another adverb. The words that usually cause trouble here are *good, bad, well; sure, surely; real, really; most, almost; awful, awfully;* and *some, somewhat:*

Chip played *well* [not *good*] in the last game. [Modifies the verb *played.*]
This paint adheres *well* [not *good*] to concrete. [Modifies the verb *adheres.*]
Almost [not *Most*] every student has a job. [Modifies the adjective *every.*]
Today my shoulder is *really* [or *very*—not *real*] sore. [Modifies the adjective *sore.*]
He was driving *really* [or *very*—not *real*] fast. [Modifies the adverb *fast.*]
This rain has been falling *steadily* [not *steady*] for a week.
The champion should win his first match *easily* [not *easy*].
You'll improve if you practice *regularly* [not *regular*].
She wants that prize very *badly* [not *bad*].

Misusing Adverbs for Adjectives as Subjective Complements

The most common verb to take the subjective complement is *be;* fortunately, mistakes with this verb are nearly impossible. A few other verbs—like *seem, become, appear, prove, grow, go, turn, stay,* and *remain,* when they are used in a sense very close to that of *be*—take subjective complements. This complement must be an adjective, not an adverb.

The house *seems empty.* [House *is* empty.]
Their plans *became apparent.* [Plans *were* apparent.]
The work *proved* very *hard.* [Work *was* hard.]

The adjective subjective complement is also used with another group of verbs, the so-called verbs of the senses. These are *feel, look, smell, sound,* and *taste:*

You shouldn't feel *bad* about this. [Not *badly.*]
His cough sounds *bad* this morning. [Not *badly.*]
At first our prospects looked *bad.* [Not *badly.*]
Doesn't the air smell *sweet* today? [Not *sweetly.*]

The verb *feel* is involved in two special problems. In the first place, it is often used with both *good* and *well.* These two words have different meanings; one is not a substitute for the other. When used with the verb *feel, well* is an adjective meaning "in good health."

The adjective *good,* when used with *feel,* means "filled with a sense of vigor and excitement." Of course, both *well* and *good* have other meanings when used with other verbs. In the second place, the expression "I feel badly" has been used so widely, especially in spoken English, that it can hardly be considered an error in usage. Many careful writers, however, prefer the adjective here, with the result that "feel bad" is usually found in written English.

Misusing a Comparative or a Superlative Form of a Modifier

Most adverbs are compared in the same way as adjectives. (For a discussion of the comparison of adjectives, see Lesson 2.) Some common adverbs cannot be compared, such as *here, now, then, when,* and *before.* As you learned in Lesson 16, we use the comparative degree *(taller, better, more intelligent, more rapidly)* in a comparison limited to two things. We use the superlative degree *(tallest, best, most intelligent, most rapidly)* for more than two things.

Two other problems, both of minor importance, are involved in comparisons. First, we do not combine the two forms *(more + er, most + est)* in forming the comparative and superlative degrees:

Later the landlord became *friendlier* [not *more friendlier*].
Please drive *slower* [not *more slower*].
Please drive *more slowly* [not *more slower*].

Second, some purists object to the comparison of the so-called absolute qualities, such as *unique* ("being the only one"), *perfect, round, exact,* and so forth. They argue that, instead of such uses as *most perfect, straighter, more unique,* the intended meaning is *most nearly perfect, more nearly straight, more nearly unique.* General usage, however, has pretty well established both forms.

Problems with Prepositions

Three reminders should be made about the use of prepositions. One problem is the selection of the exact preposition for the meaning intended.

Idioms Using Prepositions

Many words, especially verbs and adjectives, give their full meaning only when modified by a prepositional phrase. In most cases the meaning of the preposition dictates a logical idiom: to sit *on* a couch, to walk *with* a friend, to lean *against* a fence, and so on. For some more abstract concepts, however, the acceptable preposition may seem to have been selected arbitrarily. Here are a few examples of different meanings of different prepositions:

agree *to* a proposal, *with* a person, *on* a price, *in* principle
argue *about* a matter, *with* a person, *for* or *against* a proposition
compare *to* to show likenesses, *with* to show differences [sometimes similarities]
correspond *to* a thing, *with* a person
differ *from* an unlike thing, *with* a person
live *at* an address, *in* a house or city, *on* a street, *with* other people

Note: Any good modern dictionary will provide information about and examples of the correct usage of prepositions.

Unnecessary Prepositions

Although at colloquial levels of language we sometimes find unnecessary prepositions used, examples like the following are improved in serious contexts if written without the words in brackets:

> I met [up with] your uncle yesterday.
> We keep our dog inside [of] the house.
> Our cat, however, sleeps outside [of] the house.
> The package fell off [of] the speeding truck.

Avoid especially the needless preposition at the end of a sentence or the repeated preposition in adjective clauses and in direct or indirect questions:

> Where is your older brother *at*?
>
> He is one of the few people *to* whom I usually feel superior *to*.
> To what do you attribute your luck at poker *to*?
> [Use one *to* or the other, but not both.]

Repeated Prepositions in Compound Units

When two words of a compound unit require the same preposition to be idiomatically correct, the preposition need not be stated with the first unit:

Correct: We were both *repelled* and *fascinated by* the snake charmer's act.

But when the two units require different prepositions, both must be expressed:

Incomplete: The child shows an *interest* and a *talent for* music. [interest . . . *for* (?)]
Correct: The child shows an *interest in* and a *talent for* music.

Incomplete: I am sure that Ms. Lewis would both *contribute* and *gain from* a summer workshop. [contribute . . . *from* (?)]
Correct: I am sure that Ms. Lewis would both *contribute to* and *gain from* a summer workshop.

NAME _____ SCORE _____

Directions: In the first space at the left, write the word or words that the italicized word modifies. In the second space write **Adj.** if the italicized word is an adjective or **Adv.** if it is an adverb.

_____ 1. Jim looked *happy* because he made an A on the test.
_____

_____ 2. Tim was *certain* that Jim had arrived yesterday.
_____

_____ 3. Arthur *certainly* thought that you had his textbook.
_____

_____ 4. On the map that mountainous road looks *straight*.
_____

_____ 5. We watched *closely* as the band went through its morning
_____   practice.

_____ 6. Jan did not feel *good* about her performance in last night's game.
_____

_____ 7. Alan went *outside* to watch the meteor shower.
_____

_____ 8. "We have only an *outside* chance of finding Racquel in this huge
_____   crowd," said Lois.

_____ 9. The distribution of that political pamphlet was quite *wide*.
_____

_____ 10. The candidate's staff distributed that political pamphlet quite
_____   *widely*.

_____ 11. The recent debate was one of the *most* exciting times in the polit-
_____   ical campaign.

_____ 12. *Most* debaters got their training in high school.
_____

_____ 13. After the treatment on his ankle, Bart did not feel *well* for about
_____   three hours.

251

252 · *Using Modifiers Correctly*

_____ 14. Bart did feel, however, that he got *good* results from the treat-
_____   ment.

_____ 15. The treatment is highly sophisticated and usually works quite
_____   *well.*

_____ 16. "I'm exhausted," whined Harry; "can we walk *slower?*"
_____

_____ 17. The *slower* pace allowed Harry to recover his energy.
_____

_____ 18. Kelly is *very* interested in political developments in Central
_____   Europe.

_____ 19. Janice ran a *better* time in the last marathon than she did in the
_____   earlier one.

_____ 20. My room looks *better* since I painted it.
_____

Directions: In the space at the left, copy the correct form given in parentheses.

_____ 1. That computer screen does not work (good, well) in a brightly lit room.

_____ 2. The (bright, brightly) lights obscure the images.

_____ 3. Cynthia's GPA has improved (considerable, considerably) in the past two semesters.

_____ 4. The color of the walls in that room is not a (true, truly) blue.

_____ 5. To improve your putting stroke, hold your putter a little more (loose, loosely).

_____ 6. Because my addition was not done (correct, correctly), my checkbook is out of balance.

_____ 7. Jill had not practiced her serve for weeks; in the match serving was (harder, more harder) than anything else.

_____ 8. Although Ronnie was not actually sick, he really looked (bad, badly).

_____ 9. "I look at that decision (different, differently) now that I know the background," said Angelo.

_____ 10. The beautiful red leaves fell (gentle, gently) to the ground when the breeze blew.

_____ 11. "I chose to read *Heart of Darkness* because it was the (shorter, shortest) book on the required list," said Jo.

_____ 12. Theresa does not feel (good, well); she thinks she is catching a cold.

_____ 13. Only one of the stocks chosen by our investment club has performed (poor, poorly).

_____ 14. "You didn't stir that paint (good, well) enough," said James; "it looks all streaky on the wall."

_____ 15. Babs is certainly smiling and happy this morning; she must feel (good, well) about the world.

_____ 16. (Sure, Surely) we can find something more exciting to do than going to that mall again.

_____ 17. Doing the research (proper, properly) did not take a great deal of time.

_____ 18. Ask Terry to come in early; she seems to think (better, more better) at that time of day.

_____ 19. The cake baking in the oven smells (wonderful, wonderfully).

_____ 20. (Almost, Most) every student will take that test tomorrow morning.

NAME _____   SCORE _____

Directions: Study these sentences for misused adjectives, adverbs, and prepositions. If you find a misused modifier, underline it and write the correct form in the space at the left. If you find a super-fluous preposition, circle it and write *omit* in the space at the left. If you find a spot that requires a preposition, write the preposition in the space at the left and use a caret (^) to show where it should be inserted in the sentence. Some sentences are correct as they stand; in these cases leave the spaces blank.

_____   1. The students' reaction to that announcement was negative; they have been talking angry for several moments now.

_____   2. Richard started work early this morning and has now completed most all of the research for his paper.

_____   3. My cup slid off of the table and splattered coffee in a wide pattern on the carpet.

_____   4. Rick said, "I stayed up late last night studying, and this morning I don't feel well at all."

_____   5. The boys polished the car real well, but the paint still doesn't look very good.

_____   6. Can you tell me where I can buy one of those special mechanical pencils at?

_____   7. "We need to try more harder," said Angela; "we haven't really accomplished much yet."

_____   8. I was intrigued and frightened by that new mystery novel about the serial killer.

_____   9. "Please work more quietly in the back of the room," said Mrs. White quite loud.

_____   10. Rose worked very diligent, but her efforts did not prove to be very fruitful.

_____   11. Walden is a really small college; it's the kind of place in which I don't feel comfortable in.

———————————— 12. The yard certainly looks differently now that we have carefully trimmed the shrubs.

———————————— 13. "My time in the race was not very good," said Martha; "I wanted to run a little more faster."

———————————— 14. Mr. Ramsey told June that she had not itemized her hours on the timecard specific enough.

———————————— 15. Jaime was sure happy that he had gotten a good grade on that extremely difficult test.

———————————— 16. The rain fell intermittently, but the wind blew continuously all afternoon.

———————————— 17. We were all amazed at Jeremy's interest and efforts for his sister's T-ball team.

———————————— 18. Loretta's brilliant performance on the balance beam seemed almost effortless.

———————————— 19. No matter how effortlessly her performance seemed, we all knew it was an exhausting routine.

———————————— 20. My confidence and respect for Mr. Tate has diminished considerably since he first came to work here.

———————————— 21. Pull that rope more tighter; I don't want the flag to slip down from the top of the pole.

———————————— 22. "Do you remember clearly where we parked the car at when we drove into the parking lot?" asked Meredith.

———————————— 23. The steps were icy but we walked very careful and did not slip.

———————————— 24. The Human Resources Department selected you because you will contribute and benefit from the conference.

———————————— 25. The pitching at last night's game was excellent, but our fielders played very badly all night long.

Lesson 26 *A Glossary of Usage*

The forms suggested in many of the entries in this glossary are those usually preferred in standard formal English—the English appropriate to your term papers, theses, term reports, examination papers in all your courses, and most of the serious papers written for your English classes. Many of the words or expressions in brackets are appropriate enough in informal conversation and in some informal papers.

Some of the entries are labeled *colloquial,* a term you should not think of as referring to slang, to forms used only in certain localities, or to "bad" English. The term applies to usages that are appropriate to informal and casual *spoken* English rather than to formal written English. However, expressions marked *substandard* should be avoided at all times.

A, an. Use *a* when the word immediately following it is sounded as a consonant; use *an* when the next sound is a vowel sound: *a, e, i, o,* or *u* (*a* friend, *an* enemy). Remember that it is the consonantal or vowel *sound,* not the actual letter, that determines the choice of the correct form of the indefinite article: *a* sharp curve, *an* S-curve; *a* eulogy, *an* empty house; *a* hospital, *an* honest person; *a* united people, *an* uneven contest.

Ad. Clipped forms of many words are used informally, such as *ad (advertisement), doc (doctor), exam (examination), gent (gentleman), gym (gymnasium), lab (laboratory), math (mathematics),* and *prof (professor).* Formal usage prefers the long forms.

Aggravate. In standard formal English the word means "make more severe," "make worse." Colloquially it means "annoy," "irritate," "exasperate."

Walking on your sprained ankle will aggravate the hurt. [*Informal:* All criticism aggravates him.]

Ain't. Substandard for *am not, are not, is not, have not.*

Am I not [not *Ain't I*] a good citizen?

The command hasn't [not *hain't* or *ain't*] been given yet.

They are not [not *ain't*] going either.

All the farther, all the faster, and the like. Generally regarded as colloquial equivalents of *as far as, as fast as,* and the like.

This is as far as [not *all the farther*] I care to go.

That was as fast as [not *all the faster*] he could run.

A lot. Always use as two words. See also *lots of, a lot of.*

A lot of. See *Lots of.*

Alright. This spelling, like *allright* or *allright,* although often used in advertising, is generally regarded as very informal usage. The preferred form is *all right.* In strictly formal usage, *satisfactory* or *very well* is preferred to *all right.*

Very well [not *Alright*], you may ride in our car.

The members agreed that the allocation of funds was satisfactory [not *all right*].

Among, between. *Among* is used with three or more persons or things, as in "Galileo was among the most talented people of

257

his age," or "The estate was divided among his three sons." *Between* usually refers to two things, as in "between you and me," "between two points," "between dawn and sunset."

Amount, number. Use *number,* not *amount,* in reference to units that can actually be counted:

the *amount* of indebtedness, the *number* of debts.

And etc. Because *etc. (et cetera)* means "and so forth," *and etc.* would mean "and and so forth." You should not use *etc.* to replace some exact, specific word, but if you do use it, be sure not to spell it *ect.* And remember that *etc.* requires a period after it.

Anywheres. Colloquial for *anywhere.* Similar colloquial forms are *anyways* for *anyway* or *anyhow, everywheres* for *everywhere, nowheres* for *nowhere, somewheres* for *somewhere.*

I looked for my books everywhere.
They must be hidden somewhere.

Apt to, liable to, likely to. *Apt to* implies a natural tendency. *Liable to* implies a negative outcome or result. *Likely to* suggests a strong possibility.

That car is apt to increase in value.

We are liable to have a bad leak unless we fix the roof.

The new vaccine is likely to cause a disappearance of chicken pox.

As, like. See *Like.*

As to whether. *Whether* is usually enough.

Awful, awfully. Like *aggravate,* these words have two distinct uses. In formal contexts, they mean "awe-inspiring" or "terrifying." Often in conversation and sometimes in writing of a serious nature, *awful* and *awfully* are mild intensifiers, meaning "very."

Because. See *Reason is because.*

Because of. See *Due to.*

Being that, being as how. Substandard for *because, as,* or *since.*

Beside, besides. These two prepositions are clearly distinguished by their meanings. *Beside* means "at the side of" and *besides* means "in addition to."

Lucy sits *beside* me in class.
Did anyone *besides* you see the accident?

Between. See *Among.*

Bring, take. *Bring* means to convey from a farther to a nearer place. *Take* means to convey from nearer to farther.

Bring home a loaf of bread from the store.
Take that book back to the library.

But what, but that. Colloquial for *that.*

Both sides had no doubt *that* [not *but what*] their cause was just.

Calculate, figure, reckon. These are colloquial for *imagine, consider, expect, think,* and similar words.

He must have *expected* [not *calculated*] that she might not be pleased to see him after he did not return her calls.

Can, may. *Can* suggests ability to do something. *May* is the preferred form when permission is involved.

Little Junior *can* already count to ten.
May [not *Can*] I borrow your pencil?

Can't hardly, couldn't hardly, can't scarcely, couldn't scarcely. Substandard for *can hardly, could hardly, can scarcely, could scarcely.* These are sometimes referred to as double negatives.

I *can hardly* [not *can't hardly*] believe that story.

We *could scarcely* [not *couldn't scarcely*] hear the foghorn.

Caused by. See *Due to.*

Consensus means an agreement of the majority; thus *consensus of opinion* is redundant. Say simply, "The consensus was . . . ," not, "The consensus of opinion was. . . ."

Continual, continuous. A fine distinction in meaning can be made if you remember that *continual* means "repeated regularly and frequently" and that *continuous* means "occurring without interruption," "unbroken."

Could(n't) care less. This worn-out set phrase indicating total indifference is a colloquialism. A continuing marvel of language behavior is the large number of people who insist on saying "I could care less" when they obviously mean the opposite.

Could of, would of, might of, ought to of, and so on. Substandard for *could have, would have,* and so on.

Couple, couple of. These expressions are fine for informal conversation, but not precise enough for more formal occasions. In writing, be specific. Say "three points," for example, or "four issues," rather than "a couple of points/issues."

Criteria. The singular noun is *criterion;* the plural is *criteria* or *criterions.* Such combinations as *"a criteria," "one criteria"* and *"these criterias"* are incorrect.

Data. Originally the plural form of the rarely used Latin singular *datum, data* has taken on a collective meaning so that it is often treated as a singular noun. "This data has been published" and "These data have been published" are both correct, the latter being the use customarily found in scientific or technical writing.

Different from, different than. *Different from* is generally correct. Many people object to *different than,* but others use it, especially when a clause follows, as in "Life in the Marines was different than he had expected it to be."

Their customs are *different from* [not *different than*] ours.

Life in the Marines was *different from* what he had expected it to be.

Different to, a form sometimes used by British speakers and writers, is rarely used in the United States.

Disinterested, uninterested. Many users of precise English deplore the tendency to treat these words as loose synonyms, keeping a helpful distinction between *disinterested* ("impartial," "free from bias or self-interest") and *uninterested* ("lacking in interest," "unconcerned"). Thus we would hope that a referee would be disinterested but not uninterested.

Due to, caused by, because of, owing to. *Due to* and *caused by* are used correctly after the verb *to be:*

His illness was *caused by* a virus.

The flood was *due to* the heavy spring rains.

Many people object to the use of *due to* and *caused by* adverbially at the beginning of a sentence, as in "Due to the heavy rains, the streams flooded," and "Caused by the storm, the roads were damaged." It is better to use *because of* or *owing to* in similar situations. *Due to* and *owing to* are also used correctly as an adjective modifier immediately following a noun:

Accidents *due to* excessive speed are increasing in number.

Note in the examples what variations are possible:

The streams flooded *because of* the heavy rains.

The flooding of the streams was *due to* the heavy rains.

The floods were *caused by* the rapid melting of the snow.

Emigrate, immigrate. To *emigrate* is to *leave* one region to settle in another; to *immigrate* is to *enter* a region from another one.

Enthuse. Colloquial or substandard (depending on the degree of a person's aversion to this word) for *be enthusiastic, show enthusiasm.*

The director *was enthusiastic* [not *enthused*] about her new program.

Everyday, every day. *Everyday* is an adjective meaning "ordinary." *Every day* is an adjective and noun combination.

Just wear your everyday clothes; don't dress up.

I wore those shoes almost every day last week.

Everywheres. See *Anywheres.*

Explicit, implicit. *Explicit* means "stated directly." *Implicit* means "implied," "suggested indirectly."

She explicitly told us to bring two pencils and ten pages of notebook paper.

The idea implicit in her statement was that we should come prepared to take the test.

Farther, further. Careful writers observe a distinction between these two words, reserving *farther* for distances that can actually be measured.

Tony can hit a golf ball *farther* than I can.

We must pursue this matter *further.*

Fewer, less. *Fewer* refers to numbers, *less* to quantity, extent, or degree.

Fewer [not *Less*] students are taking courses in literature this year.

Food costs *less,* but we have less money to spend.

Figure. See *Calculate.*

Fine. Colloquial, very widely used, for *well, very well.*

The boys played *well* [not *just fine*].

Graffiti. The singular form is *graffito.* In serious writing *graffiti* takes a plural verb. Avoid combinations such as "a graffiti," "this graffiti," etc.

Had(n't) ought. *Ought* does not take an auxiliary.

You *ought* [not *had ought*] to apply for a scholarship.

You *ought not* [not *hadn't ought*] to miss the lecture.

Hardly. See *Can't hardly.*

Healthy, healthful. *Healthy* means "having health," and *healthful* means "giving health." Thus a person or an animal is healthy; a climate, a food, or an activity is healthful.

Immigrate. See *Emigrate.*

Implicit. See *Explicit.*

Imply, infer. Despite the increasing tendency to use these words more or less interchangeably, it is good to preserve the distinction: *Imply* means "to say something indirectly," "to hint or suggest," and *infer* means "to draw a conclusion," "to deduce." Thus you *imply* something in what you say and *infer* something from what you hear.

Incredible, incredulous. An unbelievable *thing* is incredible; a disbelieving *person* is incredulous.

In regards to. The correct forms are *in regard to* or *as regards.*

Inside of. *Inside* or *within* is preferred in formal writing.

We stayed *inside* [not *inside of*] the barn during the storm.

The plane should arrive *within* [not *inside of*] an hour.

Irregardless. Substandard or humorous for *regardless.*

The planes bombed the area *regardless* [not *irregardless*] of consequences.

Is when, is where. The *is-when, is-where* pattern in definitions is clumsy and should be avoided. Write, for example, "An embolism is an obstruction, such as a blood clot, in the bloodstream," instead of "An embolism is where an obstruction forms in the bloodstream."

Kind, sort. These words are singular and therefore should be modified by singular modifiers. Do not write *these kind, these sort, those kind, those sort.*

Those kinds [not *those kind*] of videos sell very well.

Who could believe *that sort* [not *those sort*] of arguments?

Kinda, sorta, kind of a, sort of a. Undesirable forms.

Kind of, sort of. Colloquial for *somewhat, in some degree, almost, rather.*

They felt *somewhat* [not *sort of*] depressed.

Learn, teach. *Learn* means "to acquire knowledge"; *teach* means "to give or impart knowledge."

Ms. Brown taught [not *learned*] me Spanish.

Leave. Not to be used for *let.*

Let [not *Leave*] me carry your books for you.

Less. See *Fewer.*

Let. See *Leave.*

Let's us. The *us* is superfluous, because *let's* means "let us."

Liable to, likely to. See *Apt to.*

Like, as, as if. The use of *like* as a conjunction (in other words, to introduce a clause) is colloquial. It should be avoided in serious writing.

As [not *Like*] you were told earlier, there is a small entry fee.

She acts *as if* [not *like*] she distrusts us.

Do *as* [not *like*] I tell you.

Line. Often vague and redundant, as in "What do you read *in the line* of books?" "Don't you enjoy fishing and other sports *along that line*?" It is better to say, more directly,

What kind of books do you read?

Don't you enjoy fishing and sports like that?

Lots of, a lot of. Used informally to mean a large extent, amount, or number, a usage that is enjoying increased acceptance. This usage should be avoided in formal writing.

A great many [not *Lots of*] people vacation here.

The storms caused a great deal [not *lots of*] of damage.

All of us owe you a great deal [not *a lot*].

As one word, **alot** is still acceptable spelling.

Mad. Colloquially *mad* is often used to mean "angry." In formal English, it means "insane."

Marge was *angry* [not *mad*] because I was late.

May. See *Can.*

Media. A plural noun referring to all mass communicative agencies. The singular is *medium.* Careful writers and speakers avoid the use of *media* as a singular noun, as in "Television is an influential media." Even more objectionable is the use of *medias* as a plural.

Might of. See *Could of.*

Most. This word is the superlative form of *much* and *many* (*much, more, most; many, more, most*). Its use as a clipped form of *almost* is colloquial.

Almost [not *Most*] all of my friends work during the summer.

Nauseated, nauseous. Despite the increasingly wide use of these words as synonyms, there are still speakers and writers of precise English who insist that *nauseated* should be used to mean "suffering from or experiencing nausea" and that *nauseous* should be used only to mean "causing nausea."

Nohow. This emphatic negative is substandard.

Not all that. A basically meaningless substitute for *not very* or *not really*; it can easily become a habit.

The movie was *not very* [not *not all that*] amusing.

Nowheres. See *Anywheres.*
Number. See *Amount.*
Of. See *Could of.*
Off of. Dialectal or colloquial for *off.*

> She asked me to get *off* [not *off of*] my high horse.

OK. This form calls attention to itself in serious writing. It is appropriate only to business communications and casual speech or writing. Modern dictionaries offer several permissible forms: *OK, O.K.,* and *okay* for the singular noun; *OKs, O.K.s,* and *okays* for the plural noun; and *OK'd, OK'ing, O.K.'d, O.K.'ing, okayed,* and *okaying* for verb forms.

Ought. See *Had(n't) ought.*
Ought to of. See *Could of.*
Owing to. See *Due to.*
Party. Colloquial for *individual* in the sense of *man, woman, person.*

> A man [not *a party*] called while you were out.

Percent, percentage. Use *percent* when referring to a specific number.

> Ten percent of the class made an A.

Use *percentage* when referring to no specific number.

> A small percentage of the class made an A.

Phenomenon, phenomena. A *phenomenon* is a single observable fact or event. *Phenomena* is a plural noun. When using either, be sure to make adjectives such as *this* and *these* and all verbs agree in number.

Plenty is a noun meaning "an abundance" and is used with the preposition *of.*

> There are plenty of jobs available.

Do not use the word as an adverb meaning "very" or "quite."

> It was plenty scary in that movie.

Pretty is an informal modifier. In writing, use *quite,* or *very.*

> The flood waters were very [not *pretty*] deep.

Quote, unquote. Although these words may be needed in the oral presentation of quoted material, they have no use in written material, in which quotation marks or indentation sets off the quoted material from the text proper.

Real, really. The use of *real,* which is an adjective, to modify another adjective or an adverb is colloquial. In formal contexts *really* or *very* should be used.

> We had a *really* [not *real*] enjoyable visit.

> The motorcycle rounded the corner *very* [not *real*] fast.

Reason is because, reason is due to, reason is on account of. In serious writing, a *reason is* clause is usually completed with *that,* not with *because, due to,* or *on account of.*

> The reason they surrendered *is that* [not *because*] they were starving.

> The reason for my low grades *is that I have poor eyesight* [not *is on account of my poor eyesight*].

Reckon. See *Calculate.*
Same. The use of *same* as a pronoun, often found in legal or business writing, is inappropriate in most other types of writing.

> I received your report and look forward to reading *it* [not *the same*].

So, such. These words, when used as exclamatory intensifiers, are not appropriate in a formal context. Sentences like the following belong in informal talk: "I am *so* tired," "She is *so* pretty," or "They are having *such* a good time."

Some. Colloquial for *somewhat, a little.*

> The situation at the border is said to be *somewhat* [not *some*] improved today.

Somewheres. See *Anywheres.*
Sort. See *Kind.*
Such. See *So.*
Suppose to, use to. Although these incorrect forms are difficult to detect in spoken

English, remember that the correct written forms are *supposed to, used to.*

Sure. *Sure* is correctly used as an adjective:

We are not *sure* about her plans.
He made several *sure* investments.

Sure is colloquial when used as an adverbial substitute for *surely, extremely, certainly, indeed, very, very much.*

The examination was *surely* [not *sure*] difficult.
The lawyer's plea *certainly* [not *sure*] impressed the jury.

Sure and. See *Try and.*

Suspicion. *Suspicion* is a noun; it is not to be used as a verb in place of *suspect.*

No one *suspected* [not *suspicioned*] the victim's widow.

Swell. Not to be used as a general term of approval meaning *good, excellent, attractive, desirable,* and so on.

Take. See *Bring.*

Teach. See *Learn.*

That there, this here, those there, these here. Substandard for *that, this, those, these.*

Them. Substandard when used as an adjective.

How can you eat *those* [not *them*] parsnips?

Try and, sure and. *Try to, sure to* are the preferred forms in serious writing.

We shall *try to* [not *try and*] make your visit a pleasant one.

Be *sure to* [not *sure and*] arrive on time.

Type. Colloquial when used as a modifier of a noun. Use *type of* or *kind of.*

I usually don't enjoy that *type of* [not *type*] movie.

Uninterested. See *Disinterested.*

Unique. In its original meaning, the word meant either "the only example" or "without a like or equal." In modern use, it has also acquired an additional meaning: "unusual." In the first sense, it cannot be modified by an adjective.

As a politician, he is unique.

She gave him a unique [*very special*] pen as a present.

Many object to the use of a modifier with *unique;* in formal writing, it is best to choose some other adjective to convey the meaning "special" or "unusual."

Use to. See *Suppose to.*

Want in, want off, want out. Colloquial and dialectical forms for *want to come in, want to get off, want to go out.* Inappropriate in serious writing.

Ways. Colloquial for *way,* in such expressions as

It is just a short *distance* [not *ways*] up the canyon.

We do not have a long *way* [not *ways*] to go.

What. Substandard when used for *who, which,* or *that* as a relative pronoun in an adjective clause.

His raucous laugh is the thing *that* [not *what*] annoys me most.

When, where clauses. See *Is when.*

Where . . . at. The *at* is unnecessary. Undesirable in both speech and writing.

Where [not *Where at*] will you be at noon?

Where is your car? [Not *Where is your car at?*]

-wise. The legitimate function of this suffix to form adverbs like *clockwise* does not carry with it the license to concoct such jargon as "Entertainmentwise this town is a dud" or "This investment is very attractive long-term-capital-gainswise."

Without. Not to be used as a conjunction instead of *unless.*

He won't lend me his car *unless* [not *without*] I fill the gas tank.

Would of. See *Could of.*

NAME _____ SCORE _____

Directions: In the space at the left, write the word or phrase given in parentheses that you consider the more appropriate form to use in serious writing.

_____ 1. Did you (imply, infer) from Jim's comment that you were (suppose, supposed) to attend that dinner?
_____

_____ 2. "If we had another hour," said the foreman, "we could (try and, try to) extend that ditch a little (farther, further)."
_____

_____ 3. (Can, May) we ask some (disinterested, uninterested) party to settle the dispute between the two unions?
_____

_____ 4. Morris (sure, surely) (could have, could of) found a better investment than that old rental property.
_____

_____ 5. "(Beside, Besides) me, there isn't anyone in the company who knows (lots of, many) people in the county government.
_____

_____ 6. "(Let's, Let's us) leave early today; we haven't gone (anywhere, anywheres) out of town recently.
_____

_____ 7. There is no doubt (but what, that) (among, between) the four of us we can figure out the puzzle.
_____

_____ 8. The (amount, number) of people standing in line is (fewer, less) today than it was yesterday.
_____

_____ 9. "I'm not (real, very) (enthused, enthusiastic) about that difficult exercise class," said Marta.
_____

_____ 10. The reason I failed that test is (because, that) I lost (almost, most) all my notes when I moved.
_____

_____ 11. The hotel was such a long (way, ways) from the restaurant that we were (plenty, very) tired by the time we walked there.
_____

_____ 12. "This is (all the farther, as far as) I can go because my backpack is getting (awfully, very) heavy," said Marge.
_____

_____ 13. (Being that, Because) winter is just around the corner, we (should have, should of) stocked up on firewood.

265

_____ 14. The (continual, continuous) dripping of that faucet severely
_____ (aggravated, irritated) my mother.

_____ 15. The graduate school has established one (real, very) rigid (crite-
_____ rion, criteria) for admission to the program.

_____ 16. (Due to, Because of) the high winds, a (couple, three) people
_____ withdrew from the bicycle race.

_____ 17. What do you (figure, think) Marcia will do now that she has won
_____ that (incredible, incredulous) prize in the lottery.

_____ 18. (That, Those) kind of question makes a test (kind of, rather) dif-
_____ ficult, don't you think?

_____ 19. (Lots of, Many) students were extremely (angry, mad) because
_____ Professor Howard postponed the test.

_____ 20. "Men, we (had ought, ought) to (learn, teach) those kids to play
_____ baseball the proper way," said Mr. Ames.

Directions: Each sentence contains two italicized words or expressions. If you think that the word or expression is inappropriate in serious writing, write an acceptable form in the space at the left. If an expression is correct, write **C** in the space.

_____
_____ 1. *Due to* the heavy rains, we will have to find *somewhere's else* for soccer practice.

_____
_____ 2. *Those criteria* we *use to* employ for selecting new managers were far too loosely worded.

_____
_____ 3. *Those kind* of admissions policies *aggravated* an already bad relationship with the local high schools.

_____
_____ 4. *Lots of* students *inferred* from your absences that you intend to drop the course.

_____
_____ 5. *Being that* her GPA has fallen a long *ways* from its original high point, Sally has started to study again.

_____
_____ 6. "Jim was *suppose* to sit *beside* me at the game," said Helen, "but he had to work."

_____
_____ 7. *Let's* ask for some help; this report is *awfully* complex.

_____
_____ 8. *Can* you find out *where* Jim bought that painting *at*?

_____
_____ 9. "*Hadn't you ought* to divide that work *between* those three workers?" asked Melvin.

_____
_____ 10. If they investigate that matter *further*, I *have* no *doubt* that they will discover a political scandal.

_____
_____ 11. "*In regards to* the campaign, the candidate has *nothing in the line of* comments at this time," said the article.

_____
_____ 12. In *a couple of* major details, the mayor's platform is *different from* his opponent's.

_____
_____ 13. Marilyn does not *suspicion* that she will get *less* money next year than she received this year.

_____
_____ 14. *These data* suggest that, *irregardless* of a person's age, a low-fat diet is beneficial.

_____ 15. A set of *them* new snowshoes would *sure* be nice for this winter.
_____

_____ 16. Alice says she *wants in on* that project because there is *plenty of*
_____ money to be made in overtime.

_____ 17. The reason I called to change my reservation is *because* I must go
_____ home early *due to* a family emergency.

_____ 18. The new model of that tractor pulls *really* well, and we are *enthu-*
_____ *siastic* about buying several for the farm.

_____ 19. Jill asked to be taken *off of* that committee because *almost* all of
_____ the members skip the meetings.

_____ 20. I *should of* guessed that Rachel would act *like* she hated all the
_____ other guests.

Exercise 26 *Appropriate Use*

NAME _____   SCORE _____

Directions: In the space at the left, write the word or phrase given in parentheses that you consider the more appropriate in serious writing.

_____   1. (Let's us, Let's) move that chair a bit (farther, further) toward the
_____   front so that we you can see the speaker.

_____   2. Before we did those drills, we all (use to, used to) make a far
_____   greater (amount, number) of errors on our essays.

_____   3. (Irregardless, Regardless) of my past failures, I think I can pass
_____   (almost, most) all of the remaining tests.

_____   4. "Well," said Mary, "you acted (as if, like) you were (real, really)
_____   angered by the boss' decision."

_____   5. (Because, Being that) I lost all my books, I had (fewer, less) notes
_____   for writing my paper.

_____   6. William said, "I (can hardly, can't hardly) believe that people still
_____   sell (that kind, those kind) of inefficient engine.

_____   7. The president (suspects, suspicions) that there is an industrial
_____   spy (somewhere, somewheres) in our company.

_____   8. We all (inferred, implied) from that speech that we (hadn't
_____   ought, ought not) to expect any bonuses.

_____   9. (Because of, Due to) rising costs, there have been (lots of, many)
_____   lay-offs in the plant.

_____   10. The (party, person) who wrote that anonymous memo couldn't
_____   be anyone (beside, besides) Raymond.

_____   11. "We (should have, should of) called Mary when we didn't get an
_____   (invite, invitation) to that dinner party," said Ralph.

_____   12. This message is (suppose, supposed) to go to the coach as soon
_____   as she walks in (that, that there) door this morning.

_____ 13. Helen's plan for replanting the garden is different (from, than)
_____ yours in (a couple, two) important ways.

_____ 14. The reason Bob left the party so early is (because, that) his
_____ daughter fell (off, off of) a swing and hurt herself.

_____ 15. My watch is (kinda, almost) ruined; I'd like to know (where,
_____ where . . .) I can buy a new one (at).

_____ 16. (Can, May) you find copies of (them, those) contracts so that I
_____ can review them?

_____ 17. (In regard, In regards) to my payment, I'll (try and, try to) mail
_____ it tomorrow.

_____ 18. "An (incredible, incredulous) thing just happened," said Ron;
_____ "my sister repaid (almost, most) all the money she owed me.

_____ 19. We ate a (healthful, healthy) lunch, but I'm already (real, really)
_____ hungry.

_____ 20. Her work is (alright, adequate), but she needs to make (a signif-
_____ icant, some kind of an) improvement to earn a raise.

Directions: Each sentence contains two italicized words or expressions. If you think that a word or expression is inappropriate in serious writing, write an acceptable form in the space at the left. If you think the expression is correct, write C in the space.

_____
_____ 1. Do you know *whether* or not *this data* have been verified by the research office?

_____
_____ 2. Mr. James *can't hardly* understand why he can't find a *couple of* strong young men to mow his yard.

_____
_____ 3. If you turn *off of* Highway 270 at the second light, you'll be just a short *way* from our house.

_____
_____ 4. Jerry's work in that situation was *plenty* effective, but he is still not *real* popular with his colleagues.

_____
_____ 5. In the late 19th century, my grandfather *immigrated* from England and moved to *somewheres* near little Rock.

_____
_____ 6. "*Leave* me *try and* find a replacement for that book you lost," said Mary helpfully.

_____
_____ 7. My teacher said I made *less* errors on this last test *due to* your excellent tutoring.

_____
_____ 8. The reason we were unable to accept your *invite* to the dance is *because* we don't own tuxedos.

_____
_____ 9. Please find enclosed a memo *in regard to* changes in personnel policy and read *same* before Tuesday's meeting.

_____
_____ 10. The trainer says that we are *supposed* to run three miles this morning and then take a *healthy* nap.

_____
_____ 11. I thought her note *implied* that she *would of* come to the meeting if she had not had a previous commitment.

_____
_____ 12. *This kind of* long, boring lecture *had ought* to be banned from the campus.

_____
_____ 13. In the next announcements, be sure *to tell* people *where* they can pick up their exams *at*.

_____
_____ 14. Maureen won the essay contest because she worked *really* hard and made *a lot of* good points.

_____ 15. That novel is *like* a healthful meal; it's good for you, but it's *not*
_____   *all that* exciting.

_____ 16. If a *couple more* people had signed up, we *could of* made that trip
_____   with no problems.

_____ 17. Jane was *incredible* when she learned that she had walked *further*
_____   than any other contestant.

_____ 18. Roberta suggested, "*Let's* ask for a different evaluator, someone
_____   who is totally *uninterested.*

_____ 19. "If I *may,* I'd like to suggest that the *amount* of time for that pro-
_____   ject be limited to no more than two hours.

_____ 20. Your solution worked *just fine,* but there is no doubt *but what* it
_____   was a very unusual approach to that problem.

6 Spelling and Capitalization

Lessons, Practice Sheets, and Exercises

Lesson 27   *Spelling Rules; Words Similar in Sound*

This lesson presents spelling rules that will help you improve your written work.

Rule 1: A word ending in silent *e* generally drops the *e* before a suffix beginning with a vowel and retains the *e* before a suffix beginning with a consonant.

After *c* or *g*, if the suffix begins with *a* or *o*, the *e* is retained to preserve the soft sound of the *c* or *g*.

Drop E *before a Vowel*

become	+ ing	—becoming	hope	+ ing	—hoping
bride	+ al	—bridal	imagine	+ ary	—imaginary
conceive	+ able	—conceivable	noise	+ y	—noisy
desire	+ able	—desirable	remove	+ able	—removable
fame	+ ous	—famous	white	+ ish	—whitish
force	+ ible	—forcible	write	+ ing	—writing

Retain E *before a Consonant*

excite	+ ment	—excitement	life	+ like	—lifelike
force	+ ful	—forceful	pale	+ ness	—paleness
hope	+ less	—hopeless	sincere	+ ly	—sincerely

Retain E *after* C *or* G *if the Suffix Begins with* A *or* O

advantage	+ ous	—advantageous	notice	+ able	—noticeable
change	+ able	—changeable	outrage	+ ous	—outrageous
manage	+ able	—manageable	service	+ able	—serviceable

(See Supplement.)

Rule 2: In words with *ie* or *ei* when the sound is long *ee*, use *i* before *e* except after *c*.

Use I *before* E

apiece	frontier	priest
belief	grieve	reprieve
fiend	niece	shriek
fierce	pierce	thievery

Except after C

ceiling	conceive	perceive
conceited	deceit	receipt

The common exceptions to this rule may be easily remembered if you memorize the following sentence: Neither financier seized either species of weird leisure.

Rule 3: In words of one syllable and words accented on the last syllable, ending in a single consonant preceded by a single vowel, double the final consonant before a suffix beginning with a vowel.

Words of One Syllable—Suffix Begins with a Vowel

ban	—banned	hit	—hitting	rid	—riddance
bid	—biddable	hop	—hopping	Scot	—Scottish
dig	—digger	quit	—quitter	stop	—stoppage
drag	—dragged	["qu"-consonant]		wet	—wettest

Accented on Last Syllable—Suffix Begins with a Vowel

abhor	—abhorrence	equip	—equipping
acquit	—acquitted	occur	—occurrence
allot	—allotted	omit	—omitted
begin	—beginner	prefer	—preferring
commit	—committing	regret	—regrettable
control	—controlled	repel	—repellent

Not Accented on Last Syllable—Suffix Begins with a Vowel

differ	—different	open	—opener
happen	—happening	prefer	—preference
hasten	—hastened	sharpen	—sharpened

Suffix Begins with a Consonant

allot	—allotment	mother	—motherhood
color	—colorless	sad	—sadness
equip	—equipment	sin	—sinful

(See Supplement.)

An apparent exception to this rule affects a few words formed by the addition of *ing, ed,* or *y* to a word ending in *c*. To preserve the hard sound of the *c*, a *k* is added before the vowel of the suffix, resulting in such spellings as *frolicking, mimicked, panicked, panicky, picnicked,* and *trafficking.*

Another irregularity applies to such spellings as *quitting* and *equipped.* One might think that the consonant should not be doubled, reasoning that the final consonant is preceded by two vowels, not by a single vowel. But because *qu* is phonetically the equivalent of *kw,* the *u* is a consonant when it follows *q.* Therefore, because the final consonant is actually preceded by a single vowel, the consonant is doubled before the suffix.

Rule 4: Words ending in *y* preceded by a vowel retain the *y* before a suffix; most words ending in *y* preceded by a consonant change the *y* to *i* before a suffix.

Ending in Y Preceded by a Vowel

boy	—boyish	coy	—coyness	enjoy	—enjoying
buy	—buys	donkey	—donkeys	stay	—staying

Ending in Y Preceded by a Consonant

ally	—allies	easy	—easiest	pity	—pitiable
busy	—busily	icy	—icier	study	—studies
cloudy	—cloudiness	mercy	—merciless	try	—tried

The Y Is Unchanged in Words Like the Following:

baby	—babyish	lady	—ladylike
carry	—carrying	study	—studying

Words Similar in Sound

Accept. I should like to accept your first offer.

Except. He took everything except the rugs.

———

Advice. Free advice [noun] is usually not worth much.

Advise. Ms. Hull said she would advise [verb] me this term. (Similarly, devi*c*e [noun] and devi*s*e [verb], prophe*c*y [noun] and prophe*s*y [verb].

———

Affect. His forced jokes affect [verb] me unfavorably.

Effect. His humor has a bad effect [noun]. Let us try to effect [verb] a lasting peace.

———

All ready. They were all ready to go home.

Already. They had already left when we telephoned the house.

All together. Now that we are all together, let us talk it over.

Altogether. They were not altogether pleased with the results.

———

Altar. In this temple was an altar to the Unknown God.

Alter. One should not try to alter or escape history.

———

Ascent. The ascent to the top of the mountain was quite steep.

Assent. The judge did not give assent to our request.

———

Bare. The bare and leafless limbs of the trees were a dark gray.

Bear. He could not bear to look at the accident.

———

Breath. His breath came in short gasps at the end of the race.

Breathe. The problem is solved; you can breathe easily now.

Canvas. We used a piece of canvas to shelter us from the wind.

Canvass. The candidate wanted to canvass every person in her precinct.

Capital. A capital letter; capital gains; capital punishment; state capital.

Capitol. Workers are painting the dome of the Capitol.

Cite. He cited three good examples.

Site. The site of the new school has not been decided on.

Sight. They were awed by the sight of so much splendor.

Climactic. The climactic moment in that movie was extremely exciting.

Climatic. According to NOAA, climatic conditions in North America have not changed much over the past 100 years.

Coarse. The coarse sand blew in my face.

Course. We discussed the course to take. Of course he may come with us.

Complement. Your intelligence is a complement to your beauty.

Compliment. It is easier to pay a compliment than a bill.

Consul. Be sure to look up the American consul in Rome.

Council. He was appointed to the executive council.

Counsel. I sought counsel from my friends. They counseled moderation. He employed counsel to defend him.

Decent. The workers demanded a decent wage scale.

Descent. The descent from the mountain was uneventful.

Dissent. The voices of dissent were louder than those of approval.

Desert. Out in the lonely desert [noun— desert], he tried to desert [verb—desert] from his regiment.

Dessert. We had apple pie for dessert.

Device. The device that controls the alarm system has malfunctioned.

Devise. We should devise a new system to cope with that problem.

Die. Old habits certainly die hard.

Dye. That dye produced a strange color in that new fabric.

Dining. We eat dinner in our dining room. Dining at home is pleasant.

Dinning. Stop dinning that song into my ears!

Fair. The decision of the umpire seemed very fair.

Fare. By plane, the fare from here to Toledo is $115.67.

Formerly. He was formerly a student at Beloit College.

Formally. You must address the presiding judge formally and respectfully.

Forth. Several witnesses came forth to testify.

Fourth. We planned a picnic for the Fourth of July.

Gorilla. The zoo has built a new habitat for the gorillas.

Guerrilla. The guerrilla forces are operating in the mountains beyond the city.

Heard. I had not heard that news.

Herd. The herd of cows moved slowly toward the barn.

Hole. The hole in my sock is growing bigger every minute.

Whole. The whole office is filled with a strange odor.

Incidence. Better sanitation lowered the incidence of communicable diseases.
Incidents. Smugglers were involved in several incidents along the border.

Instance. For instance, she was always late to class.
Instants. As the car turned, those brief instants seemed like hours.

Its. Your plan has much in its favor. [Possessive of *it.*]
It's. It's too late now for excuses. [Contraction of *it is, it has.*]

Later. It is later than you think.
Latter. Of the two novels, I prefer the latter.

Lead. Can you lead [lēd—verb] us out of this jungle? Lead [lĕd—noun] is a heavy, soft, malleable metallic element.
Led. A local guide led us to the salmon fishing hole.

Loose. He has a loose tongue. The dog is loose again.
Lose. Don't lose your temper.

Meat. We did not have any meat at lunch.
Meet. We intend to meet you after lunch.
Mete. The judge will mete out the punishment tomorrow.

Passed. She smiled as she passed me. She passed the test.
Past. It is futile to try to relive the past.

Patience. The teacher has little patience for lame excuses.
Patients. Twelve patients will be discharged from the hospital today.

Personal. Write him a personal letter.
Personnel. The morale of our company's personnel is high.

Pore. For hours they pored over the mysterious note.
Pour. Ms. Cook poured hot water into the teapot.

Precede. The Secret Service agents always precede the President when he enters a building.
Proceed. They all left the building and proceeded immediately to the parking lot.

Precedence. Tax reform takes precedence over all other legislative matters.
Precedents. The judge quoted three precedents to justify his ruling.

Presence. We are honored by your presence.
Presents. The child received dozens of Christmas presents.

Principal. The principal of a school; the principal [chief] industry; the principal and the interest.
Principle. He is a man of high principles.

Quiet. You must keep quiet.
Quite. The weather was quite good all week.

Rain. A soaking rain would help our crops greatly.
Reign. Samuel Pepys was briefly imprisoned during the reign of William III.
Rein. Keep a tight rein when you ride this spirited horse.

Right. Take a right turn at Oak Street.
Rite. Taking that course is a rite of passage for many students.
Write. Please write me a letter when you arrive.

Scene. The last scene in that movie was exceptionally touching.
Seen. I had not seen Frank for two weeks.

Sense. That statement makes a great deal of sense to me.
Since. Ten more people have arrived since we got here this morning.
Scents. The scents of those flowers are not easy to distinguish.

Sent. We sent a copy of the report to you yesterday.
Cent. We won't pay another cent.

Shone. The cat's eyes shone in the dark.
Shown. He hasn't shown us his best work.

Stationary. The benches were stationary and could not be moved.
Stationery. She wrote a letter on hotel stationery.

Statue. It was a statue of a pioneer.
Stature. Athos was a man of gigantic stature.
Statute. The law may be found in the 1917 book of statutes.

Than. She sings better than I.
Then. He screamed; then he fainted.

Their. It wasn't their fault. [Possessive pronoun.]
There. You won't find any gold there. [Adverb of place.]
They're. They're sure to be disappointed. [Contraction of *they are*.]

Thorough. We must first give the old cabin a thorough [adjective] cleaning.

Threw. The catcher threw the ball back to the pitcher.
Through. The thief had entered through [preposition] a hole in the roof.

To. Be sure to speak to her. [Preposition.]
Too. He is far too old for you. [Adverb.]
Two. The membership fee is only two dollars. [Adjective.]

Waist. She wore a beautiful silver belt around her waist.
Waste. Save every scrap; don't let anything go to waste.

Weather. The weather last week was very cold.
Whether. Do you know whether Jim has arrived?

Whose. Whose book is this? [Possessive pronoun.]
Who's. I wonder who's with her now. [Contraction of *who is.*]

Your. I like your new car. [Possessive pronoun.]
You're. You're not nervous, are you? [Contraction of *you are.*]

Supplement

Rule 1: A few common adjectives with the suffix *able* have two correct spellings:

likable/likeable, lovable/loveable, movable/moveable, sizable/sizeable, usable/useable

Rule 3: Dictionaries show two spellings for the *ed* and *ing* forms (and a few other derived forms) of dozens of verbs ending in single consonants preceded by single vowels. In general, the single-consonant spelling is usually found in American printing; some of the dictionaries label the double-consonant spelling a British preference.

biased/biassed, canceling/cancelling, counselor/counsellor, diagraming/diagramming, equaled/equalled, marvelous/marvellous, modeled/modelled, totaling/totalling, traveler/traveller

NAME _____ SCORE _____

Directions: Each of the following sentences contains three italicized words, one of which is misspelled. Underline each misspelled word and write it, correctly spelled, in the space at the left.

_____ 1. Two *different pieces* of *equiptment* are needed to complete that part of the paint job.

_____ 2. *Accept* for Audrey, everyone in the club had a *preference* for that new *colorless* cola drink.

_____ 3. The sailmaker will *alter* that piece of *canvass* to make it run *past* the end of the cockpit.

_____ 4. The *opening* of that *writting* lesson was *altogether* too difficult for most people in the class.

_____ 5. "Is it *conceivable* that Tom can do a *thorough* job in the time *alloted*?" asked Andrea.

_____ 6. Two of the men are *too* short to play the *role* opposite Ms. France, who is *extremly* tall.

_____ 7. A *removable* cover would be a *desireable* feature for a billiards table, if it is not *excessively* expensive.

_____ 8. The architects will *advice* the board about selecting a *site* for the stable for the *donkeys.*

_____ 9. It is *regretable* that we do not have the *capital* needed to fund the construction of a new *dining* hall.

_____ 10. Jan's *references* made her the *preffered* candidate; therefore, the *personnel* office offered her the job.

_____ 11. Any change in our *hireing policies* seems *unlikely* at this time.

_____ 12. One of Raymond's favorite *activities* is a *leisurely* walk along the lakeshore among *it's* beautiful trees.

_____ 13. After the two *incidence,* the *duties* of the *cashiers* were simplified considerably.

279

_____ 14. "*Your* not likely to find better *opportunities* for *studying* migratory birds," said the guide.

_____ 15. *There fourth* attempt to climb the mountain failed at the *iciest* part of the trail.

_____ 16. New cars are *fitted* with very *servicable batteries*.

_____ 17. She was an *adorable* baby, but she seemed to *loose* all her charming *qualities* as she grew older.

_____ 18. The firefighters made the difficult *dissent* from the top floor by *rappelling* down the exterior *past* the fire zone.

_____ 19. Anne has *committed* herself to taking an *extremely* technical *coarse* in mechanical engineering.

_____ 20. One of the *presence* Marty *received* for his birthday contained large *quantities* of various chocolate candies.

_____ 21. Winning that tournament against such *fierce* competitors was *quiet* an *achievement*.

_____ 22. The *principle* reason Arline is *quitting* that job is that she finds it very *boring*.

_____ 23. The people *living* on Shorewood Road hope that the city *counsel* will provide funds for *repaving* its surface.

_____ 24. All the team members had a different reaction to the *weird, unforgetable occurrences* at the season's end.

_____ 25. The students who took that course have *shone* a *noticeable improvement* in their math scores.

_____ 26. *Latter* that day the three *buddies* gathered at the *desert* campsite for a steak dinner.

_____ 27. In his *journeys* around the West, Martin collected large *quantities* of *fascinateing* relics.

_____ 28. "Those were the *noisiest*, most *irritable* children we've ever had *picnicing* with us," said the guide.

_____ 29. The race leaders were *adversely effected* by the *changeable* winds and the high waves.

_____ 30. In all *likelihood* this year's team will *lose* more games *then* last year's.

NAME _____   SCORE _____

Directions: Each of the following sentences contains three italicized words, one of which is misspelled. Underline each misspelled word and write it, correctly spelled, in the space at the left.

_____   1. Intensive *studies* of that problem by *you're committee* have provided no solution up to this point.

_____   2. *Unmanageable* salary demands by that *fameous* player did not cause the owner to *alter* her position.

_____   3. I do not know *whose* book that is *lying forgoten* on our living room table.

_____   4. The *changable* weather did not have any great *effect* on the size of the crowd *coming* to see the game.

_____   5. *Writting* reports is fast *becoming* the only way people use *their* computers.

_____   6. "Wally, for *instance,* is only the *forth* person today to ask for the *allotted* travel money," said Al.

_____   7. *Happyness* and joy *reigned* in the office after Mr. Alcott explained the *desirable* terms of the contract.

_____   8. Those *presence* at the birthday party produced a *noisy* kind of *excitement* among the children.

_____   9. A *lifelike statue* of the three boyish heroes of the *dessert* war was unveiled today.

_____   10. *Dinning* in our ears through the entire morning was the *altogether* horrible sound of the *begining* trumpet class.

_____   11. Any *descent* effort on her part probably would have earned a *different* response from the *hopeful* crowd.

_____   12. We *poured* over our notes for hours, but we found nothing *notably* important about work *stoppages*.

_____   13. Does new federal law take *precedents* over *personnel* policies *formerly* in effect in our company?

_____ 14. Denice seemed *knowledgeable* about computers, but she has *shown* no ability at *compilling* reports.

_____ 15. After the *festivities* my *neice* took my wife and me out for a *quiet* meal at a local restaurant.

_____ 16. The new *management counsel* has met several times but has *expressed* no opinion on quality control.

_____ 17. The *studious priest* went to the *capital* building to testify in the hearings.

_____ 18. "Jim *denies* that his view of the incident is *biased* by his *earlyer* experiences," said Yolanda.

_____ 19. The *attorneys councilled* us to move rapidly to correct that *regrettable* mistake.

_____ 20. Everyone *complimented* the women in the *brideal* party for the beauty of their *dresses.*

_____ 21. We replaced the office *stationary* because our new printer is not *equipped* to handle odd-sized *envelopes.*

_____ 22. The crew is *all ready removing* the tarpaulin although the rain has not yet completely *stopped.*

_____ 23. We were *lead* to *believe* that we had not used up our *allotment* of funds for studying the election results.

_____ 24. If Jim is forced to choose between his *studies* and a nap, he *usualy* chooses the *latter.*

_____ 25. As a beginning golfer, Julie *preferred coarses* that had the *easiest* finishing holes.

_____ 26. The *exciteable* crowd responded *immediately* to the *imaginative* story told by the lecturer.

_____ 27. The staff has made every *conceivable* effort to find a more *servicable copier* for the office.

_____ 28. Isn't that *they're equipment gathering* dust on that shelf in the back room?

_____ 29. No one is *happier then* Joan about the *arrival* of the new office manager.

_____ 30. A person of your *statute* in the community could *easily* obtain *complimentary* tickets to that playoff game.

Lesson 28 *Plurals and Capitals*

This lesson covers the formation of plurals and the conventions for using capitals.

Plurals

Plurals of most nouns are regularly formed by the addition of *s*. But if the singular noun ends in an *s* sound *(s, sh, ch, x, z), es* is added to form a new syllable in pronunciation:

crab, crabs	foe, foes	kiss, kisses	tax, taxes
lamp, lamps	box, boxes	church, churches	lass, lasses

Nouns ending in *y* form plurals according to Rule 4. (See Lesson 27.)

toy, toys	army, armies	fly, flies	attorney, attorneys
key, keys	lady, ladies	sky, skies	monkey, monkeys

Some words ending in *o* (including all musical terms and all words having a vowel preceding the *o*) form their plurals with *s*. But many others take *es:*

alto, altos	folio, folios	tomato, tomatoes
piano, pianos	hero, heroes	potato, potatoes

For several nouns ending in *o,* most modern dictionaries give both forms. Here are some examples, printed in the order they are found in most dictionaries. The first spelling is the more common one:

banjos, banjoes	frescoes, frescos	lassos, lassoes	volcanoes, volcanos
buffaloes, buffalos	grottoes, grottos	mottoes, mottos	zeros, zeroes
cargoes, cargos	halos, haloes	tornadoes, tornados	

Some nouns ending in *f* or *fe* merely add *s;* some change *f* or *fe* to *ves* in the plural; and a few *(hoofs/hooves, scarfs/scarves, wharves/wharfs)* use either form. Use your dictionary to make sure:

leaf, leaves	life, lives	half, halves	wolf, wolves
roof, roofs	safe, safes	gulf, gulfs	elf, elves

A few nouns have the same form for singular and plural. A few have irregular plurals:

deer, deer	ox, oxen	child, children	goose, geese
sheep, sheep	man, men	foot, feet	mouse, mice

Many words of foreign origin use two plurals; some do not. Always check in your dictionary:

alumna, alumnae
alumnus, alumni
analysis, analyses
appendix, appendixes, appendices
basis, bases
beau, beaus, beaux
curriculum, curriculums, curricula
memorandum, memorandums, memoranda
tableau, tableaus, tableaux

bon mot, bons mots
crisis, crises
criterion, criteria
datum, data
thesis, theses
focus, focuses, foci
fungus, funguses, fungi
index, indexes, indices

Note: Do *not* use an apostrophe to form the plural of either a common or a proper noun.

Wrong: Our neighbor's, the Allen's and the Murray's, recently bought new Honda's.
Right: Our neighbors, the Allens and the Murrays, recently bought new Hondas.

Capitals

A capital letter is used for the first letter of the first word of any sentence, for the first letter of a proper noun, and often for the first letter of an adjective derived from a proper noun. Following are some reminders about situations that cause confusion for some writers.

1. Capitalize the first word of every sentence, every quoted sentence or fragment, and every transitional fragment. (See Lesson 14.)

   The building needs repairs. How much will it cost? Please answer me.
   Mr. James said, "We'll expect your answer soon." She replied, "Of course."
   And now to conclude.

2. Capitalize proper nouns and most adjectives derived from them. A proper noun designates by name an individual person, place, or thing that is a member of a group or class. Do not capitalize common nouns, which are words naming a group or class:

   Doris Powers, woman; France, country; Tuesday, day; January, month; Christmas Eve, holiday; Shorewood High School, high school; Carleton College, college; *Mauretania,* ship; Fifth Avenue, boulevard; White House, residence

   Elizabethan drama, Restoration poetry, Chinese peasants, Indian reservation, Red Cross assistance

3. Do not capitalize nouns and derived forms that, although originally proper nouns, have acquired special meanings. When in doubt, consult your dictionary:

   a set of china; a bohemian existence; plaster of paris; pasteurized milk; a mecca for golfers; set in roman type, not italics

4. Capitalize names of religions, references to deities, and most words having religious significance:

   Bible, Baptist, Old Testament, Holy Writ, Jewish, Catholic, Sermon on the Mount, Koran, Talmud

5. Capitalize titles of persons when used with the person's name. When the title is used alone, capitalize it only when it stands for a specific person of high rank:

> I spoke briefly to Professor Jones. He is a professor of history.
> We visited the late President Johnson's ranch in Texas.
> Jerry is president of our art club.
> Tonight the president will appear on national television.

6. Capitalize names denoting family relationship but not when they are preceded by a possessive. This rule is equivalent to saying that you capitalize when the word serves as a proper noun:

> At that moment Mother, Father, and Aunt Lucy entered the room.
> My mother, father, and aunt are very strict about some things.

7. Capitalize points of the compass when they refer to actual regions but not when they refer to directions:

> Before we moved to the West, we lived in the South for a time.
> You drive three miles west and then turn north on the Pacific Highway.

Do not capitalize adjectives of direction modifying countries or states:

> From central Finland the group had emigrated to northern Michigan.

8. Capitalize names of academic subjects as they would appear in college catalog listings, but in ordinary writing capitalize only names of languages:

> I intend to register for History 322 and Sociology 188.
> Last year I took courses in history, sociology, German, and Latin.

9. In titles of books, short stories, plays, essays, and poems, capitalize the first word and all other words except the articles *(a, an, the)* and short prepositions and conjunctions. (See Lesson 19 for the use of italics and quotation marks with titles.)

> Last semester I wrote reports on the following: Shaw's *The Intelligent Woman's Guide to Socialism and Capitalism,* Joyce's *A Portrait of the Artist as a Young Man,* Pirandello's *Six Characters in Search of an Author,* Poe's "The Fall of the House of Usher," Yeats's "An Irish Airman Foresees His Death," Frost's "Stopping by Woods on a Snowy Evening," and Muriel Rukeyser's "The Soul and Body of John Brown."

Note: Traditionally, a capital letter begins every line of poetry. This convention, however, is not always followed by modern poets; when you quote poetry, be sure to copy exactly the capitalization used by the author.

NAME _____   SCORE _____

Directions: Write the plural form or forms for each of the following words. When in doubt, consult your dictionary. When two forms are given, write both of them.

1. ally   _____   _____

2. alumna   _____   _____

3. axis   _____   _____

4. beau   _____   _____

5. box   _____   _____

6. cameo   _____   _____

7. cookie   _____   _____

8. cupful   _____   _____

9. diagnosis   _____   _____

10. handkerchief   _____   _____

11. lackey   _____   _____

12. lasso   _____   _____

13. louse   _____   _____

14. man-of-war   _____   _____

15. memento   _____   _____

16. mongoose   _____   _____

17. princess   _____   _____

18. referendum   _____   _____

19. saleswoman   _____   _____

20. scarf   _____   _____

21. sheaf   _____   _____

22. Thomas   _____   _____

23. tomato   _____   _____

24. turkey   _____   _____

25. wolf   _____   _____

Directions: The following sentences contain fifty numbered words. If you think the word is correctly capitalized, write **C** in the space at the left with the corresponding number. If you think the word should not be capitalized, write **W** in the space.

_____ _____ _____ (1) The Secretary of the local Chamber Of Commerce directed
1   2   3   1   2   3   4

_____ _____ _____   us to the Museum Of Business And Industry, telling us to
4   5   6   5   6   7   8   9

_____ _____ _____   go through Prospect Park, turn left on Underwood Avenue,
7   8   9   10   11   12   13

_____ _____ _____   and walk three blocks North.
10 11 12   14

_____ _____ _____ (2) Ms. Edith Leary, who taught me Latin and Social Studies
13 14 15   15   16   17

_____ _____ _____   at North Bend Junior High School, is engaged to marry a
16 17 18   18   19   20   21   22

_____ _____ _____   young Professor of Journalism at the local Community
19 20 21   23   24   25

_____ _____ _____   College; he recently earned a Ph.D. degree from Princeton.
22 23 24   26   27 28   29

_____ _____ _____ (3) On New Year's Day Uncle Frank and two of my Cousins
25 26 27   30   31   32   33   34

_____ _____ _____   joined us, and we watched the broadcast of the
28 29 30

_____ _____ _____   Tournament Of Roses parade and the Rose Bowl football
31 32 33   35   36   37   38   39

_____ _____ _____   game.
34 35 36

_____ _____ _____ (4) Before dismissing the class, Professor Bacon told us that
37 38 39   40

_____ _____ _____   over the Christmas Holiday We should all read Joyce's
40 41 42   41   42

_____ _____ _____   *Portrait Of The Artist As A Young Man.*
43 44 45   43   44 45   46   47 48   49   50

_____ _____ _____
46 47 48

_____ _____
49 50

NAME _____ SCORE _____

Directions: Write the plural form or forms for each of the following words. When in doubt, consult your dictionary. When two forms are given, write both of them.

1. alley _____ _____

2. alumnus _____ _____

3. basketful _____ _____

4. battery _____ _____

5. brother-in-law _____ _____

6. cherry _____ _____

7. crisis _____ _____

8. folio _____ _____

9. fowl _____ _____

10. freshman _____ _____

11. gaff _____ _____

12. half _____ _____

13. index _____ _____

14. loaf _____ _____

15. mango _____ _____

16. mass _____ _____

17. moose _____ _____

18. oaf _____ _____

19. placebo _____ _____

20. potato _____ _____

21. Smith _____ _____

22. tableau _____ _____

23. terminus _____ _____

24. volley _____ _____

25. waitress _____ _____

Directions: The following sentences contain fifty numbered words. If you think the word is correctly capitalized, write **C** in the space at the left with the corresponding numbers. If you think the word should not be capitalized, write **W** in the space.

1	2	3
4	5	6
7	8	9
10	11	12
13	14	15
16	17	18
19	20	21
22	23	24
25	26	27
28	29	30
31	32	33
34	35	36
37	38	39
40	41	42
43	44	45
46	47	48
49	50	

(1) The Librarian told me that, although there are other good Encyclopedias, the *Britannica* and the *Americana* are the ones most often used by Juniors and Seniors at our High School.
(1 = Librarian, 2 = Encyclopedias, 3 = Britannica, 4 = Americana, 5 = Juniors, 6 = Seniors, 7 = High, 8 = School)

(2) The speaker continued: "The Polynesians of the South Pacific were responsive, for the most part, to the teachings of the early Christian Missionaries."
(9 = The, 10 = Polynesians, 11 = South, 12 = Pacific, 13 = Christian, 14 = Missionaries)

(3) At Horace Mann Junior High School I first read Frost's "Stopping By Woods On A Snowy Evening" in an eighth-grade Literature class.
(15 = Horace, 16 = Mann, 17 = Junior, 18 = High, 19 = School, 20 = Stopping, 21 = By, 22 = Woods, 23 = On, 24 = A, 25 = Snowy, 26 = Evening, 27 = Literature)

(4) Last weekend I took a bus to the Twin Cities and visited Aunt Laura, Uncle Winston, and two Cousins I had never met before.
(28 = Twin, 29 = Cities, 30 = Aunt, 31 = Uncle, 32 = Cousins)

(5) Following Professor Logan's advice, I registered for English 67, Zoology 132, and an introductory course in Journalism.
(33 = Professor, 34 = English, 35 = Zoology, 36 = Journalism)

(6) A retired Professor whom Father knows recommended that I go to some small College in the East and concentrate on Liberal Arts courses during my first two years.
(37 = Professor, 38 = Father, 39 = College, 40 = East, 41 = Liberal, 42 = Arts)

(7) At our Girl Scout meeting last week, Amy Jenkin's Mother showed us a beautiful blanket she had bought last Winter in Southwestern Arizona at a store that sells products made by Native Americans.
(43 = Girl, 44 = Scout, 45 = Mother, 46 = Winter, 47 = Southwestern, 48 = Arizona, 49 = Native, 50 = Americans)

Lesson 29 *Spelling List*

This list includes words frequently misspelled by high-school and college students. Each word is repeated to show its syllabic division. Whether this list is used for individual study and review or in some kind of organized class activity, your method of studying should be the following: (1) Learn to pronounce the word syllable by syllable. Some of your trouble in spelling may come from incorrect pronunciation. (2) Copy the word carefully, forming each letter as plainly as you can. Some of your trouble may come from bad handwriting. (3) Pronounce the word carefully again. (4) On a separate sheet of paper, write the word from memory, check your spelling with the correct spelling before you, and, if you have misspelled the word, repeat the learning process.

abbreviate	ab-bre-vi-ate	audience	au-di-ence
absence	ab-sence	auxiliary	aux-il-ia-ry
accidentally	ac-ci-den-tal-ly	awkward	awk-ward
accommodate	ac-com-mo-date	barbarous	bar-ba-rous
accompanying	ac-com-pa-ny-ing	basically	ba-si-cal-ly
accomplish	ac-com-plish	beneficial	ben-e-fi-cial
accumulate	ac-cu-mu-late	boundaries	bound-a-ries
acknowledge	ac-knowl-edge	Britain	Brit-ain
acquaintance	ac-quaint-ance	bureaucracy	bu-reauc-ra-cy
acquire	ac-quire	business	busi-ness
across	a-cross	calendar	cal-en-dar
additive	ad-di-tive	candidate	can-di-date
admissible	ad-mis-si-ble	cassette	cas-sette
aggravate	ag-gra-vate	category	cat-e-go-ry
always	al-ways	cemetery	cem-e-ter-y
amateur	am-a-teur	certain	cer-tain
among	a-mong	chosen	cho-sen
analysis	a-nal-y-sis	commission	com-mis-sion
analytical	an-a-lyt-i-cal	committee	com-mit-tee
apartheid	a-part-heid	communicate	com-mu-ni-cate
apparatus	ap-pa-ra-tus	communism	com-mu-nism
apparently	ap-par-ent-ly	comparative	com-par-a-tive
appearance	ap-pear-ance	competent	com-pe-tent
appreciate	ap-pre-ci-ate	competition	com-pe-ti-tion
appropriate	ap-pro-pri-ate	completely	com-plete-ly
approximately	ap-prox-i-mate-ly	compulsory	com-pul-so-ry
arctic	arc-tic	computer	com-put-er
argument	ar-gu-ment	concede	con-cede
arithmetic	a-rith-me-tic	condominium	con-do-min-i-um
association	as-so-ci-a-tion	conference	con-fer-ence
astronaut	as-tro-naut	confidentially	con-fi-den-tial-ly
athletics	ath-let-ics	conscience	con-science
attendance	at-tend-ance	conscientious	con-sci-en-tious

conscious	con-scious	foreign	for-eign
consistent	con-sist-ent	forty	for-ty
continuous	con-tin-u-ous	frantically	fran-ti-cal-ly
controversial	con-tro-ver-sial	fundamentally	fun-da-men-tal-ly
convenient	con-ven-ient	generally	gen-er-al-ly
counterfeit	coun-ter-feit	ghetto	ghet-to
criticism	crit-i-cism	government	gov-ern-ment
criticize	crit-i-cize	graffiti	graf-fi-ti
curiosity	cu-ri-os-i-ty	grammar	gram-mar
curriculum	cur-ric-u-lum	grievous	griev-ous
decision	de-ci-sion	guarantee	guar-an-tee
definitely	def-i-nite-ly	guerrilla	guer-ril-la
describe	de-scribe	harass	ha-rass
description	de-scrip-tion	height	height
desperate	des-per-ate	hindrance	hin-drance
dictionary	dic-tion-ar-y	humorous	hu-mor-ous
difference	dif-fer-ence	hurriedly	hur-ried-ly
dilapidated	di-lap-i-dat-ed	hypocrisy	hy-poc-ri-sy
dinosaur	di-no-saur	imagination	im-ag-i-na-tion
disappear	dis-ap-pear	immediately	im-me-di-ate-ly
disappoint	dis-ap-point	impromptu	im-promp-tu
disastrous	dis-as-trous	incidentally	in-ci-den-tal-ly
discipline	dis-ci-pline	incredible	in-cred-i-ble
dissatisfied	dis-sat-is-fied	independence	in-de-pend-ence
dissident	dis-si-dent	indispensable	in-dis-pen-sa-ble
dissipate	dis-si-pate	inevitable	in-ev-i-ta-ble
doesn't	does-n't	influential	in-flu-en-tial
dormitory	dor-mi-to-ry	initiative	in-i-ti-a-tive
during	dur-ing	intelligence	in-tel-li-gence
efficient	ef-fi-cient	intentionally	in-ten-tion-al-ly
eligible	el-i-gi-ble	intercede	in-ter-cede
eliminate	e-lim-i-nate	interesting	in-ter-est-ing
embarrass	em-bar-rass	interpretation	in-ter-pre-ta-tion
eminent	em-i-nent	interrupt	in-ter-rupt
emphasize	em-pha-size	irrelevant	ir-rel-e-vant
enthusiastic	en-thu-si-as-tic	irresistible	ir-re-sist-i-ble
entrepreneur	en-tre-pre-neur	irritation	ir-ri-ta-tion
environment	en-vi-ron-ment	knowledge	knowl-edge
equipment	e-quip-ment	laboratory	lab-o-ra-to-ry
equivalent	e-quiv-a-lent	laser	la-ser
especially	es-pe-cial-ly	legitimate	le-git-i-mate
exaggerated	ex-ag-ger-at-ed	library	li-brar-y
exceed	ex-ceed	lightning	light-ning
excellent	ex-cel-lent	literature	lit-er-a-ture
exceptionally	ex-cep-tion-al-ly	livelihood	live-li-hood
exhaust	ex-haust	loneliness	lone-li-ness
existence	ex-ist-ence	maintenance	main-te-nance
exorbitant	ex-or-bi-tant	marriage	mar-riage
experience	ex-pe-ri-ence	mathematics	math-e-mat-ics
explanation	ex-pla-na-tion	memento	me-men-to
extraordinary	ex-traor-di-nar-y	miniature	min-i-a-ture
extremely	ex-treme-ly	miscellaneous	mis-cel-la-ne-ous
familiar	fa-mil-iar	mischievous	mis-chie-vous
fascinate	fas-ci-nate	misspelled	mis-spelled
February	Feb-ru-ar-y	mortgage	mort-gage

mysterious	mys-te-ri-ous	remembrance	re-mem-brance
naturally	nat-u-ral-ly	repetition	rep-e-ti-tion
necessary	nec-es-sar-y	representative	rep-re-sent-a-tive
ninety	nine-ty	respectfully	re-spect-ful-ly
ninth	ninth	respectively	re-spec-tive-ly
nowadays	now-a-days	restaurant	res-tau-rant
nuclear	nu-cle-ar	rhetoric	rhet-o-ric
obedience	o-be-di-ence	rhythm	rhythm
oblige	o-blige	ridiculous	ri-dic-u-lous
obstacle	ob-sta-cle	robot	ro-bot
occasionally	oc-ca-sion-al-ly	sacrilegious	sac-ri-le-gious
occurrence	oc-cur-rence	sandwich	sand-wich
omission	o-mis-sion	satellite	sat-el-lite
opportunity	op-por-tu-ni-ty	satisfactorily	sat-is-fac-to-ri-ly
optimistic	op-ti-mis-tic	schedule	sched-ule
original	o-rig-i-nal	scientific	sci-en-tif-ic
pamphlet	pam-phlet	secretary	sec-re-tar-y
parallel	par-al-lel	separately	sep-a-rate-ly
parliament	par-lia-ment	sergeant	ser-geant
particularly	par-tic-u-lar-ly	significant	sig-nif-i-cant
partner	part-ner	similar	sim-i-lar
pastime	pas-time	sophomore	soph-o-more
performance	per-form-ance	spaghetti	spa-ghet-ti
permissible	per-mis-si-ble	specifically	spe-cif-i-cal-ly
perseverance	per-se-ver-ance	specimen	spec-i-men
perspiration	per-spi-ra-tion	speech	speech
persuade	per-suade	strictly	strict-ly
politics	pol-i-tics	successful	suc-cess-ful
possession	pos-ses-sion	superintendent	su-per-in-tend-ent
practically	prac-ti-cal-ly	supersede	su-per-sede
preceding	pre-ced-ing	surprise	sur-prise
prejudice	prej-u-dice	suspicious	sus-pi-cious
preparation	prep-a-ra-tion	syllable	syl-la-ble
prevalent	prev-a-lent	synonymous	syn-on-y-mous
privilege	priv-i-lege	synthetic	syn-thet-ic
probably	prob-a-bly	technology	tech-nol-o-gy
procedure	pro-ce-dure	temperament	tem-per-a-ment
proceed	pro-ceed	temperature	tem-per-a-ture
processor	pro-ces-sor	together	to-geth-er
professional	pro-fes-sion-al	tragedy	trag-e-dy
professor	pro-fes-sor	truly	tru-ly
pronunciation	pro-nun-ci-a-tion	twelfth	twelfth
propaganda	prop-a-gan-da	unanimous	u-nan-i-mous
psychiatrist	psy-chi-a-trist	undoubtedly	un-doubt-ed-ly
psychological	psy-cho-log-i-cal	unnecessarily	un-nec-es-sar-i-ly
pursue	pur-sue	until	un-til
quantity	quan-ti-ty	usually	usu-al-ly
questionnaire	ques-tion-naire	various	var-i-ous
quizzes	quiz-zes	vegetable	veg-e-ta-ble
realize	re-al-ize	video	vid-e-o
really	re-al-ly	village	vil-lage
recognize	rec-og-nize	villain	vil-lain
recommend	rec-om-mend	Wednesday	Wednes-day
regard	re-gard	whether	wheth-er
religious	re-li-gious	wholly	whol-ly

NAME _____ SCORE _____

Directions: Each sentence contains two words from the first half of the spelling list. In each one of these words at least one letter is missing. Write the words, correctly spelled, in the spaces at the left.

_____   1. This election our can—date for mayor is facing very weak
_____   comp—tition.

_____   2. The cost of the new equip—ent for the factory will be
_____   ex—rbitant.

_____   3. Excessive cutting of the forests has had a disast—us effect on the
_____   envi—nment.

_____   4. Our tourist group was dis—pointed with the ac—modations
_____   provided at the resort.

_____   5. The workmen did an excel—nt job of removing the graf—ti that
_____   had been spray-painted on the bare wall.

_____   6. After two lengthy confe—nces the representatives of the two war-
_____   ring tribes settled their main dif—nces.

_____   7. All of us are enthus—tic about the new series of for—gn films
_____   being shown at the local cinema.

_____   8. Martha was slightly embar—sed by her husband's attempt to tell
_____   the group what he thought was a hum—us story.

_____   9. A person is not elig—ble for this position if he or she is more
_____   than fo—ty years old.

_____ 10. In a bus—ess letter ordinary words will be written out in full, not
_____   ab—viated.

_____ 11. Many local residents crit—ized the mayor for his appear—nce at
_____   an environmental rally.

_____ 12. In her younger days she had participated in many ath—etic
_____   events, at a strictly amat—r level, of course.

_____ 13. Jerome counted am—ng his a—uaintances several actors and
_____   writers.

_____ 14. We had several severe snowstorms dur—ng the month of
_____   Feb—ary.

_____ 15. I al—ays try to attend every meeting of the hospitality com—tee.
_____

_____ 16. In the ab—ence of the regular teacher, dis—pline in the class-
_____   room became quite lax.

_____ 17. Many members of the aud—nce were clearly dis—tisfied with
_____   the performance of the substitute singers.

_____ 18. In the seventh grade Tidwell's favorite subjects were arith—tic
_____   and English gram—r.

_____ 19. The ambassador im—diately notified her gover—ent of the new
_____   development.

_____ 20. Ms. Cromwell gives her students contin—us practice in using the
_____   unabridged diction—y.

_____ 21. Ms. Lee closed her remarks with an approp—ate reminder:
_____   "Remember, children, curi—ity has killed many a cat."

_____ 22. You will find this free desk calen—r very conv—nt for recording
_____   your appointments.

_____ 23. The foreman conc—ded the fact that Lucas had been a hard-
_____   working and comp—tent assistant.

_____ 24. The clumsy, a—ward boy accident—y dropped the heavy wrench
_____   on his foot.

_____ 25. Draper used nothing except famil—r, worn-out argu—ents in
_____   his debate with the reigning champion.

Exercise 29   *Spelling*

NAME _____   SCORE _____

Directions: Each sentence contains three italicized words from the first half of the spelling list. One of the three words is misspelled. Underline the misspelled word and write it, correctiy spelled, in the space at the left.

_____ 1. The side wall of the *delapidated* shed was almost *completely* covered with *graffiti*.

_____ 2. Any *conscientious* student realizes that a *dictionery* is a *convenient* source of useful information.

_____ 3. *Attendance* at our lectures in *February* is *allways* quite low because of the bad weather.

_____ 4. *During* the demonstration an *awkward* lab assistant dropped a piece of *equiptment* and broke it.

_____ 5. Dr. Albertson *acknowledged* that some students find *compulsery* military training *beneficial*.

_____ 6. A *foreign* student told the *conferrence* participants of the *experiences* she had when the rioting began.

_____ 7. All of us were *fascinated* by the *impromtu* speech given by the *eminent* critic.

_____ 8. The *harassed* teacher was making a *desparate* attempt to maintain *discipline* in his overcrowded classroom.

_____ 9. The *embarrassed entrepreneur* gave the stockholders an unsatisfactory *explaination* for the decline in profits.

_____ 10. *Generally* speaking, Mark's father *dosen't* approve of any new *government* regulation.

_____ 11. Cynthia's *heighth certainly* should make her *eligible* to be a member of the junior-class basketball team.

_____ 12. Mr. Conway *hurriedly* explained that he has never numbered the accused man *among* his *acquaintances*.

———————————— 13. His main *arguement* is that *athletic competition* between the two schools is a good thing.

———————————— 14. The *audiance*, I'm afraid, did not fully *appreciate* the work done by the *amateur* actors.

———————————— 15. Craig's *conscience* should bother him because of the many *absence* reports he has *accummulated* this semester.

———————————— 16. The youngsters *especially* enjoyed Ms. Lane's *humorous discription* of her broken-down cabin at Lake Wilderness.

———————————— 17. *Approximately* three hundred students live in the *dormitory*, although it was designed to *accomodate* only two hundred.

———————————— 18. The publisher is *franticly* trying to locate *forty* pages that mysteriously *disappeared* from the manuscript.

———————————— 19. *Apparently* someone had *accidently* spilled some ink on Ms. Singer's new *calendar*.

———————————— 20. Mr. Linden *finally* managed to *aquire* the vacant lot *across* the street from his house.

———————————— 21. The owner of the *computer* store reports that *business* this year has been mildly *dissappointing*.

———————————— 22. "The *committee* members thank you for your *competant analysis* of the problem," said the chairperson.

———————————— 23. Some of the parents are *extreamly dissatisfied* with the *curriculum* recently adopted by the school.

———————————— 24. I will *concede* that the *commission accompolished* much good at its last meeting.

———————————— 25. Linda *immediately* accepted the offer to teach *arithemetic* in an *excellent* school district in Alaska.

NAME _____   SCORE _____

Directions: Each sentence contains two words from the second half of the spelling list. In each of these words at least one letter is missing. Write the words, correctly spelled, in the spaces at the left.

_____   1. Tomorrow you will have an op—tunity to interview the new
_____   sup—tendent of schools.

_____   2. Several mischiev—us students were being noisy in the school
_____   lib—ry.

_____   3. Ben decided that he couldn't write an orig—al short story
_____   because he was lacking in im—gination.

_____   4. Prof—sor Salyer said that it should be clear to anyone that
_____   par—lel lines will never meet.

_____   5. At the first class session I met my new lab—atory par—ner.
_____

_____   6. "We prob—ly won't be able to get a decent meal in this tiny
_____   vil—ge," complained Sue.

_____   7. The committee chairperson has sched—led a meeting for next
_____   We—sday.

_____   8. Having been suc—sful in business, she decided to enter pol—tics
_____   and seek election to the Senate.

_____   9. Ms. Stanwood's sec—tary rarely mi—pells a word in a business
_____   letter.

_____   10. Allan said that he could not rec—mend a rest—rant in his
_____   hometown.

_____   11. The clerk informed Beth that it is not permis—ble for a freshman
_____   or a soph—ore to register for Physics 344.

_____   12. At the company picnic more than ni—ty tuna fish sand—ches
_____   were eaten.

_____   13. In my lit—ature class this term we studied four Shakespearean
_____   comedies and three tra—dies.

299

_____ 14. This kind of prop—anda plays upon people's pre—udices.
_____

_____ 15. "Your interp—tation of the poem is most int—esting," Ms. Stan-
_____   wood said to Bruce.

_____ 16. When their house burned, the family lost pract—ly all of their
_____   pos—sions.

_____ 17. Stan admitted that his knowl—ge of math—atics is limited.
_____

_____ 18. The director finally p—rsuaded Andy to play the part of the
_____   vil—n in the next production of the drama club.

_____ 19. Last winter the temp—ture oc—sionally dropped below the
_____   freezing level.

_____ 20. Jane's birthday is the nin—h of February; her brother's birthday
_____   is the twel—h of June.

_____ 21. The new radio announcer made a few r—diculous errors in his
_____   pron—ation of foreign place names.

_____ 22. A few malcontents repeatedly inter—pted the mayor's welcom-
_____   ing spe—ch.

_____ 23. "Perhaps I am unduly opt—mistic, but I believe this problem will
_____   soon be solved satisfact—ly," said the chairman.

_____ 24. To our great su—prise, the waiter then proc—ded to remove all
_____   of the dishes from our table.

_____ 25. Luke's free time is often devoted to crossword puzzles, word
_____   games, and simi—r pa—times.

NAME _____ SCORE _____

Directions: Each sentence contains three italicized words from the second half of the spelling list. One of the three words is misspelled. Underline the misspelled word and write it, correctly spelled, in the space at the left.

_____ 1. A *representative* of the Red Cross spoke to our class; her *speech* was *truely* inspirational.

_____ 2. The Swansons *usually* do not remove their Christmas tree *untill* *Twelfth* Night.

_____ 3. You are *liable* to get a parking ticket, because *paralell* parking is not *permissible* on this street.

_____ 4. This *pamphlet* contains a *particularly intresting* chapter on public school financing.

_____ 5. *Together* they visited a *psychiatrist* who *pursuaded* them to work out a compromise.

_____ 6. In *politics* many discussions are made up of equal parts of *rhetoric* and *propoganda*.

_____ 7. The *sergeant* then *proceeded* to return to the *villiage*.

_____ 8. Mario now *recognizes* the fact that he was unduly *predjudiced* against the institution of *marriage*.

_____ 9. To our great delight and *surprise*, we were allowed to make a tour of the *nuclear labratory*.

_____ 10. Bertha brought home with her two *miniature* silver teapots as *momentos* of the exciting *occasion*.

_____ 11. Our neighborhood *restaurant* makes excellent *sandwitches* but badly overcooks most *vegetables*.

_____ 12. Entering students fill out *various questionaires* that presumably reveal their *knowledge* of basic subjects.

_____ 13. On *Wednesday* Lorraine had her first *oppertunity* to serve as a substitute teacher in a *ninth*-grade class.

_____ 14. Many *influential* leaders of *religious* groups consider the novel offensive, even *sacreligious.*

_____ 15. The *temperature* continued to rise, and I noticed beads of *prespiration* on my *partner's* forehead.

_____ 16. After reading several *specimans* of Laura's poetry, *Professor* Ashton *recommended* that she sign up for his advanced class.

_____ 17. "Any *repetition* of this kind of *mischievious* behavior will result *inevitably* in your dismissal," warned the foreman.

_____ 18. "I'm *naturally optomistic,* and I *really* believe that I can do a good job," said Barry.

_____ 19. The dean's *secretary* asked me *wheather* I was a junior or a *sophomore.*

_____ 20. My *original schedual* left me with *practically* no time for recreation.

_____ 21. The *preceeding* semester Ben had taken two *literature* courses that required much research in the *library.*

_____ 22. The men were warned *specifically* to say nothing in *reguard* to the *preparations* being made for the invasion.

_____ 23. "That young man shows that he has *initiative* and *intelligence,*" said the boss, "but I fear that he lacks *preserverance.*"

_____ 24. "I also have in my *possesion* a limited *quantity* of used word *processors* to sell at bargain prices," he concluded.

_____ 25. The manager of the theater *interrupted* the *performance* to announce that *lightening* had struck a car in the parking lot.

NAME _____ SCORE _____

Directions: A sentence may have no misspelled words, one misspelled word, or two misspelled words. Underline the misspelled words and write them, correctly spelled, in the spaces at the left.

_____
_____   1. If the apparatus in the laboratory has been damaged, some arrangment should be made to have it replaced.

_____
_____   2. The new dormatory will accommodate approximately ninety girls in a very pleasant enviomment.

_____
_____   3. The commission, meeting in continuous session for seven hours, accompolished an extraordinary amount of work.

_____
_____   4. Its apparent that the new law supersedes the original one, which has been ignored by practically everyone.

_____
_____   5. Our candidate is a man who has spent over fourty years in national politics.

_____
_____   6. The president of the sophomore class conferred with Professor Haley in regard to the mysterious occurrence.

_____
_____   7. The woman who lives across the street from the restaurant is an acquaintance of mine.

_____

_____   8. The retiring superintendent made his usual speach in which he recommended continued studying of reading, writeing, and arithmetic.

_____
_____   9. Undoubtedly the members of the committee will be unanimous in their voting on the proposed pay raise.

_____
_____   10. Wednesday is the twelfth day of below-freezing temperatures, and the village is completely isolated.

_____
_____   11. Nowdays a high-school diploma is certainly no guarantee of an adequate livelihood.

_____
_____   12. The enthusastic support of the principal of the school was particularily significant in the light of later events.

_____ 13. "If you cannot subdue the mischievious boys by peaceable
_____ means, a little force is permissible," said Sergeant Loomis.

_____ 14. You should seize this opportunity to continue your education
_____ and to travel in foreign lands.

_____ 15. The constant interruptions from disatisfied members of the
_____ audience finally forced us to postpone the preformance.

_____ 16. I acknowledge the fact that your acheivement has been an
_____ extremely admireable one.

_____ 17. For settling questions of grammar and pronunciation, you will
_____ find this dictionary absolutely indispensable.

_____ 18. On the ninth day of February my pardner and I found a desire-
_____ able vacant building for our new video store.

_____ 19. The propaganda in that pamphlet should appear ridiculous to
_____ any moderatly intelligent reader.

_____ 20. Durring the prolonged applause the athelete maintained his awk-
_____ ward position on the parallel bars.

Writing Paragraphs and Essays

Section 1 *An Overview of College Writing*

Although it may come as a surprise to you, you will be called on to do a great deal of writing in college and in your career. Lecture notes, essays, research papers, and tests are the very stuff of which college courses are made. Memorandums, letters, e-mail correspondence, reports, and proposals are basic tools in almost any career you can name. And all this writing, whether in or out of college, is in great measure a key to your progress and success. In fact, in many large organizations, people are known to those in other areas more through their written work than through personal contact. Often progress and promotion ride as much on the quality of written work as on any other factor. Writing skills, then, will be a major factor in your success.

Writing is also an effective tool for learning. Writing about a subject leads to greater understanding and control of the material itself and new connections to other facts and concepts. Writing out lecture notes and textbook materials in your own words, for example, will give you better control of those materials and will help you to connect the new materials with facts and concepts you learned earlier.

In the previous sections of this book, you examined the operating principles of the language and applied those principles to writing correct, effective sentences. Now you need to learn to combine those sentences into paragraphs and the paragraphs into papers that will fulfill your college writing assignments.

The assignments you receive in college may range from a single paragraph narrating an event in your life to a complex research paper. Look briefly at a list of these possible assignments:

1. *Personal Essays*
   - Recount an event in your life, explaining its importance.
   - Discuss your position on the approaching presidential election.
2. *Essay Tests*
   - Answer two of the following three questions, using well-developed paragraphs and complete sentences in your answer.
3. *Essays and Discussions*
   - Explain the causes of structural unemployment in our country today.
   - Discuss the ramifications of using gene threapy to treat diseases.

4. *Critical Papers*
   - Evaluate the enclosed proposal for the construction of a new dam.
   - Assess the legacy of industry irresponsibility toward the environment in the United States.

5. *Persuasive or Argumentative Papers*
   - Argue for or against the use of government spending to retrain displaced workers.
   - Discuss the arguments against universal military training in the United States.

6. *Documented Papers*
   - After thorough research into the subject, write a paper discussing the use of nuclear power in this country. Be sure to discuss the history, the current situation, and the arguments for and against continued use and further development.

Although this list may seem extremely diverse and the types of writing quite varied, you can take comfort in the fact that underneath this diversity and complexity lies a fairly straightforward process that can be applied to all types of writing. You need only to learn one set of steps, the basic writing process, in order to deal effectively with any writing project you might face.

The Writing Process

Writing is a process, a set of steps, not a project that is started and finished in a single session. Often people believe that successful writers have happened onto a secret method of production that allows them, almost by magic, to sit down and write out a nearly perfect draft on the first try. This happens only rarely and always to writers with long experience; most people can assume that good writing rises out of slow, painstaking, step-by-step work.

The steps in the writing process group themselves naturally into two phases, and each phase requires an approach, a mind-set, that is quite different from the other. In the first phase, composing, you should be very free and creative. Think of this phase as a search, an adventure, an opportunity to try out many possibilities for ideas, content, and strategies. In the second phase, editing, you must be very critical of the materials you have composed. This is the time when you must evaluate, rewrite, reject, and correct the materials you developed while composing.

You must be careful not to mix the modes of operation. Don't edit when you should be composing. Don't delete materials, or decide not to pursue an idea, or ponder the correctness of a mark of punctuation. Such distractions will almost certainly stop your flow of ideas. But don't allow yourself to be free and creative when you are working as an editor. Keeping a word that is not quite right or failing to cut out a section that does not fit will produce papers that lack focus and are full of distractions. Remember that each phase in the process is separate and distinct. Each one requires separate and distinct attitudes toward the work at hand.

The following brief explanation provides a general introduction to the steps that make up the writing process. In later sections you will see these steps applied to different types of writing; those applications will illustrate minor changes to suit specific types of writing.

Composing

Step 1. Select or identify the subject.

Basic Question: What should I write about? Or (if the assignment is very specific): What does the assignment require me to write about?

Strategy: Select the subject on the basis of these questions:
- Are you and your reader interested in it?
- Do you have enough knowledge to write on it? If not, can you locate enough?
- Can you treat the subject completely within the length allotted for the assignment?

Step 2. Gather information about the subject.

Basic Question: What do I know about the subject? More importantly, what do I need to know to write about this subject fully and effectively?

Strategy: Record what you know, whether the information comes from recollection or research. Seek more information where necessary. ("A Few Words Before Starting" (pages 311–315) will give you some helpful hints about this process.) Continue research and writing until you arrive at Step 3.

Step 3. Establish a controlling statement, or thesis, for the paper.

Basic Question: Exactly what can I say about this subject on the basis of the information and ideas I developed in Step 2?

Strategy: Continue to gather information and write about the subject until a specific idea develops. Write out that idea in a single sentence.

Step 4. Select specific items of support to include in the paper.

Basic Question: What ideas, facts, and illustrations can I use to make the thesis completely clear to the reader?

Strategy: Review the stockpile of materials gathered in Step 2. Select from these materials only those ideas, facts, and illustrations that will develop and support the thesis.

Step 5. Establish an order for presenting the materials you have selected.

Basic Question: What is the most effective order for presenting the materials I have selected?

Strategy: Choose an order of presentation that offers your reader a logical progression for the development of your idea. The orders used in paragraph development are sometimes useful in developing an order for an essay. (See pp. 330–340.) Write the draft in any order you choose, starting with the easiest section. Assemble the draft in the order you have selected.

Step 6. Select a technique.

Basic Question: What is the most effective technique for presenting the materials I have selected?

Strategy: Explore different writing techniques to determine which one best complements your thesis and supporting materials.

Step 7. Write the first draft.

Basic Question: What will the materials look like when presented in the order I have chosen?

Strategy: Write out a complete version of the paper, following the plan developed in the first five steps.

Revising

Before you begin to revise the first completed draft of the paper, be sure that you shift from the role of composer/writer to the role of critic or editor. You have before you a completed product, not a perfect product. You must examine that product with a critical eye, testing and weighing each part to be sure that it is as good as it can be.

Step 8. Assess the thesis of the draft.

Basic Question: Is the thesis a proper expression of your knowledge on the subject?

Strategy: Read each supporting paragraph or section of the essay individually and create a sentence outline by writing a topic statement for each one. From the topic statements produce a thesis statement for the draft. Compare it to the original thesis. If there are differences between the two, create a new, better thesis.

Step 9. Assess the content.

Basic Question: Does each paragraph or section offer genuine support for the thesis?

Strategy: Check the topic statement for each paragraph or section to be sure each one supports the new thesis. Remove and replace any paragraph or section that does not support the thesis.

Step 10. Assess the order of presentation.

Basic Question: Does the order of presentation provide the reader with a logical progression or pathway through the essay?

Strategy: Try different orders of presentation, shifting sections around to see if you can find a better order than the one you used for the first finished draft.

Step 11. Assess the paragraphs.

Basic Question: Is each paragraph unified and complete? Is each paragraph developed following the best possible method of development?

Strategy: Using the sentence outline created above, check the content of each paragraph to be sure it develops one idea and only one idea. Check the content to be sure that the paragraph contains enough specific, concrete details to make the topic statement clear to the reader.

Step 12. Assess the technique.

Basic Question: Does this technique present my thesis and supporting materials in the best way possible?

Strategy: Consider whether other techniques might better complement your thesis.

Step 13. Correct the mistakes in the draft.

Basic Question: What errors in grammar and mechanics do I need to correct?

Strategy: Read each sentence as an independent unit, starting at the end of the paper and working to the beginning. Reading "backward" in this fashion assures that you will not make mental corrections or assumptions as you read.

Step 14. Write the final draft.

Basic Question: What form shall I use for the final copy of the paper?

Strategy: Follow the guidelines for manuscript preparation specified by your teacher, printing or typing the final copy on plain white paper. Be sure to read the final copy carefully for errors.

The Process in Action

These steps can be followed with only minor changes for any writing assignment. Study the steps carefully as we apply them to various types of assignments. Make the steps second nature to you, a set of habits followed anytime you write. The more you practice, the greater will be your facility in writing.

Before we begin to examine the writing process as it applies to specific projects in college writing, take a few moments to study the results that a professional writer can achieve using these steps—or similar ones—in writing an article about a personal experience.

The setting for the experience and the article is Australia; the writer is an editor of *Car and Driver*, a magazine for auto enthusiasts. The occasion is a trip across the Outback, a sparsely settled region in the interior of Australia. The author and a passenger are driving on a 1,500-mile trip to survey Australian methods of improving auto safety. They have been driving in desolate country almost all day when, late in the afternoon, they encounter a washed-out bridge and must double back to find a new route.

A Drive in the Outback, with Second Chances

DAVID ABRAHAMSON

It took less than two seconds. The stab of oncoming headlights, a blur of looming sheet-metal in the center of the windshield, a jabbing reaction at the steering wheel and then that awful, indelible noise. And then an unearthly silence, as if nature itself knew that something irrevocable had happened and that a moment—maybe much more—was needed for the reality to be dealt with.

I had been driving fast most of the afternoon. Not really at the car's limit, but well above the posted speed. I enjoy fast driving for its own sake, and this new and isolated environment seemed to urge me on. After all, Australia's wide open spaces are exactly that, and we'd encoun-

tered less than one car an hour in either direction of the towns. And besides, Baker, my passenger, didn't seem to mind. We were in the middle of a long, sweeping right-hander when suddenly the windshield was filled with another set of headlights. Coming at us, in the middle of the road, was a monstrous truck. The left front corner of the truck cab buried itself in the left front door of our car. The sound was absolutely deafening. Bits of metal and glass were everywhere. The impact ripped the watch off my wrist and the lenses out of my glasses. But I was lucky. Because it was a righthand-drive car, as the driver I was at least three feet away from the point of impact. Passenger Baker, however, was not.

The true violence of the crash took place almost in his lap. Part of his seat was torn up and out of its mount. The door and a section of the roof were battered in toward his head and left shoulder. We were both wearing lap-and-shoulder seat belts at the time. Mine saved my life. Baker's did too, but in the process broke his collarbone and badly bruised a few essential internal organs. A grisly tradeoff.

How and why had the accident happened? What exactly had been my mistake? Long after I'd returned to the United States, long after Baker had recovered from his injuries, I was still asking myself those questions. Now, almost a year later, the answers are clear. And they go far beyond any chance encounter on a strange road in a strange land, even beyond the crushing sense of remorse I felt at the time. And they tell me something about who I was and what I might be. I enjoyed driving, and a big part of that enjoyment came from taking a number of risks. Risks I thought were calculated, but in truth were not. Rather they were part of a glorious game, imbued with notions of independence, willful mobility and a heavy dose of virility. I'd had more than my share of near misses, but they merely served to prove the range of my skills at the wheel—my ability to judge relative speed and distance, the speed of my reflexes, the correctness of my kinesthetic

instincts. In my car at speed, there was never any hint of my own mortality. Or of anyone else's. So the accident had to happen. Maybe not with that truck on that blind curve on the far side of the Earth, but somewhere. It has less to do with the law of averages than the laws of physics. Roads are a decidedly hostile environment, peopled with an unknown number of other drivers who are certain to do the wrong thing at the wrong time. And no amount of skill, real or imagined, can save you. Sweet reason is the only defense. Prudence, moderation and caution are not the stuff of grand illusions, unbridled exuberance and youthful panache. But they're great for survival.

And that, in the end, is what my experience boils down to. I now see, as I did not before, that my survival (and that of others who choose to ride with me) is at stake. I've never seen myself as a particularly courageous person, but I've always enjoyed sports containing an element of risk: parachuting, scuba-diving, alpine skiing and the like. Strange that something as mundane as an auto accident should, at age 30, give me my first glimpse of my own mortality. Thinking back to that evening south of Bombala, I am certain that I never want to hear that awful sound again. But I also never want to forget it.

Following the writing process as we have outlined it, the writer would have asked himself these questions in the first phase:

1. What should I write about?

   My Australian trip, or some part of it. The most memorable and important part of the trip was the terrible accident near Bombala, in which my passenger Bill Baker was injured.

2. What do I know or remember about the trip and, more specifically, about the accident?

   Beginning with the plane ride from San Francisco, I can record as background material all the things we did on the flight, in Sydney, and on the trip itself. I will record in greatest detail the auto trip, focusing as closely as possible on the moments before and after the crash. I'll continue to write until I reach a statement or conclusion about that accident and its meaning to me now.

3. Exactly what can I say about this subject, the accident? What impression has it made on me?

   The accident changed my view of my driving skills and the importance of those skills in preserving my safety while I drive. I never want to hear the awful sound of the crash again, but I never want to forget it, either.

4. What details, facts, illustrations, and observations can I use to make that thesis clear to my reader?

I will use visual details and facts surrounding the crash itself. I'll include the aftermath of the crash, the time while we wait to take Baker to the hospital. Finally, I'll record my thoughts on and impressions of the importance and meaning of the accident.

5. What order will most effectively present these supporting materials?

Because this piece is basically a narrative, a story about my Australian trip, I'll follow chronological order, but I'll use a few details of the actual crash to catch my readers' interest in the introduction.

6. What will the materials look like when I actually write out a first completed version of the article? [You have read the final version of the essay. The rough draft contained much more material.]

I will cut out distracting material that weakens my statement.

A Few Words Before Starting

Getting started is often the most difficult part of writing. We all have a tendency to avoid the blank page and the work involved in filling it meaningfully. Writing will always be hard work, but three preliminary exercises will help make getting started a little easier.

Strengthen your muscles so that you can write with ease

You would not go mountain climbing or run a marathon without getting in shape; you should not expect writing to be enjoyable unless you are in shape for it. Do the following exercises:

- Sit in a place where you can watch people passing by. Writing as rapidly as possible, jot down a description of all that occurs, noting sizes, shapes, descriptions, and other visual details.
- Writing continuously, sign your name or copy other words down as many times as you can in two minutes.
- Without stopping, write everything that comes into your head when you read the following words:

submarine

photosynthesis

chocolate milkshake

You should do these exercises on a regular basis, changing the words in the third exercise to any others that come to mind from your daily life or current events in the news.

The goal of these exercises is to make you comfortable as a writer, to develop the ability and the patience to write for extended periods without fatigue or frustration. You should work on these exercises until you can write for fifteen minutes without a break or an hour with two short breaks.

Free your mind to write without constraints

In the first phase of the writing process, composing, you need to write freely without editing what you write. "Free writing," or "stream-of-consciousness writing" is a way of learning about your subject, a way of making new connections within it. It allows you to record at random all the ideas that come to mind on your subject. In fact, you will probably bring to mind ideas that are technically off the subject of your paper. Don't be afraid to record these stray ideas, as they will often lead back to the subject from a direction that you had not imagined before.

Free writing is especially valuable when you are writing a paper based on personal experience because it allows you to make something important out of that experience. It is also valuable in writing papers of opinion or papers stating a personal position on a controversial subject. Only through extensive writing can you define your opinion or position clearly and firmly. A would-be comic once said, "I don't know what I think until I see what I've written." He may have intended the statement as a joke, but it is, in fact, the truth. Writing about your opinions and ideas helps you to form those opinions and ideas. Be sure to write extensively, randomly, freely, on all such writing assignments before you formulate your final thesis.

Free writing also has an important place in writing more objective papers, papers based on research and written notes. After you have completed your research and put your note cards in reasonably good order, you should read through them two or three times to get a sense of the content. After reading the notes, set them aside and begin to write freely about the subject.

At least two good things should come out of this free writing. First, it will help you to formulate a position on the subject that is your own and not the opinion of the writers you covered in your research. You learn about your subject when you write about it.

Second, free writing will allow you to write about your subject in your own voice rather than in the voices of the writers you read during your research. Without free writing, your writing will sound like every other research paper ever written because we tend to take on the tone and style of the writers we have recently read. Through free writing you can move away from the voices of those other writers and into your own voice. The paper you produce will be uniquely "you," rather than a generic, sounds-like-all-the-other-papers-ever-written sort of production.

Explore your topic extensively

There are various specialized techniques that will help you gather information and formulate your ideas on your writing projects.

Brainstorming. One technique closely allied to free writing is called **brainstorming** or **clustering**. Brainstorming is a *nonlinear, free association* drill. In this drill, the writer sits quietly with pen and pencil, or at a typewriter, and records words and phrases on a particular subject as they come to mind. To understand how brainstorming works, suppose for a moment that you are taking a United States history or political science course. Your assignment says "Write a paper on American politics." Write the name of the subject on a sheet of paper

American Politics

and then record the words and ideas that come to mind—without editing or limiting the list.

American Politics

Democrat   Republican   liberal   conservative   neo-liberal
Constitution   Bill of Rights   John F. Kennedy
radicalism   William F. Buckley   The Boston Tea Party
The Sixties   The Civil Rights Movement

Note that brainstorming will not work in a vacuum. If you have never studied, or even thought about, American politics, you will not have any associations to make. If you have the background to make constructive associations, however, brainstorming can help you in two ways.

First, brainstorming can help to isolate a manageable topic within a subject area. An assignment that simply says: "Write a paper on American politics" requires a good deal of probing and restriction before a workable topic for a paper emerges. Clearly, you can't write a paper fully exploring American politics in ten pages, or even in a whole semester. To write a successful paper, you will need to restrict and focus your thinking to a single aspect of the subject area.

> Thus you might move from John F. Kennedy to the idea that he became president in 1960 to the idea that the Civil Rights Movement began in the late fifties and early sixties to the idea that there must have been some relationship between his administration and the Civil Rights Movement.

At that point you might suspect that you have hit on a workable topic and move off to the library to do some preliminary work on a bibliography and some background reading.

Second, brainstorming can help you to make connections between ideas within a subject area. Writing about one concept can lead to a second concept. Writing about the second concept can lead to a third and then a fourth.

> So you might begin to think on a general subject—grades—
>
> and then about grades in high school
>
> and then about your greater motivation in college
>
> and then about your lack of real effort in high school
>
> and then about your much better grades in college
>
> and then about the marked improvement in your grades . . .

At this point, you might make a connection between better grades and greater motivation. From there you might move to a comparison between low motivation in high school and higher motivation in college, and then, **by brainstorming again on that concept,** you might develop several reasons why low motivation existed in high school and higher motivation existed in college.

At that point, you can choose a direction for the paper, depending on the focus required in the assignment. If the assignment asks for a personal paper—observations on your grades and experiences in high school and college—then you must continue into additional brainstorming and then into free writing and other techniques to gather information on the topic.

If, on the other hand, you can move into an objective examination of motivation and grades in high school and college, you can go to the library for bibliography work and preliminary reading.

To develop a paper on personal experience, you can employ the five questions used by journalists to develop articles:

1. **WHO** is involved?
2. **WHAT** happens?
3. **WHEN** does it happen?
4. **WHERE** does the event occur?
5. **WHY** does it happen?

Don't limit yourself to one-word or brief answers. Employ free writing techniques when you answer the questions. Don't answer the question "Who?" by saying, "John and Mr. Smith." Write about John and Mr. Smith. Explore the answers to each question extensively in a free writing mode.

Next, explore your topic by asking questions that focus on parts and relationships that exist in and around your topic. Suppose your assignment asks you to explore some aspect of business in modern Japan. After examining the general subject, you discover that Japanese business executives use a special style of management that has sparked considerable interest among managers in the United States. You might begin your exploration by looking at the topic in three ways.

1. Examine the discrete parts of the topic itself:

   What are the *distinctive features* of Japanese management style?

2. Examine the topic as a whole.

   How do these features *work together as a system?*

3. Examine the place of the topic within the general subject matter.

   How does Japanese management style *fit into the overall subject* we call management?

Or, phrased in a different way, you might ask yourself:

· How do I identify this subject?
· How do I differentiate it from others in the same general area?
· What are the important parts or aspects of this subject?
· What is the physical appearance of these parts?
· What examples of this subject occur in real life?
· How does this subject compare and/or contrast with others of the same general type?

Analogies and Metaphors. Some writers find it useful to construct *analogies* and *metaphors* on a subject. When you make an analogy, you examine ways in which one concept is like another concept.

> My brother, who plays Little League baseball, is a ballplayer out of the Rickey Henderson mold: he is quick on his feet, aggressive, a singles hitter most of the time, and, above all, he loves the game more than anything else in his life.

The writer's brother is unlike Rickey Henderson in a thousand ways, including age, size, and success in the game. But the writer, by recognizing the similarities between the two people, can begin to explore his brother's personality in greater depth. Analogies help both you and a reader learn a little bit more about an idea.

In the same way, on personal topics, it is possible to construct metaphors and similes, figures of speech that establish comparisons.

> Red Grange was *like a will-o'-the-wisp,* dancing and dodging his way through opposing teams to become the greatest running back in the early history of football.

> The invading army *was a tornado,* moving where it wished and destroying everything in its path.

Sometimes even metaphors that seem ridiculous can be productive.

> If your father were an automobile, what make and model would he be?

> He might be a 1938 Cadillac, very classy, but a trifle old-fashioned in some ways.

Images such as these can provide insight that can lead to new information and new insights, if you follow them up with additional reading and writing on the subject.

Using the Senses. Certain subjects can be explored through the senses. Recording visual aspects (shapes, sizes, and colors, for example) or recording words that describe sounds, smells, and textures might offer insights into the subject.

All these methods of exploring a subject and refining a subject into manageable parts simply open areas for reading and writing on a subject. They help you with Step 2 of the writing process, gathering materials. The resulting notes and written materials must not be confused with a first, complete draft or the final draft of a paper. They constitute the raw material of a paper, material that must be evaluated, accepted, rejected, placed in order in the draft, and written out for revision. They are not the finished product; they are background to help with production of that finished product.

So don't wait for inspiration or good beginnings. Write what you can write as well as you can write it. If you can't think of a good way to start, start any way you can. If you can't think of exactly the right word, use a close approximation. Time and condition and the freedom to write without editing will improve your ideas; careful attention to revision and correction will improve the quality of your written expression. Practice and more practice will lead to success.

In the next section you will closely examine a very important type of college writing, the essay test.

Writing Exercises for an Overview of College Writing

1. Each day for the first two weeks of your experience in using the writing sections of this book, follow the instructions on pages 310–311 for getting in shape to write.

2. Follow the steps in the writing process illustrated with "A Drive in the Outback, with Second Chances," and write about an experience in your own life.

3. Find an example of personal writing about an experience or an attitude. Read it to locate the controlling statement, or thesis, (Step 3 in composing). Then outline the supporting details to show how they develop (or fail to develop) that idea.

Section 2   *Taking Essay Tests*

Essay tests provide an excellent opportunity to apply your writing skills. An answer to an essay test question requires you to work within a very narrow subject area to produce a concise, complete written statement in a short period of time. These tight limitations of time and space force you to be precise in the formulation of a statement about an idea or concept and to distinguish carefully between materials essential to your answer and those that are only related to it. Finally, essay tests often require that you present your answer in a single well-developed paragraph. Working on test taking, then, is very practical; success on tests will improve your grades. Beyond that, and perhaps more important, practice in writing essay test answers will develop your ability to write successful paragraphs.

Getting Ready

The best preparation for taking any test is consistent, effective study throughout the term. In addition, however, the use of special strategies for the last few days before the test will improve your chances of success. Begin your final preparations for the test a few days in advance so that you will have ample time to study and assimilate the material. Follow these suggestions as you study.

Step 1. Make an overview or survey of the materials you have covered for the test. Look for periods, trends, theories, and general conclusions. Try to pinpoint important concepts and basic ideas in the materials. You may find it useful to consult a general encyclopedia for an overview or a summary of the subject areas to be covered by the test. If the subject is technical or complex or is part of an advanced course, consult an appropriate specialized encyclopedia or reference work in that field.

Step 2. Write a series of questions encompassing the major items that you have located. Cover broad areas of material. Use the seven types of direction or command words listed on pages 320–322 to devise a list of questions covering the material you identified in Step 1. Try each type of command word to determine if questions of that type apply to the material. Are there, for example, lists, or comparisons, or definitions, or discussions that seem to rise naturally from the materials? Formulate questions that cover the materials. In six to ten broad-scope questions of your own, you should be able to cover all the possible questions that the teacher may ask. If you have covered all the material in your own questions, you will not be surprised by any questions on the exam.

Step 3. Read your outline, notes, and other materials, looking for answers to the questions you have composed. As you read and review, outline the answers, commit the outlines to memory, and use them as guides during the test. Write out answers to any questions that are difficult for you.

Step 4. Review the outlines, the materials, and the answers to your questions the afternoon before the test. Then put the whole thing aside and get a good night's rest.

Step 5. Just before going in to take the test:

- Eat a high-energy snack; fruit is a good choice. Coffee, orange juice, or tea will also help. Do some calisthenics or whatever else is necessary to make you alert.
- Get your equipment ready: pens, pencils, erasers, paper or examination booklets, and scratch paper. Take what you will need so that you will not worry about supplies once you enter the room.
- Arrive a few minutes early for the test. Get yourself and your equipment arranged. Relax for a few seconds before the work begins.

Taking the Test

No student—or at least not very many students—can earn a high grade on a test without proper preparation. But good preparation alone will not guarantee success. You need a strategy for taking tests, a strategy that will help you to decide which questions to answer, what order to use in answering the selected questions, and what organization to use for each question.

When you have made the best possible preparations for taking the test and are in the classroom with the test in your hands, do two things before you write:

1. **Read the test from start to finish,** beginning with the directions. Decide which questions you know the most about. Determine the point value of each question. Answer first the questions you know the most about. Answering them first will ease you into the test, develop your confidence, and keep you from wasting time on questions you can't answer well anyway. Use any remaining time to do the best you can on the rest of the questions.

   Always follow the directions. If options allow you to choose certain questions from a group, be sure you understand the options and make your choices based on your knowledge and on the point value of the questions. Don't waste time on a question of low point value when you could be answering a question with a high point value. Invest your time wisely.

2. **Make careful preparations before you write.** Adapt the first four steps in the writing process to guide you in writing the answers.

   Step 1. Identify the subject. On a test, the teacher has selected the subject for each question. Your job is to identify that subject correctly. A question that asks for a discussion of the causes of the Great Depression is not properly answered by a discussion of the characteristics of the Roaring Twenties. Make sure you answer the question that is asked.

   Step 2. Review what you know about the question. Recall your outlines and notes. Bring to mind the practice answers you wrote in your review exercises. Make notes of these on a sheet of paper. Try to remember as much material as you can. List any special or technical words related to the subject.

   Step 3. Decide exactly what the question asks for and what overall statement you are able to make and support in response to the question. Before you write, construct a specific statement of the idea or concept that you intend to develop in writing your answer. This point, or main idea, will come out of the materials you reviewed in Step 2.

Step 4. Carefully select supporting materials, examples, explanations, and other data that will serve to establish and clarify the main idea. You will have pulled together a considerable amount of material in your quick review. Not all of it will fit exactly the statement you are making; not all of it will be especially effective in your answer. Select materials that will establish and reinforce your point as effectively as possible within the constraints of time and space.

Preparing Your Answer

Let's assume that you have read the test carefully, have selected your questions, and have decided to answer this problem first:

> Select one of the seven species of sea turtles and discuss its physical appearance, its habitat and geographic distribution, and its status in both present numbers and population trends.

Step 1. Step 1 requires careful identification of the subject matter covered in the question. The problem refers to sea turtles, not to all kinds of turtles. In fact, it asks for a discussion of just one of the seven species of sea turtles. It also asks for only three rather simple pieces of information about that species:

1. What is the physical appearance of that species?
2. In what type of habitats is the species found, and where are these habitats located?
3. How many individuals of this species are estimated to be alive, and is that number increasing or decreasing?

Only the last point is at all tricky. *Status* in this question refers to the species' survival potential based on what the estimated living population is and on whether it is increasing or decreasing worldwide.

Step 2. Step 2 is to collect material, to recall what you know about a single species of sea turtle. Remembering the textbook material, your lecture notes, and the brief outside reading assignment you reviewed, you jot down the following notes:

> *Actually 7 species—only three much covered in class. One stood out because commercial importance (food & other products)—green turtle.*
>
> *Large: 3 to 6 feet from front to back over curve of upper shell (carapace; lower shell, plastron).*
>
> *Weighs 200–300 lb. average but reaches 850 lb. some specimens. Color from green-brown to near black.*
>
> *Scutes (bony plates) clearly marked. Head small compared to body.*
>
> *Occurs almost worldwide in warmer waters shallow enough to allow growth of sea grass turtles eat.*
>
> *Present status questionable. Not endangered because lrg. pops. in remote areas—under pressure and declining in pop. areas. Needs protection. First protective law in Caribbean, passed 1620. Used extensively for food by early sailors, who killed mainly females coming on shore to lay eggs. Now used for cosmetics and jewelry.*
>
> *Large green turtles make good zoo exhibits. W. Indian natives make soup of them.*

Nesting habits: Female beaches and lays approx. 100 eggs in shaped hole. First hatchlings on top of nest push out sand covering them and leave. Those on bottom crawl out using sand first hatchlings displaced and crushed shells of vacated eggs as platform. 100 eggs right number—fewer places top of nest too low in hole, more requires nest too deep for last hatchling to escape. Recent increase in ecological pressure because women use more cosmetics based on turtle oil.

These notes, jotted down hastily (perhaps more sketchily on an actual test than in the example), produce enough information to allow you to move to Step 3.

Step 3. In Step 3 you must determine what you can say in response to the question. Before you can make that determination, you must know exactly what the question directs you to do. These directions are usually given at the beginning of the question, and, although their exact wording may vary, they generally fall into one of the following categories:

- **List, name, identify**
  These words require short-answer responses that can be written in one or two complete sentences. Do exactly what the question asks; don't try to expand the scope of the question.

  Example: Name the presidents who served in the military prior to becoming president.

  The word *identify* suggests that you ought to mention the two or three most important facts about a person or a subject area, not just any facts that come to mind. You would thus identify Eisenhower as a military commander and U.S. president, not as a West Point graduate who played golf.

- **Summarize, trace, delineate**
  An instruction to *summarize* asks that you give an overview or a capsule version of the subject.

  Example: Summarize Senator Smith's position on tax reform.

  An answer to this question would provide a three- or four-sentence statement of the main points of Smith's position. The words *trace* and *delineate* usually ask that you describe the steps or process that brought some event to pass.

  Example: Trace the life cycle of the monarch butterfly.

  The answer requires a listing of the steps in the development of the butterfly from egg to adulthood.

- **Define**
  The instruction *define* usually asks that you establish the term within a class and then differentiate it from the other members of the class. "A parrot is a bird" establishes the word *parrot* in a class, and "found in the tropics and capable of reproducing human speech" is an attempt at differentiation. You should be careful to add enough elements

of differentiation to eliminate other members of the class. For instance, as the myna is also a tropical bird capable of reproducing speech, you must complete your definition of *parrot* by specifying such items as size, color, and habitat.

- **Analyze, classify, outline**
  These command words imply a discussion of the relationship that exists between a whole and its parts. *Analyze* asks that you break an idea, a concept, or a class down into its integral parts.

  Example: Analyze the various political persuasions that exist within the Republican party.

  This question asks that you look at the Republican party and identify the various categories of political belief ranging from right to left. *Classify* asks that you position parts in relation to a whole.

  Example: Classify the following parts of an automobile as to location in engine, steering, or drive shaft:
  1. Ball joint
  2. Piston ring
  3. Pinion gear

  Outline requires that you break down an idea or a concept into its parts and show how the parts support and reinforce each other. Whether you arrange your sentences in the form of a whole paragraph or in a listing of main headings and subheadings, your outline must show how the idea or concept is made up of smaller parts and how these parts relate to the idea and to each other.

  Example: Outline Senator Random's position on emission controls for automobiles.

  This question requires that you state Senator Random's position and its supporting points.

- **Discuss, explain, illustrate**
  This type of command word is probably the most general of all the possible directions for essay tests. The request here is that you expose, in detail, the idea, concept, or process in question. Single simple sentences will not suffice to answer such instructions. You must provide all pertinent information and write enough so that your readers have no questions, no gaps left in their information, when they've finished reading. Often such questions can be answered by making a statement of the idea or process and providing examples to illustrate your statements. In fact, if the instruction is *illustrate*, examples are required.

  Example: Discuss the effect of depriving a child of physical affection in the first three years of its life.

  The answer could be given by making a statement or statements of the effects and giving examples of each.

- **Compare, contrast**

  A question that asks you to compare, or to compare and contrast, is simply asking that you discuss the similarities and differences between two or more subjects.

  Examples: Compare the military abilities of Grant and Sherman.
  Make a comparison between Smith's plan and Jones's plan for shoring up the value of the dollar overseas.
  What are the similarities and differences between racketball and squash?

  All these example questions ask you to establish categories—for example, skill in tactics, ability to motivate, and so on, as they relate to Grant and Sherman—and to explain how the subjects are alike or different in the areas you establish.

- **Evaluate, criticize**

  This type of question is probably the most difficult because it requires that you know what is correct or best or ideal and that you assess the assigned topic against that ideal.

  Example: Evaluate Eisenhower as a leader in foreign affairs.

  The question is, "What are the characteristics of a leader in foreign affairs and how does Eisenhower measure up in each of these categories?" To answer this question, you must know the subject *and* the ideal equally well.

Now let's examine the sample problem again:

> Select one of the seven species of sea turtles and discuss its physical appearance, its habitat and geographic distribution, and its status in both present numbers and population trends.

The subject area is clear: any one of the seven species of sea turtles. The direction, the instruction word, is *discuss* which means make a statement and support it. The direction is clear: discuss the physical appearance, the habitat and general distribution, and the current status of any one of the seven species of sea turtles.

Your opening statement should be simple and direct. It need not state all the facts and details; indeed, it should not try to. It is designed to serve only as a guide for the development of your answer. For this problem, your statement might read:

> The green turtle is a large green-to-black sea turtle residing in warm, shallow waters all over the world; it is numerous but is declining in populated areas.

Step 4. Step 4 requires that you select from the collected materials those items that will develop your statement. Select specific details to explain each area within the statement. For the first section, physical appearance, your notes contain the following concrete details:

1. Size—three to six feet from front to back over the shell; average weight—200–300 pounds, record is 850 pounds.

2. Coloration—greenish brown is lightest color, almost black when splotches are close together.
3. Shape of flippers, head, tail. [Note that these items are not in the original list. New materials often come to mind during preparations.]

You can fill in the other sections by selecting other information from your collection of materials. Do not include any materials that do not specifically develop or illustrate the statement that controls the answer. Provide ample development, but do not pad. For example, in your collection of supporting materials, the long discussion of the nesting habits and the number of eggs laid by the green turtle does not fit into the answer. The material is interesting, it concerns the green turtle, but it does *not* fit any of the three categories in the question. Don't use materials simply because they relate to the general subject. Use only materials that support the answer to the specific question.

Writing the Answer

At this point you have before you on scratch paper:

1. A basic idea.
2. Supporting materials for that basic idea.

These will be useful in writing the answer, but they are not the answer. They are the *content* for the answer. Now you must gather this content into grammatically correct, complete sentences that present the material in a logical, relevant order.

The best way to provide order for your answer is to modify your statement to suggest the order that you intend to follow. This modification will help your reader to follow your answer. A sentence combining elements of the question with a suggestion of your answer's focus offers a good beginning and adequate control:

> Of the seven species of sea turtles, the green turtle is the largest and the most widely distributed, but it is nearing endangered status because it has commercial value.

Note that the sentence establishes your topic, the green turtle, and defines the aspects that you will discuss by using key words from each of those areas:

1. *Largest* leads to a physical description.
2. *Most widely distributed* leads naturally to a discussion of habitat and distribution.
3. *Nearing endangered status* opens the discussion of population size and trends.

The sentence relates your answer to the question and will keep you from wandering into irrelevancy. Try to make your first sentence as specific as possible, but be sure that you can expand on it. A statement that the green turtle is "an interesting species" is little help in controlling the answer because it does not focus on the question. You are not concerned with how interesting the species is; you are concerned with its appearance, its habitat and distribution, and its status. The entire answer to this sample question might read as follows:

Of the seven species of sea turtles, the green turtle is the largest and the most widely distributed, but it is nearing endangered status because it has commercial value. It is a large turtle, measuring between 3 and 6 feet in length over the top of the shell and weighing on the average 200–300 pounds. The largest specimens are over 5 feet in length and weigh 800–1000 pounds. The upper shell (carapace) is light to dark brown, shaded or mottled with darker colors ranging to an almost black-green. The lower shell (plastron) is white to light yellow. The scales on the upper surface of the head are dark, and the spaces between them are yellow; on the sides of the head, the scales are brown but have a yellow margin, giving a yellow cast to the sides of the head. The shell is broad, low, and more or less heart-shaped. The green turtle inhabits most of the warm, shallow waters of the world's seas and oceans, preferring areas 10–20 feet deep where it can find good sea grass pastures for browsing. The turtles prefer areas that have many potholes, because they sleep in the holes for security. In numbers and population trends, the status of the green turtle is in doubt. It is under great pressure in highly populated areas such as the Caribbean Sea, where it is avidly hunted for food and for use in making jewelry and cosmetics. However, because it occurs in large numbers in remote areas, it is not technically an endangered species at this time. It needs better protection in populated areas so that its numbers will not decline any further.

Assignments and Exercises

The suggestions offered in this section will not improve your ability to take tests unless you practice applying them in your own work. Here are some suggested exercises to apply the principles:

1. Analyze your performance on a recent essay test and discuss the ways in which following the suggestions in this chapter might have improved your performance.

2. Assume that you are enrolled in a course in American history and must take an essay test on the Revolutionary War. The materials covered include the textbook, your lecture notes, your outside readings, and two films. Write a paragraph describing your preparations for the test.

3. As a practice test, write answers to the following questions on the chapter you have just read on taking essay tests.

   • Discuss the preparations for taking a test up to the point where you enter the test room.

   • Describe the process by which you would decide which questions to answer (if given options) and in which order you would answer them.

   • Name and define four of the seven instruction-word categories often found in test questions, discussing the kinds of materials that each word requires in its answer.

   • Describe the final form the answers should take. Include a discussion of opening statements and development.

A paragraph is a group of sentences (or sometimes just one sentence) related to a single idea. The paragraph originated as a punctuation device to separate ideas on paper and to assist readers in keeping lines separate as they read. Thus, each paragraph begins on a new line, and its first word is indented a few spaces from the left margin.

The Effective Paragraph

The function of a paragraph is to state and develop a single idea, usually called a **topic.** The topic is actually the subject of the paragraph, what the paragraph is about. Everything in the paragraph after the statement of the topic ought to **develop the topic,** to explain and define, to discuss, to illustrate and exemplify the topic. From the reader's point of view, the content of the paragraph should provide enough information and explanation to make clear the topic of the paragraph and the function of the paragraph in the essay or the chapter.

The Topic Sentence

The first rule of effective paragraph writing is as follows:

Usually, declare the topic of the paragraph early in a single sentence (**called the** *topic sentence*).

Look back to the sample answer to an essay test question on page 305. Note how the first sentence paraphrases a significant part of the question and provides direction for the answer by telling briefly what the answer will contain. It is, in other words, a topic sentence. Every paragraph you write should contain a sentence that names what the paragraph is about and indicates how the paragraph will proceed. It may do so in considerable detail:

> Although the green turtle—a large, greenish-brown sea turtle inhabiting warm, shallow seas over most of the world—is not yet generally endangered, it is subject to extreme pressure in populated areas.

or rather broadly:

> The green turtle is one of the most important of the seven species of sea turtles.

Both of these statements name a specific topic, the green turtle, but neither sentence stops with the name. A sentence that reads "This paragraph will be about green turtles" is not a complete topic sentence because it does not suggest the direction that the rest of the paragraph will take. Unlike the incomplete topic sentence, both good examples are phrased so that a certain type of development must follow. The first example anticipates a discussion that will mention size, color, habitat, and distribution but will focus on the green turtle's chances for survival. The second example anticipates a discussion that will develop the assertion the species is one of the most important of the sea turtles. Note that neither example tries to embrace the whole idea of the paragraph. The topic sentence should lay the foundation for the paragraph, not say everything there is to be said.

Sometimes a paragraph has no topic sentence; occasionally the topic sentence occurs at the end of the paragraph. These exceptions are permissible, but the early topic sentence is more popular with both writers and readers because it helps in three ways to produce an effective message:

1. It defines your job as a writer and states a manageable objective—a single topic.
2. It establishes a guide for your development of the basic idea. You must supply evidence of or support for any assertion in the topic sentence. The topic sentence is only a beginning, but it predicts a conclusion that the paragraph must reach.
3. It tells your reader what the paragraph is going to contain.

Notice how the italicized topic sentence in the following paragraph controls the paragraph and provides clear direction for the reader:

Of all the inventions of the last one hundred years, *the automobile assembly line has had the most profound effect on American life.* The assembly line provided a method for building and selling automobiles at a price many could afford, thus changing the auto from a luxury item owned by the wealthy few to an everyday appliance used by almost every adult in America. Universal ownership and the use of the automobile opened new occupations, new dimensions of mobility, and new areas of recreation to everyone. In addition, the automobile assembly line provided a model for the mass production of television sets, washing machines, bottled drinks, and even sailboats. All these products would have been far too expensive for purchase by the average person without the introduction of assembly-line methods to lower manufacturing costs. With the advent of Henry Ford's system, all Americans could hope to possess goods once reserved for a select class, and the hope changed their lives forever.

The italicized sentence states the topic and the purpose of the paragraph: The paragraph is going to argue that the assembly line, more than any other invention, changed America's way of life. The writer is controlled by this sentence because everything in the paragraph should serve to support this argument. Readers are assisted by the sentence, for they know that they can expect examples supporting the position stated in the sentence.

Complete Development

Writing a good topic sentence is only the first step in writing an effective paragraph, for an effective paragraph provides complete development of the topic; that is, it tells the readers all they need to know about the topic for the purposes at hand. This is the second basic rule of effective paragraph writing: **Always provide complete development in each paragraph.**

Complete development tells readers all that they need to understand about the paragraph itself and the way the paragraph fits into the rest of the essay or chapter. Complete development does not necessarily provide all the information the reader *wants* to know; rather, the reader receives what is *needed* for understanding the topic and its development (the internal working of the paragraph) and the relationship between the paragraph and the paper as a whole (the external connection). As an illustration of that rather abstract statement, read the following paragraph, which gives a set of instructions for a familiar process:

> Another skill required of a self-sufficient car owner is the ability to jump-start a car with a dead battery, a process that entails some important do's and don't's. First, make certain that the charged battery to be used is a properly grounded battery of the same voltage as the dead one. Put out all smoking material. Connect the first jumper cable to the positive terminal of each battery. Connect one end of the second cable to the negative terminal of the live battery, and then clamp the other end to some part of the engine in the car with the dead battery. DO *NOT* LINK POSITIVE AND NEGATIVE TERMINALS. DO *NOT* ATTACH THE NEGATIVE CABLE DIRECTLY TO THE NEGATIVE TERMINAL OF THE DEAD BATTERY. A direct connection is dangerous. Choose a spot at least 18 inches from the dead battery. Put the car with the live battery in neutral, rev the engine, and hold it at moderate rpm while starting the other car. Once the engine is running, hold it at moderate rpm for a few seconds and disconnect the NEGATIVE cable. Then disconnect the positive cable. It is wise to take the car to a service station as soon as possible to have the battery checked and serviced if necessary.

While the instructions in this paragraph are clear and will enable anyone to start a car with a dead battery, the reader may have certain questions in mind after reading the paragraph:

1. What is a properly grounded battery?
2. Why is it necessary to extinguish smoking materials?
3. To what parts of the engine may one attach the negative cable?
   (After all, attaching it to the fan will have exciting results.)
4. What is the danger of making a direct connection?

Also, there are at least two important steps left out of the process:

> Before connecting the two batteries,
> 1. Remove the caps to the cells of both batteries.
> 2. Check the fluid levels in the cells of both batteries.

Without these steps in the process, the car with the dead battery will start, but there is a chance of explosion. A paragraph that lacks material, that is not fully developed, probably won't explode. But it probably won't succeed, either. Questions raised in the mind of the reader will almost always weaken the effect of the paragraph. Sometimes the omissions are so important that the reader will miss the point or give up altogether in frustration.

Most of the time, you can write a well-developed paragraph by following three very simple steps:

1. Make the topic statement one clear, rather brief sentence.
2. Clarify and define the statement as needed.
3. Illustrate or exemplify the topic statement concretely where possible.

As an example of the use of this three-step process, follow the development of a paragraph written to answer the question, "What is the most important quality that you are seeking

328 · *Writing Effective Paragraphs*

in an occupation?" The student's answer, found after much preliminary writing and a good bit of discussion, led to the following topic sentence and rough paragraph:

> Above all other qualities, *I want to have variety in the tasks I perform and in the locations where I work.*
>
> I know I must do the general line of work for which I'm trained, but I want to do different tasks in that work every day if possible. Repeating the same tasks day after day must be a mind-numbing experience. Our neighborhood mechanic does one tune-up after another, five days a week. A doctor friend tells me that 90 percent of her practice involves treating people ill with a virus, for which she prescribes an antibiotic against secondary infection. I want no part of that sort of humdrum work. Variety means doing a different part of a job every day, perhaps working on the beginning of one project today and the completion of another tomorrow, or working on broad concepts one day and details the next. I'd also like to work at a different job site as often as possible. The field of architecture is one area that might suit me. I could work in drafting, and then switch to field supervision, and move from that task to developing the overall concepts of a large project. By doing this, I could vary my assignments and the locations of my work.

Following the three simple steps given above, you might revise this paragraph to read as follows:

Topic Sentence {	Some people want salary and others want big challenges, *but in my career I want variety, in both assignment and work location,* more than
Clarification and Definition {	any other single quality. As much as possible, I want to do a different part of a job every day. Perhaps I could work on the beginning of one project and shift to the completion of another, or work on details for a while and then shift to broad concepts involved in planning. For this reason architecture looks like a promising field for me. I could work in
Concrete Example {	drafting and detailing, move next to on-site supervision, and then shift to developing the design concepts of a major project. I know that doing the same task in the same place would be a mind-numbing experience for me. Our family doctor says that 90 percent of her practice consists of treating patients who have a routine virus infection, for which she routinely prescribes an antibiotic against secondary infection. Our neighborhood mechanic spends all his time doing tune-ups. I want none of that humdrum sort of work. Variety is the spice of life; it is also the ingredient that makes work palatable for me.

Unity

Effective paragraphs have two other characteristics: unity and coherence. It would seem to be easy to maintain unity in a paragraph. After all, by definition a paragraph should deal with only one idea that is completely developed. Second and subsequent ideas should be handled in separate paragraphs. Sometimes, however, ideas can trick you if you don't pay close attention to your topic sentence. A student wrote this paragraph on strawberries some years ago:

> Strawberries are my favorite dessert. Over ice cream or dipped in powdered sugar, they are so good they bring tears to my eyes. My uncle used to grow strawberries on his farm in New Jersey. Once, I spent the whole summer there and my cousins and I went to the carnival. . . .

Things went pretty far afield from strawberries as the paragraph continued, and you can see how one idea, "used to grow strawberries on his farm," led to a recollection of a delightful summer on that farm and opened the door to a whole new idea and a change in form from discussion to narration. "Strawberries" and "that summer on the farm" are both legitimate, interesting, and perfectly workable topics for a paragraph. But they are probably not proper for inclusion in the same paragraph. Unity demands that each topic be treated in a separate paragraph. One paragraph handling one idea equals unity.

Coherence

In paragraph writing, the term *coherence* is used to describe a smooth flow between sentences within the paragraph. In other words, the sentences follow one another without abrupt changes. An effective paragraph reads smoothly, flowing from start to finish without choppiness to distract the reader.

The first step in establishing coherence occurs when you decide how you are going to develop the paragraph. (We shall discuss the various ways in which a paragraph can be developed in the next section.) The way in which you decide to develop the paragraph will help to establish coherence because it will produce a flow and a movement in the paragraph and because it will serve as a frame for providing details of development. There are, however, other writing strategies that contribute to coherence. Three of these strategies are discussed next.

Repetition of Nouns and Use of Reference Words.

> My father asked me to dig some postholes. After I finished that, he told me the truck needed washing. It is Father's pride and joy, but I'm the one who has to do such jobs.

These three short sentences show a fairly clear pattern of development that in itself establishes coherence. Events occur one after another, establishing a chronological order for the development of the entire paragraph. But note how strongly the repeated nouns and reference words knit the sentences together within the paragraph:

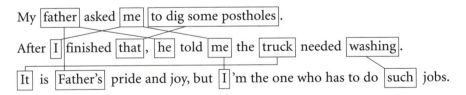

Use of Temporal Words: Conjunctions and Adverbs.
Although a series of short, abrupt sentences may create chronological coherence, the paragraph may not read smoothly:

> I drove to the corner. I stopped for a light. A car smashed into the back of mine. I got out rubbing my neck. The driver of the other car sat behind the wheel and wept. I realized that the other driver was an elderly, gray-haired man.

A writer, sensing that something is lacking from the paragraph, might revise it this way:

I drove to the corner. *While* I was stopped for a light, a car smashed into the back of mine. *As* I got out, rubbing my neck, the driver of the other car sat behind the wheel and wept. Only *then* did I realize that the other driver was an elderly, gray-haired man.

Two features of the revision have improved on the original draft. The first and most obvious is the addition of the words *while, as,* and *then* to connect the sentences by declaring the chronological sequence. Second, *while* and *as* convert short sentences into dependent clauses, thus replacing four choppy sentences with two longer ones and eliminating the jog-trot rhythm that gave the reader hiccups.

Transitional Words and Phrases At or Near the Beginning of Sentences. Coordinating conjunctions*; adverbs like *however, moreover, therefore, consequently, similarly,* and *thus;* and expressions like *on the other hand, in addition,* and *for example* can produce subtle transitional effects rather like that of reference words. They force the reader to recollect the preceding material, thus making a tie between the thoughts they introduce and what has already been stated. When you read *But* at the beginning of a sentence, the author is declaring to you in loud tones, "You are to interpret the forthcoming statement as being in opposition or in contrast to what you have just read." *Moreover,* in the same place, suggests that what is coming is an addition to the last remarks; *consequently* means "as a result of what I have just stated."

The ploy of cementing the parts of a paragraph together with these words and phrases is used by nearly every writer. It is a perfectly good device, but unfortunately it is also a seductively easy one. The unwary writer larding sentences with *however*'s and *therefore*'s in search of elegance and poise may get into trouble with logic. "Sam drank too much on our dinner date. Consequently he threw up," may leave one wondering whether the nausea stemmed from the liquor or the date.

Patterns for Paragraphs

Now that you know the characteristics of an effective paragraph—topic sentence, complete development, unity, and coherence—you can examine the different ways in which a paragraph can be developed with these characteristics. Over the years writers have created several recognizable development patterns for paragraphs. These patterns are useful for presenting certain types of information for specialized purposes within an essay. You should recognize and practice these development patterns so that you can use them in your own writing.

Comparison/Contrast

The identification of like and unlike qualities is the aim of comparison/contrast. When you compare, contrast, or compare and contrast two or more people, ideas, attitudes, or

---

*Disregard the myth that there is something wrong with starting a sentence with *and, but, for, or, nor, yet,* or *so.* Do realize, however, that these words at the opening of a sentence provide a special effect and call attention to themselves and to what follows them. Don't overuse them, and be sure of your purpose when you do launch a statement with one.

objects, you examine items that fall within the same general group or class and, after this examination, point out ways in which the items are similar and dissimilar. Common test questions or paper assignments that require this type of paragraph pattern read as follows:

> Compare the attitudes of General Patton and Bertrand Russell toward war and the maintenance of a standing army.
>
> Compare the effects of heroin and marijuana on the human body.
>
> Compare orange juice and lemon juice in respect to taste, vitamin C content, and usefulness in cooking.

Note that in each statement there is a large class that includes the subjects of the comparison:

> Patton and Russell were both famous people who held carefully developed attitudes toward war. [If one had no attitude on war, the comparison couldn't be made.]
>
> Heroin and marijuana are both drugs that act on the human body.
>
> Orange juice and lemon juice are both citrus products.

One of the most useful ways to employ comparison/contrast in any paragraph is to create an understanding of an unfamiliar concept by showing how that concept is like or unlike a more familiar concept.

> If you know the stereotype of the Texan—loud, boisterous, bragging about his state and his own possessions—you could appreciate my friend Jack because he is the exact antithesis of that stereotype. He is quiet. . . .

In a business or investment course you might want to compare stocks and bonds as investment instruments. Begin by listing the qualities of a common stock and the qualities of a bond side by side.

A bond is:	A stock is:
1. an instrument used by investors.	1. an instrument used by investors.

Note how this first point in each list establishes that the two objects of comparison are members of the same large class and can therefore be compared and contrasted.

2. a certificate of indebtedness.	2. a representation of ownership of a fraction of a company.
3. a promise to repay a specific number of dollars.	3. worth the selling price on any day, whether more or less than the purchase price.
4. payable on a specified date.	4. sold anytime, but not ever payable as is a bond.
5. sold at a specific rate of interest.	5. not an interest-drawing instrument; rather, it earns a share of profits.

For a geology course, you might want to compare types of rocks.

Rocks can be divided into three groups:

Igneous	*Sedimentary*	*Metamorphic*
Formed when molten rock material called *magma* cools and solidifies.	Formed from deposits of older rocks or animal or plant life that are deposited on each other and jointed by pressure or natural chemicals.	Formed when old rocks change under heat or pressure. They do not divide easily into subgroups.
One type (extrusive) is forced out by pressure from within the earth; for example, a volcano erupts and spews out lava, which, if cooled quickly, becomes glassy or forms small crystals such as obsidian or pumice.	Three types: *Classic*—formed of older rock pieces. *Chemical*—formed of crystallized chemicals. *Organic*—formed of plant and animal remains.	

Here, once you have made your list, you will discover that a detailed comparison of the three basic types of rocks is impossible in a single paragraph because of the enormous complexity of the subject. About all that can be dealt with in a single paragraph is a very broad comparison of the three major groups of rocks.

A comparison of the two muscle groups—skeletal and smooth—for a course on human anatomy can be more detailed because the two groups have a number of things in common. The two groups can be compared on the basis of:

	Skeletal	*Smooth*
1. Location	Attached to skeleton.	Found in blood vessels, digestive system, and internal organs.
2. Function	To move legs, arms, eyes, and so on.	To move food for digestion, contract or expand blood vessels—varies by location.
3. Structure	Long, slender fibers bundled together in parallel, contain many nuclei.	Arranged in sheets or in circular fashion, contain one nucleus.
4. Contraction	Rapid, only when stimulated by nerve; stimulus can be voluntary or involuntary.	Slow, rhythmic; cannot be controlled consciously (voluntarily); stimulated by nerves or by hormones.

It is possible to develop a paragraph of comparison/contrast in two different ways. The first pattern is clearly illustrated in the list of muscle characteristics: The qualities of both muscle groups are listed numerically in the same order. This pattern is useful if you are comparing only a limited number of characteristics. A second pattern, because it focuses the comparison point by point, provides better control of longer or more complicated topics. A paragraph comparing stocks and bonds might read as follows:

> Although stocks and bonds are both common investment instruments, they differ in several important aspects and thus appeal to different types of investors. A bond is a certificate of indebtedness; a share of stock represents ownership of a percentage of a company. A bond involves a promise to repay a specified amount of money on a day agreed on in advance. Because it represents ownership, stock must be sold to obtain its value, and it is worth only the selling price on a given day, never a guaranteed amount. A bond earns money in the form of interest at a fixed rate, but stocks share in the profits, partial distributions of which are called *dividends*. Thus the value of a bond, if held to its date of maturity, is fixed, and the periodic interest paid by many bonds is relatively secure. A stock, on the other hand, changes its value on the basis of market conditions and its rate of return on the basis of the profitability of the company. The risk in a bond is the risk that inflation will reduce the value of its fixed number of dollars and its fixed rate of return; stocks risk a possible decline in the general market and a possible reduction of profits that might erode the sale price and the dividends. So bonds are useful where security of investment is a high priority and protection against inflation is not vital. Stocks fit an investment portfolio in which some risk is acceptable and a hedge against inflation is very important.

In the point-by-point pattern bonds and stocks are compared in respect to the following categories:

1. The nature of the instrument itself
2. The way the value of the instrument is established
3. The method of earning money
4. The relative security of the two instruments
5. The risks inherent in each one
6. The situations in which each might be useful as an investment

As an exercise in comparison/contrast, you might try writing a paragraph on the two groups of muscles using each of the comparison/contrast patterns described earlier.

Definition

We have all read definitions; they are the subject matter of dictionaries. In writing, a paragraph of definition serves to establish meaning for words, concepts, and attitudes. Suppose on a test, you found the following instruction:

> Define a *boom-vang* and say how it is used in sailing.

The correct response to such an instruction would be a paragraph of definition. Clearly paragraphs of definition ought to follow the same rules of presentation and development that a dictionary does. Let's examine two definitions that follow the pattern used in dictionaries.

> Basketball is a game played by two teams on a rectangular court having a raised basket at each end. Points are scored by tossing a large round ball through the opponent's basket.

> Football is a game played with an oval-shaped ball by two teams defending goals at opposite ends of a rectangular field. Points are scored by carrying or throwing the ball across the opponent's goal or by kicking the ball over the crossbar of the opponent's goalpost.

Notice that both examples begin by identifying their opening words as the names of games. Next, they specify the

- Number of teams in a game
- Number of players on each team
- Type of playing area
- Way in which scoring occurs
- Shape of the ball

This is the classic pattern of definition: First, classify the word within a class or group; second, differentiate the word from other members of its class:

> Football is a game ... [Identify class]
>
> played by two teams
> of eleven players each
> on a rectangular field.   [Differentiate football from other games.]
>
> Scoring occurs by crossing
> opponent's goal in a special way.

    If you are writing a paragraph of definition, however, you ought to offer more than just classification and the basic points of differentiation. You should provide illustrations, examples, and comparisons of the term being defined to terms that might be familiar to your reader. Doing this is often called **extending the definition.** The additional information helps your reader to understand and assimilate the information that you are offering. Examine the following paragraph defining football and note how basic definition and extension are combined to make an effective presentation:

On any Saturday or Sunday afternoon in the fall, hundreds of thousands of Americans travel to stadiums, and millions more sprawl out in front of television sets to witness the great American spectator sport, football. In simplest form, a definition of football states that it is a game played on a large field by two teams of eleven players and that scoring is accomplished by carrying or throwing an oval ball across the opponent's goal line or by kicking the ball between two uprights called *goalposts.* But such literal definition scarcely does justice to the game or to its impact on Americans. For it is more than a game or a sport; it is a happening, a spectacle, a ritual that is almost a religious experience for its devotees. The game catches them with its color: a beautiful green field surrounded by crowds dressed in a galaxy of hues, teams uniformed in the brightest shades ever to flow from the brush of deranged artists. It holds these fans with its excitement: the long pass, the touchdown run, the closing-minutes' drive to victory. But above all the game seems to captivate them with its violence, with dangers vicariously experienced, with a slightly veiled aura of mayhem. This element of danger draws casual viewers and converts them into fanatic worshippers of the great American cult-sport, football.

    Finally, a word of warning about constructing definitions: A fundamental rule is that a definition must not be circular. A useful definition does not define a term by using a related form of the term itself. To define the word *analgesic* by saying that it causes analgesia means nothing unless the reader knows that *analgesia* means absence or removal of pain. To define *conservatism* as a philosophy that attempts to conserve old values doesn't really add much to a reader's understanding. Thus the rule: **Do not use in the definition a form of the word being defined.**

Analysis

Chemists analyze compounds to isolate and identify their components. Economists analyze the financial data of the nation to determine the factors contributing to recessions. Sports commentators analyze games to explain the strengths leading to a victory.

Analysis is the act of breaking a substance or an entity into its components. It is possible to analyze a football team and to point out the various positions: ends, tackles, guards, and the rest. An army can be broken into infantry, artillery, and engineers. A piano is made up of parts: keys, strings, sounding board, and so on.

A paragraph of analysis provides information derived from this act of breaking into parts, usually by listing, defining, and explaining the parts of the whole in question. As an example, suppose you wanted to analyze that rarest of animals, the good driver. You might begin by listing for yourself the characteristics of the good driver:

The good driver possesses:

- Technical competence
- Physical skills
- Sound judgment
- Emotional stability

A paragraph analyzing the qualities of a good driver might read this way:

Every American over age fourteen wants to drive, does drive, or just stopped driving because his or her license was revoked. Not every American—in fact, only a very few Americans—can be counted in the ranks of good drivers. Good drivers must possess technical competence in the art of driving. They must know the simple steps of starting, shifting, and braking, and the highly sophisticated techniques of feathering the brakes and the power slide, for example. In addition they must possess physical skills, such as exceptional eye–hand coordination, fast reflexes, outstanding depth perception, and peripheral vision. They must also possess good judgment. What speed is safe on a rain-slick highway? How far can a person drive without succumbing to fatigue? What are the possible mistakes that the approaching driver can make? And besides the answers to these questions and the technical and physical skills listed above, good drivers possess steel nerves to cope with that potentially lethal emergency that one day will come to everyone who slips behind the wheel of a car. Only with these qualities can a person be called a good driver and be relatively sure of returning home in one piece.

Caution: When you divide or break an entity into its elements, be sure that you establish parallel categories. It is not proper, in analyzing an automobile's major systems, for example, to list

- Frame
- Body
- Drive train
- Engine
- Piston rings

Although the first four items could possibly be called major systems, piston rings are a small part of a large system, the engine, and should not be included in a list of major systems. The rule for analysis is: **Keep categories parallel.**

Process Analysis. A process paragraph is a form of analysis that examines, in the order in which they must occur, the steps involved in an action or a sequence of actions. The most common sort of process analysis is a recipe: To make a rabbit stew, first catch a rabbit, and so forth. Instructions for building stereo receivers or flying kites or cleaning ovens are all process analyses. In addition to instructions, process analysis can be used to trace the steps involved in a historical event. This type of analysis would be required to answer an essay test question that begins with the word *trace* or *delineate.* The following paragraph provides a set of instructions:

> Changing the oil and the filter in your car is a simple process, and "doing it yourself" can save several dollars every time you change the oil. First, go to an auto parts store or a discount store and buy the oil and the oil filter specified for your car. At the same time, buy an oil filter wrench, the only specialized tool necessary for this job. Don't buy these items at your gas station; prices are lower at the other stores. In addition, you will need an adjustable wrench and a pail or bucket low enough to fit under the car to catch the old oil as it drains from the crankcase. Don't lift the car on a bumper jack. Simply crawl under the car and locate the drain plug for the crankcase. From the front of the car the first thing you see underneath will be the radiator—the thing with the large hose running from the bottom. That hose runs to the engine, the next piece of equipment as you work your way back. On the bottom surface of the engine is the drain plug, usually square with a few threads visible where it screws into the oil pan. Place the pail or bucket beneath this plug. Fit the wrench to the plug by adjusting its size. Turn the plug counterclockwise until it falls out of its hole into the pail. Don't try to catch it; the oil may be hot. While the oil drains into the pail, find the oil filter on one side of the engine, usually down low. (It will look exactly like the one you bought.) Reach up (or perhaps down from the top, whichever is easier) and slip the circle of the filter wrench over it. Pull the wrench in a counterclockwise direction and take off the old filter. Put the new filter on in exactly the opposite way, tightening it clockwise by hand until it is snug. Scoop the drain plug out of the cooled oil and put it back in place, tightening it firmly with the adjustable wrench. Now find the oil filler cap on the top of the engine and pour in the new oil. Tighten the filler cap firmly. Dispose of the old oil at a collection station and wipe your hands clean. Finally, record the mileage for this change somewhere so that you will know when the next change is due.

A process paragraph that traces a historical development might seem somewhat more difficult to write than a set of instructions. Essentially, however, tracing the steps in a historical process follows the same form as instructions. Instructions tell a reader to do this, then that, then another thing; a paragraph tracing the steps in a historical process tells a reader first this happened, then that, then another thing. The major difference is that the historical event has already occurred and the paragraph is written in the past tense. Examine the following paragraph, which traces the transformation of the computer from mainframe to microcomputer, and notice how its pattern (this happened, then that, then another thing) follows the pattern of the instructions in the previous example (do this, then that, then the other thing):

> The first computer was made from vacuum tubes about as big as a bread box, and the collection of them filled up a room the size of a classroom. The tubes were inordinately sensitive to changes in temperature and humidity, and the smallest speck of dust caused them to go berserk. They were expensive to build and expensive to maintain; therefore they were operated only by highly trained technicians. Anyone who wished to use the computer was forced to deal with the people in the white lab coats, an inconvenient arrangement at best. The first step in reducing the size

and increasing the reliability of the computer was the invention of transistors, small, inexpensive devices that control the flow of electricity. They are solid and durable, and, most important, they can be made very small. Scientists soon discovered that transistors could also be hooked together into integrated circuits known as *chips*; the chips could contain tremendous amounts of circuitry, an amount comparable to the wiring diagram of an office building, on a piece of silicon no bigger than your thumbnail. Finally, scientists and computer experts developed the microprocessor, the central works of a computer inscribed on a chip. Presto! The way was opened for the development of a microcomputer about the size of a bread box.

Causal Analysis. Causal analysis, as the name implies, is an analysis of the causes leading to a given outcome. On an essay test, you might be asked to explain or discuss the reasons for a lost war, a victory in an election, a depression, or the collapse of a bridge. In your life outside school, you might be called on to explain why you have selected some occupation or particular college or why you wish to drop out of school to hike the Appalachian Trail for four or five months.

Causal analysis differs from process analysis in that it does not necessarily involve a chronological sequence. Instead, it seeks the reasons for an outcome and lists them (with necessary discussion) in either ascending or descending order of importance. A process analysis concerned with the growth of inflation in the last seventy-five years might trace the fall of the dollar's value and the actions and reactions of government and consumers at intervals of ten years. A causal analysis on the same subject would give the reasons why the dollar has declined in value and why the reactions of government and consumers have produced progressively worse conditions. Causal analysis might also be used to explain why a course of action has been taken or ought to be taken.

It is important that the United States curb inflation over the next few years. Inflation at home is reducing the value of the dollar overseas, making it very difficult for Americans to purchase products from other countries. German automobiles, even those that once were considered low-cost transportation, have increased in price dramatically in the last few years. At home, rapid price increases have made it very difficult for salary increases to keep pace with the cost of living. In spite of large pay increases over the past few years, factory workers have shown little or no gain in buying power; prices have climbed as workers' wages have increased, leaving workers with nothing to show for a larger paycheck. Inflation has been especially hard on retired people who live on a fixed income. They receive only a set number of dollars and do not benefit from pay increases as do wage earners. But while the income of retired people has remained the same, prices have increased; thus they cannot buy the same amounts as they could previously. Unchecked inflation works a hardship on all of us, but it is especially hard on those whose income does not increase to match the increases in prices.

Causal analysis might also be used to explain the reasons why someone holds a particular position or opinion. A student explained her love of sailing as follows:

A sailboat, a broad bay, and a good breeze form the most satisfying combination in the world of sport. To be sailing before a brisk wind across an open expanse of water allows—no, requires—cooperation with the forces of nature. Working with the wind in moving the boat provides us one of the few times when we are not forced to ignore, or work against, or even overcome the natural rhythms and functions of the universe. Too much of daily life pits us against those forces; finding them on our side, aiding us in a worthwhile project, is indeed a pleasure. The boats used are in themselves very pleasant. They do not bang or clank, nor do they spout vile fumes or foul the air, suddenly explode, or cease to function altogether. Instead, they offer the soft, sliding sounds of the bow slipping through the sea, the creak of ropes and sails, and the gentle, soothing hum of the standing rigging pulled tight by the pressure of wind on sails. Most important, sailing puts us in close contact, in communion, with that most basic element, the sea. The sea remains constant; winds or storms may stir the surface, but the depths are never moved. The sea always has been and always will be, or so it seems. It offers constancy and permanence in the midst of a world where flux and change are the only constants. Is it any wonder that sailing is such a delight, such a joy?

Exemplification

One of the simplest yet most effective paragraphs states its topic and then uses examples to define and clarify it. The following paragraph explains its topic by using examples:

Youth and beauty are grand attributes, and together they are a wonderful possession. But television commercials and programs extol youth and beauty to such an extreme that those not so young and less than beautiful are made to feel inferior. Cars, beer, clothes, and even lawn mowers are almost always pictured with lithe, beautiful women of tender age or well-muscled young men with luxuriant, well-groomed hair. Cosmetics are always portrayed in use by people who have almost no need of them. Beauty, and especially youthful beauty, sells goods, we surmise, and those who do not become young and beautiful after buying the car or ingesting the iron supplement are obviously unfit to share the planet with the favored ones. And the programs themselves emphasize youthful beauty. There are few homely, few truly decrepit people who play regularly in any series. Any family, and any individual, who cannot compare with those perfect people ought to be exiled from the land of the lovely. We are left to believe that only the beautiful young are acceptable.

Description and Narration

Two important development patterns remain: *description* and *narration*. Each of these patterns involves a direction or a movement. Description requires movement through space: The writer's eye moves through a given space, picking out selected details in order to create an effect. Narration demands movement through time: The writer creates a progression through time, providing details selected to convey a story and its impact. The success of each pattern depends on the careful selection of details of physical qualities or of action and on the vivid presentation of these details.

In *Huckleberry Finn* Mark Twain has Huck give a beautiful description of a sunrise on the Mississippi:

. . . we run nights, and laid up and hid daytimes; soon as night was most gone, we stopped navigating and tied up—nearly always in the dead water under a tow-head; and then cut young cottonwoods and willows and hid the raft with them. Then we set out the lines. Next we slid into the river and had a swim, so as to freshen up and cool off; then we set down on the sandy bottom where the water was about knee deep, and watched the daylight come. Not a sound, anywhere—perfectly still—just like the whole world was asleep, only sometimes the bull-frogs a-cluttering, maybe. The first thing to see, looking away over the water, was a kind of dull line—that was the woods on t'other side—you couldn't make nothing else out; then a pale place in the sky; then more paleness, spreading around; then the river softened up, away off, and warn't black any more, but gray; you could set little dark spots drifting along, ever so far away—trading scows, and such things; and long black streaks—rafts; sometimes you could hear a sweep screaking; or jumbled up voices, it was so still, and sound come so far; and by-and-by you could see a streak on the water which you know by the look of the streak that there's a snag there in a swift current which breaks on it and makes that streak look that way; and you see the mist curl up off the water, and the east reddens up, and the river, and you make out a log cabin in the edge of the woods, away on the bank on t'other side of the river, being a wood-

yard, likely and piled by them cheats so you can throw a dog through it anywhere; then the nice breeze springs up, and comes fanning you from over there, so cool and fresh, and sweet to smell, on account of the woods and the flowers; but sometimes not that way, because they've left dead fish laying around, gars, and such, and they do get pretty rank; and next you've got the full day, and everything smiling in the sun, and the song-birds just going it!

Two qualities of this description are important for you to note. First, notice the direction or movement of the unfolding picture. Beginning with the dim view of the far bank, the narrator observes traces of paleness in the sky. He then notes that the river has softened up "away off"; notice the logical progression from sky to horizon to river. After he gives details of the changing sights and sounds at river level, the mist curling up from the river focuses his attention again on the sky as the "east reddens up." Then he returns to the river and develops the picture as new details become visible in the light of morning. This movement from mid-picture to background to foreground to background to foreground follows a sensory logic, an order of increasing visibility as the sun rises and the light increases. It is important to select an order of presentation (or, as here, a logic) and to stick with the order, whether it be left-to-right, right-to-left, middle-to-left-to-right, or any other easily followed combination. Second, Twain provides details that appeal to the senses:

Color:	dull line of woods pale sky river changing from black to gray dark spots and black streaks east reddening
Sound:	complete absence of sound bullfrogs a-cluttering sweep screaking jumbled up voices song birds
Smell:	woods flowers dead fish
Motion:	dark spots drifting snag in swift current mist curling up off the water
Touch:	cooling off in water sitting on sandy bottom of river cool breeze springing up

Supply your reader with sensory appeal. Keep your description lively and colorful.

In another section of *Huckleberry Finn,* Twain provides us with a heart-stopping piece of narration, the killing of the old drunk, Boggs.

So somebody started on a run. I walked down the street a ways, and stopped. In about five or ten minutes, here comes Boggs again— but not on his horse. He was a-reeling across the street towards me, bareheaded, with a friend on both sides of him aholt of his arms and hurrying him along. He was quiet, and looked uneasy; and he warn't hanging back any, but was doing some of the hurrying himself. Somebody sings out—"Boggs!"

I looked over there to see who said it, and it was that Colonel Sherburn. He was standing perfectly still, in the street, and had a pistol raised in his right hand—not aiming it, but holding it out with the barrel tilted up towards the sky. The same second I see a young girl coming on the run, and two men with her. Boggs and the men turned round, to see who called him, and when they see the pistol the men jumped to one side, and the pistol barrel came down slow and steady to a level—both barrels cocked. Boggs throws up both of his hands, and says, "O Lord, don't shoot!" Bang! goes the first shot, and he staggers back clawing at the air—bang goes the second one, and he tumbles backwards onto the ground, heavy and solid, with his arms spread out. That young girl screamed out, and comes rushing, and down she throws herself on her father, crying, and saying, "Oh, he's killed him, he's killed him!" The crowd closed up around them, and shouldered and jammed one another, with their necks stretched, trying to see, and people on the inside trying to shove them back, and shouting, "Back, back! give him air, give him air!"

Colonel Sherburn he tossed his pistol onto the ground, and turned around on his heels and walked off.

Again, two aspects of the narrative are important. The order is simple, straight chronology. But notice the action words. The girl comes on the run, the men jump, Boggs staggers. Few forms of the verb *to be* intrude to slow the action, and no statements of thought or emotion stop the progression. All of the impact and emotion is conveyed through action, and that use of action is the essence of good narrative.

A Final Note

Good paragraphs are not necessarily restricted to a single pattern of development. Sometimes it is necessary to include more than one pattern of development in a paragraph. A narration, for example, may demand a passage of description. And quite often it is useful to combine patterns to produce a desired effect. The following paragraph on spider webs illustrates such a combination of patterns. The predominant device used here is analysis: The larger unit, spider webs, is broken down into three separate types or categories. But the writer uses an additional strategy; he clarifies his analysis by comparison/contrast, pointing out like and unlike details of the three kinds of spider webs:

Web-spinning spiders construct three kinds of webs. The first type is the tangled web, a shapeless helter-skelter jumble attached to some support such as the corner of a room. These webs are hung in the path of insects and serve to entangle them as they pass. The second type of web is the sheet web. This web is a flat sheet of silk strung between blades of grass or tree branches. Above this sheet is strung a sort of net, which serves to knock insects into the sheet. When an insect hits the sheet, the spider darts out and pulls it through the webbing, trapping the insect. Finally, perhaps the most beautiful of the webs, is the orb. The orb web consists of threads that extend from a center like a wheel's spokes and are connected to limbs or grass blades. All the spokes are connected by repeated circles of sticky silk, forming a kind of screen. Insects are caught in this screen and trapped by the spider.

Don't hesitate to shift methods where a switch is useful. Do so with care, however, and keep in mind that a new method of development might suggest the need for a new paragraph.

Exercises for Patterns for Paragraphs

1. Examine the following facts and observations about two methods for recording and playing music and other sound:

   - Cassette tapes can stretch and lose sound quality.
   - Compact discs are resistant to damage.
   - Compact discs maintain their sound quality.
   - Cassette tapes are less expensive than compact discs.
   - Cassette tapes can be damaged by tangling or unwinding.
   - In general, sound quality on compact discs is higher than sound quality on cassette tapes.

   Write a paragraph of comparison/contrast discussing the merits of these two media.

2. Write a paragraph giving directions for preparing your favorite dessert. Include every step and provide enough detail and information for a beginning cook to be able to make the dessert successfully. Check your work by preparing the dessert following your instructions.

3. Write a description of one of the buildings on your campus. Provide sufficient detail so that a person can identify the building that you are describing. Do not use the name, the location, or any identifying colors in the description.

Once you have mastered the steps in the writing process by creating paragraphs, you will need to make only a few adjustments to follow that same process in writing a longer essay, the sort of essay you might be assigned in a college class in biology, business, or English. After all, whether you are writing essay tests or special paragraph arrangements, or full length essays, the writing process we described on pages 306–308 is the same.

Composing

Let's assume you need to develop a paper for your English class. Because the paper is a class assignment, the first step requires a look at the nature of class assignments and the problems of defining the subject and limiting it to an appropriate, manageable length.

Step 1. Select the Subject

Usually writing assignments fall into one of three categories.

1. **Very General:**   Write a two-page paper on something we've covered in this course.
2. **Somewhat Specific:** Write a two-page paper on some aspect of the novel *Huckleberry Finn.*
3. **Very Directive:**   Write a two-page paper explaining why Huck Finn's experiences led him to make his final statement: "Aunt Sally's going to adopt me and sivilize me and I can't stand it. I been there before."

The very general assignment grants considerable latitude in the selection of a subject for a paper. Often this latitude will prove more of a problem than a blessing because it is necessary to find something to write about that you *and* the teacher consider interesting and worthwhile. It is of little value to write a fine paper and find that the teacher (the grader) thinks the topic so insignificant that the whole effort can't be worth more than a C. The best approach here is to review the textbook, your lecture notes, and previous tests (if any); to select from these an important content area, concept, or personality; and to use that selection as a starting point for your work. Be sure to choose an area that interests you, an area about which you have some knowledge and some readily accessible sources of information. Once you have made this initial selection, you have converted the assignment from "general" to "somewhat specific." Next, you need to restrict the area you selected or were assigned so that you can develop it fully within the assigned length of the paper. Suppose, for example, the assignment said to write a two-page paper on *Huckleberry Finn*. Several areas are open to you:

1. Autobiographical aspects of the novel
2. Problems of plot and structure
3. Problems of characterization
4. Philosophical aspects of the novel

For the selection or restriction process, choose one of the areas and make a final selection of a topic within that area. The final selection should be fairly small in scope, something manageable within two pages. In the example of *Huckleberry Finn,* the process of restriction might look like this:

Philosophical aspects of the novel

1. The relationship between individuals and society
2. Huck Finn's attitude toward the world as he saw it
3. Why Huck's experiences led him to say that he couldn't stand to be "sivilized"

The final version of the topic (Number 3) is probably limited enough for it to be treated adequately within the assigned length. The topic asks a single question about one person. It should be possible to answer that question and offer examples supporting your answer in two pages.

Note that the way in which your teacher states the assignment dictates the starting point for your work. A general assignment requires that you go through three stages:

1. Selection of a general subject area
2. Selection of a portion or phase of this general area to form a limited subject area
3. Final selection of a specific limited topic within the limited subject area

A somewhat specific assignment completes the first two stages for you by limiting you to a general area. You need deal with only the third stage to complete the restriction process for this assignment. A very directive assignment accomplishes all three stages and leaves you free to begin work on the organization of the paper itself.

Step 2. Gather Information

Once you have established your topic, you need to establish what you know about the topic. Continuing with our *Huckleberry Finn* example, what were Huck's experiences? Why did they make him want to avoid Aunt Sally's attentions? List some of the experiences he had in the "sivilized" world. Here are some possibilities:

1. The confining life at the Widow Douglas's home and Miss Watson's efforts to teach Huck manners and religion
2. The brutal shooting of Boggs by Colonel Sherburn and the mob violence of the attempted lynching that was faced down by Sherburn's single-handed capacity for even greater violence
3. The Grangerford—Shepherdson feud
4. Huck's obvious pleasure at living outside civilization with Jim on Jackson's Island and on the raft

While other experiences may come to mind as you work on the paper, this list leads directly to Step 3.

Step 3. Establish a Controlling Statement

The controlling statement, or **thesis,** serves the longer essay much as the topic sentence serves the paragraph. The topic sentence states the subject of the paragraph and tells what will be said about it. The thesis statement controls the writer before the paper is written by defining the subject and what is to be said about the subject. It keeps the writer from wandering away from the subject; sometimes it is so specific that it establishes the order in which the essay will be arranged. Reviewing your list of Huck's experiences, the thesis statement for your paper is obvious:

> Huck could not stand to be "sivilized" because his experiences in civilization were confining, frightening, or dangerous.

Step 4. Select Specific Items of Support

Keeping the thesis statement in mind, you need to select from the book experiences and observations that will clearly illustrate the conditions in civilization. All the possible pieces of evidence listed above can be used to point out the conditions that Huck wanted to avoid. Even the pleasant experiences with Jim on Jackson's Island serve to make the bad experiences more vivid. As you select the content, you produce an outline, which is a simple list of the points you wish to make in support of your thesis. Each point in the outline then becomes a paragraph of support in your short paper. In a longer paper, more than one paragraph may be required to develop a single point.

Step 5. Establish an Order of Presentation

Several orders are possible, but the easiest one to follow is to take the materials in the order in which they occur in the book.

Step 6. Write the First Draft

Begin by writing an introduction. The introduction might read this way:

> At the close of the novel *Huckleberry Finn,* Huck concludes his story by saying that he intends to "light out for the Territory" because Aunt Sally intends to "sivilize" him, and he feels that he can't stand any more efforts to make him an upstanding, moral, and religious citizen. His attitude is understandable, for his experiences in society as it existed along the Mississippi were confining, unpleasant, or downright terrifying.

We will discuss introductions again in the next section.

Continue now to the **paragraphs of development.** Paragraphs of development are the paragraphs you write to support your thesis. In this example, the paragraphs of development will discuss Huck's experiences with the "sivilized" world.

> Huck's experiences of "home," or at the two places where he lives at the opening of the novel, are decidedly unpleasant. The home of Widow Douglas and Miss Watson tends to oppress and constrict a boy's natural energy and interests. Regular meals eaten with careful manners and polite small talk work against Huck's tendency to roam at will through the woods. Lectures on morality

and religion tend to confuse him. If one can obtain his or her desires through prayer, why are folks poor, or sick, or crippled? If being good makes one blessed, why is Miss Watson so sour and seemingly unhappy? Life with Pap may be more free from the repressions of etiquette, but it also has its frightening side of drunkenness, violence, and delirium tremens. So Huck decides to leave these situations behind to look for something better.

Something better turns out to be life on the river with Jim, the runaway slave. They meet on Jackson's Island and camp there for a time. Their experiences on the island are mostly pleasant: loafing, camping, fishing, and generally hanging out, all of which suit Huck just fine. The idyll is interrupted by a snakebite (from which Jim recovers) and is ended by the threat of a search party coming out to find Jim. Jim is a slave and, by all the measures of that day, less than human, but in reality he is the only truly civilized person Huck meets in his travels. Jim loves Huck and cares for him, in spite of Huck's tendency to play cruel jokes on him. He shelters Huck from the knowledge of Pap's death and doesn't reject Huck after he discovers the hoax of Huck's dream fabrication when they have been separated in a fog. It is ironic that the only civilized person Huck meets is not considered truly human by those who regard themselves as civilized.

The other people Huck meets in his travels do very little to improve his suspicious view of the world. He and Jim happen upon some fairly terrible people as soon as they venture out on the river: slave hunters, the gamblers who are trying to kill their partner, and a nonhuman agent of civilization, a steamboat that runs them down and puts Huck back on shore. There he meets the Grangerfords, gentlemen and ladies all, living in a fine house and enjoying prosperity. The Grangerfords are aristocrats and moral churchgoing people who have only one fault: They are engaged in a murderous, generations-old feud with the Shepherdsons. One Sunday afternoon Huck witnesses an outbreak of this feud that leaves most of the people from both families dead.

Fleeing from the killing, Huck returns to the river and finds Jim. They continue down the river. Later they meet the King and the Duke, two great con artists who dupe the people in a nearby town and are eventually tarred and feathered for their efforts. During the adventures with the King and the Duke, Huck witnesses the shooting of the harmless drunk Boggs and the attempted lynching of Colonel Sherburn, the man who shot him. Taken on balance, most of Huck's experiences on shore are grim and frightening, good reasons for his lack of enthusiasm for civilization.

Even the last episode of the book does little to increase Huck's desire to live in the civilized world. Huck comes by chance on the home of Tom Sawyer's Aunt Sally and adopts Tom's identity. When Tom shows up, he is introduced as Cousin Sid. Jim is also on the plantation, being held as a runaway slave. The two boys, with Tom leading, enter an incredible plot to free Jim, although, as Tom knows but conceals, Jim has already been freed. After a series of cops-and-robbers antics, the plot resolves into what looks like a happy ending. It is revealed that Jim is free, Pap is dead, and Huck's personal fortune, presumed lost, is intact. Aunt Sally offers to adopt Huck and raise him properly so that he can become a successful, civilized adult. At this point Huck reviews his situation. Life in town and his misadventures on shore with the Grangerfords, the King and the Duke, Sherburn, and others suggest only bad experiences to come if he accepts Aunt Sally's offer. His time with Jim, living free and easy on the river, seems wonderfully pleasant, compared to those recollections. Little wonder, then, that he decides to "light out for the Territory."

This completes the writing process through the writing of the rough draft. We shall review these steps and the remaining steps in the process in the second example of this section.

Sample Business Paper Development

With the first stage of the writing process fresh in your mind, follow how you might apply it in writing a paper of six to eight paragraphs for a business course.

Suppose your class has been studying men who have greatly influenced American business, past and present, and the assignment is to write a paper of about 800 words discussing the contributions of one of these men.

1. ***Select the Subject.*** Several names come to mind from the history of American business: F. W. Taylor, Thomas Watson, Douglas McGregor, Alfred Sloan, Frederick Herzberg. But perhaps the most interesting and certainly one of the most important contributors to the theory and practice of business in America is Peter F. Drucker. His contributions are famous and respected in this country and abroad, and they have been cataloged and discussed in two well-respected books. Thus Drucker's contributions meet the criteria for selection as a subject. They are important and interesting, and information on them is readily available.

2. ***Gather Materials.*** What is there to know about Peter Drucker? From your class notes, texts, and outside readings, you might jot down the following notes:

   He has written twenty-seven books and many articles on business. He was born in Vienna, Austria. Father was a college teacher in America. Drucker started his career as a bookkeeper and a writer. He left Germany early in WWII. Went to London and worked in a bank. Then worked for American newspapers as a British correspondent. Worked for the U.S. government during the war, then taught at two colleges, moving in 1950 to New York University, where he taught till 1970.

   His first consulting job was a massive study of General Motors Corporation, a study highly critical of its management systems. From this work he wrote *The Concept of the Corporation,* a book that was the beginning of management thought in the modern sense of the word. His latest book, *Management: Tasks—Responsibilities—Practices,* is a very broad study of modern management philosophy and practices.

   He continues to consult for major corporations, but he requires that the client come to him in California. He charges $1,500 a day and still manages to stay booked up far in advance.

   Drucker is well-known as a teacher. He taught first at NYU in a special program for active business people. He now teaches in the Claremont Graduate School in California, a position he has held since 1971. Drucker loves teaching so much that some believe he would pay to do it if necessary. He especially enjoys teaching those who are currently employed in management positions. He uses a case-study method of his own invention, not following accepted case-study methods from other colleges. His case studies are short and are not loaded with data and statistics. Instead they concentrate on analysis and on finding the right questions to ask in a given situation. Often high-level executives attend his classes for enrichment and pleasure, even though they do not need any further course work or degrees to augment their careers. His associations in the classroom often ripen into rich and enduring friendships.

Much more information could be collected about Drucker, and more probably would be needed to fill an essay of eight hundred words. But this is enough material to allow us to move to the next step.

3. ***Establish a Controlling Statement.*** It is clear from the information gathered about Peter Drucker that he is active in three general areas of business: as a teacher, consultant, and writer. But the key word in the assignment is *contributions,* not *activity.* The fact that Drucker has been active as a writer does not automatically mean that he has made a contribution to the theory and practice of American business in his writings. That remains to be determined; you must return to the information gathered in Step 2 to

see what is known about his *contributions*. (**Note:** It is not uncommon to discover that writing the statement for a paper [Step 3] requires a return to the information-gathering stage [Step 2] to find additional information to use in formulating the thesis statement.)

The information already collected provides only a suggestion of Drucker's contributions: he wrote a book that was the "beginning of management thought in the modern sense of the word." Now you must collect information directly related to this.

Further reading in books and articles about Peter Drucker indicates two very important areas of contribution, one theoretical and the other practical, which you summarize as follows:

In the theory of management, Drucker was the first to identify the corporation as a whole as something that needed management and that could be managed. Prior to his work, discussions of corporation management were rather fragmented, dealing with isolated problems such as accounting and materials handling. Drucker developed a theory for the operation of the entire corporation.

On the practical side, Drucker developed the concept of the manager and his or her role in the corporation, and he has written guides to the day-to-day functions of those in management. He has worked as a consultant for major corporations, and the solutions to their problems have filtered to other companies and influenced institutions such as schools and hospitals. He also did initial work on ideas that later were more fully developed by others: The "hygiene" theory of the effects of wages on motivation and the theories of motivation often labeled X and Y were initially discussed in Drucker's works, at least in concept, and were developed by other writers, Herzberg and McGregor in particular.

The addition of this information to the information previously collected provides a solid basis for working on Step 3, establishing the statement.

The nature of Drucker's contributions is now clear enough for you to try writing a statement about them. Such a statement might read:

Peter Drucker has made both a theoretical and a practical contribution to American business.

or

Peter Drucker was the first to develop a theory of the nature and function of the corporation, and he has made practical application of that theory to the day-to-day work of the manager through his writings and his work as a consultant. He also did initial work on concepts fully developed by others.

The second version captures most of what needs to be said, but the order is jumbled and the statement is too wordy. A better version is

Peter Drucker developed the overall concept of the corporation, its place in society, and its operation; he also began work on specific concepts that were later developed by other men. His practical work as writer and consultant has provided direction to many managers.

Now you are ready to move to Step 4.

4. *Select Specific Items of Support.* You can shape the controlling statement into a general outline for a paper and get an idea of the kinds of materials you will need to support the statement.

Drucker's Contributions

- Developed theory and concept of the corporation.
- Began work on concepts later fully developed by others.
- Provided practical applications of those theories in writings and in consulting work.

To develop the first point in the outline, you will need to discuss the state of management theory when Drucker began his work. Then you will need to explain how he developed his theory, where he first began to publish it, and, in general terms, what that theory of the corporation and its management is. For the second point, you need to identify the concepts that Drucker began to develop, the people who completed that development, and the name or the final form of those concepts. A discussion of his more practical books and some of the guidelines in them can be joined with a brief discussion of his work as a consultant to present the third point in the outline.

5. *Establish an Order of Presentation.* There is an order already built into the outline from the materials collected in Step 2: first, theories and concepts of the corporation as a whole, then specific theories, and then practical applications of those theories. This order also seems to arrange the contributions in descending order of importance, taking the larger, more global contributions first and moving to less important theories and practical matters next. It would be possible to reverse that order and work from least important to most important, from practical to theoretical. But such a progression does not seem to suit the materials as well as the first order, so you should present the materials in the draft in the order suggested by the outline.

6. *Write the First Draft.* It might seem logical to begin writing a draft of a paper with the beginning, the introduction. If a clear, effective introduction comes to mind rather handily, begin with the introduction. But do not wait with pen in hand for the perfect introduction to appear on the page. Make one attempt at an introduction; if nothing comes of that first attempt, begin to write the body of the paper wherever you find the writing easiest, even if you begin with what is actually the last paragraph in the essay. Get the material written and then put the paper in the proper order. Write, don't wait for the inspiration.

There are two elements in Step 6 of your business paper development that need to be discussed in greater detail. These are the introduction to your topic and the conclusion of your paper.

The Introduction

The introduction should serve two important functions. *First,* and more important, the introduction must catch the interest of the reader. *Second,* it must give the reader an idea of the direction the paper will take. This sense of direction may come from a restating of the thesis statement you developed in Step 3 or from a paraphrase of your thesis statement. On the other hand, you may provide a sense of direction by offering a general identifying statement of the topic. For the paper on Peter Drucker a paraphrase of the Step 3 statement might read:

> Peter Drucker developed a philosophy of the corporation, devised specific concepts within that philosophy, and showed managers how to make a practical application of that philosophy.

Identifying the topic and making a general statement of the ideas to be covered might produce:

> Of all those who have helped to develop our ideas of the nature and workings of the corporation, Peter Drucker is among the most important.

With this effort to provide a sense of direction, you must also catch the reader's interest. If you have trouble thinking of methods for developing introductions, you might try one of the following strategies:

- Use a quotation or a paraphrase of a striking statement:

  > Peter Drucker is, in the words of C. Northcote Parkinson, "preeminent among management consultants and also among authors of books on management."

- Cite an important fact or statistic:

  > Prior to the writing of *The Concept of the Corporation,* the idea of the corporation as an entity that needed management did not exist. Drucker invented the corporate society.

- Recount an anecdote:

  > "What *is* your business?" the famous consultant asked the directors of a firm that made bottles. "Everyone knows," responded the chairman, "that we make bottles for soft drinks and other foods." "I disagree," replied the consultant to the astounded board. After a pause to let his words sink in, he continued, "Your business is not the making of bottles; you are in the packaging business." With that one question Peter Drucker, America's foremost business consultant, opened the board's eyes and provided new direction for a foundering company.

- Use a dictionary definition:

  > The dictionary defines a corporation as a group of individuals legally united to conduct business. Peter Drucker defines the corporation as the cornerstone of our society.

- Set up a contrast between two ideas:

  > The original management consultant was really an efficiency expert, timing workers on an assembly line and suggesting ways of improving their speed and productivity. Peter Drucker's work is as far removed from that practice as the supersonic transport is from the Wright brothers' first plane.

As you become a more experienced writer, you will find less and less need for these strategies. Use them now, but feel free to experiment as your confidence grows.

The Conclusion

Always provide a conclusion for your paper. As a rule, a short sentence of summary or a restatement of the topic will suffice. The function of a conclusion for a short paper is to let the reader know that the paper has been completed, to provide a sense of "finished-ness." Don't leave the reader with the impression that he or she ought to be looking for more material. Don't try to provide an extensive restatement or summary for a short paper. And be very careful that you never use the conclusion to introduce a new point or add additional information. A one-sentence conclusion should be ample for most college essays.

Revising

The first completed draft of the paper on the contributions of Peter Drucker might read this way:

Of the business people, scholars, and writers who have attempted to analyze and influence the business world of the twentieth century, none has made a greater contribution or been more interesting to observe than Peter Drucker. Drucker is a teacher, a consultant, and a writer who has drawn from each role to construct a philosophy or theoretical concept of the corporation and a workable application of the theory to actual business problems and challenges. In theory and in practice, Drucker has been a major influence on American business for the last fifty years.

In the minds of many, Drucker is the person who almost single-handedly invented the idea of the corporation. Prior to Drucker's introduction of the idea in *The Concept of the Corporation,* the study of business management was the study of individual problems such as accounting or materials handling. Drucker changed that view and suggested that the corporation was an entity, a whole, and needed to be managed as a whole, not as a series of isolated services or problems. Much of this book, and the ideas within it, arose from a massive study of General Motors under-taken in 1943. Having examined the operation of that company in great detail, and having reported that he thought it was managed chaotically, he set about developing a unified view of the corporation and its management. He did develop such a view and, in the process, suggested that the key institution and the chief influence on the future of the Western world would be the corporation, complete with assembly lines. This view of the corporation as a whole and his real-ization that the corporation was a major political, social, *and* economic force have made Drucker a major contributor to the present-day theory of business.

Drucker has written extensively in the area of management and has been a leader in the development of important concepts in specific areas of management. He was a leader, or at least an important forerunner, of the management system commonly called *management by objec-tives* (MBO). He first used the term in his book *The Practice of Management* and says he first heard it used by Alfred Sloan in the 1950s. Essentially, MBO tries to focus the attention of man-agers on their objectives. Managers of the old school had always asked themselves, "What do I do?" Drucker turned their attention from the process to the product or objective and said that the proper question is "What do I wish to accomplish?" That principle of management is now so commonplace in business and government that it seems always to have existed. Two concepts in the area of motivation were suggested by Drucker and developed by others. The first is the now famous "hygiene" theory of compensation, which says that wages and certain other condi-tions of employment do not cause high morale and motivation; instead they prevent low morale and allow other positive motivators to have an impact on the workers. These *hygiene factors* do not increase motivation and production, but motivation and the accompanying higher pro-duction cannot occur without them. Drucker also was an early contributor to the theories of motivation commonly called *Theory X* and *Theory Y,* which are widely discussed by writers such as Douglas McGregor. Theory X says that people are motivated best by threat and fear, by neg-ative or extrinsic motivation; Theory Y counters that people are better and further motivated by satisfaction of their basic needs and by appeals to their sense of participation and involvement. These ideas are well known and widely used today; Drucker was a major contributor to their early development.

But Drucker is no airy theorist incapable of practical work. He is a consultant whose services are heavily sought by industry and government. He is in such demand that he can charge $1,500 a day for his services and never lack clients. He is a consultant who does not try to provide clients with an answer to their problems. Rather, he tries to point out what the proper questions are and to help the clients find the answers. In early work with a manufacturer of glass bottles, he shocked the executive committee by asking them what business the firm was in. Silence followed the question, and then the chairman replied with a hint of anger in his voice, "We make glass bottles for soft-drink makers and others." "No," replied Drucker, "your business is not making bottles. You are in the packaging business." That answer, coming from an unusual perspective, greatly altered the executives' view of the company and its problems and led to solutions never suspected by the executive committee. Drucker constantly advises his clients to build from strength, to use the abilities that each person possesses, and to structure assignments so that no manager is forced to work long in an area where she or he is weak. Managers of the old school always looked at weaknesses and worked for their correction. Drucker said, "Forget the weaknesses. Put the person in a position where his weaknesses will not matter; use and develop the strengths of each employee."

Drucker has raised the art of consulting to new heights, making practical applications of the theories of management he developed. As a writer he has been an important contributor to the practical side of management. *The Effective Executive* is full of good advice to managers, advice useful on a day-to-day basis. His later book, *Management: Tasks—Responsibilities—Practices,* has in it long sections that are intensely practical. Even his more theoretical works have a practical bent. Arjay Miller, former president of Ford Motor Company, says that *The Concept of the Corporation* was "extremely useful in forming my judgments about what was needed at Ford. It was, by considerable margin, the most useful and pragmatic publication available and had a definite impact on the postwar organizational development within the Ford Motor Company" (*Drucker: The Man Who Invented the Corporate Society,* 1976, p. 32). Peter Drucker, philosopher, theorist, and practical authority, is, without doubt, a major figure in the history of American business and a man who helped to shape and form the corporation as we know it today.

Materials for this essay were taken from John J. Tarrant, *Drucker: The Man Who Invented the Corporate Society* (Boston: Cahners Books, Inc., 1976) and from Tony H. Bonaparte and John E. Flaherty, eds., *Peter Drucker: Contributions to Business Enterprise* (New York: New York University Press, 1970). Drucker's latest book is *Managing for the Future* (Truman Talley Books/Dutton, 1992).

Keep in mind the completed version of the paper that comes out of Step 6 is *not*—repeat, *not*—the final version of the paper. Step 6 produces a rough draft, a version suitable for revision and not much else. Think of that draft as a good start, but remember that it is still a long way from completion. Use the remaining steps of the writing process in revising your draft. Wait a day or two (if possible) between completing the draft and undertaking the revision.

Follow the seven steps in the revision process (p. 308) to produce the best paper possible.

Step 7. Assess the Thesis of the Draft

Basic Question: Is the thesis a proper expression of your knowledge on the subject?
Strategy: Read each supporting paragraph or section of the essay individually and write a topic sentence for each one. From the topic statements produce a thesis statement

for the draft. Compare it to the original thesis. If there are differences between the two, create a new, better thesis. Omit the introduction from the outline; it does not provide support for the thesis.

Paragraph 2.   Drucker invented the idea of the corporation as we know it.
Paragraph 3.   Drucker has written extensively and developed important concepts in management.
Paragraph 4.   Drucker is more than a theorist; he is a consultant who is much in demand.
Paragraph 5.   Drucker has shown managers how to apply his ideas.

These five topic sentences agree with or add up to the thesis statement as originally written and refined. The thesis statement is an accurate reflection of the information gathered in Step 3.

Step 8. Assess the Content

Basic Question: Does each paragraph or section offer genuine support for the thesis?
Strategy: Check the topic statement for each paragraph or section to be sure each one supports the new thesis. Remove and replace any paragraph or section that does not support the thesis.

All the content seems to support the thesis. No material develops an idea outside of the thesis, and there is adequate support of the thesis.

Step 9. Assess the Order of Presentation

Basic Question: Does the order of presentation provide the reader with a logical progression or pathway through the essay?
Strategy: Try different orders of presentation, shifting sections around to see if you can find a better order than the one you used for the first finished draft.

The order of the paragraphs works from theory to practice and also has some movement forward in time. Thus the order seems to be logical.

Step 10. Assess the Paragraphs

Basic Questions: Is each paragraph unified and complete? Is each paragraph developed following the best possible method of development?
Strategy: Using the topic sentences from the sentence outline, check the content of the paragraph to be sure it develops one idea and only one idea. Check the content to be sure that the paragraph contains enough specific, concrete details to make the topic statement clear to the reader. Evaluate the introduction and conclusion separately as a single unit.

Introductions serve two basic purposes:

1. They catch the interest of the reader and identify the subject.
2. They state the thesis or set the direction for the essay.

The introduction tries to catch the interest of the reader by making a connection between students of business and Drucker, a preeminent teacher, writer and consultant.

The last sentence of the introduction suggests the thesis of the essay. The conclusion closes out the essay by offering a slightly rewritten version of the last sentence of the introduction.

The paragraphs of support each develop a single idea and have sufficient detail to make the paragraph complete.

Step 11. Correct the Mistakes in the Draft

Basic Question: What errors in grammar and mechanics do I need to correct?
Strategy: Read each sentence as an independent unit, starting at the end of the paper and working to the beginning. Reading "backward" in this fashion assures that you will not make mental corrections or assumptions as you read.

- Check each sentence for errors in completeness (Lesson 13), subject–verb agreement (Lesson 22), pronoun–antecedent agreement (Lesson 23), pronoun case (Lesson 24), dangling or misplaced modifiers (Lesson 14), and the use of prepositions (Lesson 25). (**Note:** As you find errors in your papers and as marked errors appear on papers returned to you, keep a record of them—either by putting a check in the appropriate lessons of this book or by marking your reference handbook. You will soon discover whether you have a tendency to repeat certain kinds of errors, and you simplify your proofreading by checking first for these errors. In a short time, you should be able to eliminate repeat faults from your writing.)
- Check each sentence for errors in punctuation; check for missing punctuation marks *and* for unneeded marks.
- Check for errors in mechanics, capitalization, and spelling.

Step 12. Write the Final Draft

Basic Question: What form shall I use for the final copy of the paper?
Strategy: Follow the guidelines for manuscript preparation specified by your teacher, printing or typing the final copy on plain white paper. Be sure to read the final copy carefully for errors.

8

Progress Tests

NAME _____   SCORE _____

Directions: Copy the subject of the sentence on the first line at the left and the verb on the second line.

_____   1. Our first sight of the dilapidated house depressed us.
_____

_____   2. There was no sign of life about the farm.
_____

_____   3. Each of the tourists carried a small camera.
_____

_____   4. Beyond the pines grew a few dwarf junipers.
_____

_____   5. This was only the first of a long series of interruptions.
_____

_____   6. Close to the summer camp is a nine-hole golf course.
_____

_____   7. He's the only one of my teenage friends with an unlisted phone number.
_____

_____   8. By this time next week most of the vacationers will have left the island.
_____

_____   9. Not one of the villagers had received the proper legal notice.
_____

_____   10. One of the bored clerks perfunctorily rubber-stamped Jane's passport.
_____

_____   11. Moments later a covey of quail rose from the large patch of weeds.
_____

_____   12. Next on the program will be three songs by the junior-high mixed chorus.
_____

_____   13. Finally, shortly before midnight, the last of the guests drove away.
_____

_____   14. On the kitchen table lay the remnants of a quick lunch.
_____

_____   15. Behind the shed was a short row of plum trees in full bloom.
_____

357

Directions: Each sentence contains two italicized words. In the space at the left, write one of the following numbers to identify the part of speech of each italicized word:

1. Noun	3. Verb	5. Adverb
2. Pronoun	4. Adjective	6. Preposition

_____ 1. The *address on* the letter was almost illegible.
_____

_____ 2. The general *addressed* the troops and urged them *on*.
_____

_____ 3. More money will be available at *some later* date.
_____

_____ 4. *Later, some* of the guests washed the dishes.
_____

_____ 5. In a firm *voice*, the sergeant demanded an *apology*.
_____

_____ 6. The teacher *voiced* the opinion that Joe's speech was needlessly *apologetic*.
_____

_____ 7. *Beyond* a doubt, the *arrival* of the Marines saved the day.
_____

_____ 8. *Doubtlessly* a large crowd will await the candidate's *arrival*.
_____

_____ 9. A *lovely* park is *close* to the campus.
_____

_____ 10. The *alert* dog guarded the prisoner *closely*.
_____

_____ 11. The sentinel was commended *for* his *alertness*.
_____

_____ 12. *Everyone* thinks your action deserves a *reward*.
_____

_____ 13. *Every* member of the squad must work *harder*.
_____

_____ 14. The children *like* an *occasional* visit to the zoo.
_____

_____ 15. *Occasionally* Julia's practical jokes *annoy* me.
_____

_____ 16. We consider these interruptions only a *minor annoyance*.
_____

_____ 17. We *worked throughout* the hot afternoon.
_____

_____ 18. You should be commended for your *enthusiastic work* on the project.
_____

_____ 19. *This* plan sounds completely *workable*.
_____

_____ 20. *This* improvement cannot be made *without* additional funds.
_____

NAME _____   SCORE _____

Directions: Identify the italicized word by writing one of the following abbreviations in the space at the left:

S.C.	[subjective complement]	I.O.	[indirect object]
D.O.	[direct object]	O.C.	[objective complement]

If the italicized word is *not* used as one of these complements, leave the space blank.

_____   1. Next Thursday afternoon might be a good *time* for our next meeting.

_____   2. You should have looked up the correct *spelling* of the word in your dictionary.

_____   3. I can have your meal *ready* for you in half an hour.

_____   4. The truck had been standing out in the sub-zero *weather* all week.

_____   5. One in high political office must avoid even a *hint* of scandal.

_____   6. In a hard-fought eighteen-hole playoff, Jeremy emerged the *winner.*

_____   7. The injured woman could give the *police* only a sketchy account of the accident.

_____   8. You should send the personnel *officer* a list of your previous employers.

_____   9. These vacuum-packed bags will keep the potato chips *crisp.*

_____   10. How *old* is that noisy, gas-guzzling car of yours?

_____   11. How many *miles* per gallon do you get from your car?

_____   12. The children were happily making *sandcastles* on the beach.

_____   13. Henry made *me* an attractive offer for my used camcorder.

_____   14. A fresh coat of paint would make this dingy room more *attractive.*

_____   15. In Chinese cooking, dried sea cucumber is an important *ingredient.*

_____   16. When will you send *me* a bill for your professional services?

_____ 17. Our new state officers are taking on an awesome *responsibility.*

_____ 18. "I want every one of these windows *spotless* by noon," said the sergeant.

_____ 19. "I want every one of these *windows* spotless by noon," said the sergeant.

_____ 20. Later the picture frames will be given three *coats* of varnish.

_____ 21. In his youth he had been looked upon as the town *buffoon.*

_____ 22. How *certain* can we be of the mayor's support for our project?

_____ 23. Which of these three samples do you consider the best *buy?*

_____ 24. *Which* of these three samples do you consider the best buy?

_____ 25. During the cook's testimony the accused man appeared *worried.*

_____ 26. After a noticeable pause the umpire called the pitch a *strike.*

_____ 27. All of us wish *you* a prosperous New Year.

_____ 28. The influx of refugees brought our *city* new problems.

_____ 29. How *wide* should we make the new path?

_____ 30. How wide should we make the new *path?*

_____ 31. Susan had been putting off a *visit* to her dentist.

_____ 32. Did Mrs. Camp offer you *any* of her famous blueberry pie?

_____ 33. Did Mrs. Camp offer *you* any of her famous blueberry pie?

_____ 34. I now feel *rested* enough for the climb to the summit.

_____ 35. How *cold* do the winters get in Anchorage?

_____ 36. *Whom* has the chairwoman chosen as her assistant?

_____ 37. This dessert must be kept very *cold* until serving time.

_____ 38. First of all, someone will give *you* an aptitude test.

_____ 39. First of all, you will be given an aptitude *test.*

_____ 40. You will find the climate here quite *moderate.*

NAME _____ SCORE _____

Directions: Each of the following sentences contains one subordinate clause. Use square brackets ([ ]) to mark the beginning and the end of each subordinate clause. Circle the subject and underline the verb of each subordinate clause. Identify the clause by writing in the space at the left one of the following abbreviations:

    Adv. [adverb clause]   Adj. [adjective clause]   N. [noun clause]

_____ 1. As the chorus marched onto the stage, a small dog followed.

_____ 2. There is much merit in what you propose.

_____ 3. The scenery collapsed at the moment when Gene stepped out from the wings.

_____ 4. Have you told your family of the plans you have made?

_____ 5. Anyone as old as your niece should know the alphabet.

_____ 6. Were I you, I'd apply for the scholarship.

_____ 7. It's unfortunate that you missed the class picnic.

_____ 8. We had nothing to eat except what was left over from lunch.

_____ 9. Theodore Roosevelt did several things that restored presidential leadership over Congress.

_____ 10. According to the legend, Medusa could change a man to stone as he was looking at her.

_____ 11. The dormitory where Julie lived housed several students from India.

_____ 12. This pamphlet explains on what bases the student essays should be judged.

_____ 13. The diamond ring Alice is wearing came originally from her aunt in Holland.

_____ 14. Do you sometimes wonder if you could handle a confining job in an office?

_____ 15. Beth looks after two small children whose mother works afternoons on the campus.

_____ 16. Mark's lawyer argued that his client was not financially liable for the damages.

_____ 17. An argument that Mark's lawyer presented questioned the financial liability for the damages.

_____ 18. Mark's lawyer's argument was that his client was not financially liable for the damages.

_____ 19. Mark's lawyer's argument that his client was not financially responsible for the damages impressed the jury.

_____ 20. Some of us wonder if you would be interested in the job.

Directions: The italicized material in each of these sentences is a subordinate clause. In the first space at the left, write **Adv., Adj.,** or **N.** to identify the clause. Within the italicized clause the word in boldface type is a complement. Identify it by writing in the second space at the left one of the following:

S.C.	[subjective complement]	I.O.	[indirect object]
D.O.	[direct object]	O.C.	[objective complement]

_____ 1. One of Jeff's difficulties is *that he is painfully **shy** in the presence of strangers.*
_____

_____ 2. *If you follow these **directions,** you will avoid really heavy traffic.*
_____

_____ 3. After you leave this class, I hope that you will practice ***what** you have learned*
_____   *here.*

_____ 4. The letter of introduction *that you sent **me*** proved very helpful.
_____

_____ 5. The car was registered in the name of Charles Albertson, a Britisher ***whom***
_____   *the FBI had been investigating.*

_____ 6. Beth has as yet told no one ***who** her bridesmaids will be.*
_____

_____ 7. We are living in a period *when crises are almost daily **occurrences.***
_____

_____ 8. I'm afraid *that I caused my **parents** some real embarrassment.*
_____

_____ 9. The substitute teacher devised some activities *that kept the youngsters **busy***
_____   *for half an hour.*

_____ 10. Uncle Jake sputtered indignantly *when the waiter reminded **him** that the cus-*
_____   *tomary gratuity is fifteen percent.*

_____ 11. The first fish ***that** Laura caught* was only five inches long.
_____

_____ 12. Several friends commented on *how **happy** Elaine looked.*
_____

_____ 13. I am sure *that the best seats for the concert are no longer **available.***
_____

_____ 14. I think you should tell the mechanic *that you consider his bill unreasonably*
_____   ***high.***

_____ 15. Although Sue has shown me *where I had been making **mistakes,*** I'm still not
_____   entirely comfortable with my new computer.

_____ 16. The board approved Mr. Barnes' suggestion *that the club make Ms. Thomp-*
_____   *son an honorary **member.***

_____ 17. An actress ***whom** none of us had ever seen before* played the part of the pros-
_____   ecuting attorney.

_____ 18. The contractor could only guess at ***what** the total cost will be.*
_____

_____ 19. Ted has been studying the pamphlet *the traffic officer gave **him.***
_____

_____ 20. Your theme will be improved, I think, *if you make your introductory para-*
_____   *graph somewhat **shorter.***

NAME _____   SCORE _____

Directions: Each sentence contains one verbal phrase. Underline the phrase and, in the space at the left, write one of the following letters to identify the phrase:

    G. [gerund phrase]   P.   [participial phrase]
    I. [infinitive phrase]   A.   [absolute phrase]

_____ 1. It might be a good idea to look into the Acme Company's offer more carefully.

_____ 2. Tomorrow being a holiday, I shall loaf most of the day.

_____ 3. Wayne's daily chores included looking after the boss's collection of African violets.

_____ 4. Do you think that granting Larsen another extension on the loan is wise?

_____ 5. I'll send you a ten-page brochure describing this tremendous real-estate opportunity.

_____ 6. Dad would sometimes let me sit on his lap while he was steering the car.

_____ 7. Troubled by these inaccuracies, one board member demanded that new auditors be hired.

_____ 8. Hatchwood was found guilty of sending an abusive, threatening letter to the mayor.

_____ 9. Can you show me how to put this new cartridge into my printer?

_____ 10. Over the weekend I did little except review my geology notes for the midterm examination.

_____ 11. Dad has done most of the cooking this week, Mother having been called for jury duty.

_____ 12. Perhaps your client might consider buying a somewhat larger piece of property.

_____ 13. The substitute teacher's first mistake was assigning the class some additional homework.

_____ 14. Another possibility would be to rent a car at the airport.

_____ 15. Three men found guilty of espionage were deported.

_____ 16. One of Paula's unusual hobbies is collecting old theater programs.

_____ 17. Keeping the younger children quiet during the long ceremony will tax your ingenuity.

_____ 18. One of the ushers will tell you when to march to the platform for your diploma.

_____ 19. Johnson returned to Memphis, having been unsuccessful in his search for a job in Atlanta.

_____ 20. Being a charitable person, Bascom graciously accepted the apology.

363

Directions: Each of the italicized words in the following sentences is used as a complement within a verbal phrase. In the first space at the left, write one of the following letters to identify the phrase:

    G. [gerund phrase]   P. [participial phrase]
    I. [infinitive phrase]   A. [absolute phrase]

In the second space, write one of the following numbers to identify the complement:

    1. Subjective complement   3. Indirect object
    2. Direct object   4. Objective complement

_____   1. You can help the committee most by providing *transportation* for the out-
_____   of-town delegates.

_____   2. It might be to our advantage to make *Chapman* a second offer for his
_____   property.

_____   3. There will be celebrating in Coalville this week, the local baseball team hav-
_____   ing won the league *pennant.*

_____   4. The excited children raced to the backyard, leaving the kitchen door wide
_____   *open.*

_____   5. These graphic pictures succeeded in making the legislators *aware* of the need
_____   for immediate action.

_____   6. The clerk, looking extremely *annoyed* by our insistence, finally summoned
_____   his supervisor.

_____   7. How many *signatures* were you able to get for our petition?
_____

_____   8. "Remember, jurors," said the attorney, "that no one actually heard my client
_____   threaten the police *officer.*"

_____   9. Beth's aunt looked after the children yesterday, our regular sitter being
_____   *unavailable.*

_____   10. A new regulation making students *eligible* for membership on college com-
_____   mittees is being considered.

_____   11. Having already sent the *bank* the February payment, Tracy was puzzled by
_____   the delinquent notice.

_____   12. Spending time with Uncle Josh is almost as unpleasant as visiting the *dentist.*
_____

_____   13. Feeling *sorry* for the embarrassed clerk, Mother paid for the broken cookies.
_____

_____   14. Have you ever thought of becoming an airline flight *attendant*?
_____

_____   15. I must find a new handball partner, Jeff Toner having left *town.*
_____

NAME _____ SCORE _____

Directions: If a sentence is correct, write **C** in the space at the left. If you find a dangling modifier, underline it and write **W** in the space.

_____ 1. In purchasing a dog for a family pet, its background is as important to consider as its appearance.

_____ 2. A boat as light as this one can be upset by sitting on the side the way you are doing now.

_____ 3. Turning the car into the driveway, my purse fell to the floor and the contents scattered all over.

_____ 4. Dad is certainly busy enough this morning without asking him to drive us to the gym.

_____ 5. Dad is certainly busy enough this morning without being asked to drive us to the gym.

_____ 6. Upon reaching nine years of age, my family moved again, this time to Omaha.

_____ 7. Having bruised her ankle while taking inventory this morning, the boss told Edith to take the afternoon off.

_____ 8. I think I'll splurge tonight and order an expensive dessert, tomorrow being payday.

_____ 9. The tapes may be used again after rewinding them.

_____ 10. The tapes may be used again after being rewound.

_____ 11. After filing away all the loose magazines and pamphlets that I have acquired this year, my shelves look quite tidy.

_____ 12. To be assured of a capacity audience, the price of the tickets must be kept low.

_____ 13. The weather having turned cold and windy, we decided to take along our parkas.

_____ 14. Exhausted after the long hours of studying, Luke's head slowly nodded and finally came to rest on the open book.

_____ 15. Notice also that, by being reversed, this coat can be used in rainy weather.

_____ 16. Notice also that, by reversing it, this coat can be used in rainy weather.

_____ 17. Notice also that, by reversing it, you can use this coat in rainy weather.

_____ 18. Meeting Lois after work, she suggested that we see a movie.

_____ 19. Yesterday, while eating lunch on the patio, a flock of crows made a raucous racket.

_____ 20. Instead of leaving the lawn mower out in the rain, it should be put away in the carport.

365

Directions: Rewrite each of the following sentences twice:
   a. Change the dangler to a complete clause with subject and verb.
   b. Begin the main clause with a word that the dangler can logically modify.

1. Having been in the army for five years, my serious reading has been neglected.

   a. _____

   b. _____

2. While mowing the grass, the long-lost gold chain was found.

   a. _____

   b. _____

3. Before applying the first coat of paint, the surface should be sanded well.

   a. _____

   b. _____

4. To be assured of a successful cake, the flour must be sifted thoroughly.

   a. _____

   b. _____

5. Having turned the horses loose, they raced for the cool, inviting stream.

   a. _____

   b. _____

NAME _____ SCORE _____

Directions: Study these paired sentences for incompleteness, misplaced modifiers, faulty parallelism, and faulty comparisons. In the space at the left, write the letter that identifies the correct sentence.

_____ 1. a. Our service department uses only factory-approved materials.
b. Our service department only uses factory-approved materials.

_____ 2. a. One of the laboratory assistants having had enough presence of mind to rush the injured student to the infirmary.
b. One of the laboratory assistants had enough presence of mind to rush the injured student to the infirmary.

_____ 3. a. Although a sergeant's pay is lower than a commissioned officer, an officer has several additional expenses.
b. Although a sergeant's pay is lower than a commissioned officer's, an officer has several additional expenses.

_____ 4. a. Our company specializes in cars of conservative design and which get good gas mileage.
b. Our company specializes in cars that are conservatively designed and get good gas mileage.

_____ 5. a. Last semester Johnny had a better grade-point average than any other fellow in his fraternity.
b. Last semester Johnny had a better grade-point average than any fellow in his fraternity.

_____ 6. a. Gladys only approves of a movie if it has a gloriously happy ending.
b. Gladys approves of a movie only if it has a gloriously happy ending.

_____ 7. a. What started the argument was Fran's casual remark that hers was the fastest of any speedboat on the lake.
b. What started the argument was Fran's casual remark that hers was the fastest of all the speedboats on the lake.

_____ 8. a. Jan had to reluctantly admit that all college students are not vitally interested in modern dance.
b. Jan had to admit reluctantly that not all college students are vitally interested in modern dance.

_____ 9. a. It was one of the greatest thrills, if not the greatest thrill, of my life.
b. It was one of the greatest, if not the greatest thrill of my life.

_____ 10. a. Minnesota, I have been told, has more lakes than any state in the Union.
b. Minnesota, I have been told, has more lakes than any other state in the Union.

_____ 11. a. The road is wide, hard-surfaced most of the way, and very few sharp curves.
b. The road is wide and hard-surfaced most of the way and has very few sharp curves.

_____ 12. a. The survey revealed that the salaries of the janitors were equal, and in some cases higher than the beginning teachers.
b. The survey revealed that the salaries of the janitors were equal to, and in some cases higher than, those of the beginning teachers.

_____ 13. a. The receptionist told me to return the questionnaire to her as soon as I finished it.
b. The receptionist told me to, as soon as I finished the questionnaire, return it to her.

_____ 14. a. Some of the more vocal fans, still complaining about Coach Driscoll's lack of imagination and new ideas.
b. Some of the more vocal fans are still complaining about Coach Driscoll's lack of imagination and new ideas.

_____ 15. a. "I admire neither the mayor's politics nor the people he associates with," said Ms. Ames.
b. "I neither admire the mayor's politics nor the people he associates with," said Ms. Ames.

_____ 16. a. The predicted rainfall will be as heavy as that of the last few days, if not heavier.
b. The predicted rainfall will be as heavy, if not heavier than, the last few days.

_____ 17. a. One unusual bit of information being that Hong Kong boasts of more Rolls Royces per square foot than any city on earth.
b. One unusual bit of information is that Hong Kong boasts of more Rolls Royces per square foot than any other city on earth.

_____ 18. a. Danny managed by December to pay off nearly half of his father's debts.
b. Danny managed to by December nearly pay off half of his father's debts.

_____ 19. a. The accident happened because the street was icy and the other driver was inexperienced and careless.
b. The accident happened because the street was icy and because of the other driver's inexperience and carelessness.

_____ 20. a. Whose ACT scores were best, yours or your twin brothers?
b. Whose ACT scores were better, yours or your twin brother's?

NAME _____ SCORE _____

Directions: Change the italicized sentence to the form indicated in the parentheses and write the two sentences as one sentence.

1. *The Jensens were in Hawaii on vacation.* They missed the dedication of the new court-house. (adverbial clause of reason) _____

   _____

2. *The Jensens were in Hawaii on vacation.* They missed the dedication of the new court-house. (absolute phrase) _____

   _____

3. *Brush the movable metal parts lightly with oil.* This will protect them against rust. (gerund phrase)_____

   _____

4. Brush the movable metal parts lightly with oil. *This will protect them against rust.* (infinitive phrase) _____

   _____

5. The survivors were flown to Ellertown by Ben Towle. *He is a local helicopter pilot.* (adjective clause) _____

   _____

6. The survivors were flown to Ellertown by Ben Towle. *He is a local helicopter pilot.* (appositive) _____

   _____

7. *I had read the editorial.* I decided to write a letter to the editor. (adverbial clause of time) _____

   _____

8. *I had read the editorial.* I decided to write a letter to the editor. (participial phrase)

   _____

   _____

9. *I had read the editorial.* I decided to write a letter to the editor. (prepositional phrase with gerund phrase object) _____

   _____

10. With our sandwiches we drank warm ginger ale. *Our meager supply of ice had melted.* (absolute phrase)_____

    _____

369

Directions: Rewrite each of the following numbered items as one complex sentence; show enough of the new sentence to illustrate the construction. In each case use the italicized subject and verb for the main clause. Use a variety of the subordinating units listed on the first page of Lesson 15.

1. I knew Stan Whipple in college. He is now a successful art auctioneer. *I was surprised* to learn this. _____

   _____

2. I spent five hours typing my research paper and *I was* exhausted and so I went to bed before nine o'clock. _____

   _____

3. This *quilt* has been in our family for over sixty years. It *was made* by my grandmother. She was twenty years old when she made it._____

   _____

4. I finished high school in June. I didn't find a job that I liked. *I returned* to summer school for a course in word processing. Word processing is a valuable skill for anyone.

   _____

   _____

5. The recipe called for chopped pecans. *I used* chopped peanuts instead. Chopped peanuts are more fitted to my limited budget. _____

   _____

6. Hank and I attended college together. That was twenty years ago. *He seemed* completely lacking in ambition. But he was intelligent. _____

   _____

7. Jackson is not a very strong student, but he is a good basketball player and so *I suppose* he'll have no trouble getting into college somewhere._____

   _____

8. Mother is usually easygoing. She rarely raises her voice. *She surprised* the family. She announced that this year she was not cooking a big Thanksgiving Day dinner. _____

   _____

9. Duncan graduated from college with a degree in pharmacy. But now *he manages* a seed company. The company is large. It is located near Lompoc, California. _____

   _____

10. Laura's uncle learned that she was majoring in journalism. *He sent* her a letter. It was stern and unequivocal. It ordered her to change her major to law. _____

    _____

*Commas and Semicolons:
Compound Units (Lessons 7, 17)*

NAME _____ SCORE _____

Directions: In each sentence a [*V*] marks a point of coordination between (1) two verbs with a coordinating conjunction, (2) two independent clauses with a coordinating conjunction, or (3) two independent clauses without a coordinating conjunction. In the space at the left, write one of the following:
    0 (no punctuation is needed)
    C (a comma is needed)
    S (a semicolon is needed)

_____ 1. "I have a new machine here," said the mechanic [*V*] "in two minutes it will analyze your car's exhaust."

_____ 2. Dr. Ellis's lecture must have impressed her audience [*V*] for dozens of people with questions crowded around her after she finished.

_____ 3. Many years ago Jerome had fished for bass and muskellunge in northern Minnesota [*V*] in those days no one worried about polluted lakes and streams.

_____ 4. Ms. Brady's comments on student themes were sometimes cruel [*V*] and did not endear her to the students in pre-engineering.

_____ 5. The living conditions of the people are improving slowly [*V*] but there is little hope for significant change.

_____ 6. The party must have been rather unexciting [*V*] for my roommate was home and in bed by ten o'clock.

_____ 7. The day-long meeting was routine and uneventful [*V*] for the visiting students from India it must have seemed quite dull.

_____ 8. Under the new law automobile drivers over seventy years of age must pass a test [*V*] otherwise their current licenses will be revoked.

_____ 9. This set of matched golf clubs normally sells for $350 [*V*] but during our anniversary sale it is available for only $265.

_____ 10. This set of matched golf clubs normally sells for $350 [*V*] during our anniversary sale, however, it is available for only $265.

_____ 11. This set of matched golf clubs normally sells for $350 [*V*] but during our anniversary sale is available for only $265.

_____ 12. A teenager carrying a noisy boom box lurched past Mrs. Howe [*V*] and sat down in the only unoccupied seat in the bus.

_____ 13. For several months General Benham had been receiving anonymous threats over the telephone [*V*] but had not reported them to the police.

_____ 14. For several months General Benham had been receiving anonymous threats over the telephone [*V*] but he had not reported them to the police.

_____ 15. The ill-mannered guard neither answered Marcy's question [*V*] nor invited her to step inside out of the rain.

_____ 16. The ill-mannered guard did not answer Marcy's question [*V*] nor did he invite her to step inside out of the rain.

_____ 17. The ill-mannered guard did not answer Marcy's question [*V*] moreover, he did not invite her to step inside out of the rain.

_____ 18. This television by itself sells for $672 [*V*] with its matching stand the price is $730.

_____ 19. The advertised price is $730 [*V*] but without the matching stand the price is only $672.

_____ 20. Ms. Shaw has used these videos in her seventh-grade class [*V*] she reports that the student response was good.

_____ 21. Ms. Shaw has used these videos in her seventh-grade class [*V*] and reports that the student response was good.

_____ 22. Ms. Shaw has used these videos in her seventh-grade class [*V*] the student response, she reports, was good.

_____ 23. Our special this week is the four-head VCR pictured in our advertisement [*V*] we are offering it at the low price of $299.

_____ 24. You'll like its on-screen menu system [*V*] and inexperienced users will appreciate its easy-to-understand panel display.

_____ 25. Ms. Stern comes to our firm well-recommended [*V*] for the past four years she headed a work force of nearly seventy people.

_____ 26. Ms. Stern should go far with our firm [*V*] for she is intelligent and hard-working.

_____ 27. Dean Lewis accepted the students' petition [*V*] and promised that he would study it carefully.

_____ 28. *Ilex opaca* is an American holly with glossy leaves and red berries [*V*] the foliage and berries are often used for Christmas decorations.

_____ 29. Juniors in this program normally take History 350 [*V*] however, Dean Tate has allowed me to substitute Political Science 107.

_____ 30. A limited number of viewers have called this movie a masterpiece [*V*] but many others are bothered by its ambiguities.

NAME _____ SCORE _____

Directions: The following sentences contain fifty numbered spots between words or beneath words. (The number is beneath the word when the punctuation problem involves the use of an apostrophe in that word.) In the correspondingly numbered spaces at the left, write **C** if the punctuation is correct or **W** if it is wrong.

1. _____
2. _____
3. _____
4. _____
5. _____
6. _____
7. _____
8. _____
9. _____
10. _____
11. _____
12. _____
13. _____
14. _____
15. _____
16. _____
17. _____
18. _____
19. _____
20. _____
21. _____
22. _____

(1) Had we known that the lecture would attract such a large audience; we[1] would have scheduled it for Farwell Hall, which has three hundred seats.[2]

(2) The average tourists'[3] equipment consists of:[4] a camera, a raincoat, dark glasses, and a guidebook.

(3) Geoffrey Chaucer, who wrote *The Canterbury Tales,*[5] is known for his realism, his humor, and his accurate observation.[6]

(4) The 1928 Olympic Games, by the way, made history[7][8] for competitive events for women were introduced.

(5) Mother was not amused when she discovered that the children had made a snowman[9] and had used one of her new golf balls for it's[10] nose.

(6) Frank Duveneck, a portrait painter who was born in Kentucky on October 9, 1848,[11] eventually settled in Cincinnati[12] where he died in 1919.

(7) "I distinctly heard someone say, 'What's[13] that guy talking about?' "[14] said the new teacher.

(8) If you didn't draw this hilarious caricature of me, I wonder who's[15] responsible for it?[16]

(9) "Please remember, my dear Miss. Scroggs,"[17] said the secretary, "that a neat[18] tidy appearance is one of the best recommendations."

(10) Dark clouds crept up from the west,[19] and the hot,[20] sultry air was ominously quiet.

(11) When Mr. Davis finally does resign[21] the position will probably be filled by one of the boss's[22] nephews.

373

23. _____ (12) When we lived there, the village was peaceful and restful, now it has been

23
24. _____ ruined by noisy ill-mannered tourists.

24
25. _____ (13) Mr. Oldham's assessment for the new paving on Elm Street being, in his
26. _____ opinion, too high; he protested to Ned Lane, a member of the council.

25   26
27. _____ (14) "Responsibility for the seating arrangement at the banquet will be
28. _____ someone else's, not your's," the chairperson told Edith.

27   28
29. _____ (15) A short, quite pathetic appeal was made to the mayor by an elderly

29
30. _____ woman whose property tax had been nearly doubled.

30
31. _____ (16) A fiery, political speech was made by our senior county commis-

31
32. _____ sioner who hopes to be reelected.

32
33. _____ (17) "This car seems to be pulling slightly to the left, I wonder if one of the

33
34. _____ tires is going flat?" said Marge.

34
35. _____ (18) Epictetus, a Greek Stoic who was originally a slave, taught in Rome until

35
36. _____ A.D. 90 when the emperor Domitian banished all philosophers.

36
37. _____ (19) This week you'll find real bargains at Shops-Mart in: light fixtures, paint,

37
38. _____ linens, and childrens' shoes.

38
39. _____ (20) "My briefcase isn't here in the car," said McCall; "I wonder if I could have

39
40. _____ left it in your office."

40
41. _____ (21) "We had a bad storm when I was out fishing in the bay two week's ago,"

41
42. _____ said Mark, who knew that Jo was a nervous landlubber.

42
43. _____ (22) The last bus from Lawrenceville having arrived with no passengers, Jim

43
44. _____ and Trudy walked slowly to their car and drove back to the farm.

44
45. _____ (23) "Let's drop the matter," said Anne impatiently. "After all these problems

45
46. _____ are nobody's business but mine."

46
47. _____ (24) Louisa is writing a book about her paternal grandmother who was a

47
48. _____ vigorous worker for womens' rights.

48
49. _____ (25) From the very first difficulties beset the planned expansion; finally

49   50
50. _____ resulting in the withdrawal of funds by the two principal backers.

NAME _____ SCORE _____

Directions: The following sentences contain fifty numbered spots between words or beneath words. (The number is beneath the word when the punctuation problem involves the use of an apostrophe in that word.) In the correspondingly numbered spaces at the left, write **C** if the punctuation is correct or **W** if it is wrong.

1. _____   (1) The treasurer's report was so long, so disorganized, and so dull that some
            1   2
2. _____   of the listeners dozed off at times.

3. _____   (2) At daybreak a crow parked itself outside our balcony and kept us awake
4. _____   with it's loud   raucous scolding.
                    3   4
5. _____   (3) The dodo and the roc, both commonly found only in crossword puz-
6. _____   zles, are similar in some respects, and different in others.
                    5   6
7. _____   (4) The dodo, a bird that is now extinct, actually lived in Mauritius but the
                                                                                7
8. _____   roc lived only in people's imagination.
                                         8
9. _____   (5) Rotary International was founded in Chicago, Illinois, in 1905, it now has
                                                            9   10
10. _____   chapters in more than seventy countries.

11. _____ (6) The Jensens sat in the airport for six long, tedious hours; their flight being
                                                              11   12
12. _____   delayed by what was called an equipment shortage.

13. _____ (7) Your equipment should consist of: heavy hiking boots, a waterproof
                                                  13
14. _____   tarpaulin, and plenty of warm clothing.
                         14
15. _____ (8) Today I received from a travel agency a new calendar; on the cover
                                                                      15
16. _____   theres a beautiful picture of the Bay of Naples.
                    16
17. _____ (9) "A team that wont be beaten can't be beaten," said Coach Wellby, who is
                             17   18
18. _____   hopelessly addicted to clichés.

19. _____ (10) In the outer lobby is a huge oil portrait of the founder of the firm; his
                                                                                    19
20. _____   stern   humorless face adding to the austerity of the surroundings.
                     20
21. _____ (11) The midterm test will cover the following materials: the class lectures to
                                                                     21
22. _____   date and chapters 2, 3, 4, and 5 of the text.
                              22

23. _____ (12) The play has received good reviews from the critics, I suppose it's
   23   24
24. _____   impossible to get tickets at this late date.

25. _____ (13) "You agree with me, dont you," Jean answered, "that my suggestion was a
   25
26. _____   reasonable one."
   26

27. _____ (14) For most of this summer Martha has been borrowing one of my

28. _____   bikes; her's is now too old and too rusty to be safe.
   27   28

29. _____ (15) Flight 723, which is scheduled to arrive here at 4:12 P.M. has been delayed
   29
30. _____   at Topeka, Kansas, because of bad weather.
   30

31. _____ (16) Coleman, the third baseman, threw down his glove, and screamed that the
   31
32. _____   runner hadn't touched the base.
   32

33. _____ (17) The art teacher, Miss. Philbrick, asked Janey if she had ever done any
   33
34. _____   professional modeling?
   34

35. _____ (18) Our neighbors, the Thomas's, have a new television set that has a much
   35
36. _____   larger picture than our's.
   36

37. _____ (19) The notice on the bulletin board announced the new schedule: breakfast
   37
38. _____   at six-thirty, lunch at eleven-thirty, and dinner at six.
   38

39. _____ (20) "After all my friends will help me out of this, they know that my word is
   39   40
40. _____   as good as my bond," said Mr. Winther.

41. _____ (21) Julia's cousin Larry studied at Heidelberg, where he became well
   41
42. _____   acquainted with Judge Coleman's only grandson Herman.
   42

43. _____ (22) "Judd shouldn't have taken offense at my remark, I merely asked him if he
   43
44. _____   was made up for a masquerade party?" said Eugene.
   44

45. _____ (23) Dr. Andrews has written articles about child psychology but his own
   45
46. _____   childrens' behavior in a group is far from admirable.
   46

47. _____ (24) "The story line, the costumes, the music—everything must be changed,"
   47
48. _____   said Cecil Burbank, the new director.
   48

49. _____ (25) Laura is the kind of person who shops downtown until five oclock, and
   49 50
50. _____   then complains about the crowded condition of the bus on her ride

             home.

NAME _____   SCORE _____

Directions: Study these sentences for (1) the correct form of a principal part of a verb, (2) the correct subject–verb agreement, and (3) the correct tense of a verb. Underline every incorrect verb and write the correct form in the space at the left. No sentence contains more than two incorrect verb forms. Some sentences may be correct.

1. After setting in the hot sun all day, every one of the petunia plants I put out this morning has wilted badly.

2. Neither Dr. Alterton nor his assistant were able to make sense of the peculiar symbols written on the wooden slab.

3. Has either of your two roommates begun to be interviewed for a job after graduation?

4. One story that I've heard is that Judge Trowbridge payed back to the bank all of the money that his nephew had stole.

5. The mayor, along with three of her top aides, has been asked to set at the head table with the visiting dignitaries.

6. "I been hunting in these woods for fifty years but never before seen a critter like that one," said the guide.

7. Stan walked into the principal's office, laid his books on the table, and says, "I've come to the end of my rope."

8. There was only seven seconds left in the game when Pete West let fly from midcourt and sank the game-winning three-pointer.

9. A news story reports that the appearance of mysterious patterns in wheat fields have become a summer diversion in southern England.

10. After the eight-o'clock bell had rang, Mr. Towle said, "The fact that the weather is bad don't mean that we won't hold classes today."

11. I like to go to the movie with you, but I saw that show last month in Dallas.

12. Don't it worry you that the price of your shares of stock have fallen by nearly thirty percent in four months?

13. Seated behind us were a woman with four children who noisily ate candy and drunk pop during the entire movie.

14. After the other officers had given their reports, the colonel said, "The evidence has shown that neither of the two incidents were the result of equipment failure."

_____ 15. There's been so many improvements made at the Lakeside Inn
_____ that it has became one of the most popular resorts in the state.

_____ 16. As we rose to leave the auditorium, Bart remarked, "I think our
_____ speaker could have chose a livelier topic to discuss."

_____ 17. In July heat records were broke on two days, but during August
_____ the range of temperatures were normal for the season.

_____ 18. Julie had just lain down for a short rest when her neighbor came
_____ running over and tells her that there was a couple of raccoons in
her vegetable garden.

_____ 19. The Associated Press reports that the search for possible sur-
_____ vivors of the earthquake have been slowed because of repeated
aftershocks that have shaken the area.

_____ 20. The magnitude of our budgetary problems have left a shadow
_____ across the legislative process; no wonder that the confidence in
our lawmakers has sank to new low levels.

_____ 21. The advertisement announcing that our entire stock of Nature's
_____ Own Vitamins are on sale has drawn huge crowds.

_____ 22. "It's been a hectic day," said Beth. "The two-o'clock bell has
_____ already rung, and I haven't eaten a bite of lunch yet."

_____ 23. "Commissioner Bunker's standards for the behavior of public
_____ servants, including himself," the editor had written, "has always
been minimal."

_____ 24. "Neither of the two Ford trucks in our lot have been drove more
_____ than forty thousand miles," said the salesperson.

_____ 25. The number of fatal accidents at the corner of Fifth and Oak has
_____ risen alarmingly over the past two years.

_____ 26. In the lobby there is a sofa and several overstuffed chairs where
_____ patients can set and read while waiting to see the dentist.

_____ 27. The leader of the gang, along with two of his followers, were lying
_____ wounded on the floor of the garage.

_____ 28. Not one of the paintings that were taken from the museum dur-
_____ ing the robbery last summer have been recovered.

_____ 29. The girls abandoned the sinking canoe and swam safely to shore,
_____ but unfortunately their pet dog drownded.

_____ 30. Has either your teacher or the school counselor spoke to you
_____ about applying for a scholarship?

NAME _____   SCORE _____

Directions: Study the following sentences for poorly used pronouns. Look for wrong case forms, misspelled possessives, vague or inexact references. Circle each incorrect pronoun. In the space at the left of each pair of sentences, write the letter that identifies the correct sentence.

_____ 1. a. In years past, the personnel director of the laboratory would inquire about an applicant's personal life, including such things as who your associates were.
  b. In years past, the personnel director of the laboratory would inquire about an applicant's personal life, including such things as who were his or her associates.

_____ 2. a. Every guy at the dorm except Jacobs, Peterson, and me has already had his spring-term class schedule approved.
  b. Every guy at the dorm except Jacobs, Peterson, and I has already had their spring-term class schedule approved.

_____ 3. a. Four of us girls got in line for the ticket sale at seven in the morning, and then we were told that the office wouldn't open until noon.
  b. Four of we girls got in line for the ticket sale at seven in the morning, and then they told us that the office wouldn't open until noon.

_____ 4. a. "I'm supposed to ride in Phil's car," said Lew, "but, just between you and I, I'd prefer to ride in someone elses."
  b. "I'm supposed to ride in Phil's car," said Lew, "but, just between you and me, I'd prefer to ride in someone else's."

_____ 5. a. "I plan to become a forester," said Tom, "because it allows you to do your bit for saving the environment."
  b. "I plan to become a forester," said Tom, "because work in forestry allows a person to do his or her bit for saving the environment."

_____ 6. a. It said on television that the finalists, whomever they are, will meet for five games in Las Vegas.
  b. According to a television report, the finalists, whoever they are, will meet for five games in Las Vegas.

_____ 7. a. Ginny told her best friend, Marge, that she should lose at least five pounds.
  b. Ginny told her best friend, Marge, "I should lose at least five pounds."

_____ 8. a. "Dad is a dedicated fisherman, and he keeps trying to get my sister and me interested in fishing," said Mary Jane.
  b. "Dad is a dedicated fisherman, and he keeps trying to get my sister and I interested in it," said Mary Jane.

_____ 9. a. Mr. Capri's lawyer produced two witnesses who he said had been present when the alleged bribe offer was made.
  b. Mr. Capri's lawyer produced two witnesses whom he said had been present when the alleged bribe offer was made.

379

_____ 10. a. "All of us administrators are pleased," said Dean Powers, "that the college is attracting many adults into its Retraining Program."
   b. "The college is attracting many adults into their Retraining Program, which pleases all of we administrators," said Dean Powers.

_____ 11. a. A tourist whom we met at a filling station in Plainview told us that the highway for the next two miles is being resurfaced.
   b. A tourist who we met at a filling station in Plainview told us that they are resurfacing the highway for the next two miles.

_____ 12. a. My younger brother is a better mathematician than me, principally because he has taken several courses in it.
   b. My younger brother is a better mathematician than I, principally because he has taken several courses in mathematics.

_____ 13. a. It clearly states in the application form that you must provide a recent black-and-white picture of yourself.
   b. The application form clearly states that applicants must provide black-and-white pictures of themselves.

_____ 14. a. The person whom the Speaker of the House appoints to make this investigation must reconcile himself or herself to a thankless chore.
   b. The person who the Speaker of the House appoints to make this investigation must reconcile themself to a thankless chore.

_____ 15. a. The car ahead of our's was weaving so erratically that I didn't want to try to pass him.
   b. The car ahead of ours was weaving so erratically that I didn't want to try to pass it.

_____ 16. a. At the first pep rally the cheerleaders told we freshmen to wear our green T-shirts at every game.
   b. At the first pep rally the cheerleaders told us freshmen to wear our green T-shirts at every game.

_____ 17. a. "Is there anyone who you really think might get more votes than I in the primary election?" asked ex-Senator Wiley.
   b. "Is there anyone whom you really think might get more votes than me in the primary election?" asked ex-Senator Wiley.

_____ 18. a. The three new owners of the Busy Bee Store maintain that you can't find another merchant in town who's prices are lower than their's.
   b. The three new owners of the Busy Bee Store maintain that there isn't another merchant in town whose prices are lower than theirs.

_____ 19. a. Your brother likes to tease you. If it wasn't he who sent you the comic valentine, who do you think it might have been?
   b. Your brother likes to tease you. If it wasn't him who sent you the comic valentine, whom do you think it might have been?

_____ 20. a. "This notebook must be someone else's," said Martin. "Mine has an American flag stenciled on its cover."
   b. "This notebook must be someone elses," said Martin. "Mine has an American flag stenciled on it's cover."

NAME _____ SCORE _____

Directions: In the space at the left, write the *number* of the correct form given in parentheses.

_____ 1. I (1. couldn't have   2. couldn't of) finished typing my term paper even if I
_____   had worked on it (1. steady   2. steadily) until midnight.

_____ 2. (1. Let us   2. Let's us) put in an extra hour on this project and finish it
_____   (1. faster   2. more faster) than in the time allotted for it.

_____ 3. "(1. Where   2. Where at) can I buy some of (1. them   2. those) huge sun-
_____   glasses like the ones you are wearing?" Ms. Tower asked Letty.

_____ 4. "I have no doubt," said Mrs. Lathrop, "(1. but what   2. that) my daughter
_____   will finally select the (1. more   2. most) expensive of the two dresses."

_____ 5. Our committee got a (1. real   2. really) early start, and by noon we had
_____   addressed (1. most   2. almost) all of the political pamphlets.

_____ 6. Coach Treadwell is (1. sure   2. surely) happy about the large (1. amount
_____   2. number) of junior-college transfers who turned out for the team.

_____ 7. "Old Hank Jones (1. use to   2. used to) appear (1. regular   2. regularly) at
_____   our church functions," said Mrs. Walker, "but I haven't seen him in months."

_____ 8. Frankly, I am (1. kind of   2. rather) surprised that our girls' team did as
_____   (1. good   2. well) as they did in the regional tournament.

_____ 9. As I stood up, ready to get (1. off   2. off of) the bus, a fire engine swerved
_____   around the corner and came (1. awful   2. very) close to us.

_____ 10. (1. Due to   2. Because of) his bad eyesight, Mel didn't do very (1. good
_____   2. well) on the map-reading part of the test.

_____ 11. "I know that your uncle will feel (1. bad   2. badly) if he doesn't receive an
_____   (1. invite   2. invitation) to the wedding," said Aunt Yolanda.

_____ 12. "I think (1. this   2. this here) purple scarf would look (1. good   2. well)
_____   with your new suit," said the salesperson.

_____ 13. Judged on (1. this   2. these) new and stricter criteria, Ludlow's essay is
_____   clearly the (1. better   2. best) of the two finalists.

———— 14. From his report, Jack sounded (1. as if   2. like) he had a (1. real   2. really)
————   good time on his trip to Florida.

———— 15. I wish Professor Lynn would talk (1. more slower   2. more slowly); I (1. can
————   hardly   2. can't hardly) take notes when he is racing to finish his lecture.

———— 16. The thing (1. that   2. what) really surprised the firefighters is that no one
————   was injured (1. bad   2. badly) in the spectacular fire.

———— 17. A (1. couple   2. couple of) friends and I work out (1. regular   2. regularly)
————   at the company's gymnasium.

———— 18. (1. Lots   2. Many) of the native people have (1. emigrated   2. immigrated)
————   because of the crop failures in their homeland.

———— 19. That flower you call an evening primrose (1. sure   2. surely) smells (1. sweet
————   2. sweetly).

———— 20. The reason the deal fell through is (1. because   2. that) at the last minute
————   the seller increased the price (1. considerable   2. considerably).

———— 21. (1. Light-complexioned   2. Light-complected) people like you and me
————   (1. shouldn't   2. hadn't ought to) stay out in the hot sun on a day like today.

———— 22. (1. Because of   2. Due to) the infection in his eye, Darrell hasn't been able
————   to study very (1. good   2. well) this week.

———— 23. Now that he has lost weight, Graham looks quite (1. different   2. differ-
————   ently) (1. from   2. than) the way he looks in these old photographs.

———— 24. "I'm (1. enthused   2. enthusiastic) about my new job," said Malcolm. "It is
————   interesting, and, best of all, it pays (1. good   2. well)."

———— 25. By your answer to Mike's question, did you mean to (1. imply   2. infer) that
————   you feel (1. bad   2. badly) about the election results?

NAME _____ SCORE _____

Directions: Each sentence has two italicized words or expressions. If you think that a word or expression is inappropriate in serious writing, write a correct form in the space at the left. If a word or expression is correct, write C in the space.

_____ 1. *Lying* at the side of the road was a plastic bag full of garbage that
_____   some tourist had apparently thrown from *their* car.

_____ 2. In this senior class there *are* only four or five people *whom* I think
_____   are capable of successful work at the graduate level.

_____ 3. The reward money was divided *among* four of *we* hikers who had
_____   turned in the fire alarm.

_____ 4. The mechanic *lay* down the wrench and explained to Roger and
_____   *I* what had to be done and what it would cost.

_____ 5. We were *plenty* surprised when we learned that there *was* only
_____   one teacher and eighteen pupils in the entire school.

_____ 6. "I doubt that fellows as short as you and *me* can play basketball
_____   *good* enough to earn a letter," Al said to Jeremy.

_____ 7. No one at headquarters was *suppose to* know *who* the new agent
_____   was reporting to in Berlin.

_____ 8. Sergeant Gross did not *suspicion* that quite a few of *we* men had
_____   been sneaking off to the movies in the village.

_____ 9. A gregarious person like Andy seems able to make *themself* feel
_____   right at home almost *anywheres*.

_____ 10. By the end of the second week every freshman should have *chosen* which social club *they* will join.

_____ 11. "Who can be *enthused* about *those kind* of video games?" asked
_____   Claire.

_____ 12. Just *like* I had predicted, after the speech there *wasn't* more than
_____   three or four questions from members of the audience.

———————————— 13. Dan was *sure* surprised to learn that everyone in class except
———————————— Marcia Lerner and *him* would have to take another test.

———————————— 14. The reason there is a critical shortage is *because* neither of the two
———————————— state-supported universities *is* turning out qualified engineers.

———————————— 15. The thief, *whoever* he was, had apparently left the warehouse
———————————— parking lot in a small truck that he had *stolen* earlier in the day.

———————————— 16. "These people speak a language that is strange to us," said the
guide, "but in truth they are really not much different *from* you
———————————— and *I*."

———————————— 17. *Has* either of the two plum trees you planted *began* to bear fruit
———————————— yet?

———————————— 18. *Due to* the icy condition of the roads, all of *we* latecomers were
———————————— given excuses today.

———————————— 19. The sale of season tickets for basketball games this year *has*
———————————— declined *considerable*.

———————————— 20. The missing climber's backpack was found *lying* at the bottom of
———————————— a small crevasse, where it had apparently *lain* for several days.

———————————— 21. Every one of the stocks that you recommended to my wife and
———————————— *me* last year *has* declined in value.

———————————— 22. All of us agree that *whoever* took the money from the Christmas
———————————— Fund was *real* desperate.

———————————— 23. The committee's choice for chairperson was Marge Bingham, not
I, in spite of the fact that my experience is much broader than
———————————— *her's*.

———————————— 24. Just between you and *me*, my parents don't approve of *me* post-
———————————— poning my senior year of college.

———————————— 25. *Whom* do you suppose could have written *them* insulting anony-
———————————— mous letters to the superintendent?

NAME _____ SCORE _____

Directions: In the spaces at the left, copy the correct forms given in parentheses.

_____
_____   1. We took a cab to the auditorium, but when we arrived the (con-ference, conferrence) had (already, all ready) begun.

_____   2. The homemade warning device, although far from perfect, is (quiet, quite) (servicable, serviceable).

_____
_____   3. The fast-talking salesman maintained that he was a (personal, personnel) friend of several New York (financeirs, financiers).

_____
_____   4. "In my lifetime I (seized, siezed) many golden (opportunities, opportunitys) but couldn't hold on to them," Mr. Caldwell answered.

_____
_____   5. "I'd hardly call this an (unforgetable, unforgettable) (dining, dinning) experience," said Sal as she set aside the bowl of luke-warm soup.

_____
_____   6. "(Neither, Niether) of your two laboratory experiments was (completely, completly) satisfactory," said the lab assistant.

_____
_____   7. The Acme Corporation has donated to the city a very (desirable, desireable) building (cite, sight, site) for the proposed convention center.

_____
_____   8. "Just to be in the (presence, presents) of such a (fameous, famous) basketball star is a great honor," said the youngster.

_____
_____   9. I haven't seen my neighbors lately; in all (likelihood, likelyhood, liklihood, liklyhood) (their, there, they're) out of town.

_____
_____ 10. Some people (beleive, believe) that the city engineer will (altar, alter) the specifications in order to attract more bidders.

_____
_____ 11. Remember, (its, it's) considered good manners to (complement, compliment) the hostess after a good meal.

_____
_____ 12. With my two time-consuming jobs, I assure you that I have no (leisure, liesure) time (activities, activitys) to speak of.

_____ 13. "Our negotiators managed to (affect, effect) an (advantageous,
_____   advantagous) settlement with the union," said Mr. Siebert.

_____ 14. (Unfortunately, Unfortunatly), similar (incidence, incidents) are
_____   being reported to the police with increasing frequency.

_____ 15. The judge (adviced, advised) the quarreling neighbors to settle
_____   their problem (peacably, peaceably) without outside help.

_____ 16. This semester Sherwood's work in mathematics has (shone,
_____   shown) a (noticable, noticeable) improvement.

_____ 17. The (principal, principle) of the school was not (deceived,
_____   decieved) by young Thompson's outlandish story.

_____ 18. After confessing to the theft, the man (lead, led) the officers to the
_____   place in the barren (desert, dessert) where he had buried the loot.

_____ 19. "I think (your, you're) being very (courageous, couragous)," said
_____   Belinda to the young firefighter.

_____ 20. "Frankly, Alice," said Marlene, "I think that your new friend is
_____   (outrageously, outragously) (conceited, concieted)."

_____ 21. The three (attornies, attorneys) representing our competitor
_____   were much younger (than, then) I had expected.

_____ 22. The bank president rewarded the (casheir, cashier) (who's,
_____   whose) quick thinking had thwarted the holdup.

_____ 23. For her (neice's, niece's) birthday Ms. Simpson sent her a box of
_____   monogrammed (stationary, stationery).

_____ 24. "I predict that our (cheif, chief) of police will (loose, lose) his job
_____   after the next election," said Alderman Whiteside.

_____ 25. After (poring, pouring) over dozens of books in the library, I feel
_____   that I have done a (thorough, through) job of researching the
                    matter.

NAME _____   SCORE _____

Directions: Each sentence contains two words from the first half of the spelling list. In each of these words at least one letter is missing. Write the words, correctly spelled, in the spaces at the left.

_____
_____   1. The new dorm—tory, which will be finished by next fall, will ac—modate three hundred students.

_____
_____   2. I am cer—n that you and your family will enjoy your tour of Great Brit—n.

_____
_____   3. The results of most of our school's ath—tic contests for the past two seasons have been dis—pointing.

_____
_____   4. In class were between thirty-five and fo—ty enthu—tic students.

_____
_____   5. The careless, a—ward boy accident—y broke one of the jars.

_____
_____   6. The new clerk in the office is sometimes embar—sed by his glaring mistakes in gram—r.

_____
_____   7. We were dis—atisfied with the poor service and the ex—rbitant price of the meals.

_____
_____   8. Caldwell is building a large apartment complex ac—oss the street from a large cem—tery.

_____
_____   9. Janice is an exception—y good student of for—n languages.

_____
_____   10. Delegates are arriving for an international confer—nce concerned with protecting the env—nment.

Directions: These sentences contain thirty italicized words from the first half of the spelling list. A sentence may have no misspelled words, one misspelled word, or two misspelled words. Underline each misspelled word and write it, correctly spelled, in a space at the left.

_____

_____

1. *Confidentially,* Mr. Burke's resignation *dosen't* make any real *difference* in our company's long-range plans.

_____

_____

2. Although only an *amateur,* Ms. Davis has *aquired* a collection of early-American pewter that is *amoung* the best in the nation.

_____

_____

3. *Finally,* late in *Febuary,* an *eminent* retired general spoke out strongly against the proposed treaty.

_____

_____

4. One of the *candidates* for mayor gave the *committee* a lengthy *explaination* of his financial dealings.

_____

_____

5. This applicant is an *efficient* worker whose wide *experience* makes her *especialy* well equipped to replace Thornton.

_____

_____

6. *Apparently* the new *apparatus* will cost the county *approximately* three thousand dollars.

_____

_____

7. *During* your college days, ownership of an *excellent dictionary* is a necessity.

_____

_____

8. The visitor's harsh *criticism* of our *goverment* was, we all agreed, not *appropriate.*

_____

_____

9. "I *allways* went to chapel when I was in school," said Uncle James. "*Attendance,* I might add, was not *compulsory.*"

_____

_____

10. *Accompaning* the letter was a brochure with a *discription* of the proposed *condominium.*

NAME _____   SCORE _____

Directions: Each sentence contains two words from the second half of the spelling list. In each of these words at least one letter is missing. Write the words, correctly spelled, in the spaces at the left.

_____
_____

1. Densmore found it nec—sary to borrow money in order to finish his sop—ore year of college.

_____
_____

2. I can rec—mend Ms. Lukens highly; I am sure that she will do the work satisfa—ly.

_____
_____

3. After speaking to Prof—r Quigley, I felt more opt—tic about being able to finish the course.

_____
_____

4. The secr—ry of the local chamber of commerce ordered a large quan—ty of the booklets.

_____
_____

5. Leonard's parents lost pract—ly all of their pos—sions in the fire.

_____
_____

6. The three of us left the chemistry lab—atory and walked to a nearby rest—nt for lunch.

_____
_____

7. The superinten—nt ordered me to return all of the books to the school lib—ry.

_____
_____

8. The teacher said that Angela's interp—tation of the poem was highly orig—nal.

_____
_____

9. Oc—sionally Jenny would su—prise the family by offering to plan and cook a meal for them.

_____
_____

10. The spe—ch instructor criticized my pron—ciation of a few historical place names.

Directions: These sentences contain thirty italicized words from the second half of the spelling list. A sentence may have no misspelled words, one misspelled word, or two misspelled words. Underline each misspelled word and write it, correctly spelled, in a space at the left.

————————————

————————————

1. You must admit that our drama club has put on several *really suc-cessful preformances.*

————————————

————————————

2. Some people look upon *politics* as a somewhat *rediculous pastime.*

————————————

————————————

3. Last month I worked overtime on *Wednesday* the *ninth* and Saturday the *twelfth.*

————————————

————————————

4. In his writings one can find many *specimans* of *propaganda* that play upon racial *prejudices.*

————————————

————————————

5. The *sergeant* and I often go to the gym to exercise on the *parallel* bars to develop grace and *rythm.*

————————————

————————————

6. My lack of *preserverence* can *undoubtably* be explained in impressive-sounding *psychological* terms.

————————————

————————————

7. I *regard* it a *privilege* to interview such a prominent member of the British *Parliament.*

————————————

————————————

8. My *pardner's schedual* is so full that he never has time for more than a hurried *sandwich* at noon.

————————————

————————————

9. "I *usualy* avoid parsnips and *similiar vegetables,*" said Mr. Jefferson.

————————————

————————————

10. I *recognize* the fact that a person of my *temperment* should *probably* avoid being around small children.

Plurals and Capitals (Lesson 28)

NAME _____ SCORE _____

Directions: Write the plural form or forms for each of the following words. When in doubt, consult your dictionary. If two forms are given, write both of them.

1. beef _____ _____

2. child _____ _____

3. curio _____ _____

4. donkey _____ _____

5. fox _____ _____

6. graffito _____ _____

7. handkerchief _____ _____

8. hippopotamus _____ _____

9. knife _____ _____

10. mouse _____ _____

11. oasis _____ _____

12. opportunity _____ _____

13. phenomenon _____ _____

14. portico _____ _____

15. process _____ _____

16. roomful _____ _____

17. species _____ _____

18. stadium _____ _____

19. syllabus _____ _____

20. trout _____ _____

21. valley _____ _____

22. variety _____ _____

23. waltz _____ _____

24. witch _____ _____

25. workman _____ _____

Directions: The following sentences contain fifty numbered words. If a word is correctly capitalized, write **C** in the space with the corresponding number. If a word should not be capitalized, write **W** in the space.

1	2	3
4	5	6
7	8	9
10	11	12
13	14	15
16	17	18
19	20	21
22	23	24
25	26	27
28	29	30
31	32	33
34	35	36
37	38	39
40	41	42
43	44	45
46	47	48
49	50	

(1) My advisor, Professor Samuels, suggested that during my
Sophomore year I take Accounting 194 and elective
courses in Economics, English History, Sociology, and
German.

(2) On their recent trip to the East, Mother and Aunt Lydia
visited the Museum Of The City Of New York, which is
on Fifth Avenue at 104th Street.

(3) Bob's native American fishing guide gave him a photograph
of Mount Baker, a snow-capped Mountain of the Cascade
Range Northeast of Seattle.

(4) The day after the Fourth Of July holiday, the Professor of my
class in American Literature tested us on our reading of Poe's
Fall Of The House Of Usher.

(5) Formerly a Captain in the United States Coast Guard, Linda's
Father is now an assistant to Secretary Watkins of the
Department Of The Interior.

NAME _____   SCORE _____

Directions: If you find a misspelled word, underline it and write it correctly at the left. (Consider an omitted or misused apostrophe a punctuation error, not a spelling error.) In the column of figures at the left, circle the numbers that identify errors in the sentence. Each sentence contains at least one of the following errors:

1. The group of words is a sentence modifier.
2. There is a dangling or misplaced modifier.
3. There is a misused verb (wrong number, tense, or principal part).
4. There is a poorly used pronoun (wrong number or case form, or inexact reference).
5. There is an error in punctuation.

_____
1 2 3 4 5   (1) A car that was backing out of the restaurant parking lot had a breifcase setting on its top but when I tried to signal them they just waved and drove off.

_____
1 2 3 4 5   (2) Last Sunday, while looking out the window of my new condominium, an ugly rat come out from some bushes and ran across the lawn.

_____
1 2 3 4 5   (3) "The simple construction of the five opening lines of the poem result in an especially pleasing rythm," Professor Quigley Houston told his class of literature majors.

_____
1 2 3 4 5   (4) The boss's inability to make quick decisions, as well as her often faulty judgment, have certianly brought about most of our companys really serious problems.

_____
1 2 3 4 5   (5) The chair of the board, to use an obvious example, a person with admireable instincts and real dedication but little skill in management.

_____
1 2 3 4 5   (6) "The fact that advance ticket sales have been dissappointing don't mean that the concert will be postponed, does it," the worried young sophomore asked.

_____
1 2 3 4 5   (7) "The preformance of our defensive backs in the last three games have been less than outstanding," said our head coach who sometimes uses understatement to emphasize his points.

_____
1 2 3 4 5   (8) Trying to decide on our route, it was pointed out that the shorter one was quite hilly and winding, therefore the shorter one would very likely take more time than the longer one.

_____
1 2 3 4 5   (9) Theres not more than three or four people in this entire city goverment whom I'd say are capable of leadership in difficult times.

_____
1 2 3 4 5   (10) The three older women always arrived at the class earlier than the other students, they also managed to quickly, carefully, and throughly complete every assignment.

1 2 3 4 5   (11) Assembling in the superintendent's office at ten o'clock, Mr. Swift asked we seven freshmen if we wanted to form an honors class?

1 2 3 4 5   (12) My neighbor's oldest son, for example, who confidently selected a course in engineering, in spite of the fact that his knowledge of mathmatics and physics were slight.

1 2 3 4 5   (13) Apparently the mischievous youngsters choice of companions have given him many oppertunities to get into real trouble.

1 2 3 4 5   (14) Although both Thelma and Mary Lou were named in the grandmother's will neither one of them have as yet received their share of the inheritance.

1 2 3 4 5   (15) How can you maintain that this dictionery is yours when someone else's name and address is stamped on its inside cover.

1 2 3 4 5   (16) Their delay in making shipments, in addition to their higher prices, have lost business for them, they're no longer serious compitition for us.

1 2 3 4 5   (17) "Just between you and I," said Eddie, "there's to many people in this elevator; let's wait for the next one."

1 2 3 4 5   (18) The amateur entrepreneur explained to my partner and I that the influx of orders from small investors have undoubtedly effected the market unfavorably.

1 2 3 4 5   (19) Bruce's face turned flaming red upon hearing that his grade on the literature midterm test was higher then anyone elses.

1 2 3 4 5   (20) I'm quiet sure that I won't get the job, I was told that to be hired a person either had to be a union member or have their apprentice card.

1 2 3 4 5   (21) The article concluded with the following sentence; "Part of the credit should go to whomever supplies the restaurant with its incredibly fresh vegetables."

1 2 3 4 5   (22) People in our neighborhood are extremely dissatisfied with the maintainence work of the Highway Department, there's still several deep potholes in our street.

1 2 3 4 5   (23) We were unhappily supprised to hear the mayor say, "Neither of these projects, although desperately needed, have been funded, our repair fund only has four thousand dollars left in it."

1 2 3 4 5   (24) There having been, if I remember correctly, two or three productions of our drama association that many in the audience nearly thought were of professional quality.

1 2 3 4 5   (25) After crossing the boundary into the next country, bad driving conditions can be expected for approximately fourty miles; the government having neglected the roads and bridges outrageously.

NAME _____ SCORE _____

Directions: If you find a misspelled word, underline it and write it correctly at the left. (Consider an omitted or misused apostrophe a punctuation error, not a spelling error.) Circle at least one of the numbers at the left:

1. The sentence is correct.
2. There is a dangling or misplaced modifier.
3. There is a misused verb.
4. There is a misused pronoun.
5. There is an error in punctuation.

_____   1 2 3 4 5   (1) While walking down the slippery wooden steps to the beach, a most embarassing thing happened to my escort and I.

_____   1 2 3 4 5   (2) In the margin of my theme Professor Jenkins had written this note: "You can now see, can't you, that the omission of two commas from this sentence have produced a humerous effect."

_____   1 2 3 4 5   (3) The eminent critic nearly spent forty-five minutes giving us an extraordinary explaination of one of the short poems we had read.

_____   1 2 3 4 5   (4) Clancy, a chunky, pleasant sophomore whom I had known in high school, stopped me and said, "Tell me, friend, what you thought about that last test we took in mathematics."

_____   1 2 3 4 5   (5) "The usual procedure," explained the receptionist, "is that Ms. Stanton's secretary or one of her assistants are on duty until five oclock on Wednesdays."

_____   1 2 3 4 5   (6) I could hardly believe what I had just heard, the superintendent had never before ever spoke so harshly to any of we students.

_____   1 2 3 4 5   (7) The frightened little boy told Mother and me that he had become separated from his parents, had wandered away from the other picnickers, and had been chased by a fierce dog.

_____   1 2 3 4 5   (8) Beyond the village of Greenville the motorist must procede cautiously, I have been told that they are resurfacing the highway for approximately ninety miles.

_____   1 2 3 4 5   (9) If anyone tells me that any child can learn to, with patient teaching, play a musical instrument, I'll give them a real arguement.

_____   1 2 3 4 5   (10) On the last night of Homecoming Week there is usualy a banquet at which the college president or the football coach give the alumni an inspirational speech.

_____   1 2 3 4 5   (11) Apparently every guy in our dorm except you and I has already had a conference with their academic adviser.

_____ (12) "The *Santa Maria* wasn't Columbus's favorite ship," explained
1   2   3   4   5   Dr. Slade. "After its destruction he is quoted as saying that it was
                             'too weighty and not suitable for making discoveries.' "

_____ (13) "There's probably only three or four boys on this team whom I
1   2   3   4   5   think stand a chance of receiving college atheletic scholarships,"
                             said Coach Wills who is normally quite optimistic.

_____ (14) "I'm absolutely sure that the suspected troublemakers about
1   2   3   4   5   whom the principal of the school has been talking are not you
                             and I," Jacklin confidently told his pal Barnhart.

_____ (15) After reading the pamphlet you brought me from the library,
1   2   3   4   5   my understanding of the history, purpose and accompolish-
                             ments of the United Nations have been broadened.

_____ (16) Unfortunately, many intelligent and conscientious high-school
1   2   3   4   5   graduates lack enough funds to go directly to college, which is
                             an outrageous situation.

_____ (17) The person whom I was referred to told me that I would have
1   2   3   4   5   to only wait a few more days before learning whether I or one
                             of the other contestants have won the first prize.

_____ (18) Having paid my fine at the local sheriff's office, our next desti-
1   2   3   4   5   nation was Centerville where I understand they also have
                             extreamly strict laws relating to speeding.

_____ (19) The personnel director replied, "Our company plans to within
1   2   3   4   5   a month or so hire a new financial adviser whom we all hope
                             will solve these troublesome problems for us."

_____ (20) "Dont it seem unusual that every one of us five trainees received
1   2   3   4   5   the same letter of recommendation from the boss?" asked Stan.

_____ (21) The police sergeant approached my roommate and me, opened
1   2   3   4   5   his notebook, and asked, "Has either one of you ever before seen
                             the hammer that was found lying near the front door?"

_____ (22) Miss Perkins was a truely dedicated teacher, she seemed always
1   2   3   4   5   ready to graciously and uncomplainingly give her time to
                             whomever came to her for help.

_____ (23) The members of the planning committee have studied these
1   2   3   4   5   problems and have become convinced that neither of the two
                             suggested remedies has been satisfactorily researched.

_____ (24) This applicant has only been studying Russian for three semes-
1   2   3   4   5   ters, his knowledge of the grammar, literature, and pronounci-
                             ation are quite limited.

_____ (25) The fact that your niece's careless handling of money could
1   2   3   4   5   result in her loosing the property to the mortgage holder don't
                             seem to trouble either she or her husband.

Appendix A

Sentence Combining

Sentence combining is a simple process designed to help you write more sophisticated and effective sentences. You began to employ combining techniques in Lesson 7 and its accompanying exercises, so the following exercises ought to be familiar to you. The exercises in Appendix A begin with the simplest kinds of combining, embedding an adjective from one sentence into another sentence, thus enriching one sentence and eliminating the other. The exercises then move through the formation of compound sentences and into complex sentences, those constructed with verbal phrases and subordinate clauses.

Every set in these exercises can be done in several ways, each one correct in its own way. The first set offers a good example of the possbilbilities:

> The man was tall.
> He was thin.
> He walked down the street.

The simplest combined form puts the adjectives tall and thin in the sentence immediately before the noun:

> The tall, thin man walked down the street.

But it is possible to move the adjectives into more emphatic positions:

> Tall and thin, the man walked down the street.
> The man, tall and thin, walked down the street.

Each of these options is correct and each creates a slightly different sentence, a sentence that draws the reader's attention to the facts in slightly different ways.

These additional combining exercises will help your writing in two ways. First, they will remind you of different ways of expressing the same idea, and thus they will expand the range of constructions you employ in your writing. Second, the exercises will focus your attention on punctuation as you make up the combinations.

Remember that every set in these exercises can be done in several ways, all of them correct. For each set, test the various ways of creating combinations and you will make yourself a more flexible and more effective writer.

Directions: Combine the sentences in each numbered unit into a single longer sentence.

1. The man was tall.
   He was thin.
   He walked down the street.

   _____

   _____

2. The tall, thin man walked down the street.
   A woman walked with him.
   She was short.
   She was blonde.

   _____

   _____

3. The man and the woman walked down the street.
   The street was dusty.
   The street was crowded.

   _____

   _____

4. The tall, thin man and the short, blonde woman walked down the dusty, crowded
     street.
   They walked slowly.
   They walked into a cold north wind.

   _____

   _____

5. The man and the woman were very cold.
   They stopped in front of a store.
   Then they went inside.
   They went inside for a cup of coffee.

   _____

   _____

Combine the sentences in each unit into a single sentence by using compound verbs.

6. Jim walked down the hall.
   He entered the last classroom on the right.

   _____

   _____

7. Robert and the girls parked the car in the student parking lot.
   They made the long walk to the library.

   _____

   _____

8. The office building is seven stories high.
   It has a long circular drive in front of it.

   _____

   _____

9. We went to the soccer field.
   Then we walked into the picnic area.

   _____

   _____

10. Tom went to the basketball game.
    Sue went to the basketball game.
    They sat at mid-court behind the team's bench.

    _____

    _____

Combine the sentences in each unit into a single sentence by putting the items into a series.

11. Joan picked up her purse.
    She picked up her umbrella.
    She picked up a set of car keys.

    _____

    _____

12. She walked slowly down the stairs.
    She got into her car.
    She drove happily off to work.

    _____

    _____

13. Jim opened the windows.
    He turned on the fan.
    Then he began to work on the test.

    _____

    _____

14. I have lost my textbook.
    I have lost my lecture notes.
    I have lost my workbook.

    _____

    _____

15. I have called all my friends.
    I have searched the trunk of my car.
    I have even looked on my desk.

    _____

    _____

Combine the sentences in each unit into a single compound sentence.

16. The bus arrived late.
    George didn't mind waiting for it.

    _____

    _____

17. The tall boy looks like a basketball player.
    He would rather study nuclear physics.

    _____

    _____

18. I spend a great deal of time at the Student Union.
    It is a wonderful place.

    _____

    _____

19. The three little boys went to the soccer game.
    They stayed only a few minutes.

    _____

    _____

20. Thunder and lightning hit the area very suddenly.
    Both teams left the field in a great hurry.

    _____

    _____

Combine these same sentences in each unit by using adverbial clauses.

21. The bus arrived late.
    George didn't mind waiting for it.

    _____

    _____

22. The tall boy looks like a basketball player.
    He would rather study nuclear physics.

    _____

    _____

23. I spend a great deal of time at the Student Union.
    It is a wonderful place.

    _____

    _____

24. The three little boys went to the soccer game.
    They stayed only a few minutes.

    _____

    _____

25. Thunder and lightning hit the area very suddenly.
    Both teams left the field in a great hurry.

    _____

    _____

Combine the sentences in each unit into a single sentence by using participial phrases.

26. The tall, slender girl walked out of the garage.
    She moved close to a blue car.
    She inspected the outside of the car for dents and scratches.

    _____

    _____

27. The girl walked up to the car.
    She opened the door of the car.
    She checked the odometer reading.

    _____

    _____

28. The girl opened the hood of the car.
    She took a wrench out of her toolbox.
    She removed a spark plug so that she could check it.

    _____

    _____

29. The girl looked at the tip of the spark plug.
    She looked very carefully.
    She shook her head sadly.

    _____

    _____

30. She replaced the spark plug.
    She closed the hood.
    She walked slowly away from the car.

    _____

    _____

Combine the sentences in each unit into a single sentence by using adjective clauses and participial phrases.

31. The lifeguard sat in the tower.
    He scanned the water carefully.
    He was looking for people in distress.

    _____

    _____

32. Only a few people were at the beach that day.
    They sat on the sand.
    They listened to their CD players.

    _____

    _____

33. The lifeguard watched the ships.
    The ships sailed by on the horizon.
    He regularly checked two people.
    The people were swimming nearby.

    _____

    _____

34. About noon the lifeguard left the tower.
    He walked slowly across the sand.
    He was carrying his umbrella and sunscreen with him.

    _____

    _____

35. He sat quietly at the lunch counter.
    He ate a hot dog with onions and pickles.
    Then he took a short nap on a bench nearby.

    _____

    _____

Combine the sentences in each unit into a single sentence by using a variety of constructions.

36. Last night three guys came to visit Jim.
    The three guys had played on his high school soccer team.
    The four of them talked until 3:00 A.M.

    _____

    _____

37. One of them is studying accounting.
    He had been a weak student in high school.
    He now works very hard at his courses.

    _____

    _____

38. He had never enjoyed school very much.
    He finds several of his courses extremely interesting now.

    _____

    _____

39. The second guy is in the Air Force.
    He is a year older than the others.
    He is studying to be an electronics technician.

    _____

    _____

40. The third guy intends to enter the state university this fall.
    He has been working in construction since he graduated from high school.

    _____

    _____

Make the first sentence in each of the following units a participial phrase or a gerund combined with a preposition.

41. The two men were installing a satellite dish on the roof.
    They found a small suitcase on the roof of the building.

    _____

    _____

42. The girls were walking slowly down the hall.
    They stopped to talk to the other students.

    _____

    _____

43. The clouds built up slowly in the west.
    They brought lightning and thunder early in the evening.

    _____

    _____

44. The players saw that defeat was certain.
    They played even harder for the rest of the game.

    _____

    _____

45. The teacher walked into the room.
    She was rolling a cart.
    The cart had a computer and an LCD projector on it.
    She was carrying a __?__ .

    _____

    _____

Combine the sentences in each unit into a single sentence by using a variety of constructions.

46. The woman was tall and slender.
    She was wearing a gray coat.
    She met a man.
    She met him in the lobby of the hotel.

    _____

    _____

47. The man was extremely young.
    He was poorly dressed.
    He had no important information to give her.

    _____

    _____

48. The man told the woman his sad story.
    She was disappointed.
    Her disappointment was extreme.
    She told him (two things).
    He was fired.
    He would never work in industrial espionage again.

    _____

    _____

49. In response, the man told her (something).
    He had just landed a job with IBM.
    The job was in their security office.

    _____

    _____

50. (Something) seems unlikely.
    The man was telling the truth.

    _____

    _____

Combine the sentences in each unit into a single sentence by using a variety of constructions.

51. The new office building down the street is finally finished.
    A few tenants are moving in.

    _____

    _____

52. Three lawyers moved into an office on the third floor yesterday.
    Today they installed a new phone system.

    _____

    _____

53. That building has fifty offices in it.
    Only six of them are occupied.

    _____

    _____

54. The rent for the offices is extremely high.
    Many of the offices are vacant.

    _____

    _____

55. The owners need to lower the rent.
    They might go into bankruptcy.

    _____

    _____

Appendix
B

Diagnostic Tests

Diagnostic Test: *Punctuation*

NAME _____ SCORE _____

Directions: In the space at the left of each pair of sentences, write the letter that identifies the correctly punctuated sentence.

_____ 1. a. "Whenever I try to study my class notes are almost unreadable," complained Ruth, "I must be more careful about my handwriting."
  b. "Whenever I try to study, my class notes are almost unreadable," complained Ruth; "I must be more careful about my handwriting."

_____ 2. a. Some of the stockholders are now wondering if the company has overextended itself by buying the two new ships.
  b. Some of the stockholders are now wondering, if the company has overextended itself by buying the two new ships?

_____ 3. a. Although the Perkinses live less than a block away from us, we hardly feel that we know them well.
  b. Although the Perkins's live less than a block away from us; we hardly feel that we know them well.

_____ 4. a. The following notice recently appeared on the bulletin board; "The editors of this years Senior yearbook have decided to dispense with the so-called humor section."
  b. The following notice recently appeared on the bulletin board: "The editors of this year's Senior yearbook have decided to dispense with the so-called humor section."

_____ 5. a. I scraped the mud and mashed insects from the windshield and Jennie sadly inspected the crumpled, rear fender.
  b. I scraped the mud and mashed insects from the windshield, and Jennie sadly inspected the crumpled rear fender.

_____ 6. a. After they had cleaned the kitchen, put the children to bed, and locked the front door, Pete and Jane looked forward to a quiet, peaceful evening.
  b. After they had cleaned the kitchen, put the children to bed and locked the front door; Pete and Jane looked forward to a quiet peaceful evening.

_____ 7. a. Some neighbors asked questions about Jim's strange friends but Mother told them that it was nobodys concern except our family's.
  b. Some neighbors asked questions about Jim's strange friends, but Mother told them that it was nobody's concern except our family's.

411

_____ 8. a. "Tryouts for the class play have been completed," Miss. Lowe, the drama coach, announced, "this year we are blessed with almost too much talent."
   b. "Tryouts for the class play have been completed," Miss Lowe, the drama coach, announced; "this year we are blessed with almost too much talent."

_____ 9. a. My office mate claims to understand horse racing, but his bets every month usually cost him a week's pay.
   b. My office mate claims to understand horse racing but his bets every month usually cost him a weeks pay.

_____ 10. a. The childrens' father made a good impression, the presiding judge, in fact, commended him for his handling of the matter.
   b. The children's father made a good impression; the presiding judge, in fact, commended him for his handling of the matter.

_____ 11. a. Coach Stannard scheduled volleyball tryouts for February 16, 1998 and nearly two dozen eager, young women turned out.
   b. Coach Stannard scheduled volleyball tryouts for February 16, 1998, and nearly two dozen eager young women turned out.

_____ 12. a. "How can we foreigners learn English," complained Carmen, "when you give different pronunciations to words like *bough, cough, dough, plough* and *slough.*"
   b. "How can we foreigners learn English," complained Carmen, "when you give different pronunciations to words like *bough, cough, dough, plough,* and *slough?*"

_____ 13. a. Located 85 miles offshore, its pipelines stretching across the ocean floor, the platform well is nearly completed and will soon begin pumping oil to the mainland.
   b. Located 85 miles offshore, its pipelines stretching across the ocean floor; the platform well is nearly completed, and will soon begin pumping oil to the mainland.

_____ 14. a. "You will remember, boys and girls, to give this brochure to your parents, won't you?" said Mr. Turner, the third-grade teacher.
   b. "You will remember, boys and girls, to give this brochure to your parents, won't you," said Mr. Turner, the third-grade teacher.

_____ 15. a. "I commend you, Lois," said the boss, "for your suggestion, but I wonder if you've thought of the engineering problems involved."
   b. "I commend you Lois," said the boss, "for your suggestion, but I wonder if you've thought of the engineering problems involved?"

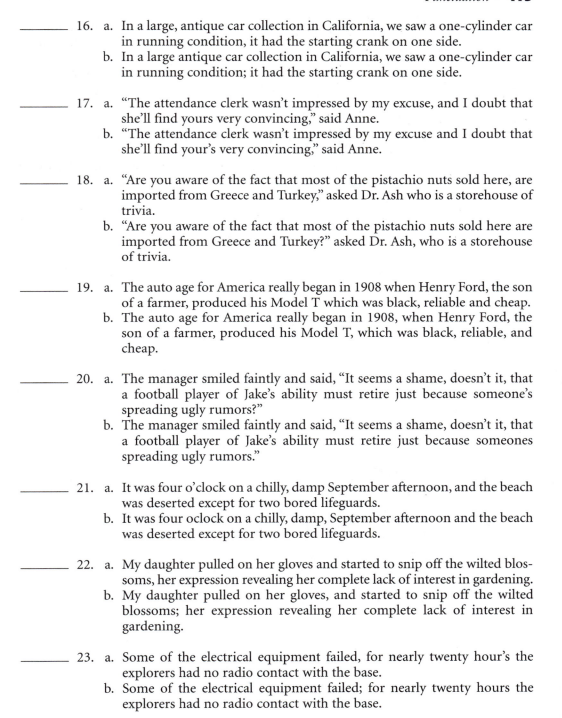

_____ 16. a. In a large, antique car collection in California, we saw a one-cylinder car in running condition, it had the starting crank on one side.

b. In a large antique car collection in California, we saw a one-cylinder car in running condition; it had the starting crank on one side.

_____ 17. a. "The attendance clerk wasn't impressed by my excuse, and I doubt that she'll find yours very convincing," said Anne.

b. "The attendance clerk wasn't impressed by my excuse and I doubt that she'll find your's very convincing," said Anne.

_____ 18. a. "Are you aware of the fact that most of the pistachio nuts sold here, are imported from Greece and Turkey," asked Dr. Ash who is a storehouse of trivia.

b. "Are you aware of the fact that most of the pistachio nuts sold here are imported from Greece and Turkey?" asked Dr. Ash, who is a storehouse of trivia.

_____ 19. a. The auto age for America really began in 1908 when Henry Ford, the son of a farmer, produced his Model T which was black, reliable and cheap.

b. The auto age for America really began in 1908, when Henry Ford, the son of a farmer, produced his Model T, which was black, reliable, and cheap.

_____ 20. a. The manager smiled faintly and said, "It seems a shame, doesn't it, that a football player of Jake's ability must retire just because someone's spreading ugly rumors?"

b. The manager smiled faintly and said, "It seems a shame, doesn't it, that a football player of Jake's ability must retire just because someones spreading ugly rumors."

_____ 21. a. It was four o'clock on a chilly, damp September afternoon, and the beach was deserted except for two bored lifeguards.

b. It was four oclock on a chilly, damp, September afternoon and the beach was deserted except for two bored lifeguards.

_____ 22. a. My daughter pulled on her gloves and started to snip off the wilted blossoms, her expression revealing her complete lack of interest in gardening.

b. My daughter pulled on her gloves, and started to snip off the wilted blossoms; her expression revealing her complete lack of interest in gardening.

_____ 23. a. Some of the electrical equipment failed, for nearly twenty hour's the explorers had no radio contact with the base.

b. Some of the electrical equipment failed; for nearly twenty hours the explorers had no radio contact with the base.

_____ 24. a. If theres one thing today's students don't need; it's more critical, admonitory, or threatening advice hurled at them by long-nosed sanctimonious adults.

          b. If there's one thing today's students don't need, it's more critical, admonitory, or threatening advice hurled at them by long-nosed, sanctimonious adults.

_____ 25. a. "A team that won't be beaten can't be beaten," shouted Coach Miller, who had a seemingly endless supply of clichés.

          b. "A team that wont be beaten can't be beaten," shouted Coach Miller who had a seemingly endless supply of clichés.

NAME _____   SCORE _____

Directions: Each of the following sentences contains three italicized words, one of which is misspelled. Underline each misspelled word and write it, correctly spelled, in the space at the left.

_____   1. "There are limitations on the length, breadth, and *heighth* of packages we ship, and the weight must not *exceed forty* pounds," the agent said.

_____   2. My present was a box of fancy *stationery;* I was *dissappointed* that I didn't *receive* something more practical.

_____   3. The food served at this rural inn is *becoming fameous* throughout Great *Britain.*

_____   4. Lathrop sought the *advise* of an *eminent psychiatrist.*

_____   5. This may sound *unbelievable* to you, but our city *library* has been struck three times by *lightening.*

_____   6. Jerry is *dissatisfied* with his new *schedual* because it does not allow him time for studying *during* the afternoons.

_____   7. In her *sophmore* year Joyce took a course in *speech* and two courses in *literature.*

_____   8. The play had *it's* first *performance* in Hartford last *February.*

_____   9. "An *acquaintance* of mine *reccommended* your *restaurant* to me," said Mrs. Watkins to the receptionist.

_____   10. The applicant attempted to flatter the interviewer by saying, "You are *undoubtably knowledgeable* about the latest *technology* in our field."

_____   11. "Your *humorous* remarks were not *appropriate* for a serious *occassion* such as this one," said the chairperson.

_____   12. I admit that my new dog behaved *deploreably* last *Wednesday* at *obedience* school.

_____ 13. The data we get from these *questionnaires* could have an *effect* on next year's hiring *proceedures*.

_____ 14. *Reference* to a *dictionary* could have quickly settled the *arguement* the two of you were having.

_____ 15. We must all *recognize* the fact that tourism is the *principle* source of income in our quaint *village*.

_____ 16. Yesterday one of the arrested men *lead* the police officers to the place where the *equipment* stolen from the *laboratory* had been hidden.

_____ 17. A *goverment* spokesperson announced that the new *satellite* will provide weather forecasters with *indispensable* data.

_____ 18. The coach happily announced a *noticeable improvement* in batting averages, *especialy* in those of our outfielders.

_____ 19. A serious accident on the highway caused us to *loose approximately ninety* minutes of valuable time.

_____ 20. A senior *pardner* of the firm *conceded* that further meetings would very likely be *necessary*.

_____ 21. "This *pamphlet* is full of the most *rediculous propaganda* I've ever read," shouted the incumbent.

_____ 22. "*Neither* of these two small countries could withstand a long *seige*," replied *Sergeant* Lewis.

_____ 23. As he presented Enid with the award, the *superintendent* said, "Here is a young person *who's courageous* fight has inspired all of us."

_____ 24. When arrested, Elaine had in her *possession* a large *quanity* of *counterfeit* money.

_____ 25. "Serving on this *committee* has been a *priviledge* and a wonderful *experience*," said the retiring chairperson.

NAME _____   SCORE _____

Directions: In the space at the left, copy from within the parentheses the form that would be appropriate in serious writing.

_____   1. Bert was surprised to learn that everyone in the class except Maria and (he, him) had to take another test.

_____   2. The thief apparently had crept through the broken ventilator grill and had (laid, lain) quietly in the storeroom until nightfall.

_____   3. Mary Ellen wasn't at the park yesterday; it hardly could have been (she, her) who tore your scarf.

_____   4. Anyone selected for the acting presidency must prepare (himself or herself, themself, themselves) for a short and thankless term of office.

_____   5. The reason I'm looking so pale is (because, that) my sunlamp needs repairing.

_____   6. Some fellow who had occupied the room before I arrived had left some of (his, their) old clothes in the closet.

_____   7. I wish someone on the school paper would write an editorial in (regard, regards) to the noise in the library reading room.

_____   8. Just between you and (I, me), Luke shouldn't expect to get off with only a lecture from the judge.

_____   9. You're convinced now, aren't you, that you (hadn't ought to, shouldn't) leave your garage unlocked?

_____   10. My sister once studied the alto saxophone but never played it (good, well) enough to be chosen for the school band.

_____   11. The robbers, (whoever, whomever) they were, must have known exactly when the workers would be paid.

_____   12. The school's new program must be effective, for there (has, have) been surprisingly few complaints from parents.

_____ 13. Not many jobs are available, (because, being that) the government has curtailed operations at the navy yard.

_____ 14. After speaking into the microphone, Laura played back the tape and commented on how (different, differently) her voice sounded.

_____ 15. "Vote for (whoever, whomever) you think is the best candidate," answered Anita's father.

_____ 16. In a political campaign every candidate makes promises that (they know, he or she knows) cannot possibly be kept.

_____ 17. Also included in the packet (is, are) a travel guide, some special trip tips, and two exceptional bonus prizes.

_____ 18. Someone should have told (we, us) ushers that the main door had not been unlocked.

_____ 19. Do you know who the man is who is (setting, sitting) at the head table next to the guest speaker?

_____ 20. As everyone knows, neither DDT nor any other insecticide (has, have) the ability to distinguish between good and bad insects.

_____ 21. If the helicopter pilot had not dropped blankets to the men stranded on the ice floe, they probably would have (froze, frozen) to death.

_____ 22. After a few months Carrie (began, begun) to have doubts about her nephew's ability to manage her investments.

_____ 23. No one could have been more surprised than (I, me) to learn of your recent marriage.

_____ 24. The gratification resulting from working on the school newspaper and other publications (outweighs, outweigh) the demands on one's time.

_____ 25. After a person has sat for five hours in the blazing sunlight listening to this kind of music, (he or she feels, they feel) numb and beaten.

NAME _____ SCORE _____

Directions: Study these paired sentences for incompleteness, dangling or misplaced modifiers, faulty parallelism, and faulty comparisons. In the space at the left, write the letter that identifies the correct sentence.

_____ 1. a. The cotton crop this year, we all hope, will be much better than last years.
   b. The cotton crop this year, we all hope, will be much better than last year's.

_____ 2. a. Because we are the parents of five active children, our washing machine is running much of the time.
   b. Being the parents of five active children, our washing machine is running much of the time.

_____ 3. a. Searching the area carefully, we finally found the tunnel entrance, expertly covered by underbrush and which the other searchers had overlooked.
   b. Searching the area carefully, we finally found the tunnel entrance, which had been expertly covered by underbrush and which the other searchers had overlooked.

_____ 4. a. The group's intention, surely a noble one, to constantly and relentlessly encourage the protection of the environment.
   b. The group's intention, surely a noble one, is to encourage constantly and relentlessly the protection of the environment.

_____ 5. a. Believing me to be a better public speaker than anyone else in the class, my parents told all the relatives that I would be the valedictorian.
   b. Being a better public speaker than anyone in the class, my parents told all the relatives that I would be the valedictorian.

_____ 6. a. Malaysia and other countries proved incapable of sheltering or unwilling to shelter all of the refugees.
   b. Malaysia and other countries proved incapable or unwilling to shelter all of the refugees.

_____ 7. a. "I neither intend to withdraw from the race nor to in any degree stop pointing out my opponent's shortcomings," Ms. Hawley replied.
   b. "I intend neither to withdraw from the race nor in any degree to stop pointing out my opponent's shortcomings," Ms. Hawley replied.

_____ 8. a. When seen from a distance, the white cliffs seem to resemble icebergs.
     b. When seen from a distance, one might think that the white cliffs were icebergs.

_____ 9. a. This popular young actor lives high in the Hollywood hills in a small apartment decorated with posters of auto races and bullfights.
     b. This popular young actor lives in a small apartment decorated with posters of auto races and bullfights high in the Hollywood hills.

_____ 10. a. The relatively small amount of flood water has not and probably won't cause any major damage.
     b. The relatively small amount of flood water has not caused and probably won't cause any major damage.

_____ 11. a. When we replaced the wooden shingles with a composition roof, the insurance company agreed to lower our annual premium quite considerably.
     b. By replacing the wooden shingles with a composition roof, the insurance company agreed to quite considerably lower our annual premium.

_____ 12. a. Commissioner Reed stated that our downtown streets are as clean, if not cleaner than, other cities.
     b. Commissioner Reed stated that our downtown streets are as clean as, if not cleaner than, those of other cities.

_____ 13. a. I already have a full enough schedule of work today without being asked to listen to you practice your speech.
     b. I already have a full enough schedule of work today without asking me to listen to you practice your speech.

_____ 14. a. The reason for our moving being that the security system at Elmhurst Manor is more modern than the old apartment.
     b. The reason for our moving is that the security system at Elmhurst Manor is more modern than that at the old apartment.

_____ 15. a. Sylvia Andrews is a self-sufficient and talented person who, since her parents died, has supported herself and her younger brothers tutoring students in mathematics.
     b. Sylvia Andrews, a self-sufficient and talented person who has supported herself and her younger brothers since her parents died tutoring students in mathematics.

_____ 16. a. My mother's paternal grandmother was one of the very few, if not the only, woman to study veterinary medicine in the early 1900s.
     b. My mother's paternal grandmother was one of the very few women, if not the only woman, to study veterinary medicine in the early 1900s.

———— 17. a. You must either return these books to the library or pay a substantial fine.
b. Either you must return these books to the library or pay a substantial fine.

———— 18. a. I hope that the yield from these tax-free bonds will be equal to, if not more than, the yield from your stocks.
b. I hope that the yield from these tax-free bonds will be equal, if not more than, your stocks.

———— 19. a. Albert's plan being to, as soon as he receives his inheritance, retire to some remote island in the South Seas.
b. Albert's plan is to retire to some remote island in the South Seas as soon as he receives his inheritance.

———— 20. a. You will be given preferred seating only if you have donated at least $200 to the Opera Guild.
b. You will only be given preferred seating if you have donated at least $200 to the Opera Guild.

———— 21. a. Ellen hopes that her tax-deductible contributions this year will be equal to, if not more than, last year's.
b. Ellen hopes that her tax-deductible contributions this year will be equal, if not more than, last year.

———— 22. a. Pietro maintains that most people in his country are easygoing, warm-hearted, friends to Americans, and having a tolerance for the ideas and ways of foreigners.
b. Pietro maintains that most people in his country are easygoing and warmhearted, are friends to Americans, and have a tolerance for the ideas and ways of foreigners.

———— 23. a. Fairhaven has one of the largest airports in the state, if not the largest.
b. Fairhaven has one of the largest, if not the largest, airport in the state.

———— 24. a. While just getting nicely adjusted to high-school life, my family moved again, this time to Baltimore.
b. While I was just getting nicely adjusted to high-school life, my family moved again, this time to Baltimore.

———— 25. a. Quickly totaling the bills, imagine my dismay on discovering that I nearly owed my entire month's salary.
b. Quickly totaling the bills, I was dismayed to discover that I owed nearly my entire month's salary.

Appendix C

Answer Key to Practice Sheets

Practice Sheet 1, page 5

1. seemed
2. knocked
3. sits
4. fell
5. came
6. offered
7. are
8. (i)s
9. own
10. echoed
11. attended
12. stands
13. appeared
14. became
15. comes
16. were
17. bought
18. hired
19. left
20. made

Practice Sheet 1, page 6

1. whine
2. trophies
3. Answers
4. puddles
5. trees
6. articles
7. first
8. None
9. pages
10. shortage
11. filly
12. lack
13. grades
14. oldest
15. boy
16. runner
17. One
18. textbook
19. call
20. shorter

Practice Sheet 2, pages 15, 16

1. 5, 5
2. 2, 6
3. 2, 5
4. 4, 1
5. 4, 6
6. 5, 5
7. 1, 3
8. 3, 4
9. 1, 4
10. 4, 5
11. 4, 2
12. 2, 5
13. 2, 6
14. 5, 4
15. 2, 6
16. 5, 4
17. 2, 5
18. 5, 4
19. 4, 4
20. 5, 6
21. 2, 6
22. 5, 4
23. 3, 5
24. 4, 4
25. 1, 6
26. 3, 5
27. 4, 1
28. 1, 4
29. 1, 1
30. 4, 1
31. 5, 5
32. 4, 2
33. 4, 5
34. 4, 6
35. 5, 3
36. 4, 5
37. 6, 5
38. 4, 1
39. 4, 5
40. 5, 4

Practice Sheet 3, page 27

1. failure
2. politician
3. player
4. leader
5. location
6. person
7. part
8. appearance
9. mystery
10. members
11. help
12. distraction
13. winner
14. source
15. efforts
16. one
17. bid
18. choice
19. friends
20. key

Practice Sheet 3, page 28

1. full
2. tired
3. sour
4. ill
5. reconciled
6. fruitless
7. ready
8. sweeter
9. dark
10. unmanageable
11. flexible
12. attractive
13. excited
14. cold
15. beautiful
16. calm
17. unlikely
18. happy
19. probable
20. obvious

Practice Sheet 4, page 35 (Note: Adverbial modifiers appear in parentheses.)

1. boys sampled one
2. sister made impression
3. Richard has read any
4. I will bookmark site
5. we watched half
6. Bob found one
7. Aunt Martha plays game
8. test will cover material
9. Dozens cleaned (up) lot
10. club appreciates gift
11. we watched bull-riding
12. you will count money
13. Mrs. Rawlings enjoys short stories
14. men crossed bridge
15. senator pointed (out) changes
16. I (wi)ll pick (up) couple
17. wife bought SUV
18. windstorm knocked (down) trees
19. Jack hit serve
20. Pam cut (up) vegetables

Practice Sheet 4, page 36

1. D.O.
2. O.C.
3. D.O.
4. O.C.
5. I.O.
6. I.O.
7. D.O.
8. I.O.
9. I.O.
10. O.C.
11. D.O.
12. D.O.
13. I.O.
14. O.C.
15. D.O.
16. O.C.
17. D.O.
18. I.O.
19. O.C.
20. I.O.

Practice Sheet 5, pages 43, 44

1. has, 3
2. must, 3
3. should, 1
4. might, 4
5. would be, 2
6. will, 4
7. had been, 1
8. should have, 1
9. has, 5
10. can, 3

11. has, 4
12. have been, 3
13. should, 4
14. is, 5
15. could, 3
16. will have, 3
17. has been, 4
18. must, 1
19. has been, 1
20. could, 2

21. must have been, 4
22. did, 2
23. had, 3
24. has been, 1
25. had, 2
26. should, 3
27. had, 5
28. (i)s, 2
29. will have, 3
30. might have, 4

31. should have been, 1
32. have, 4
33. could have been, 3
34. will, 5
35. might, 4
36. must, 3
37. would have, 5
38. did, 4
39. should, 3
40. does, 3

Practice Sheet 6, page 53

1. 3, could be seen
2. 4, will be allowed
3. 3, has been met
4. 3, is being considered
5. 5, have been kept

6. 4, will be given
7. 3, would be appreciated
8. 4, will be sent
9. 5, might be considered
10. 3, should have been paid

Practice Sheet 6, page 54

1. cookies
2. copies
3. What
4. proposal
5. car
6. that
7. errors
8. Whom
9. Who
10. assistant
11. whom
12. color
13. Who
14. What
15. whom

Practice Sheet 7, pages 61, 62

1. C
2. 0
3. S
4. C
5. S
6. C
7. 0
8. S
9. S
10. C
11. S
12. S
13. C
14. S
15. C
16. S
17. S
18. C
19. S
20. C
21. C
22. C
23. C
24. C
25. S

Practice Sheet 8, pages 73, 74

1. 6
2. 5
3. 7
4. 8
5. 4
6. 3
7. 7
8. 10
9. 5
10. 1
11. 3
12. 1
13. 9
14. 8
15. 7
16. 7
17. 10
18. 2
19. 1
20. 9
21. 8
22. 5
23. 10
24. 1
25. 3
26. 1
27. 9
28. 8
29. 5
30. 10
31. 4
32. 1
33. 9
34. 7
35. 10
36. 1
37. 3
38. 1
39. 8
40. 1

Practice Sheet 9, page 83

1. books
2. high school
3. flight
4. watch
5. Dick Lee
6. road
7. someone
8. Dallas
9. mystery
10. spot
11. Julie Ross
12. theme
13. report
14. house
15. 1938

Practice Sheet 9, page 84

1. woman, who. . .started
2. fellow, whose car I had borrowed
3. those, who arrive late
4. dog, whenever . . . down the street
5. One, who is older than I am
6. man, who lives downstairs
7. person, who wrote . . . life
8. Speech 301, which . . . course
9. scouts, who hadn't called . . . tenth grade
10. sofa, where I was lying
11. time, (when) our boat . . . of the lake
12. everything, Dad . . . in the paper
13. James, whose . . . mine
14. table, where . . . his lunch
15. subject, she was assigned

Practice Sheet 10, page 95

1. S.C.	5. S.	9. S.	13. Ap.	17. D.O.
2. S.	6. S.	10. S.	14. D.O.	18. D.O.
3. D.O.	7. O.P.	11. D.O.	15. Ap.	19. S.C.
4. D.O.	8. S.C.	12. Ap.	16. D.O.	20. O.P.

Practice Sheet 10, page 96

1. D.O. (where . . . keys)
2. S.C. (that . . . high)
3. D.O. (where . . . is)
4. D.O. (that . . . again)
5. S.C. (that . . . him)
6. S.C. (what . . . store)
7. S. (that . . . exam)
8. D.O. (that . . . exam)
9. Ap. (that . . . exam)
10. D.O. (that . . . referendum)
11. D.O. (that . . . overcharged)
12. S.C. (that . . . fee)
13. S. (Whoever . . . driveway)
14. S. (that . . . date)
15. O.P. (how . . . luxuries)
16. S. (Why . . . pension)
17. D.O. (that . . . made)
18. Ap. (that . . . defeated)
19. D.O. (if . . . wealth)
20. D. O. (he . . . voted)

Practice Sheet 11, page 107

1. D.O.	5. S.C.	9. S.C.	13. S.C.	17. S.
2. D. O.	6. S.	10. O.P.	14. O.P.	18. O.P.
3. O. P.	7. O.P.	11. S.	15. D.O.	19. D.O.
4. S.	8. D.O.	12. O.P.	16. S.	20. S.C.

Practice Sheet 11, page 108

1. Adv.	5. Adj.	9. Adv.	13. N.	17. Adv.
2. Adj.	6. Adv.	10. N.	14. Adv.	18. N.
3. N.	7. N.	11. N.	15. Adv..	19. Adj.
4. N.	8. N.	12. N.	16. N.	20. N.

Practice Sheet 12, pages 117, 118

1. ___, G(erund)	8. Martha	16. Anyone	24. ___
2. Ms. Wood, I(nfinitive)	9. ___	17. ___, I	25. scholarship
3. clothes	10. boys, G	18. ___, I	26. girls
4. books	11. stories	19. singer, I	27. boys
5. ___	12. man	20. ___, G	28. boy
6. ___, I	13. job, G	21. family	29. ___
7. brother	14. ___	22. bridge	30. team, I
	15. fans	23. reporter, G	

Practice Sheet 13, pages 129, 130

1. F	6. F	11. F	16. F	21. S	26. F
2. S	7. S	12. S	17. S	22. F	27. F
3. F	8. F	13. F	18. F	23. S	28. S
4. F	9. F	14. F	19. F	24. F	29. F
5. S	10. S	15. S	20. F	25. S	30. S

Practice Sheet 14, page 139

1. A	3. B	5. B	7. B	9. A
2. A	4. A	6. B	8. B	10. B

Practice Sheet 14, page 140

1. A	3. B	5. A	7. B	9. B	11. A	13. A or B	15. B
2. A or B	4. A	6. A	8. B	10. A	12. A	14. A or B	

Practice Sheet 14A, pages 143, 144

1. A	4. A	7. B	10. A	13. A	16. A	19. A
2. B	5. A	8. B	11. A	14. A	17. A	20. B
3. B	6. A	9. A	12. B	15. A	18. A	

Practice Sheet 15, page 151

1. 1	3. 3	5. 6	7. 3	9. 4	11. 4	13. 6	15. 5
2. 2	4. 2	6. 1	8. 5	10. 1	12. 2	14. 1	

Practice Sheet 15, page 152

1. Yesterday I met Charles Atwood, our new computer programmer.
2. . . . Charles Atwood, who is our new computer programmer.
3. After checking all the printed circuits, the technician replaced. . . .
4. Spraying some lubricant on the drawer slides will stop the squeaking.
5. Spray some lubricant on the drawer slides to stop the squeaking.
6. The team having selected a new coach, the public relations department. . . .
7. After the team selected a new coach, the public relations department. . . .
8. Having finished the paint job on my car, I put all the paints. . . .
9. Although Jim sent out ten resumes last month, he has received no replies yet.
10. Because Jim received no replies to the ten resumes, he will send out twenty this month.

Practice Sheet 16, page 159

1. A	3. A	5. B	7. B	9. A
2. B	4. A	6. A	8. A	10. A

Practice Sheet 16, page 160

1. B	3. A	5. B	7. B	9. A
2. A	4. A	6. B	8. B	10. A

Practice Sheet 17, pages 167, 168

1. 2, 1 singers, . . . time,
2. 4, 3 shelves, . . . colorful,
3. 2, 3 forward, . . . tall,
4. 3, 4 cold, . . . wind,
5. 2, 1 press, . . . brake,
6. 5(4), 2 leaving, . . . locks,
7. 3, 4 wailing, . . . hills,
8. 3, 5 intricate, . . . since,
9. 4, 2 schools, . . . tunnels,
10. 1, 3 VCR, . . . obscure,
11. 4, 3 grass, . . . hasty,
12. 5, 3 that, . . . passionate,
13. 5(4), 3 applauding, . . . dark,
14. 4, 2 projector, . . . slides,
15. 1, 3 play-offs, . . . cheaper,
16. 2, 1 computer, . . . sets,
17. 4, 3 jacket, . . . long,
18. 3, 2 bearded, . . . catcher, . . . quickly,
19. 4, 3 infield, . . . long,
20. 2, 1 French, . . . Russian,

Practice Sheet 18, page 177

1. 2 Island,
2. 4 package, . . . opinion,
3. 6 expected,
4. 5 today,"
5. 2 March, . . . school,
6. 6 Yolanda, . . . died,
7. 3 children, . . . Mary,
8. 1 Alma, . . . drive,
9. 2 Marshall, . . . department,
10. 1 Mel,
11. 2, today, . . . geography,
12. 6 yesterday,
13. 1 Richard, . . . accuracy,
14. 1 City,
15. 1 children, . . . Street,

Practice Sheet 18, page 178

1. R
2. N , faded . . . use,
3. N , where . . . replaced,
4. N , desperately . . . paper,
5. R
6. N , which . . . laboratories,
7. R
8. N , who . . . Texas,
9. N , which . . . ago,
10. R
11. R
12. N , who . . . accountant,
13. R
14. N , who . . . program,
15. R

Practice Sheet 19, page 189

1. W person's, yours
2. W shareholders'
3. W "Where's, subscribers
4. W I'm, They're
5. W twenty-first, twenty-one
6. C
7. W station's
8. W Yours
9. W finishers for their running time. . .
10. W Kelly's
11. W who's, buses, o'clock
12. C
13. C
14. W places
15. W founder's

Practice Sheet 19, page 190

1. The mayor said, "I have ordered a new car phone."
2. General Steiner answered, "I do not intend. . . ."
3. Ramona Rice replied, "I have never met. . . ."
4. Mrs. Overholt asked, "Why did the bridge club skip . . . ?"
5. Did you tell me, "The new map shows . . . "?
6. The announcement clearly stated that only members . . . would be admitted. . . .
7. The moderator of the debate said that the reporter . . . would ask . . . .
8. The first graders said in chorus that every time they plan . . . rains and they can't go.
9. Why didn't I see the little sign that said that the instructions were taped . . . carton?
10. Captain Manley came over to our group and asked if anyone who knew . . . would come over and help them.

Practice Sheet 20, page 197

1. C
2. W Ms. . . . D.C.
3. C
4. W NASA
5. W etc.
6. C
7. W tape!" she screamed.
8. W MBA
9. W Mr.
10. W No. 3, p. 101.
11. W Smith Creek, W. Va.?" asked Martin.
12. C
13. W Ms. . . . would arrive.
14. C
15. C

Practice Sheet 20, page 198

1. 1, 4 trip, Maine,
2. 1, 2 skyscraper, its
3. 1 River,
4. 1, 2 grimly, yours
5. 4, watch,
6. 2, 3 idea; o'clock, Charley's
7. 1, 2 theirs," Ron,
8. 1, 2, 4 Fosters neighbors, California,
9. 1, 3 early; us,
10. 1, 2, 4 situation, club's account,

Practice Sheet 21, pages 209, 210

1. begun, paid
2. did, gave
3. written, taken
4. swore, broken
5. swum, lay
6. ridden, fallen
7. frozen, drank
8. grown, worn
9. seen, became
10. climbed, tore
11. spent, eaten
12. gone, spoken
13. chosen, driven
14. flung, seen
15. run, come
16. stood, crept
17. set, told
18. spent, lent
19. lay, raised
20. swung, clung

Practice Sheet 21, pages 211, 212

1. shone, C
2. C, worn
3. came, C
4. C, worn
5. C, sit

6. take, torn
7. C, C
8. spoken, drowning
9. C, is
10. C, C

11. rung, begun
12. have been, seen
13. spoken, saw
14. C, sank
15. to leave, C

16. yelled, C
17. C, chosen
18. sitting, frozen
19. C, began
20. lie, eaten

Practice Sheet 22, page 221

1. were
2. is
3. sit
4. are
5. is
6. has
7. has
8. has
9. have
10. were
11. is
12. is
13. enjoy
14. has
15. were

Practice Sheet 22, page 222

1. become
2. is
3. C
4. has made
5. is
6. C
7. are
8. have enabled
9. (there) are
10. have
11. is
12. was
13. are
14. C
15. is

Practice Sheet 23, pages 231, 232

1. B, it's
2. A, their
3. B, she
4. A, themself
5. B, It
6. B, one
7. A, their
8. B, you, you
9. B, them
10. B, which
11. A, you
12. B, their
13. A, they
14. A, It
15. B, they

Practice Sheet 24, page 241

1. 4
2. 3
3. 5
4. 1
5. 1
6. 5
7. 1
8. 4
9. 2
10. 4
11. 1
12. 6
13. 1
14. 4
15. 2
16. 2
17. 4
18. 5
19. 4
20. 1

Practice Sheet 24, page 242

1. Whom
2. who
3. us
4. me
5. she
6. yours
7. he
8. whomever
9. whoever
10. she
11. anybody's
12. us
13. who's
14. I
15. who
16. whom
17. me
18. who
19. me
20. whoever

Practice Sheet 25, pages 251, 252

1. Jim, Adj.
2. Tim, Adj.
3. thought, Adv.
4. road, Adj.
5. watched, Adv.
6. Jan, Adj.
7. went, Adv.
8. chance, Adj.
9. distribution, Adj.
10. distributed, Adv.
11. exciting, Adv.
12. debaters, Adj.
13. Bart, Adj.
14. results, Adj.
15. works, Adv.
16. walk, Adv.
17. pace, Adj.
18. interested, Adv.
19. time, Adj.
20. room, Adj.

Practice Sheet 25, pages 253, 254

1. well
2. bright
3. considerably
4. true
5. loosely
6. correctly
7. harder
8. bad
9. differently
10. gently
11. shortest
12. well
13. poorly
14. well
15. good
16. Surely
17. properly
18. better
19. wonderful
20. Almost

Practice Sheet 26, pages 265, 266

1. infer, supposed
2. try to, farther
3. May, disinterested
4. surely, could have
5. Besides, many
6. Let's, anywhere
7. that, among
8. number, fewer
9. very, enthusiastic
10. that, almost
11. way, very
12. as far as, very
13. Because, should have
14. continuous, irritated
15. very, criterion
16. Because of, three
17. think, incredible
18. That, rather
19. Many, angry
20. ought, teach

Practice Sheet 26, pages 267, 268

1. Because of, somewhere else
2. C, used to
3. Those kinds, C
4. Many, C
5. Because, way
6. supposed, C
7. C, very
8. C, where (at)
9. Ought you, among
10. C, C
11. In regard to, no comments
12. C, C
13. suspect, C
14. C, regardless
15. those, surely
16. wants to work on, C
17. that, because of
18. C, C
19. off, C
20. should have, as if

Practice Sheet 27, page 279, 280

1. different
2. Except
3. alter
4. writing
5. allotted
6. extremely
7. desirable
8. advise
9. regrettable
10. preferred
11. hiring
12. its
13. incidents
14. You're
15. Their
16. serviceable
17. lose
18. descent
19. course
20. presents
21. quite
22. principal
23. council
24. unforgettable
25. shown
26. Later
27. fascinating
28. picnicking
29. affected
30. than

Practice Sheet 28, page 287

1. allies
2. alumnae
3. axes
4. beaux, beaus
5. boxes
6. cameos
7. cookies
8. cupfuls, cupsful
9. diagnoses
10. handerkerchiefs, handkerchieves
11. lackeys
12. lassos, lassoes
13. lice
14. men-of-war
15. mementos, mementoes
16. mongooses, mongeese
17. princesses
18. referenda, referendums
19. saleswomen
20. scarves, scarfs
21. sheaves
22. Thomases
23. tomatoes
24. turkeys
25. wolves

Practice Sheet 28, page 288

1. W	6. W	11. C	16. W	21. C	26. W	31. C	36. W	41. W	46. C
2. C	7. C	12. C	17. W	22. C	27. C	32. C	37. C	42. W	47. W
3. W	8. W	13. C	18. C	23. W	28. C	33. C	38. C	43. C	48. W
4. C	9. C	14. W	19. C	24. W	29. C	34. W	39. C	44. W	49. C
5. C	10. C	15. C	20. C	25. W	30. C	35. C	40. C	45. W	50. C

Practice Sheet 29, pages 295, 296

1. candidate, competition
2. equipment, exorbitant
3. disastrous, environment
4. disappointed, accommodations
5. excellent, graffiti
6. conferences, differences
7. enthusiastic, foreign
8. embarrassed, humorous
9. eligible, forty
10. business, abbreviated
11. criticized, appearance
12. athletic, amateur
13. among, acquaintances
14. during, February
15. always, committee
16. absence, discipline
17. audience, dissatisfied
18. arithmetic, grammar
19. immediately, government
20. continuous, dictionary
21. appropriate, curiosity
22. calendar, convenient
23. conceded, competent
24. awkward, accidentally
25. familiar, arguments

Practice Sheet 29A, pages 299, 300

1. opportunity, superintendent
2. mischievous, library
3. original, imagination
4. professor, parallel
5. laboratory, partner
6. probably, village
7. scheduled, Wednesday
8. successful, politics
9. secretary, misspells
10. recommend, restaurant
11. permissible, sophomore
12. ninety, sandwiches
13. literature, tragedies
14. propaganda, prejudices
15. interpretation, interesting
16. practically, professions
17. knowledge, mathematics
18. persuaded, villain
19. temperature, occasionally
20. ninth, twelfth
21. ridiculous, pronunciation
22. interrupted, speech
23. optimistic, satisfactorily
24. surprise, proceeded
25. similar, pastimes

Index

430

compare, contrast, as instruction words in essay test, 322

Comparison
forms of, 156–157
incomplete, 156
writing paragraphs of, 330–333

Comparison, adverb clause of
ambiguity in, 70
case of pronoun in, 237
ellipsis in, 69

complected, 258

complement, compliment, 276

Complements. *See* Direct object; Indirect object; Objective complement; Subjective complement

Completeness
acceptable fragments, 127
types of fragments, 125–126

Complex sentence
defined, 67

Compound modifiers, hyphen with, 185

Compound numbers, hyphen with, 185

Compound sentence
defined, 58
instead of two sentences, 147
overuse of, 147
punctuation of, 58, 163

Compound subjects, number of verb with, 218

Compound verb
method of subordination, 147
no comma with, 59

Concession, adverb clause of, 69

Conclusion of essay, 350–351

Condition
adverb clause of, 68
subjunctive mode in, 207
unexpressed conjunction in, 69

Conjugation
defined, 9
of *earn, grow, be,* 9–10

Conjunction
defined, 58

Conjunctive adverb
defined, 59
semicolon with, 59

Connotation, 403

consequently, 59

consul, council, counsel, 276

contact, 258

continual, continuous, 258

Contractions, apostrophe with, 183–184

Contrast
forms of, 156, 157
writing paragraphs of, 330–331

contrast, as instruction word in essay test, 322

Coordinate adjectives, comma between, 164

Coordinating conjunction
in compound sentence, 59
defined, 58
overuse of, 147
punctuation with, 59, 163

Coordination
defined, 58
overuse of, 147

Correlatives, position of, 136

could(n't) care less, 258

could of, 258

couple, 258

criteria, 259

criticize, as instruction word in essay test, 322

Dangling modifiers
correcting, 137–138
defined, 136
elliptical clauses, 138
gerund phrases, 137
infinitive phrases, 137
participial phrases, 136

Dashes, 185

data, 259

Dates, commas with, 175

decent, descent, dissent, 276

define, as instruction word in essay test, 320–321

Definitions
in dictionaries, 400
writing paragraphs of, 333–334

Degree
adverbs of, 11
See also Comparative degree; Superlative degree

Degrees following names, commas with, 175

Delayed direct object
infinitive phrase as, 104
noun clause as, 90

Delayed subject
infinitive phrase as, 104
noun clause as, 90

delineate, as instruction word in essay test, 320

Demonstrative pronoun
defined, 3
vague reference of, 227–229

Denotation, 403

Dependent clause. *See* Adjective clauses; Adverb clauses; Noun clauses; Subordinate clause

Derivation of words, 404

Description
sensory appeal in, 339
writing paragraphs of, 338–340

desert, dessert, 276

Dialectal forms of verbs, 205

Dialogue, 127

Dictionaries, 397–405

different from, different than, 259

dining, dinning, 276

Direct address, commas with, 174

Direction, adverbs of, 11

Directions, not capitalized, 285

Direct object
case of pronoun as, 236
contrasted with object of preposition, 33
defined, 31
following passive verb, 48
gerund phrase as, 103
infinitive phrase as, 105
noun clause as, 89

Direct question, question mark with, 194

Direct quotation, punctuation with, 174, 185–186

discuss, as instruction word in essay test, 321

disinterested, uninterested, 259

do
as auxiliary verb, 41
emphatic form, 41
misuse, 220
in negatives, 51
in questions, 49

Double comparison, 156

Drucker, Peter, 347–354

due to, 259

e, silent spelling rule, 273

earn, conjugation of, 9–10

either . . . or, 136

Ellipsis, 69

Elliptical clauses
after *than, as,* 69–70
ambiguity in, 70
dangling, 138

emigrate, immigrate, 259

enthuse, 259

er/more, est/most, 11, 157

Reference of pronouns, 225–226
Reference words, to achieve coherence, 329
Reflexive pronouns
  as complement, 21–22
  defined, 4
  misuse, 4
Regular verbs, 10, 204–205
Relative adjective, relative adverb, 79
Relative pronoun
  antecedent of, 80
  defined, 79
  number of, 219
  to subordinate adjective clause, 80
  vague reference of, 229
Religious terms, capital letters with, 284
rest, number of, 219
Restrictive modifiers
  adjective clauses, 79–80, 81, 173
  no commas with, 80, 173
  participial phrases, 114, 173
  prepositional phrases, 173
Result, adverb clause of, 68
Revising, 308, 351
Run-on sentence. *See* Comma fault/comma splice

same, 262
-self pronouns, 4
Semicolons, 59, 164
Senses
  exploring subjects through, 315
  verbs of, 25, 248–249
Sentence
  defined, 1
  incomplete, 125
  variety, 148–149
Sentence fragment
  correcting, 126
  defined, 125
Sentence patterns. *See* Alterations of basic sentence patterns; Basic sentence patterns
Sequence of tenses, 206
Series, commas with, 163–164
shine, principal parts of, 204
shone, shown, 277
sight. See cite, site, sight
Simple sentence, 1–2, 58, 67

since, introducing adverb clause, 68
Single quotation marks, 187
sit, set, 205
site. See cite, site, sight
Slang
  dictionary label for, 401
  quotation marks with, 186
so, such, 262
some, 248, 262
somewheres. See anywheres
so that, introducing adverb clause, 68
Speaker in dialogue, commas with, 174
Spelling
  in dictionary, 397–398
  variant, 397
Spelling list, 291–293
Spelling rules, 273–275
Split infinitive, 135
Squinting modifier, 135
s-sound, plural of nouns ending in, 283
States, abbreviations and postal symbols of, 193
stationary, stationery, 277
statue, stature, statute, 277
Subject
  case of pronoun as, 236
  defined, 1
  gerund phrase as, 103
  infinitive phrase as, 104
  noun clause as, 89
  prepositional phrase as, 103
Subjective complement
  adverb misused for adjective, 248
  case of pronoun as, 237–238
  defined, 24
  following passive verb, 48
  gerund phrase as, 103
  infinitive phrase as, 104
  noun clause as, 89
  subject-verb agreement, 217
Subject of infinitive
  case of pronoun as, 105, 236
  defined, 105
  preceded by *for*, 105
Subjects, academic, capital letters for, 285
Subjunctive mood, 207–208
Subordinate clause
  defined, 67
  tense in, 206–207
  used as sentence, 125

Subordinating conjunctions
  and completeness, 125
  defined, 65–66
  introducing adverb clauses, 67–68
  introducing noun clauses, 89
Subordination
  defined, 67
  method of, 147–148
such . . . that, introducing adverb clause, 68
Suffix
  defined, 3
  to form adjectives, 10–11
  to form nouns, 3
summarize, as instruction word in essay test, 320
Superlative degree
  defined, 11
  est/most, 11, 157
  misuse, 157, 249
  with more than two things, 11
suppose, as auxiliary verb, 41
sure, 248, 262
sure and. See try and, sure and
suspicion, 262
swell, 262
Syllabic division of words, hyphens with, 185
Synonyms, dictionary source of, 402–403

"Tag" questions, commas with, 174–175
Tense
  confusion between past tense and past participle, 203–204
  defined, 9
  forms, 9–10
  sequence of, 206
  shifting, 207
  use of six tenses, 39
Test taking, 317–324
than
  case of pronoun following, 237
  introducing adverb clause, 69
than, then, 277
that
  introducing adjective clause, 80
  introducing adverb clause, 68
  introducing noun clause, 89
  relative pronoun, 79
  in restrictive adjective clause, 81

Credits

Dictionary entries for *indigestible* and *decimate* are reproduced by permission from *The American Heritage Dictionary of the English Language, Third Edition,* © 1996 by Houghton Mifflin Company.

Dictionary entries for *grow, enthuse,* and *monstrous* are reproduced from *Merriam-Webster's Collegiate® Dictionary, Tenth Edition,* © 1996. Used with permission from Merriam-Webster, Incorporated.

Dictionary entries for *hijack, lead,* and *flyball* through *fly-cast* are reproduced from *Random House Webster's College Dictionary,* © 1996 by Random House, Incorporated. Used with permission.

Dictionary entries for *curriculum, curriculum vitae,* and *goodly* through *goofy* are reproduced with permission of MacMillan General Reference USA, a Simon & Schuster MacMillan Company, from *Webster's New World Dictionary, Third College Edition (Updated).* Copyright © 1988, 1991, 1994 by Simon & Schuster, Incorporated.